Middle English Literature

Blackwell Guides to Criticism

Editor Michael O'Neill

The aim of this new series is to provide undergraduates pursuing literary studies with collections of key critical work from an historical perspective. At the same time emphasis is placed upon recent and current work. In general, historic responses of importance are described, and represented by short excerpts, in an introductory narrative chapter. Thereafter landmark pieces and cutting edge contemporary work are extracted or provided in their entirety according to their potential value to the student. Each volume seeks to enhance enjoyment of literature and to widen the individual student's critical repertoire. Critical approaches are treated as 'tools', and not articles of faith, to enhance the pursuit of reading and study. At a time when critical bibliographies seem to swell by the hour and library holdings to wither year by year, the *Blackwell Guides to Criticism* series offers students privileged access to and careful guidance through those writings that have most conditioned the historic current of discussion and debate as it now informs contemporary scholarship.

Published volumes

Corinne Saunders	*Chaucer*
Francis O'Gorman	*The Victorian Novel*
Emma Smith	*Shakespeare's Comedies*
Emma Smith	*Shakespeare's Histories*
Emma Smith	*Shakespeare's Tragedies*
Roger Dalrymple	*Middle English Literature*

Middle English Literature

A Guide to Criticism

Edited by Roger Dalrymple

Blackwell
Publishing

BLACKWELL PUBLISHING
350 Main Street, Malden, MA 02148-5020, USA
108 Cowley Road, Oxford OX4 1JF, UK
550 Swanston Street, Carlton, Victoria 3053, Australia

First published 2004 by Blackwell Publishing Ltd

Library of Congress Cataloging-in-Publication Data

Middle English literature: a guide to criticism / edited by Roger Dalrymple.
    p.   cm. – (Blackwell guides to criticism)
Includes bibliographical references and index.
    ISBN 0-631-23289-3 (alk. paper) – ISBN 0-631-23290-7 (pbk. : alk. paper)
    1. English literature – Middle English, 1100-1500 – History and criticism – Handbooks, manuals, etc.   I. Dalrymple, Roger, 1971–   II. Series.
    PR255.M5 2004
    820.9′001 – dc22

                                      2003025563

A catalogue record for this title is available from the British Library.

Set in 10 on 12½ pt Caslon
by SNP Best-set Typesetter Ltd., Hong Kong
Printed and bound in the United Kingdom
by TJ International Ltd, Padstow, Cornwall

The publisher's policy is to use permanent paper from mills that operate a sustainable forestry policy, and which has been manufactured from pulp processed using acid-free and elementary chlorine-free practices. Furthermore, the publisher ensures that the text paper and cover board used have met acceptable environmental accreditation standards.

For further information on
Blackwell Publishing, visit our website:
http://www.blackwellpublishing.com

For Martin Nichols

Contents

Contents Arranged by Middle English Text / Author

Preface

This book offers an introduction to the central critical traditions that have THE AIMS OF formed in reading and writing about Middle English literature. Each chapter THIS GUIDE brings together a cross-section of critical work, varied in approach and idiom, but united in engaging a common critical concern or interpretative theme. The individual chapters tell the story of how eight key critical themes have been addressed by such contrasting approaches as historicism, textual criticism, literary anthropology, New Criticism, psychoanalysis and gender studies. In the course of each chapter, connections and contrasts between critical approaches are drawn out and guidance is given to related work and further reading. Extracts from major critics exemplify different approaches at greater length. Not all authors and critical approaches could be included, though signposts to many of these can be found in the Notes and Further Reading at the end of each chapter and in the Bibliography at the end of the book. The book aims to cover a wide range of both critical approaches *and* Middle English texts: you can read about philology or queer theory, Chaucer's works or anonymous lyrics between the covers of this *Guide*.

A handbook of this length cannot hope to represent the state of the entire critical landscape as it stands at the start of the twenty-first century (nor can an individual editor gain sight of its every contour). Instead, the *Guide* brings together a range of major critical approaches that demonstrate the rich variety of contemporary Middle English studies.

The *Guide* can be used in two ways. Read from cover to cover, it offers an USES OF overview of major developments in Middle English criticism over the past THIS GUIDE century. Read piecemeal, it can be used to resource critical reading around a particular text, group of texts, or theme. Readers looking for criticism on, say, gender and medieval literature or allegory and medieval literature will find these chapters relatively free standing. Readers looking for criticism on specific authors – Chaucer, Gower, Hoccleve and so on – will also be able to turn straight to the relevant extracts and overviews. To support the book's two uses, two separate tables of contents are prefaced to the *Guide*: the first Contents organizes the material by critical theme; the second Contents organizes the material by Middle English text.

In the various essays extracted in each chapter, original notes and references are given at the end of each extract, while my own editorial glosses (for example, to Middle English words) are given at the foot of the page, cued by lower-case letter.

CHAUCER
CRITICISM
Critical approaches to Middle English texts are generally pioneered in relation to the most celebrated medieval English writer, Geoffrey Chaucer. Feminist readings, critical historicist readings, psychoanalytic readings – all established their presence in the field through initial work on Chaucer. Accordingly, a book on Middle English studies must make room for the substantial critical literature on this poet – but just how much? As the inevitable leading man in the story of Middle English studies, Chaucer's presence risks crowding so many other players off the stage. For this reason (and because this *Guide* is designed as a companion volume to Corinne Saunders's excellent *Blackwell Guides to Criticism: Chaucer* of 2001), an attempt has been made to keep critical work on Chaucer in relatively modest proportion to work on other writers. 'The Father of English poetry' merits his place in the pages that follow – but so do Margery Kempe and the Paston women.

Acknowledgements

I have a lengthy list of debts, but it is a pleasure to acknowledge them all. For their own inspiring practice of Middle English criticism, grateful thanks are due to my students past and present. I owe a long-standing debt to the exemplary critics at Goldsmiths's College, London, especially Rob Beddow, Andrea Clough, David Margolies and Tim Parnell, and at Collyer's, Horsham: Paul Clarke, Richard Jacobs, Penny Maynard and, above all, Martin Nichols to whom this book is dedicated.

Warmest thanks go to my colleagues, who have been generous with their support and advice at every stage: Justine Crump, Katherine Duncan-Jones and Fiona Stafford at Somerville; Hugh Gazzard, Isabel Rivers and Peter McDonald at St Hugh's. Grateful thanks also go to Debbie Quare, librarian at St Hugh's, who cheerfully retrieved many an EETS volume from the stacks.

I owe a great debt to the medievalist friends and colleagues who have given generously of their encouragement and advice: Elizabeth Archibald, Anthony Bale, Helen Barr, Joyce Boro, Caroline Cole, Helen Cooper, James Daybell, Vincent Gillespie, Tony Grand, Douglas Gray, Nicola McDonald, Caroline Palmer, Matthew Pearson, Ad Putter, Elizabeth Robertson, Miri Rubin, Lucinda Rumsey, Paul Strohm, John Watts and Kevin Whetter. Particular debts are owed to Marilyn Corrie and Corinne Saunders for helpful advice at the planning stage, and to Helen Barr and Jason Lawrence for reading and commenting on chapters. My thanks also go to those at Blackwell Publishing who have expertly guided the project from start to finish: Sue Ashton, Emma Bennett, Ally Dunnett, Leanda Shrimpton and Karen Wilson.

Special thanks are also due to Lorna Arnold, Ian Bowman, Nat Chase, Andrew Geoghegan, Rupert Giles, Lam Ho, Julie Norman, Emma Plaskitt and Rikky Rooksby. Love and thanks, as always, to my family and to Sean.

The editor and publisher wish to thank the following for permission to use copyright material:

David Aers, '"In Arthurus Day": Community, Virtue and Individual Identity in *Sir Gawain and the Green Knight*' from *Community, Gender and Individual Identity: English Writing, 1360–1430* (Routledge, 1988), reprinted by permission of the Taylor and Francis Group Ltd.

Helen Barr, 'Constructing Social Realities' from *Socioliterary Practice in Late Medieval England* (Oxford University Press, Oxford, 2001).

Piero Boitani, 'The Religious Tradition' from *English Medieval Narrative in the Thirteenth and Fourteenth Centuries* (Cambridge University Press, 1982).

John M. Bowers, 'Economics' from *The Politics of Pearl: Court Poetry in the Age of Richard II* (D. S. Brewer, 2001), reprinted by permission of Boydell & Brewer Ltd, Woodbridge.

D. S. Brewer, 'The hoole book' from *Essays on Malory*, ed. J. A. W. Bennett (Clarendon Press, Oxford, 1963), reprinted by permission of Oxford University Press.

Sheila Delany, 'Sexual Economics, Chaucer's Wife of Bath and *The Book of Margery Kempe*' from *Writing Woman: Women Writers and Women in Literature: Medieval to Modern* by Sheila Delany, copyright © 1983 by Sheila Delany. Used by permission of Schocken Books, a division of Random House, Inc.

E. Talbot Donaldson, 'Patristic Exegesis in the Criticism of Medieval Literature: The Opposition' from *Critical Approaches to Medieval Literature: Selected Papers from the English Institute, 1958–59*, ed. Dorothy Betherum (Columbia University Press, 1960).

Laurie A. Finke and Martin B. Schichtman, 'No Pain, No Gain: Violence as Symbolic Capital in Malory's *Morte Darthur*', *Arthuriana* 8, 1998, reprinted by kind permission of the authors.

Kathryn Hume, 'Intellectual and Religious Interpretations' from *The Owl and the Nightingale: The Poem and its Critics* (The University of Toronto Press, 1975).

Tim William Machan, 'Authority' from *Textual Criticism and Middle English Texts* (The University Press of Virginia, Charlottesville and London, 1994).

Jill Mann, 'Allegorical Buildings in Mediaeval Literature', *Medium Ævum* 63 (1994), reprinted by permission of the Society for the Study of Medieval Languages and Literature, Magdalen College, Oxford, and the author.

David Mills, 'Characterisation in the English Mystery Cycles: A Critical Prologue', *Medieval English Theatre* 5 (1983), reprinted by permission of the English Department, Lancaster University.

Alastair Minnis, 'Literary Theory and Literary Practice' from *Medieval Theory of Authorship* (Scolar Press, 1984, © Medieval Theory of Authorship), reprinted by kind permission of Ashgate Publishing Group, Aldershot, and the author.

Lee Patterson, '*Troilus and Criseyde* and the Subject of History' from *Chaucer and the Subject of History* (Routledge, 1991), reprinted by permission of the Taylor and Francis Group Ltd.

Derek Pearsall, 'John Lydgate: The Critical Approach' from *John Lydgate* (Routledge and Kegan Paul, 1970), reprinted by permission of the Taylor & Francis Group Ltd.

Elizabeth Robertson, 'Medieval Medical Views of Women and Female Spirituality in the *Ancrene Wisse* and Julian of Norwich's *Showings*' from *Feminist Approaches to the Body in Medieval Literature*, ed. Linda Lomperis and Sarah Stanbury (University of Pennsylvania Press, Philadelphia, 1993).

A. C. Spearing, 'Early Medieval Narrative Style' from *Readings in Medieval Poetry* (monograph) (Cambridge University Press, 1987).

Paul Strohm, 'Middle English Narrative Genres' from *Genre: Forms of Discourse and Culture* 13 (1980), reprinted by permission of Professor Timothy S. Murphy, editor of *Genre* and the author.

Thorlac Turville-Petre, 'Three Languages' from *England the Nation: Language, Literature, and National Identity, 1290–1340* (Clarendon Press, Oxford, 1996), reprinted by permission of Oxford University Press.

Diane Watt, '"No Writing for Writing's Sake": The Language of Service and Household Rhetoric in the Letters of the Paston Women' from *Dear Sister:*

Medieval Women and the Epistolary Genre, ed. Karen Cherewatuk and Ulrike Wiethaus (University of Pennsylvania Press, Philadelphia, 1993).

Siegfried Wenzel, 'The Poets' from *The Sin of Sloth: Acedia in Medieval Thought and Literature* by Siegfried Wenzel. Copyright © 1967 by the University of North Carolina Press. Used by permission of the publisher.

Hugh White, 'Division and Failure in Gower's *Confessio Amantis*', *Neophilologus* 72 (1988), 600–616, reprinted with the kind permission of Kluwer Academic Publishers, Dordrecht, The Netherlands.

Every effort has been made to trace copyright holders and to obtain their permission for the use of copyright material. The editor and publisher will gladly receive any information enabling them to rectify in subsequent editions any error or omission.

1

Authorship

The author-based emphasis of early Middle English criticism. The displacement of the author by New Criticism. Historical enquiry and changing models of authorship: Derek Pearsall on Lydgate. Medieval literary theory and authorship: Alastair Minnis on Chaucer. Textual criticism and authorship: Tim William Machan on Henryson.

We can gain an initial picture of the diversity and richness of Middle English literary criticism by considering some of the contrasting approaches taken to the question of authorship. Important critical work has explored various dimensions of medieval authorship, thereby intervening in some enduring critical questions. Is biographical information admissible as literary evidence? Is authorial intention recoverable and, if so, is it always relevant to literary interpretation? Should the medieval writer be regarded as an historical presence inhering in the text, a rhetorical construct or a 'function of discourse'?

In much of the earliest medieval scholarship the question of authorship was central and the shared conception of 'the author' generally unproblematic. Many of the literary investigations of nineteenth- and early twentieth-century scholars were focused upon the attribution of anonymous works to *known* authors, the uncovering of further biographical information about those authors, and the location of literary works in precise contexts. Author-identification conferred status on a text. Thus a 1904 survey of Middle English literature authored some of the anonymous lyrics upon the poet of *The Owl and the Nightingale*: 'the question arises, whether some of the religious lyrics . . . did not come from the hand of the same poet. We lack materials for a decisive answer.'[1] Likewise, for a long time, almost the entire corpus of the anonymous Middle English alliterative verse tradition was ascribed by scholars to mysterious Scottish poet 'Huchoun' on the slender basis of a cryptic late-medieval allusion. Next to nothing was known about any such writer; nothing material was gained by the identification. But the historicist temper of scholarship at this time meant that Middle English studies drew validation from attributing anonymous texts to historical authors.

SEEKING THE
AUTHOR IN
EARLY
HISTORICIST
SCHOLARSHIP
The author-based emphasis of this earlier phase of criticism might often blur the line between fact and speculation. A 1914 portrait of the poet Laȝamon shows this trend:

> [Laȝamon's] charming preface exhibits the character of the author in unmistakable wise. A simple-hearted man, we observe, tender and devout, a sincere booklover, an honest scholar, a faithful son. Evidently Layamon worked not for promotion or favour, not at the instigation of a patron in power, but for the love of learning, for his people's good. His office was to read the service in a little country church, and in this retirement he found hours of leisure, which he improved for study.[2]

The search for the authors behind some of the most cherished Middle English works dominated early scholarship. Attempts to unmask the poet or poets behind the alliterative *Pearl, Patience, Purity,* and *Sir Gawain and the Green Knight* were a case in point. Osgood raised speculation on authorial identity in his 1906 edition of *Pearl*;[3] the following year Gollancz linked the poems with Chaucer's contemporary Ralph Strode.[4] In 1928 Cargill and Schlauch presented new candidates John Donne (no relation of the Renaissance poet) and John Prat, two secular clerks officiating in a noble household in the reign of Edward III,[5] while in 1932 Chapman proposed an Augustinian friar based in fourteenth-century York, one John of Erghome.[6] Though concern with author-identification would lessen in the second half of the century, Davenport's 1978 study of 'the *Gawain*-poet' makes clear just how central the notion of common authorship has proved to be to the critical reception of the four poems: 'Though the *Gawain*-poet may not have existed, it has proved necessary to invent him.'[7]

It was a similar story in early scholarship on chief Middle English Arthurian, Sir Thomas Malory. Until the late nineteenth century, little more

> But though he be nameless, the poet's personality and background are so vividly impressed on his work that one may be forgiven the somewhat hazardous task of attempting to evolve an account of his earlier life from mere conjecture and inference. Such an attempt, though fanciful, at all events serves to link together certain facts and impressions, and with this reservation cannot but prove helpful. If documentary evidence is ever discovered, hypothetical conjecture will no doubt be put to a very severe test.[8]

1921: Israel Gollancz speculates on the author behind the *Pearl* poems.

was known of the author of *Le Morte Darthur* than is indicated in William Caxton's preface to his 1485 edition of the text. In the 1890s, however, the independent researches of Oskar Sommer and George Lyman Kittredge, a figure who would dominate this early phase of scholarship, unearthed the biography of one Sir Thomas Malory of Newbold Revel, Warwickshire.[9] Shortly afterwards, Martin identified a second Thomas Malory, this one hailing from Huntingdonshire.[10] Which, if either, was our Arthurian? Heated debate would follow through the twenties (Chambers, 1922; Hicks, 1928; Vinaver, 1929),[11] thirties (Baugh, 1933)[12] through to the sixties when William Matthews's *Ill-framed Knight* proposed yet another identification for the author of the *Morte*.[13] Benson's 1976 study remained tentative, avoiding 'making any assumptions about Malory's life',[14] and as late as 1987 R. M. Lumiansky declared the case still open: 'as things now stand we cannot give a sure answer to the question, Who was our Sir Thomas Malory?'[15] Only in the mid-1990s would P. J. C. Field's persuasive espousal of the Newbold Revel Thomas appear to seal the case – for now at least.[16]

By contrast, under the influence of the Anglo-American New Criticism that first entered literary studies in the 1930s and 1940s, authorship slipped down the critical agenda. For New Critics, authorial intention was irrecoverable, extrinsic to a text's artistic integrity and irrelevant to critical analysis. To base a critical case on authorial intention was to commit 'the intentional fallacy' in W. K. Wimsatt and Monroe Beardsley's influential phrase.[17] The influence of this critical approach registered in the field of medieval studies in a variety of ways, not least in the fresh impetus given to study of the *anonymous* tradition. It was in this critical phase that the anonymous works of 'the *Pearl*-poet' were studied anew: no longer distracted by the search for an historical figure on whom to author the poems, criticism might now focus on the craftsmanship of the texts, their rich symbolism, characterization and textual form. And with the sidelining of 'the author' came the emergence of 'the narrator'. Today, most critical discussion of Chaucer's *General Prologue* or of *Pearl* would take as read the significance and centrality of the respective narrator figures. In reality, 'Chaucer the pilgrim' and 'the Pearl-dreamer' arrived in critical discourse only fifty odd years ago, placed there by E. Talbot Donaldson and Charles Moorman respectively:

- *E. Talbot Donaldson* (1954): I think it time that [Chaucer the Pilgrim] was rescued from the comparatively dull record of history and put back into his poem. He is not really Chaucer the poet . . .[18]
- *Charles Moorman* (1955): I would suggest that the quickest way to come to the heart of the poem would be to waive entirely all questions of allegory and symbolism and to concentrate not upon the figure of the girl but upon that of the narrator.[19]

New Criticism and Authorship

Key

[handwritten marginal note: so many midevng texts are anonymus raises there issues]

While New Criticism displaced the author, later theorists were to pronounce that author dead (the structuralist polemic of Barthes) or to recast the author as a constructed and provisional category rather than a stable historical presence (the post-structuralist contention of Foucault). Such theories of authorship were of deep importance across literary studies, though it seemed some particular ramifications followed for medieval studies. Since so many medieval texts are anonymous, and the biographical record for even the known authors relatively sketchy, a 'dead' or absent author could seem particularly pertinent.

> Our own categories and models for authorship do not often overlap with what can be deduced from Middle English terminology and practice. The relatively rare word *writere* in Middle English is as likely to indicate the scribe as the composer of a literary work; the term *poet* is not in widespread use before the fourteenth century . . . Contemporary understandings of authorship often revolve around either the notion of individual genius (derived from the Romantic conception of the 'artist') or that of property rights over a text (as expressed in laws governing copyright or plagiarism). Authorship in the Middle Ages was more likely understood as participation in an intellectually and morally authoritative tradition, within which . . . a writer might fill one of several roles, copying, modifying, or translating, as well as composing.[20]

1999: Reflections on medieval authorship in the landmark volume, *The Idea of the Vernacular*, ed. Wogan-Browne, Watson, Taylor and Evans.

HISTORICISM AND AUTHORSHIP
Some of the most valuable and enduring criticism on the topic has emphasized the historical conditions impinging upon the practice and understanding of medieval authorship. In the pre-copyright age of manuscript culture, where derivative and well-worn stories were cherished above new-fangled (what we would call 'original') fictions, authorial roles were conceived along different lines. C. S. Lewis made this point memorably in *The Discarded Image* of 1964:

> I doubt if [medieval audiences] would have understood our demand for originality or valued those works in their own age which were original any more on that account. If you had asked Laȝamon or Chaucer 'Why do you not make up a brand-new story of your own?' I think they might have replied (in effect) 'Surely we are not yet reduced to that?'[21]

Hand in hand with this prizing of tradition over invention comes a less-elevated notion of the literary artist in medieval theories of authorship. Some of the most important critical studies of the anonymous literature of the

Middle English period have emphasized this different conception of the author, as in Rosemary Woolf's 1968 study of the religious lyrics:

> In the Middle Ages the writers of religious lyrics were not thought of as men with keener powers of observation and with greater sensibility than others, only as more learned and more articulate. The worth of a poem was guaranteed, not by the dignity of the author, but by the dignity of the source that he used. Since this attitude is reflected in the style and feeling, it must also become ours, even though it is counter to modern literary preconceptions. For, whereas in studying later poetry we justifiably search for an author with a distinctive cast of mind and sensibility, in treating the medieval lyric we must consider a way of thought and a particular emotional bias that was not peculiar to one man but that for centuries characterized medieval devotion.[22]

A central current of Middle English criticism thus stresses the conceptual and material differences between modern and medieval notions of authorship. One such historically relative view is set out in our first extract where Derek Pearsall considers the question of medieval authorship through the case-study of prolific fifteenth-century poet John Lydgate. The extract restores the historical context of Lydgate's poetry. It stresses the prevailing notions of authorship available to a poet of his day and maintains that these should inform our modern critical reception of his work. Not the post-Romantic distiller of experience, nor the *poeta vates* of classical literary theory, Lydgate is described by Pearsall more as a material craftsman, moulding poetic matter in accordance with traditional and inherited forms.

Pearsall's historical approach to the question of authorship sets out to account for the wide discrepancy between Lydgate's reputation in his own day (he was widely read: a high-status writer with royal patronage) and his general reputation today (he's little read: most literary histories have him as a rather pious and prolix moralizer). A dialogic dimension thus defines the extract as Pearsall reveals conceptions of authorship and poetic theory to be shifting, provisional and protean.

Extract from Derek Pearsall, 'John Lydgate: The Critical Approach', in *John Lydgate* (London: Routledge and Kegan Paul, 1970), pp. 4–10.

[. . .] Certain things should be admitted straightaway. One is that Lydgate is unusually prolific. Something like 145,000 lines of verse are attributed to him, twice as much as Shakespeare, three times as much as Chaucer, and there can be no sense in which this works to his advantage. No one who wrote so much can be anything but a hack, we may think, and protect ourselves from what looks like an unrewarding task by simply dismissing the man and his work as unworthy of our attention. This is a defensive reaction, and an easy one, offering plentiful opportunity for witty gibes at the poet's expense. Behind it, however, lie a whole series of unreasoned assumptions about the nature of poetry. Poetry, it is assumed, is the distillation of experience, the precious record of moments of heightened perception, moments which can, possibly, be induced in the act of poetic creation, but which are bound to be rare. There is only so much heightened perception to go round, and a handful of exquisite lyrics or a slim volume of verse are the best guarantee that a poet has had some share in it. This fastidious notion of poetry, which partially accounts for its valetudinarian state now, may be sharply contrasted with the rude health of the medieval, indeed pre-Romantic view that poetry is different only in form and style, not in kind, from other forms of discourse. Poetry must therefore be much more comprehensively defined for the Middle Ages, and for Lydgate, whom I shall take in this book to be himself a comprehensive definition of the Middle Ages. Lydgate's work includes very little that would nowadays be accommodated in poetic form, perhaps only 'a handful of lyrics'. For the modern equivalents of other poems, we should have to look in history-books, encyclopaedias, the Complete Family Doctor, devotional manuals, books of etiquette, souvenir programmes, collections of maxims. Above all – and this is the significant point – we should have to look in the novel, the modern 'hold-all'. The immense bulk of Lydgate's work, therefore, is in itself significant, apart from its physically deterrent quality, only as a mark of changing fashions and attitudes to poetry.

Having said this, one is of course aware of the limitations of this kind of historical relativism. The historical approach, in this case the attempt to understand a much wider concept of poetry in the fifteenth century, is no more than an approach. It offers an explanation of literature in the light of history, but not as history; and the explanation only serves to prepare the mind for understanding. Lydgate's vast output is a historically explicable phenomenon, but it remains true that, although all of his poems engage our interest (as the ways of a man with words in poetry always command interest), some of them are more interesting than others, not because they are more 'poetic', but because they deal with subjects that are intrinsically more important. That Lydgate should have written a 'Treatise for Laundresses'[1] is a salutary and salubrious reminder of the comprehensiveness of his range in poetry, but to give it more weight than that would be quaint antiquarianism. What one would like to establish is a picture of Lydgate as a highly professional and skilful craftsman in a wide range of related literary arts, capable of turning his hand to an epithalamion as well as an epic, an exposition of the Mass as well as a satire on women's fashions in headgear, working like a mason or a sculptor or a mural-painter, not like a *poeta vates*.[a] For him, poetry is a public art, its existence conditioned and determined by outer needs and pressures, not by inner ones. In this sense, all his poetry is occasional poetry. Writing of a Romantic poet, one would be tempted to create, even if there were no extant chronological evidence, a chronological structure in which each poem was so placed as to illustrate the growth of the poet's mind, or some mythical prototype of it. The pressures would be recognised as inward, a struggle towards self-expression. Problems (such as Byron's) of which self to express, might need more sophisticated handling, but would still tend to be evaluated in terms of the accuracy and intensity of the response to inward pressures. It is not profitable to study a medieval poet like Lydgate in this way – fortunately so, for we lack much of the chronological evidence we should need. There is development in his writing, but it is a development of style, or rather the development of new styles, not of poetic personality. Lydgate's personality is a matter for curiosity only, for it is of the supremest irrelevance to the understanding of his poetry. Every mask he puts on is a well-worn medieval one, and it is well to recognise these masks for what they are, otherwise we may find ourselves interpreting poems like the *Testament* as personal documents. The coherence of his work as a whole is to be found, not in terms of its relation to his inner self or to any concept of the self-realising individual consciousness, but in terms of its relation to the total structure of the medieval world, that is, the world of universally received values, traditions, attitudes, as well as, and more significantly than, the world of 'real life'.

These generalisations about Lydgate are aimed at medieval poetry in general, ill-advisedly, it may seem, in view of the many qualifications one would need to make in connection with Chaucer. Chaucer's personality is obviously interesting to us, and in a significant literary way, not out of mere curiosity. His playing off of real against assumed attitudes constitutes one of his characteristic signatures, and he talks about himself and provokes interest in himself far more than other medieval poets. Chaucer, in fact [. . .] is not a very representative medieval poet – any more than Shakespeare is a representative Elizabethan dramatist. However, he remains a medieval poet, and the above reservations are over-scrupulous if they suggest any regard for the romantic-biographical interpretation of Chaucer's work, in which his poetry, dated or undated, may be stretched on a Procrustean bed of the 'three periods',[b] and made to fit some fashionable theory as to the growth of realism or the emancipation from rhetoric. So tenacious is the hold of this literary biography that works like the *Clerk's Tale*, for which there is little evidence as to precise date,

[a] poet, bard.
[b] Early Chaucer criticism divided his works into the French, Italian and English periods.

are assigned, because of their 'non-realistic' qualities, to an early period, thus completing and strengthening the circle of hypotheses.

There is one further point to make about Lydgate's prolific output. I have suggested that this needs understanding as a historical phenomenon, as a mark of the wider scope of poetry in his time, and qualified this suggestion by drawing attention to the fact that some poems will be intrinsically more interesting, by virtue of their subject-matter, than others. It is also true, obviously, that sometimes he will write less well than at others, when his attention and interest is not fully engaged. Every craftsman has his off-days, when his mind is not on his job – perhaps because he did not fancy the job in the first place. The historical approach is not intended to blanket discrimination between the better and the worse, though it should try to ensure that the discrimination is properly based. The bad poems are bad, not because of their subject, but because of what Lydgate does, or fails to do with them. The *Pilgrimage of the Life of Man* stretches to 26,000 lines, but fails because at no time does Lydgate attempt to shape, control or master his material; he merely goes through the motions of versifying in the most mechanical manner possible. Clearing the ground of rubbish like this will help us to see and examine what is truly representative and intrinsically worthwhile. It is on these poems that judgment must be based. The first task is to understand what Lydgate is trying to do, and for this every discipline, every kind of historical information, is relevant. Understanding can then inform judgment on the good and the less good.

Two further charges against Lydgate, apart from that of having written so much, can be considered in their wider implications in order to establish this historical reorientation. They are the two most deadly weapons in the critical armoury – that he is prolix, and that he is dull. Prolixity is certainly a characteristic feature of Lydgate's style. No poet can mark time with such profuse demonstrations of energy, can so readily make twenty words do the work of one. Sometimes it is difficult to slow down the processes of the mind to the breathless snail's pace of his verse. Yet it would be fair to recognise that prolixity (sometimes due to diffuseness of syntax) is deliberately cultivated by Lydgate. Translating the Prologue to the *Fall of Princes*, he says, following Laurent de Premierfait:

> For a story which is nat pleynli told,
> But constreynyd undir woordes fewe
> For lak of trouthe, wher thei be newe or old,
> Men bi report kan nat the mater shewe;
> These ookis grete be nat doun ihewe
> First at a stroke, but bi long processe,
> Nor longe stories a woord may not expresse.[2]

Of course, like most of Lydgate's comments on style and the art of poetry, this
is a formula, and one could set beside it numerous equally stereotyped formulae in which he asserts that his main design is to 'eschewe prolixite'.[3] Both
attitudes may be traced back to the rhetoricians of the twelfth century, who
set side by side their recommendations for 'amplification' and 'abbreviation'.[4]
But in them, as in Lydgate, abbreviation is of little more than formal interest,
and is totally swamped in amplification, the governing principle in medieval
stylistics. In academic theory, a poem essentially provides a theme for amplification, and the prize goes to the man who can go on saying the same thing
longest without repeating himself – *varius sit et tamen idem.*[a5] Academic theory
is one thing, of course, and poetic practice is another. Obviously poems leap
the confines of the rhetorical exercise, but the school-training in amplification
which Lydgate and every other educated medieval poet would have received
must have exerted a powerful and lasting influence on their style. It would not
be unprofitable, for instance, to make a study of Chaucer's *Troilus* as an *amplificatio* of Boccaccio's *Filostrato*, paying particular attention to the use of devices
such as exclamation, apostrophe and description, all listed by Geoffrey among
the forms of amplification. In these and other ways Chaucer gives the story
its rich and full-bodied quality, its wholeness or *integritas.*[6] Amplification is
still the basis of sixteenth century poetic, under the name of *copie* or copious-
ness,[7] and Shakespeare, though he mocks *copie* in Touchstone,[8] still uses its
machinery to construct long speeches.

In Lydgate, we may assume, rhetorical precept coincided happily with a
natural tendency to prolixity, and no doubt reinforced it. It is not difficult to
recognise his natural verbosity in this stanza:

> The rounde dropis of the smothe reyn,
> Which that discende and falle from aloffte
> On stonys harde, at eye as it is seyn,
> Perceth ther hardnesse with ther fallyng offte,
> Al-be in touchyng, water is but soffte;
> The percyng causid be force nor puissaunce
> But of fallyng be long contynuaunce.
>
> (*Fall*, II, 106–12)

But we must recognise, too, that Lydgate is consciously writing according to
accepted canons of taste, and that his deliberate unfolding of 'Constant drip-
ping wears away a stone' is as skilful in its own way as the aphorism itself in
another way. And though Lydgate is by nature long-winded, he knows when
this kind of elaborate tautology is not appropriate, and can write in a com-

---

[a] let it be different and yet the same.

paratively abbreviated, aphoristic style, as in the series of short moralistic poems with gnomic refrains,[9] or in the fable of the *Churl and the Bird*. Lydgate's expansiveness clearly forms part of a deliberate poetic style.

It looks perverse to us, though, and again, if we are not to assume some gigantic aberration on the part of the Middle Ages, it is necessary to reshape our minds to the major change of taste which has taken place in attitudes to poetry. Poetry is now admired for its economy of expression, its compression, compactness and intensity. Every line must be packed with significant imagery, every rift loaded with ore. Eliot's dedication of *The Waste Land* to Ezra Pound, *il miglior fabbro*, records his debt to the better craftsman, whose skill enabled him to unburden the poem of the conventional paraphernalia of linguistic communication, and to boil it down to its essence. Syntax itself is something of a handicap, in this view of poetry. Small wonder, then, that medieval poetry, Chaucer included, is found to be diffuse,[10] and that the search for fine lines is unrewarding. Any that one prises out of Chaucer – 'Singest with vois memorial in the shade'[11] – are fortuitous and uncharacteristic, and Eleanor Hammond's attempt at a *florilegium*[a] of fine lines in Lydgate[12] is a strange lapse of understanding and taste in a great scholar. Medieval poetry characteristically produces its effects over longer stretches, the stanza or the verse-paragraph, and the comparatively free metrical systems of alliterative verse, even Chaucer's verse, are designed to operate over longer passages, not in single lines. Associated with this tendency, are a relaxed kind of syntax and a wide use of free-running paratactic constructions which make translation of medieval verse into modern logical units so difficult.

All these features, of course, have to do with something else, as well as being the general consequences of a particular poetic theory. They are the features of verse composed for oral delivery. Amplification, tautology, diffuseness of sense and looseness of syntax, are not only acceptable but desirable to the listening audience, which has no opportunity to linger over close-packed lines, and which will welcome as well as recognise the familiar phrase.[13] Every medieval poet has a store of tags and formulae which he will use to establish this pattern of communication. Some have nothing else, perhaps, while others, like Chaucer, have such leisured control over the medium that they can afford to uncoil the formulae into new and ambiguous contexts. But for the most part the stereotyped nature of medieval poetic expression is better referred to conditions of delivery than to lack of 'originality', in its prevailing form a largely modern concept. It is not necessary to suggest that Lydgate's poems were habitually read aloud to a listening audience, though there is evidence in plenty in the fifteenth century for the persistence of this method of publica-

[a] anthology.

tion, alongside even more evidence for the growth of the habit of private reading.[14] The argument need only assume that the stylistic traditions of orally delivered verse were more tenacious than the conditions which produced them.

The revolution in reading habits produced by the invention of printing is one clue to the shift in attitude we have been discussing, and to the growth of a non-rhetorical poetic which finds Lydgate's prolixity excessively burdensome. I talked a moment ago of the difficulty of accommodating the mind to the leisurely processes of Lydgate's verse, but the mind referred to was of course an exceptional mind, the modern mind, trained to incredibly specialised kinds of short-cutting and short-circuiting of perception by generations of print-culture.[15] It may seem ridiculous to suggest that there might be value in training the mind to move more slowly, but a flexible attitude to the possibility is probably better than the assumption that things have never been better. Intensity is one standard of judgment for poetry, but not the only one.

Comparisons of medieval with modern poetic theory can help us with some of our problems of recovery, by illustrating to us the limited and relative application of such theories, and the inadequacy of assuming that any one of them is right, absolutely. Sometimes, though, the comparisons reveal such totally opposed points of view that one seems to be comparing not different manifestations of the same thing but different things. As has been said, poetry occupied the central literary position in the Middle Ages; it could be regarded as the highest form of discourse, but it existed also as the workaday form, the tool to which the professional craftsman naturally stretched his hand for a story, a treatise, a political pamphlet. Literary prose remained the specialised medium, though one sees its range being extended in the later fifteenth century, in the work of Malory, and Caxton's ambitious translations. The situation was already changing, and it is now changed completely. Poetry is now highly specialised, the property of an élite; the central literary position is occupied by the novel. The growth of the novel to accommodate virtually every kind of literary experience provides the major literary development of the last two centuries. Many of these kinds of experience have been taken over from poetry – historical and didactic interests, for instance – and it might be said therefore that we should be prepared to transfer to earlier poetry some of the appetites now satisfied by the novel, and in particular appetite itself. Novels are so much the staple of our literary diet that we hardly notice we are reading them, and we certainly do not find it necessary as we begin to read always to summon our faculties for a major literary experience. Some novels are more important than others, of course, but so are some medieval poems. The point is that the natural literary element in which we move is the novel, whereas in the fifteenth century it was verse. Lydgate's diffuseness and pro-lixity should therefore be referred, for a standard of comparison, to the dif-fuseness and prolixity of eighteenth and nineteenth century prose fiction, of Richardson, Scott, Dickens and Thackeray. Voluminousness is their natural condition, and to ask for them to be briefer would be to ask for them not to be.

Notes

1   *Minor Poems*, ed. H. N. MacCracken, Part II (EETS, OS 192, 1934), p. 723.
2   *Fall of Princes*, I, 92–8.
3   For example, *Fall*, II, 2565.
4   For instance, Geoffrey of Vinsauf, in his *Poetria Nova*; Evrard the German, *Labor-intus*; John of Garland, *Poetria*. See E. Faral, *Les arts poétiques du XIIe et du XIIIe siècle* (Paris, 1923), pp. 218, 348, 380.
5   Geoffrey of Vinsauf, *Poetria Nova*, 225: in Faral, *Les arts poétiques*, p. 204.
6   See G. T. Shepherd, 'Troilus and Criseyde', in D. S. Brewer (ed.), *Chaucer and Chaucerians: Critical Studies in Middle English Literature* (London: Thomas Nelson and Sons, 1966, pp. 65–87), pp. 77–81.
7   One of the most widely used text-books in the sixteenth century was Erasmus's *De duplici copia verborum ac rerum*, of which there were sixty editions between 1512 and 1536: see T. W. Baldwin, *William Shakespeare's Small Latine and Lesse Greeke*, 2 vols (Urbana, IL, 1944), I, 99; II, 176.
8   *As You Like It*, V. i. 52.
9   *Minor Poems*, ed. MacCracken, Part II, pp. 744–847.
10 See A. C. Spearing, *Criticism and Medieval Poetry* (London: Edward Arnold, 1964), pp. 16–18.
11 *Anelida*, 18, quoted by C. S. Lewis, *The Allegory of Love: A Study of Medieval Tra-dition* (Oxford: Oxford University Press, 1936), p. 201. Matthew Arnold's choice (in 'The Study of Poetry', *Essays in Criticism*, second series) is 'O martyr souded in virginitee', from 'The Prioress's Tale', *The Canterbury Tales*, ed. F. N. Robinson, 2nd edn (Boston MA: Houghton Mifflin, 1957), VII, 579.
12 Eleanor P. Hammond (ed.), *English Verse between Chaucer and Surrey* (Durham, NC: Duke University Press, 1927), pp. 81–2.
13 K. Sisam (ed.) *Fourteenth Century Verse and Prose* (Oxford: Clarendon Press, 1921), p. xxxix. The standard works on this subject are H. J. Chaytor, *From Script to Print: An Introduction to Medieval Vernacular Literature* (Cambridge: Cambridge University Press, 1945); Ruth Crosby, 'Oral Delivery in the Middle Ages', *Speculum* 11 (1936), 88–110, and 'Chaucer and the Custom of Oral Delivery', *Speculum* 13 (1938), 413–32.
14 See H. S. Bennett, 'The Author and his Public in the 14th and 15th Centuries', *Essays and Studies* 23 (1937), 7–24.
15 There is much on this subject, and a great many other subjects, in H. M. McLuhan, *The Gutenberg Galaxy* (London: Routledge and Kegan Paul, 1962).

Pearsall's sympathetic approach to Lydgate takes its place in a wide body
of criticism on the English and Scottish Chaucerians, those various poets,
Hoccleve, Lydgate and Henryson among them, who set out to imitate
Chaucerian writing and even to augment the Chaucerian canon in the century
following his death in 1400. As work on these figures has increased (Brewer
on Chaucerians in 1966; Gray on Henryson in 1979; Burrow on Hoccleve
in 1994, for example),[23] so has an awareness that the establishment of Chaucer
as 'founding father' of English poetry took place early in the critical reception
of his work. Seth Lehrer's 1993 study *Chaucer and his Readers: Imagining
the Author in Late Medieval England* draws on Foucauldian conceptions of
'the author' to describe the startling extent of Chaucer's influence upon his
followers:

> The construction of the author according to a social ideology carries with it
> . . . a set of implications for all those who would write after his example. As
> Foucault points out, there is perhaps an unavoidable sense of genealogy to
> authorship, one that I think may help explain the maintenance of 'father
> Chaucer' for the fifteenth century . . . Rephrased in Foucault's terms, all fif-
> teenth-century poetry remained 'within the field of discourse' Chaucer had
> initiated. To put it more bluntly, we might say that to be a poet in the fifteenth
> century was by necessity to be a Chaucerian.[24]

How did 'father Chaucer' conceive of his own poetic art? Our second
extract takes up the issue. Since Alastair Minnis's foundational 1984
study *Medieval Theory of Authorship* many scholars have been inclined to
consider Chaucer's poetic method in the light of the scholastic literary theory
of his own day. Drawn from this study, the following extract shows how many
of the most immediate models of medieval authorial practice available
to Chaucer were those displayed in the scholastic Latin compendiums
and compilations put together by such figures as Vincent of Beauvais,
Bartholomew the Englishman and Brunetto Latini. As these names indicate,
Minnis places the authorship question in a European context, Christian
Latinity forming the bridge between insular and continental authorial practice. Rather than seeking to apply modern literary theory to medieval texts,
Minnis's approach draws upon this body of medieval literary theory to explore
Chaucer's conception of his own authorial role. In our extract, Minnis
describes the role of medieval *compilator* or compiler, a role distinct from *auctor*
or author, to illuminate Chaucer's sophisticated authorial stance in the
Canterbury Tales. In a critical approach that aims to draw closer to the historical reception of Chaucer's work in his own time, Minnis argues that in the
practice of the medieval compilers, Chaucer discovered both 'a literary role and
a literary form'.

Extract from Alastair Minnis, 'Literary Theory and Literary Practice', in *Medieval Theory of Authorship: Scholastic Literary Attitudes in the Later Middle Ages* (London: Scolar Press, 1984), pp. 198–203.

[. . .] We are now in a position to examine the role of 'rehearsing' compiler which Chaucer assumed in the *Canterbury Tales*, wherein the fictitious narrative of a pilgrimage to Canterbury provides the rationale for the compilation. As compiler, Chaucer proposes to 'rehearse' the words of other men as accurately as he can, without being responsible for what they say:

> But first I pray yow, of youre curteisye,
> That ye n'arette it nat my vileynye,[a]
> Thogh that I pleynly speke in this mateere,
> To telle yow hir wordes and hir cheere,
> Ne thogh I speke hir wordes proprely.
> For this ye knowen al so wel as I,
> Whoso[b] shal telle a tale after a man,
> He moot *reherce* as ny[c] as evere he kan
> Everich a word, if it be in his charge,
> Al speke he never so rudeliche and large,[d]
> Or ellis he moot telle his tale untrewe,
> Or feyne thyng, or fynde wordes newe . . .
> Also I prey yow to foryeve it me,
> Al have I nat set folk in hir degree
> Heere in this tale, as that they sholde stonde.
> My wit is short, ye may wel understonde.
> (General Prologue, lines 725–46; italics mine)

The idiom in which this self-depreciation is couched displays the influence of the compiler's stock disavowal of responsibility. One may compare Vincent's[e] remark, 'I added little, or almost nothing, of my own', or Ashenden's[f] expressed desire 'to compile sentences, adding nothing out of my own head' or, indeed,

---

[a] don't ascribe it to my boorishness.
[b] whoever.
[c] nearly.
[d] uncouthly and freely.
[e] Vincent of Beauvais.
[f] John Ashenden, compiler of a fourteenth-century reference book on astrology.

Chaucer's own protestation that his *Treatise on the Astrolabe* was not 'founden of my labour or of myn engyn'. In the General Prologue, Chaucer the compiler seems to be protesting that he has not 'founden' the *Canterbury Tales* 'of my labour or of myn engyn'.

As compiler, Chaucer cannot be held responsible for, for example, the words of the churlish Miller:

> . . . this Millere
> He nolde[a] his wordes for no man forbere,
> But tolde his cherles tale in his manere.
> M'athynketh[b] that I shal *reherce* it heere.
> (I, lines 3167–70; italics mine)

What he is doing, in the technical sense, is 'rehearsing' the *materia* ('mateere') of the pilgrims; the *intentio* ('entente') of the compiler is stated to be a good one:

> . . . demeth[c] nat that I seye
> Of yvel *entente*, but for I moot[d] *reherce*
> Hir tales alle, be they bettre or werse,
> Or elles falsen[e] som of my mateere.
> (I, lines 3172–5; italics mine)

A reporter deserves neither thanks nor blame for what he repeats without fabrication or alteration: 'Blameth nat me . . .'. CRUCIAL.

But, of course, many medieval compilers were accustomed to including something out of their own heads, of adding some personal assertion to their reportage. Vincent appeared in his *Speculum maius*[f] as the *auctor*; Ralph Higden indicated personal assertions within his work by the initial 'R'; in the passages marked with his name, the more aggressive John Trevisa delivered his own opinions and sometimes criticised his sources. The most ostensibly personal assertions of Chaucer the pilgrim are the two tales he tells, namely, Sir Thopas and Melibee.

Chaucer's sense of combining and organising diverse materials may owe something to the compilers' theory and practice of *ordinatio partium*. The major medieval compilations were compendious, containing *materiae* to cater

[a] would not.
[b] I think.
[c] judge.
[d] must.
[e] misrepresent.
[f] *Greatest Mirror.*

for a wide range of demands and tastes. Vincent of Beauvais prided himself
on the amount of diverse materials he had managed to include in his
Speculum maius.[1] Brunetto Latini explained that his *Trésor* combined both
teaching and delight:

> This book is called 'Treasury'. For, just like the lord who wishes in one small
> place to collect something of great worth, not only for his delight, but to increase
> his power and protect his position in both war and peace, places in it the most
> valuable things and the most precious jewels that he can, to the best of his ability;
> just so is the body of this book compiled from wisdom, as one which is drawn
> from all the parts of philosophy concisely into one digest.[2]

Brunetto's practice may have influenced Gower's conception of the scope of
his *Confessio amantis*, which comprises both 'lust' and 'lore':[a] certainly, the
Latin commentary stresses the point that Gower compiled extracts from
chronicles, histories and the sayings of the (pagan) philosophers and poets.[3]
When Higden described the *ordinatio* of his *Polychronicon*,[b] he explained how
he had taken various things from various sources and had reorganised them in
accordance with new principles.[4] His fifteenth-century translator renders the
relevant passage as follows: 'In whom alle things excerpte of oþer men ar
broken in to smalle membres, but concorporate here liniamentally; thynges of
disporte be admixte with saddenes, and dictes ethnicalle to thynges religious,
that the ordre of the processe may be obseruede . . .'[5]

In the *Canterbury Tales* also, 'thynges of disporte be admixte with saddenes,
and dictes ethnicalle to thynges religious'. Chaucer aimed at being compendious, at providing 'Tales of best sentence and most solaas', 'cherles tales' and
noble tales, 'myrie' tales and 'fructuous' tales, pagan tales and Christian tales.[6]
When the host stops Chaucer the pilgrim from completing the Tale of Thopas,
he urges him to tell something 'in which ther be som murthe or som doctryne'
(VII, line 935), making it clear that different standards apply to different types
of tale. The major reference-books of the day may be regarded as having provided the general precedents for the combinations of 'murthe' and 'doctrine',
of 'lust' and 'lore', practised by Chaucer in the *Canterbury Tales* and, indeed,
by Gower in the *Confessio amantis* and Jean de Meun in the *Roman de la Rose*.

Of course, the nature of Chaucer's diverse *materiae* is not identical with the
nature of the diverse *materiae* of a compiler like, for example, Vincent of
Beauvais.[7] The point is rather that both writers drew on a common corpus of
literary theory; they described their different diversities in a similar way. Moreover, Vincent 'ordinated' materials in relation to chapters, books and *tituli*,
whereas Chaucer 'ordinated' materials in relation to tales and tellers; both

[a]   entertainment and instruction.
[b]   *Universal History*.

writers shared basic principles of hierarchical or 'encapsulating' structure.[8] It is as if Chaucer derived certain principles of order from compilations and from the explanations of *ordinatio* which accompanied them, principles which he chose to apply in his own way.

Moreover, Chaucer and Vincent (among other compilers) shared the principle of the reader's freedom of choice (*lectoris arbitrium*). In the case of Vincent, this means that the reader can isolate and believe whatever things he wishes to believe: no attempt has been made to force the *auctores* to speak with one voice, and it is up to the reader to make his own choice from the discordant *auctoritates* offered to him.[9] Chaucer also is interested in the freedom of the reader. If a reader does not want a tale like the Miller's Tale, there are many other types of 'mateere' on offer:

> . . . whoso list it [the Miller's Tale] nat yheere,
> Turne over the leef and chese another tale;
> For he shal fynde ynowe, grete and smale,
> Of storial[a] thyng that toucheth gentillesse,[b]
> And eek moralitee and hoolynesse.
>
> (I, lines 3176–80)

The common principle involved is that a compiler is not responsible for his reader's understanding of any part of the *materia*, for any effect which the *materia* may have on him and, indeed, for any error or sin into which the *materia* may lead a reader. 'Blameth nat me if ye chese amys', warns Chaucer; 'Avyseth yow, and put me out of blame' (I, lines 3181, 3185).

But perhaps the most intriguing facet of Chaucer's exploitation of the principles of *compilatio* is the way in which he seems to have transferred the compiler's technique of authenticating sources to his 'sources', the Canterbury pilgrims. All the major compilers habitually authenticated their sources by stating that the 'rehearsed' words were the proper words of their *auctores*, and by carefully assigning the extracted *auctoritates* to their respective *auctores*. Likewise, Chaucer has his narrator explain that the words he 'rehearses' are the proper words of the fictitious pilgrims. In order to 'speke hir wordes properly', he must give 'everich a word' that each pilgrim uttered, 'al speke he never so rudeliche and large' (General Prologue, lines 729–34). The 'wordes' of a churl like the Miller are proper to the Miller, who

> . . . nolde[c] his wordes for no man forbere,
> But tolde his cherles tale in his manere . . .
> The Millere is a cherl, ye knowe wel this;

[a] historical.
[b] nobility.
[c] would not.

> So was the Reve eek and othere mo,
> And harlotrie[a] they tolden bothe two.
>
> (I, lines 3167–84)

The device of organising diverse *materiae* by distributing them amongst diverse fictional characters was not new: we have already noted its use by Jean de Meun. What was new was the kind of attention paid to what the fictional characters said.

Chaucer's professed concern for the *ipsissima verba*[b] of his pilgrims seems to parallel the concern of a compiler like Vincent of Beauvais for the actual words of his *auctores*. For example, in the first chapter of his *apologia*, Vincent complains bitterly about textual corruptions in manuscripts, which make it difficult to understand the authors' meanings and, indeed, to know which *auctor* is responsible for whatever *sententia*.[c] [10] Moreover, he feels obliged to point out that he has used not the *originalia* of Aristotle but collections of 'flowers' extracted from the *originalia* by brother friars who could not always follow the order of the words in Aristotle's text, although in every case they tried to follow the meaning.[11] Merely to preserve the meaning is not good enough for Chaucer the compiler, who is determined to preserve the proper words of each pilgrim without 'feigning' anything or adding 'wordes newe':

> Whoso shal telle a tale after a man,
> He moot reherce as ny as evere he kan
> Everich a word, if it be in his charge,
> Al speke he never so rudeliche and large,
> Or ellis he moot telle his tale untrewe,
> Or feyne thyng, or fynde wordes newe.
> He may nat spare, althogh he were his brother;
> He moot as wel seye o word as another.
>
> (General Prologue, lines 731–8)

In sum, it may be argued that Chaucer treats his fictional characters with the respect that the Latin compilers had reserved for their *auctores*. The 'lewd compilator' has become the compiler of the 'lewd'. [. . .]

Notes

1   See especially 'Vincent of Beauvais, *Speculum maius, apologia totius operis*', cap. iv, ed. A. D. v. den Brincken, 'Geschichtsbetrachtung bei Vencenz von Beauvais', *Deutsches Archiv für Erforschung des Mittelalters*', 34 (1978), 469–70.

[a] bawdy talk.
[b] words themselves.
[c] short moral statement.

2   Brunetto Latini, *Li Livres de Tresor*, ed. F. J. Carmody (Berkeley, CA: University of California Press, 1948), p. 16.

3   See the gloss pr. G. C. McCaulay (ed.), *The English Works of John Gower* (EETS, ES 81, 82 [1900–1]), i, 3–4. For the argument that Brunetto Latini influenced Gower, see ibid., ii, 522; cf. H. C. Mainzer, 'A Study of the Sources of the *Confessio amantis* of John Gower', unpublished DPhil thesis (Oxford University, 1967), esp. pp. 38–40.

4   *Polychronicon Ranulphi Higden: together with the English translations of John Trevisa and of an unknown writer of the fifteenth century*, ed. C. Babington and J. R. Lumby (London, 1865–86), i, 16.

5   Ibid., i, 17.

6   For these quotations see *The Works of Geoffrey Chaucer*, ed. F. N. Robinson, 2nd edn (Oxford: Oxford University Press, 1957), i, lines 798, 3169; vii, line 964; x, line 46 (cf. vii, lines 2790–817).

7   But there is some overlap: see P. Aiken, 'Vincent of Beauvais and Dame Pertelote's Knowledge of Medicine', *Speculum* 10 (1935), 281–7; 'The Summoner's Malady', *Studies in Philology* 33 (1936), 40–4; 'Vincent of Beauvais and the Green Yeoman's Lecture on Demonology', *Studies in Philology* 35 (1938), 1–9; 'Chaucer's Legend of Cleopatra and the *Speculum historidle*', *Speculum* 13 (1938), 232–6; 'Vincent of Beauvais and Chaucer's *Monk's Tale*', *Speculum* 17 (1942), 56–68; 'Vincent of Beauvais and Chaucer's Knowledge of Alchemy', *Studies in Philology* 41 (1944), 371–89.

8   For the idea of 'encapsulating' structure, cf. J. Burrow, *Ricardian Poetry* (London, 1971), pp. 57–68, 86, 92.

9   *Apologia totius operis*, cap. viii (ed. v. den Brincken, p. 477).

10   Ibid., cap. i (pp. 465–6).

11   Ibid., cap. x (pp. 479–80).

Authors and their meanings are also central concerns of a further branch of Middle English studies – textual criticism. Rooted in the study of medieval manuscripts and early printed books, Middle English textual criticism aims to recover, often from complex textual traditions, the words that authors originally wrote. Textual critics set out to discriminate authorial readings from scribal readings and to establish the 'best' text among variant manuscript versions. Growing initially out of biblical scholarship, Middle English textual criticism has increasingly evolved editorial principles suited to the study of medieval texts. High-profile debates over how best to edit the multiple texts of such works as Langland's *Piers Plowman* have led to a growing awareness that editorial choices are also *interpretative* and *evaluative* choices. The roles of textual critic and literary critic are closely allied. As the 1992 collaborative volume *Crux and Controversy in Middle English Textual Criticism* put it:

TEXTUAL CRITICISM AND AUTHORSHIP

> [T]he words on the modern printed page bear an indeterminate relation to what the author originally wrote. Worse still, it may be impossible ever to discover what the author originally wrote – and worst of all, it may be that conventions

of text production in the medieval period render the concept of an original, authorial text simply irrelevant.[25]

Among the aims of textual criticism, then, is the attempt to move towards a form of reception of the medieval work that is more in line with the experience of the work's primary audience or audiences. The challenge this poses can be substantial: in an important work of textual criticism, Ralph Hanna III points out how, even in the case of so central a writer as Chaucer, the authorial picture that emerges from modern printed editions is far removed from the one we would glean if presented only with medieval manuscripts:

> [M]odern forms of reception differ from either Chaucerian holograph or fifteenth-century manuscripts. We typically consume Chaucer through a single-volume *The Works of . . .* edition, and such a book addresses a professional necessity that is ours and neither the author's nor scribes'. For the evidence shows that, whatever Chaucer thought of his own authoriality, he was remarkably negligent about 'publishing' and made no effort at collecting a *Works*.[26]

Drawn from another work of textual criticism, our final extract is focused upon late fifteenth-century Scottish author Robert Henryson. In discussing Henryson's 'Fable of the Lion and the Mouse', Tim William Machan draws attention to a further model of authorship current in the late Middle Ages, that of the 'maker'. In the wider study from which the extract is drawn, Machan aims to define the key concepts of 'author', 'work' and 'text' with reference to 'the discourse of medieval manuscripts' rather than any extrinsic body of literary theory, medieval or modern. In our extract, the discussion turns to the question of authorship and authority as Machan studies the fable's staging of an encounter between Henryson himself and his esteemed forebear Aesop: classical *auctor* meets vernacular maker.

Extract from Tim William Machan, 'Authority', in *Textual Criticism and Middle English Texts* (Charlottesville: University of Virginia Press, 1994), pp. 126–31.

[. . .] The late Middle English contest over vernacular authority is perhaps clearest in the *Moral Fables* of Robert Henryson,[1] for there, in the fable of *The Lion and the Mouse*, it is dramatized. This is the seventh fable of the thirteen in the collection,[2] and by this point Henryson has effected two important emphases in the collection. First, having announced his interest in literary authority in the Prologue, he has gradually and self-consciously begun to assert his own rhetorical importance in the tales he tells. For example, in the *Moralitas*[a] to *The Sheep and the Dog*, which precedes *The Lion and the Mouse*, he claims to have been a viewer of, a participant in, the events he narrates (1282–5). And second, he has gradually shifted the focus of his concern from the foolishness of one cock (in the first fable) to the issue of God's presence in this world (in the sixth). Given its subject and this emphasis on Henryson's rhetorical significance in his own moralizing poem, then, the seventh fable can profitably be examined for the way its rhetoric mediates the late medieval conflict over authority.

The Lion and the Mouse opens with [a] cluster of literary conceits and devices: In a 'ioly sweit seasoun'[b] (1321) of late spring, early summer the narrator 'rais[c] and put all sleuth[d] and sleip asyde' to go to 'ane wod . . . allone but gyde'[e] (1326–27), where he confronts a *locus amoenus*[f] in which he has a dream. While such a cluster emphasizes Henryson's self-consciousness as a narrator, it is also in this overtly, even overdetermined metatextual context that Aesop appears. In the ancient poet the Scots writer confronts both the specific writer of whom he claims to be only a translator and also, more generally, one of the genuine *auctores* of medieval culture.[3] Even though Aesop was an *auctor* considered especially valuable for adolescents, the meeting itself thus has the potential to be emblematic of a broader meeting between *auctores* and makers. In this regard, it is noteworthy that such a meeting between maker and *auctor* is unprecedented in the Aesopic tradition in general and in the *Moral Fables* in particular. Furthermore, even in comparison to generally similar encounters, such as that between Dante and Vergil or Gavin Douglas and Mapheus Vegius, Henryson's experience is distinguished by the rhetorical and thematic complexity with which the encounter is treated.

That this meeting between maker and *auctor* is in fact representing larger cultural issues becomes more apparent when, after Aesop appears, he is described as the very emblem of the conventional poet:

> Ane[g] roll off paper in his hand he bair,
> And swannis pen[h] stikand vnder his eir,
> Ane inkhorne, with ane prettie gilt pennair,[i]
> Ane bag off silk, all at his belt he weir.
>
> (1356–9)

[a] Moral epilogue.
[b] jolly sweet season.
[c] rose.
[d] sloth.
[e] a wood . . . without a guide.
[f] beautiful place.
[g] A.
[h] quill pen.
[i] gilded penholder.

This is not the misshapen Aesop of legend but a distinguished, imperious figure 'with ane feirful face' (1361).[4] There is thus an immediate contrast between the ancient writer, who confidently advances towards Henryson ('he come ane sturdie pace' [1362]), and Henryson himself, who is still reclining 'amang thir bewis bene'[a] (1346). Significantly, Aesop speaks first (1363) and sits down *beside* Henryson (1366), thereby both imaging his superiority once again but also implying a certain familiarity with the Scots writer. The language here is especially striking in this regard. Aesop's first words are 'God speid, my *sone*' (1363, emphasis added), and that 'word' (1364) is not only pleasing to Henryson but also well known ('couth') to him. Whether the intended meaning of *word* is 'utterance' or 'single lexical item', the implication is that Henryson has customarily viewed Aesop as his figurative father, the name with which he initially addresses him ('Welcome, father' [1366]) and which he later reprises with a reference to Aesop's 'fatherheid' (1399); in turn, throughout the Prologue Aesop refers to Henryson as his 'sone' (1370, 1382, 1388). To be sure, such language might be used between any social or ecclesiastical superior and subordinate, but the wider cultural context here implies a more specific application: Henryson affirms Aesop as his figurative father in the sense that the genuine *auctores* are the fathers of the vernacular makers and nascent authors. Indeed, if the Scots poet presents the ancient as his father, he also regards him as his 'maister' (1367, 1377, 1384), and throughout the dialogue Henryson's language is deferential and includes both rhetorical concessions (e.g., 'Displeis ȝow not' [1367]) and the invariable use of the honorific plural pronouns 'ȝe' and 'ȝow'. Furthermore, the syntax he uses to phrase his final request to Aesop is as elaborately circumspect as that used either by Beowulf or by Sir Gawain for their own respective famous requests:

> 'ȝit,[b] gentill schir,'[c] said I, 'for my requeist,
> Not to displeis ȝour fatherheid, I pray,
> Vnder the figure off ane brutall beist,
> Ane morall fabill ȝe wald denȝe[d] to say.'
> (1398–1401)[5]

Given the profound respect that Henryson evinces for Aesop, it is perhaps not surprising that he conducts himself as an innocent by asking Aesop to declare his 'birth . . . facultye, and name' (1368). It is surprising, however, that Aesop reveals his 'winning is in heuin for ay' (1374), inasmuch as the historical Aesop was unambiguously pagan. But in converting Aesop to a Chris-

---

[a] pleasant boughs.
[b] Yet.
[c] Sir.
[d] deign.

tian now residing in Heaven, Henryson eliminates the one potentially com-
plicating aspect of his author's background and in effect provides, through
Aesop's eventual acquiescence to Henryson's demands, divine confirmation of
the theoretical positions he here dramatizes. It is also perhaps surprising that
Henryson should now, after he himself has clearly recognized the 'fairest man
that euer befoir' (1348) he saw and after this 'man' has clearly identified himself
(1370–6), additionally demand that Aesop clarify his literary accomplishments
in order to confirm his identity. Yet Henryson thereby forces himself (and the
reader) to pause and consider the qualities and accomplishments of this representative *auctor*, and Henryson's questions thus further the discussion of literary authority in the passage:

> 'Ar 3e not he that all thir fabillis wrate,[a]
> Quhilk in effect, suppois[b] thay fen3eit be,
> Ar full off prudence and moralitie?'
> (1379–81)[6]

When Henryson asks Aesop for a composition that meets one set of
criteria put forth in the Prologue to the *Moral Fables* – that the work be
both rhetorically pleasing ('ane prettie fabill' [1386]) and ethically beneficial
('Concludand with ane gude moralitie' [1387]) – Aesop refuses. But he does
so not because the composition Henryson requests is theoretically impossible
– not because poetry cannot be simultaneously rhetorical and ethical – nor
because it is impertinent for a maker to make such a demand of an *auctor* but
because, in Aesop's words, '"quhat[c] is it worth to tell ane fen3eit taill, / Quhen[d]
haly preiching may na thing auaill?"' (1389–90). As Aesop elaborates this view
(1391–7), it becomes clear that from his now-divine perspective the corrup-
tion and decadence of the world have rendered useless his ethical 'taillis' if not
ethical instruction itself. Despite what would seem to be the unchangeable and
irrefutable nature of his position, however, the narrator does in fact persuade
him to tell a tale, not by the cogency of any further arguments but simply by
the power of his own rhetoric. As a result, during the course of the dialogue
Henryson moves from passivity, when he remains reclining to meet Aesop, to
activity, when he is not silenced by Aesop's objections but is in fact able to
silence them through rhetoric.

In this regard, it seems especially significant that the fable Aesop tells is
The Lion and the Mouse, for this fable and its *Moralitas* offer the most explicit
political and social commentary in all of the *Moral Fables*.[7] Henryson may well

---

[a] that wrote all these fables.
[b] although.
[c] what.
[d] when.

be 'cautious' in having Aesop tell this traditional story of a mouse that, having been freed by a lion, in turn releases the lion from a net in which it has been trapped.[8] But in view of the way that the Prologue to the fable foregrounds the issue of literary authority, another motivation for this particular tale at this particular point in the *Moral Fables* is possible. In telling a fable that is moralized as an account of the ideal social balance between king and commons, Henryson, through Aesop, confidently assumes what would become the Renaissance role of the adviser to and supporter of a prince.[9] It is this role that Aesop, in his final paternal and authorial gesture, explicitly transfers to the vernacular poet:

> My fair child,
> Perswaid the kirkmen ythandly to pray[a]
> That tressoun of this cuntrie be exyld,
> And iustice[b] regne, and lordis keip thair fay[c]
> Vnto thair souerane lord baith nycht and day.
> (1615–19)

As rhetorical representations of larger cultural concerns, Henryson's unique dialogue with Aesop and the subsequent telling of *The Lion and the Mouse* thus enact a usurpation of authorial voice and authority by a vernacular writer. Up to this point in the *Moral Fables* Henryson has feigned to be merely a translator, passing on the text of an auctor. By drawing Aesop into a narrative that purports to be the translated text of Aesop, Henryson renders Aesop and his work part of the fiction and, consequently, undermines the authority that is imputed to him as an auctor and the efficient cause of the fables. Moreover, in silencing Aesop's objections and evidently compelling him to tell a story and in relying on rhetoric alone to achieve this end, Henryson appropriates for himself the dominant, authoritative role in the dialogue. Having usurped the rhetorical voice of his auctor – that is, authorship – Henryson thus by extension usurps his responsibility for the *Fables* – his authoritativeness. Moreover, since Aesop tells a fable of social criticism and since Aesop's composition is exposed as the production of Henryson himself, the Scots poet also assumes Aesop's ability to make ethical utterances that have authorization. What Henryson dramatizes, in effect, is the birth of the vernacular author whose father is literary authority and whose mother is vernacular language ('mother toung' [31]). The *Moral Fables* is thereby in part a poem motivated by cultural and linguistic anxieties over the status of vernacular writers. In order

---

[a] Persuade the ecclesiastics to pray constantly.
[b] justice.
[c] faith.

to replace Aesop, his father figure, Henryson first needs to legitimate a famil-ial connection between the Antique or patristic fathers and the vernacular sons. But of necessity, for Henryson's rhetorical resolution of the conflict over authority to make sense, it requires a cultural context in which the issue is not yet resolved. Indeed, this attempt at legitimation, which would not receive broad institutional support in England for at least another hundred years, only serves to confirm the fact that the authority of the vernacular writer was still, in the late fifteenth century, a contested issue.[10]

Notes

1 Denton Fox (ed.), *The Poems of Robert Henryson* (Oxford: Clarendon Press, 1981).
2 My discussion supports the arguments that assert that the order of the fables in the Bassandyne print is Henryson's. See Fox, *Poems*, pp. lxxv–lxxxi. A detailed discussion of the relevant issues lies outside the scope of my argument, though I would like to note that the 'literary' evidence marshaled in support of the textual evidence of Bassandyne does not at all seem to me inadmissible or beside the point; indeed, such evidence has long been used in arguments about the intended order of the *Canterbury Tales*. The agreement of this evidence seems formidable: It is the Bassandyne order in which Howard Roerecke has demonstrated thematic coherence and symmetrical patterning ('The Integrity and Symmetry of Robert Henryson's *Moral Fables*', unpublished dissertation, Pennsylvania State University, 1969), George D. Gopen the aesthetic complexity of three 'simultaneously func-tional symmetries' ('The Essential Seriousness of Robert Henryson's *Moral Fables*: A Study is Structure', *Studies in Philology* 82 [1985], 42–59), and A. C. Spearing an artful utilization of the sovereign midpoint. As Spearing notes, 'It seems unlikely that an organization so ingenious in itself and so appropriate to the meaning of the central tale and of the whole series could have occurred by chance' ('Central and Displaced Sovereignty in Three Medieval Poems', *Review of English Studies* n.s. 33 [1982], 256). While it is possible that a later redactor and not Henryson himself is responsible for the order, I would argue that such a redac-tor would have had to have had a more sophisticated understanding of author-ship and literary structure than Henryson. And then even if this were the case, this understanding remains a significant statement of vernacular medieval aesthetics.
3 On Aesop as an auctor, see Ernst Robert Curtius, *European Literature and the Latin Middle Ages*, trans. W. R. Trask (New York: Pantheon, 1953), pp. 49–50, and Alastair Minnis, *Medieval Theory of Authorship: Scholastic Literary Attitudes in the Later Middle Ages* (London: Scolar Press, 1984), p. 161.
4 In Caxton's translation of Rinuccio's *Life*, e.g., Aesop 'had a grete hede/large vysage/longe Iowes/sharp eyen/a short necke/corbe backed/grete bely/grete legges/and large feet' (Caxton, *Caxton's Aesop*, ed. R. T. Lenaghan [Cambridge, MA: Harvard University Press, 1967], p. 27).

5   See *Beowulf*, 426–32, and *Sir Gawain*, 343–7 (see *Sir Gawain and the Green Knight*, ed. J. R. R. Tolkein and E. V. Gordon, 2nd edn, rev. N. Davis [Oxford: Oxford University Press, 1967]).

6   In the *Inferno*, in what is perhaps the *locus classicus* of confrontations between vernacular writers and *auctores*, Dante also demands the identity of the figure he meets. But there it is clear that Dante, unlike Henryson, does not in fact recognize the figure. It also may be noted that though Dante, like Henryson, is deferential to his *auctor*, he never challenges and overrules him the way the Scots poet does; when Vergil leaves Dante in the Earthly Paradise, it is because the Latin poet himself recognizes the limitations of his knowledge. See *Inferno* 1.61–87 and *Purgatorio* 27.127–43. Similarly, in the prologue to his translation of Mapheus Vegius's thirteenth book of the *Aeneid*, Gavin Douglas ('Threttene Buik of Eneados', in Anne Cox Brinton (ed.), *Maphaeus Vegius and his Thirteenth Book of The Aeneid* [Stanford: Stanford University Press, 1930]) asks about the identity of the *auctor* he meets because he does not know who he is – 'I saw зou nevir ayr.' This meeting, however, is presented comically – Vegius beats the Scots poet 'twenty rowtis apoun [his] rigging' because of Douglas's reluctance to translate the thirteenth book – though Douglas is nonetheless deferential to his *auctor* and acts according to his wishes.

7   Critics have interpreted Henryson's rendition of 'The Lion and the Mouse' in a variety of ways, though they all agree on the political nature of the piece. See, for example, Matthew P. McDiarmid, *Robert Henryson* (Edinburgh: Scottish Academic Press, 1981), pp. 15–16; Spearing, 'Central and Displaced Sovereignty', pp. 254–6; Denton Fox, 'The Coherence of Henryson's Work', in Robert Yeager (ed.), *Fifteenth Century Studies: Recent Essays* (Hamden, CT: Archon Books, 1984), p. 277; C. David Benson, 'O Moral Henryson', in Robert Yeager (ed.), *Fifteenth Century Studies: Recent Essays* (Hamden, CT: Archon Books, 1984), p. 227; and George D. Gopen (ed.), *The Moral Fables of Aesop* (Notre Dame, IN: University of Notre Dame Press, 1987), p. 22.

8   So Robert L. Kindrick asserts in *Robert Henryson* (Boston, MA: Twayne, 1979), p. 105.

9   See Richard Firth Green, *Poets and Princepleasers: Literature in the English Court in the Middle Ages* (Toronto: University of Toronto Press, 1980).

10   See further Tim William Machan 'Robert Henryson and Father Aesop: Authority in the *Moral Fables*', *Studies in the Age of Chaucer* 12 (1990), 193–214.

Further Reading

For a different take on the question of medieval authorship, see Anne Middleton, 'William Langland's "Kynde Name": Authorial Signature and Social Identity in Late Fourteenth-century England', in Lee Patterson (ed.), *Literary Practice and Social Change in Britain, 1380–1530* (Berkeley, CA: University of California Press, 1990), pp. 15–81. Roland Barthes' essay on 'The Death of the Author' can be found in his *Image–Music–Text*, trans. Stephen Heath (New York: Hill and Wang, 1977), pp.

142–8, and Michel Foucault's 'What is an Author?', in David Lodge (ed.), *Modern Criticism and Theory: A Reader* (London: Longman, 1988), pp. 196–210. Criticism on Thomas Hoccleve has shown that 'autobiographical poetry' in Middle English, though rare, was not an impossibility: J. A. Burrow, 'Autobiographical Poetry in the Middle Ages: The Case of Thomas Hoccleve', *Proceedings of the British Academy* 68 (1982), 389–412, and Nicholas Perkins, *Hoccleve's Regiment of Princes: Counsel and Constraint* (Cambridge: D. S. Brewer, 2001).

Chapter Notes

1   Bernhard Ten Brink, *History of English Literature*, trans. Horace M. Kennedy (London: George Bell and Sons, 1904), p. 218.
2   William Henry Schofield, *English Literature from the Norman Conquest to Chaucer* (London: Macmillan, 1914), pp. 350–1.
3   C. G. Osgood (ed.), *Pearl* (Boston: Heath and Co., 1906).
4   Israel Gollancz, '*Pearl, Cleanness, Patience* and *Sir Gawain*', in A. W. Ward and A. R. Waller (eds), *The Cambridge History of English Literature* (Cambridge: Cambridge University Press, 1907), pp. 320–34 (p. 332).
5   O. Cargill and M. Schlauch, '*The Pearl* and its Jeweller', *PMLA* 43 (1928), 105–23.
6   Coolidge Otis Chapman, 'The Authorship of *The Pearl*', *PMLA* 47 (1932), 346–53.
7   W. A. Davenport, *The Art of the Gawain-poet* (London: Athlone Press, 1978), p. 1.
8   Israel Gollancz (ed.), *Pearl: An English Poem of the Fourteenth Century* (London: The Medieval Library, 1921), pp. xl–xli.
9   H. Oskar Sommer (ed.), *Le Morte Darthur* (London, 1889–91), Vol. II, pp. 1–2; George Lyman Kittredge, 'Who was Sir Thomas Malory?', *Harvard Studies and Notes in Philology and Literature* 5 (1896–7), 85–106.
10 Alfred T. Martin, 'Sir Thomas Malory', *Athenaeum* 30 (1897), 353–4; 'The Identity of the Author of *Le Morte Darthur*', *Archaeologica* 56 (1898), 165–77.
11 E. K. Chambers, *Sir Thomas Malory* (Oxford: Oxford University Press, 1922); Edward Hicks, *Sir Thomas Malory, his Turbulent Career* (Cambridge, MA: Harvard University Press, 1928); Eugène Vinaver, *Malory* (Oxford: Oxford University Press, 1929), Appendix I.
12 A. C. Baugh, 'Documenting Sir Thomas Malory', *Speculum* 8 (1933), 1–29.
13 William Matthews, *The Ill-framed Knight: A Skeptical Inquiry into the Identity of Sir Thomas Malory* (Berkeley, CA: University of California Press, 1966).
14 Larry D. Benson, *Malory's Morte Darthur* (Cambridge, MA: Harvard University Press, 1976), p. ix.
15 R. M. Lumiansky, 'Sir Thomas Malory's *Le Morte Darthur*, 1947–1987: Author, Title, Text', *Speculum* 62 (1987), 878–97 (883).
16 P. J. C. Field, *The Life and Times of Sir Thomas Malory* (Cambridge: D. S. Brewer, 1993).

17   Wimsatt and Beardsley's essay first appeared in W. K. Wimsatt, *The Verbal Icon: Studies in the Meaning of Poetry* (Lexington: University of Kentucky Press, 1954).

18   E. Talbot Donaldson, 'Chaucer the Pilgrim', *PMLA* 69 (1954), 928–36 (928).

19   Charles Moorman, 'The Role of the Narrator in *Pearl*', *Modern Philology* 80 (1955), 73–81 (74).

20   Jocelyn Wogan-Browne, Nicholas Watson, Andrew Taylor and Ruth Evans (eds), *The Idea of the Vernacular: An Anthology of Middle English Literary Theory, 1280–1520* (Exeter: University of Exeter Press, 1999), pp. 4–5.

21   C. S. Lewis, *The Discarded Image: An Introduction to Medieval and Renaissance Literature* (Cambridge: Cambridge University Press, 1964), p. 211.

22   Rosemary Woolf, *The English Religious Lyric in the Middle Ages* (Oxford: Clarendon Press, 1968), pp. 5–6.

23   Derek Brewer (ed.), *Chaucer and Chaucerians: Critical Studies in Middle English Literature* (London: Thomas Nelson and Sons, 1966); Douglas Gray, *Robert Henryson* (Leiden: E. J. Brill, 1979); John Burrow, *Thomas Hoccleve, Authors of the Middle Ages 4* (Aldershot: Variorum, 1994).

24   Seth Lehrer, *Chaucer and his Readers: Imagining the Author in Late Medieval England* (Princeton, NJ: Princeton University Press, 1993), p. 11.

25   Alastair Minnis and Charlotte Brewer (eds), *Crux and Controversy in Middle English Textual Criticism* (Cambridge: D. S. Brewer, 1992), p. x.

26   Ralph Hanna III, *Pursuing History: Middle English Manuscripts and their Texts* (Stanford: Stanford University Press, 1996), p. 176.

2

Textual Form

Formalism, New Criticism and textual form in Middle English texts. Critical approaches to the 'unity' of medieval texts. Robert Jordan's theory of 'inorganic structure'. Derek Brewer on form in the Morte Darthur. *Hugh White on the form of Gower's* Confessio Amantis.

We can trace a second route through the varied terrain of Middle English criticism by considering the recurrent concern of textual form. Many critical readings seek an entry point into a text through study of its form, surveying structure, arrangement and the inter-relations between constituent parts. It was not always so. The formalist emphasis is slighter in late-Victorian and early twentieth-century scholarship where antiquarian and historical interests took precedence.[1] Historicists treasured medieval literature as a repository of ancient customs, manners and mores, as a source for the study of legend and folktale (see chapter 6). They looked beyond superficies of style and structure in search of precise historical contexts for works or real-life identifications for, say, Chaucer's pilgrims or Malory's knights. The shift away from these historicist and literalist approaches was speeded by the influence of the Russian Formalism of the early twentieth century. Led by theorists Victor Shklovsky and Roman Jakobson, the Formalists set aside extrinsic contexts of history and authorial biography, focusing instead on the intrinsic verbal and technical elements of the literary text.[2] Their approach permeated academic English studies with the rise of the formalist and ahistorical New Criticism of the 1930s and 1940s whose enduring legacy means that, today, a share of formal analysis will feature in almost any sample of Middle English criticism.

Did medieval writers and audiences share this concern with literary form? More learned authors could, after all, draw upon a small amount of literary theory on the matter. Geoffrey of Vinsauf, celebrated authority on rhetoric in the Middle Ages (see chapter 4), famously likened poetic composition to the fabrication of the solid structures of a building. His simile is quoted by Pandarus in Book II of Chaucer's *Troilus and Criseyde*:

> For everi wight* that hath an hous to founde*   person   build
> Ne renneth naught the werk for to begynne
> With rakel* hond, but he wol bide a stounde*,   hasty   wait a while
> And sende his hertes line* out fro withinne   imaginary guiding line
> Aldirfirst* his purpos for to wynne.   first of all
>   (1, 1065–9)

But if medieval texts can be likened to buildings, readers have found many of these textual edifices to be ramshackle, fragmentary and haphazard. Medieval writers' conceptions of form often seem to differ markedly from our own. While texts such as *Gawain and the Green Knight* or *Pearl* might impress modern readers as balanced, self-enclosed and carefully wrought works, others seem much looser in structure. Langland's *Piers Plowman*, Chaucer's *Canterbury Tales*, Gower's *Confessio Amantis* – each work challenges modern notions of artistic coherence; each has provoked resourceful critical attempts to uncover these works' elusive unity.

To unify the *Canterbury Tales*, some critics stressed continuity and realism, plotting a geographically correct running-order for the tales (Furnivall) and real-life identifications for the pilgrims (Manly).[3] Others sought unity in symbolism, enfolding each separate element of the *Tales* in an over-arching allegorical scheme (Tupper),[4] while others sought unity in the pilgrims' dramatic interplay – a 'human comedy' (Kittredge) or 'roadside drama' (Lumiansky).[5] Still others stressed the unifying role of the pilgrimage frame. This was the case set out in Ralph Baldwin's 1955 study, *The Unity of the Canterbury Tales*, where the architectural metaphors of Geoffrey of Vinsauf were applied to Chaucer's poem:

> An examination of the beginning and the ending of the *Tales*, the only masonry of our edifice on which Chaucer laboured without the help of his editors, reveals that they fulfil an architectonic function, hitherto overlooked, and that they sustain the story as they reinforce each other. They make the pilgrimage not a frame but a dynamic entity.[6]

Later, Helen Cooper's important study of 1983, *The Structure of the Canterbury Tales*, took up the question of textual form with recourse to a different metaphor. Rather than a fragmentary building, the *Tales* were now viewed as a jigsaw. Some pieces were missing but the overall design might still be picked out:

> The tales firmly joined in the separate fragments make recognisably coherent patterns, even though it may still be obscure as to how they might all eventu-

ally fit together and what the finished jigsaw would look like. And the pieces do join together, as much recent criticism has stressed: the *Canterbury Tales* is not a ragbag of unrelated narratives.[7]

A similar story might be told for the reception of Gower's *Confessio Amantis*, Langland's *Piers Plowman* and a range of other Middle English texts where the question of textual form has been foremost in critical reception. Indeed, the formalist and ahistorical emphases of New Criticism made unity of form a criterion of literary excellence, a legacy reflected in the many mid-century critical writings on the unity of medieval texts. (From Chaucer studies alone one could point to the unifications of *The Parlement of Foules* by Lumiansky (1948) and Stillwell (1950);[8] Muscatine's stress on form in *The Knight's Tale* of 1950;[9] or Ruggiers' 1953 unification of the patently unfinished *House of Fame*.)[10]

I have attempted in this paper to show the poem to be a really finely built structure, the nave for the people, the choir for the clergy, yet, like many a church in the Middle Ages, so crowded with tombs, rood-screens, chantries and side altars, that the total effect is a most curious blending of order and confusion.[11]

1929: Wells's essay on the construction of *Piers Plowman* already draws on architectural metaphors to make sense of textual form.

THE PROBLEM OF UNITY

Since medieval texts so often challenge modern notions of form, some critics have suggested that substantially different aesthetic conceptions must have applied in the Middle Ages – conceptions that must be recovered if valid formalist criticism is to be practised. If the medieval writer nursed a conception of formal unity at all, they argue, it can hardly have been identical to the 'organic unity' prized in literary criticism since Coleridge first identified the quality in Shakespeare: 'The organic form . . . is innate; it shapes as it develops itself from within, and the fullness of its development is one and the same with the perfection of its outward form.'[12] What were the factors that shaped medieval texts along such different lines from this model? For A. C. Spearing in 1964, one determining factor was orality. In his *Criticism and Medieval Poetry*, Spearing stressed the likely effect of oral delivery upon the structure of medieval texts. Far from nurturing 'organic' form, oral delivery would more likely create serial, episodic narrative structures:

This means that a long work, such as, for instance, Chaucer's *Troilus and Criseyde*, will tend to be constructed less as a single whole than as a series of episodes. Each episode will be developed semi-independently, and we shall be unable to find in the complete work the Aristotelian kind of unity which has a single plot as its centre or 'soul'.[13]

Where Spearing stressed orality, C. S. Lewis's *The Discarded Image* (also appearing in 1964) emphasized the role of rhetoric in bringing a digressive shape to medieval literature. Lewis suggested that literary digressions:

> can be regarded as an expression of the same impulse we see at work in much medieval architecture and decoration. We may call it the love of the labyrinthine; the tendency to offer to the mind or the eye something that cannot be taken in at one glance, something that at first looks planless though all is planned.[14]

JORDAN AND INORGANIC STRUCTURE

Shortly afterwards, Robert M. Jordan published a detailed study of the structure of Chaucer's major poetry. Drawing his aesthetic vocabulary from both rhetorical theory and architecture, Jordan emphasized the aggregative and quantitative character of medieval literary composition. His influential *Chaucer and the Shape of Creation* of 1967 described how any coherence we might find in medieval works is better characterized as a 'mechanic' rather than 'organic' unity:

> Regarding his poems as finite, limited illusions, the medieval poet developed modes of formalism which in the light of modern theory will seem mechanical and artificial but which in truth express assumptions – about both life and art – which are fundamentally and enduringly human.[15]

Jordan described the medieval writer as working with 'a quantitative approach to literary structure', disposing literary materials into a preconceived shape, section by section, quite unlike the organic literary creation envisaged by post-Romantic criticism (compare Derek Pearsall's view of Lydgate as craftsman in chapter 1).

> Whether in consequence of the depletion of prime philological materials or an increasing general interest in aesthetic values, medieval English studies have taken a pronounced critical turn since World War II. All things considered, this has been a fortunate development; for two or three preceding generations of medievalists left the question of artistic achievement embarrassed, either by their silence or by their impressionism and affectivity. Perhaps a majority, conditioned by classical criteria and nineteenth-century exemplars, took mainly an antiquarian and historical interest in what was very often literature seemingly careless of formal requirements.[16]

1968: Arthur K. Moore observes a turning tide in Middle English formalist criticism.

These formalist approaches to Middle English led to a wide critical recogni- GOTHIC
tion of a distinct 'Gothic aesthetic' infusing medieval texts. Inspired by such FORMS
works of art history as Erwin Panofsky's *Gothic Architecture and Scholasticism*
(1957) and Emile Mâle's *The Gothic Image* (1958),[17] critics such as Charles
Muscatine had emphasized how this 'Gothic aesthetic' was one of unity-in-
diversity, juxtaposing disparate modes and materials. In his *Chaucer and the
French Tradition* of 1957, Muscatine argued how this aesthetic illuminates the
mixed modes and varied structures of Chaucer's poetry. Unity of form might
be present in these texts after all, but it would reside not in an 'organic unity'
but, paradoxically, in diversity and juxtaposition – in plenitude of expression
and in the skilful arrangement of disparate and disjunctive literary materials.
Just as the sculpture of the medieval mason might frame a saint's visage alongside the anarchic grotesquerie of the Green Man, so the medieval writer might
take equal delight in blending earnest with game, sacred with profane, comedy
with tragedy, high style with low.

> Medieval literary theory does not lean heavily on the ideas of form, structure,
> and coherence, preferring rather to dwell on the methods of amplification and
> ornamentation, which in too many cases obliterate form and structure.[18]

1972: Charles Muscatine's *Poetry and Crisis in the Age of Chaucer* pursues
questions of form.

Such were the dominant approaches to textual form down to the mid-
1960s, the date of our first extract. (On the rival tradition of 'exegetical criticism', where texts were unified at the allegorical level, see chapter 5.)[19] The
extract reflects one of the most dramatic debates on unity to have taken place
in Middle English criticism, centred upon one of the most enduring of
medieval English texts – Sir Thomas Malory's *Morte Darthur*.

By the early decades of the twentieth century Malory's prose tale of King DEBATES ON
Arthur and the Round Table knights had long been known to readers as a UNITY: THE
single, unified text, printed in 1485 by William Caxton under the title *Le Morte* CASE OF
Darthur. With its twenty-one chapters covering Arthur's birth, reign and MALORY'S
death, the *Morte* had the narrative sweep of a nineteenth-century novel. But *MORTE*
in 1947 this notion was challenged when Eugène Vinaver re-edited the text *DARTHUR*
under the controversial title *The Works of Sir Thomas Malory*. As his title suggests, Vinaver saw Malory's text not as a continuous, unified tale but as eight
separate romances: 'instead of a single work subordinate to an imaginary principle of "structure", we now have before us a series of works reflecting in an
ever-changing panorama of incident and character a genuine variety of

narrative forms and fancies.'[20] The editor's case rested upon the scribal evidence of the recently discovered Winchester manuscript, in which formal *implicits* and *explicits* split Malory's work into eight separate parts.

The resulting 'unity debate' was heated. A 'unitarian' school of Malory criticism quickly formed to counter the Vinaver thesis, the best of it acknowledging that a new aesthetic vocabulary was needed if coherence was to be claimed without recourse to the anachronistic notion of 'organic unity'. In the United States the unity case was advanced by Wilson's 'How Many Books Did Malory Write?' (1951)[21] and Lumiansky's 'The Question of Unity in Malory's *Morte Darthur*'.[22] In England, the case for unity was influentially set out by D. S. Brewer, first in 1952 in an article on 'Form in the *Morte Darthur*'[23] and, again, in expanded form in the collaborative volume *Essays on Malory* of 1963 – the source of our first extract. Though embracing source study and historicism, Brewer's critical approach bases itself firmly on the central propositions of New Criticism: the literary work is to be judged 'in and for itself alone'; authorial intentions are 'undiscoverable and unimportant, except in so far as they reveal themselves in the book'. The result is a classic formalist intervention in the Malory debate, one that challenged Middle English studies to evolve a more apposite and nuanced vocabulary for describing the form of medieval works.

Extract from D. S. Brewer, 'The hoole book', in *Essays on Malory*, ed. J. A. W. Bennett (Oxford: Clarendon Press, 1963), pp. 42–52.

[. . .] Our difficulty in discussing the form of the *Morte Darthur* is partly due to the lack of satisfactory descriptive and critical terms for the kind of literary experience that Malory gives us. It is natural for those who are dissatisfied with the idea of completely separate romances to assert some kind of unity for Malory's work. But obviously unity here cannot mean structural unity of a kind we expect from a modern novel, or that we find in an ancient epic; and the term unity (which I have used in the past) is probably misleading and should be abandoned. If we assert the connectedness of the constituent works we shall be on safer ground, but there are not specific connexions everywhere, and the term does not include those impressions of unity of atmosphere and of underlying concepts which Professor Vinaver himself has never denied, and which are an important part of the general literary effect. Perhaps the best term, of a useful elasticity, is *cohesion*.[1] The cohesion of Malory's *Works* is greater than that of the separate works of a modern novelist, though it is different from that Coleridgean concept of 'organic unity' with which we now approach a work of art.

The emphasis must be on 'the work of art'. In the last resort, when all has been learnt than can be known of authorship and source, Malory's work must be judged, like any other, in and for itself alone. It is the more important to emphasize this in Malory's case because, as Professor Vinaver has shown us, Malory had a peculiar relation to his sources. He has rehandled them, to be sure, in accordance with his own strong feeling for form and moral content, but he is also completely at their mercy. Unless they move him, he cannot move. The essence of the matter was put by a reviewer of Vinaver's edition in *The Times Literary Supplement* (7 June 1947): 'we are not reading the work of an independent artist. . . . Whatever he does, Malory's personal contribution to the total effect cannot be very great, though it may be very good.' When we look at Malory's work – or works – we are not looking at the work of one man, but perhaps of a dozen, far separated in time and space, occupation and outlook. Each writer built on what had been made before. The work of art is cumulative and transcends any one, or any group, of its makers. Malory's very dependence on his sources makes us insist, paradoxically, that in terms of art neither the sources nor Malory himself are of the least importance. Malory's personal contribution is less than the book as a whole, and the book may create effects of which Malory is little more than the scribe.

Here is perhaps the root of the differences, which, after all, are rather of emphasis and nomenclature than of principle, between Professor Vinaver and those who are reluctant to accept the complete divisions proposed in his great edition of 1947 and further emphasized in his edition of *The Death of King Arthur*. In his major edition Professor Vinaver was chiefly concerned to show the nature and as it were the machinery of Malory's personal contribution. That he has brilliantly succeeded, and in so doing has made an important contribution to our understanding of Malory's work, and of an important phase in literary history, is beyond dispute. But it may also be argued that in his perfectly proper and highly illuminating emphasis on Malory's personal contribution, and perhaps because of his own vast knowledge of the whole Arthurian *corpus*, he has taken for granted what needs equal emphasis in an aesthetic judgement: that is, the inherent tendencies to cohesion of that *corpus*, and Malory's reflection of that tendency to cohesion, even while he simplified its complexities. His simplification, indeed inevitably made the cohesion more evident.

Yet I do not wish to underestimate Malory's personal contribution even to the sense of cohesion in the whole Arthurian *corpus*. At the very least he brought out what was only suggested, and the completed work shows that his whole attitude to the material differed from his predecessors'. Professor Vinaver's consciousness of Malory's dependence on, yet divergence from, his sources sometimes leads him to measure Malory against the French and find him wanting, where to the less learned reader it seems merely that Malory is attempting and achieving something different. A minor example of this is Malory's detail of the twenty thousand pounds it cost the Queen to find Lancelot (*W*, p. 831),[2] which Professor Vinaver once deplored and Professor Lewis defended. Granted the different premises, each critic is right. But if we judge Malory's work by the standards of its source, rather than by its effectiveness within its own context, we may miss, or misinterpret, the special quality of the work of art itself.

Thus for two opposite reasons, Malory's dependence on his sources, and Malory's differences from his sources, we must make a clear distinction between Malory's personal contribution and the actual book he left. Sometimes the effect of the book is due primarily to Malory's source, and sometimes it is due primarily to Malory's own personal contribution. Fascinating and important as it is to distinguish, guided by Professor Vinaver, between what is derived and what is personal,[3] such a distinction cannot affect our final judgement on the total work of art, which must be judged in its own right, as a whole, obeying its own laws, holding and shaping the reader's imagination by its own power. (I do not deny the value of anything that will help us to a clearer understanding of the work of art, especially in places where it is obscure or to some extent unsuccessful; a knowledge of the sources is particularly relevant to understanding much of Malory, and the knowledge that Professor Vinaver has put at our disposal enormously increases our understanding and enjoyment of Malory's aims and achievements.)

When, therefore, we disregard the peculiar mixture of source and personal contribution in Malory's book, and look 'at the thing in itself, as it really is', we shall be more than ever impressed by a sense of its cohesion. How far that impression is due to Malory's sources does not for the moment matter. It would not even matter if Malory's personal contribution had only been to attempt to break down that sense of cohesion; it is still there. And in fact the case is not so desperate. It is possible to show, thanks to Professor Vinaver's own edition, that there are bonds still left between the various tales, and that Malory also made a deliberate attempt to link the beginnings and ends of his tales together. It is also possible to show that the tales could not have been put together in any order other than the present one; that the succession of romances has a cumulative effect; and that there is a kind of shapeliness in the whole book, even though the shape is one that is difficult to describe.

We must first emphasize what is indeed indisputable, the unity of tone and atmosphere, the continual moral concern of a special kind. All the tales are concerned with the romance of knight-errantry, of strange adventures in which the wrongs of the oppressed are to be righted, and in which the High Order of Knighthood is justified and glorified. There is certainly a development in

Malory's concept of true morality, and certainly the earlier books are fiercer, more primitive; but the same conception of the moral quality of knightliness, most movingly expressed in Ector's lament for Lancelot, underlies them all.

Then all the stories are concerned with the same kind of people, and all these people are associated with the same central group, the court of Arthur. Indeed, one of Malory's great achievements is his portrayal of this passionate, limited and aristocratic society, with its own standards of success and failure.

Next, within this society some half-dozen characters are dominant in most of the tales and continually recur. Of these Arthur and Lancelot are the most important. Now it is very noticeable that the tales, in the order that we have them, observe the proper sequence of events in the lives of Lancelot and Arthur. There is a biographical continuity observed throughout the tales which effectively links them together. This is worth exploring. Its existence reduces to minor proportions certain apparent inconsistencies in the treatment of minor characters. There are no inconsistencies (though perhaps some lack of realism) in the presentation, in due order, throughout all the tales, of the lives of the chief characters.

The passage of time, and the development of character and event are particularly strongly felt in the first two and last three tales. The first two tales show us the birth of Arthur, his first flowering as a knight, and his triumph as a great king over many lands – though with this essential theme there are, in Spenserian terms, 'other adventures intermedled'. The second tale, of Arthur's war against Rome, is especially interesting because in it the young Lancelot appears for the first time. He is rapidly brought forth as a hero subsidiary to Arthur alone; and Professor Vinaver shows that Malory invents almost everything that is said about Lancelot in this tale, while diminishing the roles that other knights have in his source. At the end of the second tale Arthur is triumphantly established as the greatest English king, ruling from Ireland to Rome, surrounded by his knights of the Round Table, devoted to the High Order of Knighthood. It seems to a reader natural and logical enough that the third tale should go on to establish in his own right the prowess of Malory's second hero, Sir Lancelot. Once Lancelot is established, the next tales reinforce the sense of continuity by going on to give the histories and to reveal the glorious deeds of other knights of the Round Table. These are the short tale of Sir Gareth and the inordinately long one of Sir Tristram. The reason why Malory leaves out the tragic end of the French tale of Sir Tristram, and leaves Sir Tristram in cheerful domesticity, is surely because these central tales of Lancelot, Gareth, Tristam, and a number of minor characters, are all devoted to the glory and success of the knights of the Round table. Arthur and Lancelot, once they have been established, recede somewhat into the background. But Arthur is the point of departure and return for all the knights, and their glory is his; while Sir Lancelot, even where he is not a central figure, is frequently mentioned as the type of ideal knight. The praise of Sir Tristram is that his fame at one time began to overshadow Sir Lancelot's, and there could be no higher praise. In these fourth and fifth books, therefore, if Arthur and Lancelot are less active it is not because they have been supplanted.

In all the French books, and in the English *Morte Arthure* which is the principal source of Malory's second tale, the story of the Roman campaign and triumph is followed forthwith by the story of Arthur's downfall. Malory places the story of Lancelot's adventures immediately after Arthur's return from Rome. Professor Vinaver argues from this that Malory was ignorant of the position of the '*Lancelot* proper' in the Arthurian cycle (*W*, p. 1398). But Malory knew, if only from the English source of his second tale, that the death of Arthur followed the Roman campaign, and he probably knew this from French tales as well. The change he introduced was probably deliberate. He postponed the tragic end and turned his second tale into a tale of triumph, possibly in tribute, as Professor Vinaver suggests, to Henry V, but also in tribute to Arthur, and to all that Arthur stands for in his imagination. The triumphant second tale establishes the chief hierophant of the Order of Knighthood. Arthur has to be established in his own greatness before we feel the greatness of his court, his knights, and the ideals they express. On the other hand the crowning of Arthur is the climax of his personal triumph. Further adventures of his own could not effectively add to it. His glory is extended in the next three tales by the glorious deeds of his knights. These anglicized paladins, with their noble achievements, by acknowledging him as their lord add their renown to his. Certainly, Malory was not interested in subtle analysis of courtly feeling, but it is fruitless to blame him for this. We must take what we can get. What we are offered is essentially the story of the Golden Age of English history, and how it came to its tragic end. So it is fitting that the time of Arthur's triumph should be separated from the time of disaster. It makes Arthur's fame in later ages more comprehensible, it allows us to dwell somewhat on the English glory of the Round Table and of the Order of Knighthood. And as a literary result, it makes the final tragedy more moving by allowing to flourish somewhat the flower which is to be so cruelly lopped; for the final tragedy is not only one of persons but of 'the flower of chivalry of the world'; of a whole noble way of life.

After the second book there are no precise notations of age, but it is nevertheless true that we have been introduced to the chief actors in their youth, and that we follow them through the glory of their maturity to their sad decline and exemplary deaths. Within this general biographical chronology, which is never violated, inconsistencies in the treatment of some minor characters are unimportant. Such as they are (and they have been over-emphasized) they tend to occur in the middle books, where the sense of the passage of time, though not neglected by Malory, is less important. Thus, taking the events in the lives of Arthur and Lancelot as our main guide, we can see a clearly perceptible progression throughout the first two books, which corresponds to the rise in Fortune's wheel; a less perceptible movement in the next three books, when Arthur's glory is at its height; and a further progressive movement in the last three books, gathering momentum especially in the last two, whose downward movement is the wheel's adverse turn. Whether or not Malory consciously intended this form is perhaps disputable. If he did not, he would not be the first or last author to have built better than he knew. In any event, Malory's conscious intentions are undiscoverable and unimportant, except in so far as they reveal themselves in the book. The test of the form I have suggested is whether it corresponds to the details of the book; whether it makes sense in itself; and whether equal sense could be made of a different arrangement of the books.

The form makes sense in itself because it describes a general chronological progression just like those in life, and also comprehensible to medieval views of life. Growth, flowering, and decay; rise, supremacy, and fall not only completely accord with normal experience, but can easily be imaged in such medieval terms as Fortune's wheel. If we disorder the tales, this general pattern which holds them together is lost. And to insist on the completely separate nature of the *Works* is inevitably to insist that there is no literary value in reading them in any specific order; to insist that there will be no loss if we read of Arthur's death, before we read of his triumph or birth. How can we insist on such a crippling procedure, once we have realized the chronological order of the tales in their present sequence?

In looking more closely at the details of arrangement we should bear in mind that for Malory the material he was arranging was historical material. For various reasons medieval writers make a different distinction from ours between *fabula* and *historia*; or rather, the two kinds intermingled for them in a way that is strange to us. Chaucer's treatment of the story of Troilus and Criseyde is perhaps the most obvious example, but there are many others.[4] Furthermore, it is well known that from the late twelfth to the early seventeenth centuries practically all Englishmen thought that Arthur was a genuinely historical figure; and it is clear both from the general situation and from his own remarks (e.g. *W*, p. 1229) that Malory shared this view. Caxton in his Preface to the *Morte Darthur* 'coude not wel denye but that there was suche a noble kyng named Arthur'. He refers to Malory's work as 'a joyous history', even if 'to gyve fayth and byleve that al is trewe that is conteyned herein, ye be at your liberté'.[. . .]

It is this 'historical' basis that does much to explain our sense of the cohesion of Malory's separate tales. It would be strange, however, if this cohesion rested only on general impressions, and the general course of the narrative. It does not. There is plenty of evidence in the actual conduct of the individual stories, in the actual words that Malory uses, which confirms our feeling, and which is indeed largely the basis of our feeling, that with whatever local failure to master the material, Malory is dealing with one tract of time, one general course of events, throughout the whole series of tales. This evidence is found in the numerous references back and forth which establish continuity and connexions throughout the various books; and in the deliberate links invented by Malory, which form bridges between the main tales, and which further confirm the need to read them in the order in which they have come down to us.

To take some of the references forward and back. In the first tale, at the end of its first section, there is a reference forward to Mordred coming to court 'as hit rehersith aftirward and towarde the ende of the MORTE ARTHURE' (*W*, p. 56). This comment is apparently not in the French original. It may refer either to the French *Mort Artu* or to Malory's own later version. If to the latter, Professor Vinaver suggests that the comment is a scribal insertion not due to Malory himself. But the comment appears in both Caxton's text and the Winchester MS, and there is no evidence that it is merely scribal. It is at least as likely to be Malory's as not. Even if Malory's, it may be due to a phrase in the actual book he was copying. But it does not matter; the effect of a phrase like this in Malory's work as we have it, whether or not in eight parts, is to bind the parts together. The likely reason for the remark, if it is indeed Malory's, is surely that he was thinking forward not particularly to his own translation, if he projected it, but to the 'future' event which was part of the whole historical Arthurian sequence, whose cohesion underlies his work. There are a number of other references to 'future' events in this first tale (for example, on pages 91, 92, 97, 126, 179–80). Some of these are unquestionably due to 'the French book'. But as I have emphasized, it is immaterial for the present purpose whether such remarks are original or due to the source, since we are dealing with a work of multiple authorship, not Malory's alone. Whether or not invented or even intended by Malory, the binding effect is there. Thus, granting all that Professor Vinaver has shown us of Malory's reducing, dissolving, simplifying power, Malory has not cut the bonds completely. He has at least left in, or put in, those references forward of which I have given examples. In at least one case he has made the reference more explicit than it was in the French, as Professor Vinaver shows us: 'Marlyon warned the kyng covertly that Gwenyvere was nat holsom for hym to take to wyff. For he warned hym that Launcelot scholde love hir, and sche hym agayne' (*W*, p. 97). The French original of this is a very obscure hint, which Malory makes perfectly plain – somewhat to the disadvantage, indeed, of Arthur's character. Malory's clarification is not the kind of remark that reveals a modern sense of organic unity in the structure of the 'whole book', but it helps to establish, like the other references forward, a sense that we are dealing with a specific tract of experience, a history linked in cause and effect. That these references come so early in the whole historical sequence surely indicates that for Malory the various stories were bound together.

It does not matter that some of the references forward are inaccurate (e.g. that on pp. 179–80): no one can be surprised if an author whose scope is so vast changes the details of his plans. These references are inaccurate inasmuch as they do not agree with the later version produced by Malory himself, because they are translated from the source Malory was following at that moment, the *Suite du Merlin*, and they refer to the Quest of the Grail. From these inaccuracies Professor Vinaver argues Malory's ignorance, when writing this first tale, of the true story of the Grail, or at least of the version he was himself to translate, perhaps years later. Even if Professor Vinaver is right, we need not be driven to denying Malory's consciousness of the total Arthurian context. He cannot have been totally ignorant of the Grail story and its effect on the story of Arthur. At the very least these references he translates would have told him a good deal in outline. And would so devoted a reader of Arthurian tales have remained in ignorance of so well known a story even if, as is not surprising, he was hazy about the details?

Just as there are references forward in the first tale there are references back in the later tales. Some of the most notable are in *The Tale of the Sankgreal* itself, where, for example, Malory, apparently unprompted by his source, deliberately refers back to the story of Balin, which is part of the first tale (*W*, p. 856ff, especially 862–3). There are similar backward glances in the final *Tale of the Death of King Arthur* (e.g. p. 1198, referring to pp. 265–6). Again, these are more like an historian's references to earlier significant incidents and causes, than an artist's attempt to build up an organic whole. But these connexions have an artistic effect; they give a sense of continuity and also, as it were, of depth. They show the effects of causes remote but not detached. They give that sense of context in human affairs which great literature usually suggests. [. . .]

Notes

1   Professor Vinaver has himself suggested the use of this term to me. I am grateful to him for this and for several other suggestions generously made to me on the subject of this essay.
2   Eugène Vinaver (ed.), *The Works of Sir Thomas Malory* (Oxford: Oxford University Press, 1947), hereafter abbreviated in the text to *W*.
3   The distinction is obviously artificial; in fact the two may merge indistinguishably. Nevertheless, the two elements exist separately.

4   Cf. my *Chaucer*, 3rd edn (London: Longman, 1961), pp. 95, 127, 148, 158 for examples from Chaucer.

FLUID AND
FRACTURED
TEXTUAL
FORMS

Brewer's article, the Malory 'unity debate' and the continued study of form in Chaucer brought about a major shift in approaches to textual form. In the Middle English criticism of the 1970s onwards we encounter a more experimental vocabulary in the elucidation of form ('mechanic unity',[24] 'generic unity'[25]) and a broader willingness to recognise fluid, amorphous and downright disunited literary forms. We might take the case study of *Piers Plowman*. Where early critics had invested effort in arguing for the poem's structural integrity (Wells in 1929, Gerould in 1945, Dunning in 1956, Lawlor in 1957),[26] Charles Muscatine's 1972 *Poetry and Crisis in the Age of Chaucer* suggested 'the best criticism of the poem suggests that what might have been a great tripartite medieval structure does not rise here, or at least that it is neither clearly outlined nor solidly based.'[27] Accordingly, the diffuse character of some other medieval literary texts came to be viewed as less problematic as new implications of literary form were addressed. In 1979 Paul Strohm applied the concept of 'mediation' from Marxist theory to medieval works to explain how literary form might plausibly be viewed as encoding social knowledge and reflecting social realities. Form takes on radical new significances in the light of this concept: 'No longer regarded either as a self-contained aesthetic structure on the one hand or a propaganda-piece on the other, the work of art becomes a creation of an artist living in society.' Form might plausibly be viewed 'as a statement conditioned by the social experiences of its author'.[28]

Though making less use of theory, Hugh White's article on the design of John Gower's *Confessio Amantis*, the concluding extract of this chapter, shares this more fluid and creative critical conception of literary form. Gower's eight-book poem, *Confessio Amantis*, is fashioned as a fictional confession in which a lover, Amans, tells Genius, priest of Venus, of his unrequited love. The resulting work stands alongside Chaucer's *Canterbury Tales* as the second major English story-collection of the late fourteenth century and, like Chaucer's poem, its overall unity and coherence of design have been questioned. This 1908 verdict on the poem's structure reflects a critical view that would endure well into the twentieth century: 'The plan of the work is not ill conceived; but, unfortunately, it is carried out without a due regard to proportion in its parts, and its unity is very seriously impaired by digressions which have nothing to do with the subject of the book.'[29]

In contrast to this perspective, White's 1988 reading of the *Confessio* views the form of Gower's encyclopedic poem as deliberately reflective of a thematic emphasis on division, fragmentation and rupture. Where Brewer's approach to his text took form in isolation, White's reading is more intentionalist, invoking the apparent designs and intentions of the author in structuring his poem. In a reading which makes use of medieval literary and theological contexts, White's extract uncovers Gower's concern with division and disunity in the very 'design and development of the poem'.

Extract from Hugh White, 'Division and Failure in Gower's *Confessio Amantis*', *Neophilologus* 72 (1988), 600–3, 607–10.

Confessio Amantis[a] has often been accused of lacking unity. Gower's commitment to both *lust* and *lore*,[b] it has been felt, leads him to yoke together essentially disparate materials: on the one hand we have the love-interest, on the other moral and political material. Coghill thought the application of a Christian moral scheme to courtly love 'preposterous'[1] and Macaulay registered a similar disquiet:

> The scheme [of the poem] itself, with its conception of a Confessor who as priest has to expound a system of morality, while as a devotee of Venus he is concerned only with the affairs of love (I. 237–280), can hardly be called altogether a consistent or happy one . . . The Confessor is continually forgetting one or the other of his two characters, and the moralist is found justifying unlawful love or the servant of Venus singing the praises of virginity.[2]

Recently, however, Alastair Minnis has suggested that Gower's materials are not incompatible; *Confessio Amantis* is a unified work, and we should endeavour to see it whole. This view rests on a conviction that throughout *Confessio Amantis* Gower's concern is ethical and that 'For Gower, the virtues of the good lover were indistinguishable from those of the good man . . .'.[3] For reasons I shall give, this modern view seems to me open to question, yet I suspect that the older view of Gower as incompetent in respect of the basic fiction of his poem is unjust. Gower is profoundly sensible of the unhappy dividedness of things, which he regards as perhaps the most significant feature of man's existence in this world. The design of the poem seems to me to reflect Gower's concern with division, and its development to illustrate how attempts to overcome division and the problems it brings almost inevitably end in failure.

---

[a] The *Confession of the Lover.*
[b] entertainment and instruction.

Gower emphasises division at an early stage of *Confessio Amantis*. Considering the mutability of all earthly things Gower refers to a *tale* in the Bible which

> as in conclusion
> Seith that upon divisioun
> Stant,[a] why no worldes thing mai laste,
> Til it be drive to the laste.[b]
>
> (Prologue, 575–8)

The *tale* is Nebuchadnezzar's dream of the statue (*Daniel*, ch. 2), which represents the degeneration of the world through different ages. Gower aligns these ages with the successive empires of the world and relates the troubles of the present age to division:

> Upon the feet of Erthe and Stiel
> So stant this world now everydiel
> Departed; which began riht tho,[c]
> Whan Rome was divided so:
> And that is forto rewe sore,[d]
> For alway siththe more and more[e]
> The world empeireth[f] every day.
>
> (Prologue, 827–33)

Of Rome's collapse we learn that

> The cause hath ben divisioun,
> Which moder[g] of confusioun
> Is wher sche cometh overal,
>
> (Prologue, 851–3)

Gower reiterates his conviction that division is responsible for the mutability of things, pushing the analysis back beyond the political into the structure of man's being:

> Division, the gospell seith,
> On hous upon another leith,

[a] stands the reason.
[b] until its time runs out.
[c] at exactly the time.
[d] to be sorely regretted.
[e] ever since, increasingly.
[f] declines.
[g] mother.

Til that the Regne al overthrowe:
And thus may every man wel knowe,
Division aboven alle
Is thing which makth the world to falle,
And evere hath do sith[a] it began.
It may ferst proeve upon a man;
The which, for his complexioun
Is mad upon divisioun
Of cold, of hot, of moist, of drye,
He mot be verray kynde[b] dye:
For the contraire of his astat[c]
Stant[d] evermore in such debat,
Til that o[e] part be overcome,
Ther may no final pes be nome.[f]
Bot other wise, if a man were
Mad al togedre of o matiere
Withouten interrupcioun,
Ther scholde no corrupcioun
Engendre upon that unite:
Bot for ther is diversite
Withinne himself, he may noght laste,
That he ne deieth ate laste.

(Prologue, 967–90)

At this very basic level man is a victim of antagonistic forces between which no truce is possible. Peace, rather than coming about through the harmonious balancing of contending forces,[4] cannot be attained until one of those forces has been overcome and rendered incapable of exerting its power. This vision of man poised between powers which cannot achieve harmonious coexistence in a balancing of the influences they exert is recurrent in *Confessio Amantis* and seems to be quintessential to Gower's sense of man's position in the universe. The idea is apparent in the lines on the relationship between the body and the soul which follow those on man's complexional constitution just quoted.

Bot in a man yit over this
Full gret divisioun ther is,
Thurgh which that he is evere in strif,
Whil that him lasteth eny lif:

[a] since.
[b] true nature.
[c] condition.
[d] stands.
[e] one.
[f] peace be achieved.

The bodi and the Soule also
Among hem ben divided so,
That what thing that the body hateth
The soule loveth and debateth;
Bot natheles fulofte[a] is sene
Of werre which is hem betwene
The fieble hath wonne the victoire.
And who so drawth into memoire
What hath befalle of old and newe,
He may that werre sore rewe,[b]
Which ferst began in Paradis:
For ther was proeved what it is,
And what desese there is wroghte;[c]
For thilke[d] werre tho[e] forth broghte
The vice of alle dedly Sinne,
Thurgh which division cam inne
Among the men in erthe hiere.
(Prologue, 991–1011)

Local victories are won in this conflict (too often by the lesser party, the body), but there will be no 'final pes' in this life. The great significance this division between soul and body holds for Gower is evident in his making it the cause of the primal sin in Paradise – and sin in turn is to be seen as 'moder of divisioun' (Prologue 1030) in the world at large.

In Book VII of *Confessio Amantis* Gower returns to the divisions between the different complexions within man and between body and soul. In his creation of man God

Hath so devided the nature,
That non til other wel acordeth:
And be the cause it so discordeth,
The lif which fieleth the seknesse
Mai stonde upon no sekernesse.[f]
(VII, 396–400)

Man is again the victim of his divided constitution. There follows a discussion of the different complexions and of the organs of the body. Though he began this section by asserting God's responsibility for man's being, Gower goes on

[a] very often.
[b] regret.
[c] brought about.
[d] that same.
[e] then.
[f] security.

to introduce the figure of Nature as a presiding force in the creation of man. There is, of course, no contradiction: Nature is functioning in her traditional role as *vicaria Dei*.[a] But, as frequently in writings which employ this personification (e.g. the *Anticlaudianus* and the *Roman de la Rose*), Nature's creative power does not extend to the soul. Nature's creativity operates in the material realm, but the soul is created directly by God, and their different origins serve to mark the essential disparity between soul and body. So, having concluded his treatment of the qualities of the complexions and the disposition of the bodily organs Gower continues:

> And thus nature his pourveance[b]
> Hath mad for man to liven hiere;
> Bot god, which hath the Soule diere,
> Hath formed it in other wise.
> Than can noman pleinli devise;
> Bot as the clerkes ous enforme,
> That lich to god it hath a forme,
> Thurgh which figure and which liknesse
> The Soule hath many an hyh noblesse
> Appropred to his oghne kinde.[c]
> Bot ofte hir wittes[d] be mad blinde
> Al onliche of this ilke point,
> That hir abydinge is conjoint[e]
> Forth with the bodi forto duelle:
> That on desireth toward helle,
> That other upward to the hevene;
> So schul thei nevere stonde in evene,[f]
> Bot if the fleissh be overcome
> And that the Soule have holi nome
> The governance, and that is selde,[g]
> Whil that the fleissh him mai bewelde[h] . . .
> Alle othre bestes that men finde
> Thei serve unto here oghne kinde,[i]
> Bot to reson the Soule serveth;
> Wherof the man his thonk[j] deserveth

[a] deputy of God.
[b] provision.
[c] appropriated to his own nature.
[d] their senses.
[e] joined.
[f] in balance.
[g] unless the Soul has completely taken over the Body, and that is rare.
[h] have power over him.
[i] own nature.
[j] thanks.

And get him with hise werkes goode
The perdurable[a] lyves foode.
                        (VII, 490–510, 515–20)

Here the conflict between soul and body is not presented as irresolvable, but, as in the case of the strife between the complexions in the Prologue, a final resolution can only be achieved through the complete removal of the influence of one of the warring parties. And there is a clear awareness that such a resolution is not often achieved. This is not the only place in *Confessio Amantis* in which Gower projects a movement out of the problematic actual towards a superior state of things in which the difficulty has been overcome, only to acknowledge the near-impossibility of reaching that state. It is a pattern which concedes the dominance of failure.[5] [. . .]

Gower's sensitivity to division and to the difficulty of reconciling the poles of divisions seems to me to find expression in the design and development of the poem. Thus Genius can be seen as a figure divided against himself. Genius is very conscious of his dual responsibility[6] to love and to morality, and he is aware that the task of doing justice to both these aspects of himself is a difficult one. At considerable length and rather hesitantly, Genius lays out for Amans' benefit the procedure he is going to adopt in order to balance his commitments (see I, 233ff). He explains that:

it is noght my comun us[b]
To speke of vices and vertus,
Bot al of love and of his lore,
For Venus bokes of nomore
Me techen nowther text ne glose.[c]
Bot for als moche as I suppose.
It sit[d] a prest to be wel thewed,[e]
And schame it is if he be lewed,[f]
Of my Presthode after the forme
I wol thi schrifte[g] so enforme,
That ate leste thou schalt hiere
The vices, and to thi matiere
Of love I schal hem so remene,[h]

[a] eternal.
[b] general habit.
[c] commentary.
[d] behoves.
[e] well disposed.
[f] ignorant.
[g] confession.
[h] apply, relate.

That thou schalt knowe what thei mene.
(I, 267–80)

Similar considerations arise at the end of Book VI and the beginning of Book VII where, indeed, the non-amatory matter of Book VII is recognised as digressive. This emphasis on the problems Genius faces in his attempt to bring together morality and love (and the acknowledgment of the digressive nature of Book VII) suggests that the two are not as easily relatable as has recently been supposed – Genius, at least, thinks that he is dealing with two clearly distinct areas. (The Latin colophon printed by Macaulay on pages 479–80 of Volume II of his edition of *Confessio Amantis* distinguishes three elements of the work: the prophecy of Daniel concerning the degeneration of earthly king-doms, dealt with in the Prologue; the education of Alexander in kingship, treated in Book VII; and what is designated the principal subject-matter of the poem, love.)

What Genius' commitment to his orthodox priesthood leads him to do is to seek, in confessing Amans, to regulate love in accordance with Christian morality. This enterprise constitutes the body of the poem. But Genius' insis-tence that love and morality are usually separate, that Venus' books do not offer anything by way of moral discourse, might lead us to wonder whether the regulation of love Genius attempts can actually be achieved. Can Genius successfully maintain both his loyalties?

Macaulay was surely right to suggest that there is something odd about a priest of Venus praising virginity (see V, 6359ff), and Genius himself seems to sense that his recommendation of married love sits a little awkwardly with a commitment to Venus:

Mi ladi Venus, whom I serve,
What womman wole hire thonk[a] deserve,
Sche mai noght thilke love eschuie[b]
Of paramours, bot sche mot suie[c]
Cupides lawe; and natheles
Men sen such love sielde[d] in pes, . . .
Bot thilke love is wel at ese,
Which set is upon mariage; . . .
A gret mervaile it is forthi,[e]
How that a Maiden wolde lette,[f]

[a] thanks.
[b] avoid that same love.
[c] follow.
[d] seldom.
[e] therefore.
[f] wait.

> That sche hir time ne besette[a]
> To haste unto that ilke feste,[b]
> Wherof the love is al honeste.
> (IV, 1467–72, 1476–7, 1480–4)

Genius is unable to condemn 'love . . . of paramours', unequivocally even though it is not 'al honeste'. But Genius' embarrassment is more obvious in his discourse on pagan beliefs. Gower does not spare Genius' blushes: he has Amans point out that Genius has said nothing about Cupid and Venus (V, 1374ff). Genius admits that he has omitted an account of the god and goddess of love 'for schame' (V, 1382) and proceeds to detail Venus' incestuous behaviour and her sponsorship of various highly unsavoury amatory activities. Thus the difficulty his service of Venus causes Genius, who also has a commitment to orthodox morality, is high-lighted.

One might try to see Genius as priest-in-charge of a very difficult parish: he can legitimately lament Venus' moral shortcomings and still be determined to serve her, perhaps to bring her into a more satisfactory moral state. But there are difficulties with this view. Firstly, there is at least one occasion on which Genius makes a claim on behalf of love which seems to be false (that, anyway, is the opinion of the marginal commentator, who is probably Gower himself). Genius claims that

> Love is an occupacion,
> Which forto kepe hise lustes save
> Scholde every gentil herte have:
> (IV, 1452–4)

The marginal note here reads 'Non quia sic se habet veritas, set opinio Amantum'. It seems that Genius' loyalty to Venus has distorted his witness to the truths of orthodox morality. At IV, 1648–82 Amans offers a firm rebuttal of Genius' recommendation that he should fight on crusade to win the favour of his lady, invoking the commandment forbidding killing, and we may be supposed to endorse Amans' position here. But more telling evidence that Genius finds his double loyalty unsustainable comes with Genius' final recommendation that Amans should abandon love. Genius reverts to the question of his double status and seems to suggest that while his priesthood presses him towards virtue, his association with love is an association with vice:

> For I behihte[c] thee that yifte[d]
> Ferst whan thou come under my schrifte,[e]

---

[a] employ.
[b] feast.
[c] promised.
[d] gift.
[e] confession.

That thogh I toward Venus were,
Yit spak I suche wordes there,
That for the Presthod which I have,
Min ordre and min astat to save,
I seide I wolde of myn office
To vertu more than to vice
Encline, and teche thee mi lore.
Forthi[a] to speken overmore
Of love, which thee mai availe,
Tak love where it mai noght faile:
For as of this which thou art inne,
Be[b] that thou seist it is a Sinne.

(VIII, 2075–88)

In the original passage in which Genius balanced his commitments (I, 233ff) he was more confident of his qualifications to speak of love than of his ability to give moral instruction. In this passage his stance seems to have changed, and he presents himself first and foremost as a spokesman of morality. He goes on to speak of the blindness of love and its tendency to subvert self-rule in the individual. Torn between two incompatibles, Genius has made his choice, and it involves a betrayal of his mistress. The attempt to reconcile reason and love has broken down, and Genius finds himself, like Amans, having to abandon his loyalty to Venus in a commitment to reason alone. One might say that a reconciliation between love and morality is proposed in the character of Genius as Gower first presents him, but that this reconciliation is found to be impossible, and that accordingly the character acts in a way that the terms of his original creation would have seemed to disallow. The fragmentation of Genius perhaps enacts Gower's sense that a genuine reconciliation of reason and love, despite the occasional precarious moment of balance, is impossible. [. . .]

Notes

1   Nevill Coghill, *The Poet Chaucer*, 2nd edn (London, 1967), p. 86.
2   G. C. Macaulay (ed.), *The English Works of John Gower*, EETS. E.S. 81, 82, 1900, 1901, p. xix. All references to *Confessio Amantis* are to this edition.
3   A. J. Minnis (ed.), *Gower's Confessio Amantis: Responses and Reassessments* (Cambridge, 1983), editor's introduction, p. 1. See further in the same volume Alastair Minnis, '"Moral Gower" and Medieval Literary Theory', pp. 50–78, and Elizabeth Porter, 'Gower's Ethical Microcosm and Political Macrocosm', pp. 135–62.
4   Contrast, for instance, Boethius' picture in Book II *metrum* 8 of the *Consolation of Philosophy*, trans. V. E. Watts (London: Penguin, 1969).

[a] Therefore.
[b] According to.

5   See V, 6395*–411* and VIII, 2330–6. The pattern seems to be operative also at VII, 633–69, which discusses the possibility of evading the influence of the stars.
6   On the genesis of Genius' doubleness, see Denise N. Baker, 'The Priesthood of Genius: A Study in the Medieval Tradition', *Speculum* 51 (1976), 277–91.

Further Reading

A general treatment of the 'Gothic aesthetic' is provided by Barbara Nolan, *The Gothic Visionary Perspective* (Princeton, NJ: Princeton University Press, 1977), and a survey of the question of unity by Arthur K. Moore, 'Medieval English Literature and the Question of Unity', *Modern Philology* 65 (1968), 285–300.
In addition to Helen Cooper's study of *The Structure of the Canterbury Tales* (London: Duckworth, 1983), Donald R. Howard's *The Idea of the Canterbury Tales* (Berkeley, CA: University of California Press, 1976), John Leyerle's 'Thematic Interlace in the *Canterbury Tales*', *Essays and Studies* 26 (1979), 107–21, and Carl Lindahl's 'The Festive Form of the *Canterbury Tales*', *English Literary History* 52 (1985), 531–74, give detailed attention to the poem's structure.
Derek Pearsall's *The Canterbury Tales* (London: Routledge, 1985) presents the most sustained counter-claim for reading the individual tales in isolation. On the question of form in Malory, the exchanges between C. S. Lewis and Eugène Vinaver in *Essays on Malory*, ed. J. A. W. Bennett (Oxford: Clarendon Press, 1963) remain a monument of Middle English scholarship. Alongside Brewer's essay, the most influential 'unitarian' work of Malory criticism was the collaborative volume edited by R. M. Lumiansky, *Malory's Originality: A Critical Study of Le Morte Darthur* (Baltimore, MD: The Johns Hopkins University Press, 1964), and the unity question would be taken up again by Stephen Knight in *The Structure of Sir Thomas Malory's Arthuriad* (Sydney: Sydney University Press, 1969).
On the complex form and structure of *Piers Plowman*, an excellent starting-point is John Alford's 'The Design of the Poem', in John Alford (ed.), *A Companion to Piers Plowman* (Berkeley, CA: University of California Press, 1988), and the form of Gower's *Confessio* is also addressed by James Simpson in *Sciences and the Self in Medieval Poetry: Alan of Lille's Anticlaudianus and John Gower's Confessio Amantis* (Cambridge: Cambridge University Press, 1995). Elizabeth Scala has recently explored new dimensions of literary structure in *Absent Narratives, Manuscript Textuality, and Literary Structure in Late Medieval England* (New York: Palgrave, 2002).

Chapter Notes

1   There were, of course, exceptions: Thomas R. Price was scrutinizing the structure of Troilus as early as 1896: '*Troilus and Criseyde*: A Study in Chaucer's Method of Narrative Construction', *PMLA* 11 (1896), 307–22.
2   Extracts from the writings of the Formalists are collected in David Lodge (ed.), *Modern Criticism and Theory: A Reader* (London: Longman, 1988), pp. 15–61.

3   Frederick J. Furnivall, *A Temporary Preface to the Six-text Edition of Chaucer's Canterbury's Tales*, Chaucer Society (London: Trubner, 1868); John Matthews Manly, *Some New Light on Chaucer* (London: G. Bell, 1926).

4   Frederick Tupper, 'Chaucer and the Seven Deadly Sins', *PMLA* 29 (1914), 237–371.

5   George Lyman Kittredge, *Chaucer and his Poetry* (Harvard, MA: Harvard University Press, 1915); R. M. Lumiansky, *Of Sondry Folk: The Dramatic Principle in The Canterbury Tales* (Austin, TX: University of Texas Press, 1955).

6   Ralph Baldwin, *The Unity of the Canterbury Tales* (Copenhagen: Rosenkilde and Bagger, 1955), pp. 15–16.

7   Helen Cooper, *The Structure of the Canterbury Tales* (London: Duckworth, 1983), p. 3.

8   R. M. Lumiansky, 'Chaucer's *Parlement of Foules*: A Philosophical Interpretation', *Review of English Studies* 24 (1948), 81–9; Gardiner Stillwell, 'Unity and Comedy in Chaucer's *Parlement of Foules*', *Journal of English and Germanic Philology* 49 (1950), 470–95. See also Robert Worth Frank, Jr, 'Structure and Meaning in *The Parlement of Foules*', *PMLA* 71 (1956), 530–9.

9   Charles Muscatine, 'Form, Texture and Meaning in Chaucer's *Knight's Tale*', *PMLA* 65 (1950), 911–29.

10   P. G. Ruggiers, 'The Unity of Chaucer's *House of Fame*', *Studies in Philology* 50 (1953), 16–29.

11   Henry W. Wells, 'The Construction of *Piers Plowman*', *PMLA* 44 (1929), 123–40 (140).

12   *Coleridge's Shakespearean Criticism*, ed. T. M. Raysor (London: Constable and Co., 1930), I, p. 224.

13   A. C. Spearing, *Criticism and Medieval Poetry*, 2nd edn (London: Edward Arnold, 1972), p. 25.

14   C. S. Lewis, *The Discarded Image: An Introduction to Medieval and Renaissance Literature* (Cambridge: Cambridge University Press, 1964), pp. 193–4.

15   Robert M. Jordan, *Chaucer and the Shape of Creation: The Aesthetic Possibilities of Inorganic Structure* (Cambridge, MA: Harvard University Press, 1967), p. 8.

16   Arthur K. Moore, 'Medieval English Literature and the Question of Unity', *Modern Philology* 65 (1968), 285–300 (285).

17   Erwin Panofsky, *Gothic Architecture and Scholasticism* (New York: Meridian Books, 1957); Emile Mâle, *The Gothic Image: Religious Art in France of the Thirteenth Century* (New York: Harper, 1958).

18   Charles Muscatine, *Poetry and Crisis in the Age of Chaucer* (Notre Dame, IN: University of Notre Dame Press, 1972), p. 73.

19   D. W. Robertson, Jr and Bernard F. Huppé, *Piers Plowman and Scriptural Tradition* (Princeton, NJ: Princeton University Press, 1951), p. 247.

20   Eugène Vinaver (ed.), *The Works of Sir Thomas Malory* (Oxford: Oxford University Press, 1947), I, p. vi.

21   R. H. Wilson, 'How Many Books Did Malory Write?', *University of Texas Studies in English* 30 (1951), 1–23.

22   R. M. Lumiansky, 'The Question of Unity in Malory's *Morte Darthur*', *Tulane Studies in English* 5 (1955), 29–39.

23   D. S. Brewer, 'Form in the *Morte Darthur*', *Medium Aevum* 21 (1952), 14–24.

24   Robert M. Jordan, 'The Non-dramatic Disunity of *The Merchant's Tale*', *PMLA* 78 (1963), 293–9 (299).

25   Norris J. Lacy, 'Spatial Form in Medieval Romance', *Yale French Studies* 51: Approaches to Medieval Romance (1974), pp. 160–9.

26   Wells, 'Construction of *Piers Plowman*'; Gordon Hall Gerould, 'The Structural Integrity of the B-text of *Piers Plowman*', *Studies in Philology* 45 (1945), 60–75; T. P. Dunning, 'The Structure of the B-text of *Piers Plowman*', *Review of English Studies* n.s. 7 (1956), 225–37; John Lawlor, 'The Imaginative Unity of *Piers Plowman*', *Review of English Studies* n.s. 8 (1957), 113–26 (125).

27   Muscatine, *Poetry and Crisis in the Age of Chaucer*, p. 75.

28   Paul Strohm, 'Form and Social Statement in *Confessio Amantis* and *The Canterbury Tales*', *Studies in the Age of Chaucer* 1 (1979), 17–40 (18).

29   A. W. Ward and A. R. Waller (eds), *The Cambridge History of English Literature*, Vol. II (Cambridge: Cambridge University Press, 1908), p. 149.

3

Genre

Genre studies in Middle English: the examples of romance and Chaucer's Troilus and Criseyde. *The reception aesthetics of Hans Robert Jauss. Paul Strohm on the classification of Middle English narrative genres. Piero Boitani on the transformation of the genre of* exemplum *in* Patience.

What were the main genres of Middle English literature? How far does familiarity with these genres help readers to classify and interpret individual works? A central strand of Middle English criticism has been dedicated to the pursuit of these questions from the earliest to the most recent critical writing. Genre studies in Middle English have revealed that notions of genre are not always continuous, that medieval writers and audiences may not have shared our sense of the generic identity of literary works. Genre studies have asked whether *Troilus and Criseyde* can usefully be labelled 'a novel', whether the *Morte Darthur* is best described as romance or tragedy, whether the genre of *Piers Plowman* can be described at all. A central and recurrent critical concern, the importance of genre in Middle English criticism can be demonstrated by glancing over the reception history of two case studies, the medieval romances and Chaucer's *Troilus and Crisyede*.

Middle English genre studies have found their richest subject in romance. The fluidity of the term 'romance' is notorious: its meanings seem never to have stood still for long. Originally used to indicate any metrical narrative in the vernacular, the term came, by the later Middle Ages, to indicate more specific tales of adventure, magic, love and chivalry. How were twentieth-century scholars to classify the genre? For some, romance was best defined in contrast to the related genre of epic. Ker famously wrote on the two genres at the close of the nineteenth century, though early in the twentieth, Griffin despaired of discovering 'any infallible criterion by means of which the two species may be distinguished'.[1] Later, Dorothy Everett's 1955 attempt to provide a 'Characterization of the English Medieval Romances' reinforced critical understanding of the amorphous nature of this genre: 'The medieval romance is of course incapable of such exact definition as some literary types'.[2] This note of caution set the tone for John Finlayson's 1980 essay, where a tentative title referred in the plural to '*Definitions* of Middle English Romance' (my emphasis).[3]

At much the same time, other genre studies defined subsets of the romance genre. Conscious of the considerable overlap between more pious romances and saints' lives, critics such as Kratins, Schelp and Crane identified such hybrid genres as 'exemplary romance' and 'secular hagiography'.[4] In the latter decades of the century, structuralist approaches to romance also played their part: studies by Susan Wittig, Carol Fewster and Robert Burlin each contributed to the critical understanding of the highly formulaic structure and style of the genre.[5] Today, most studies will avoid strict definitions of romance: it seems more apt to describe 'family resemblance' between related kinds of narrative, or to describe romance as mode rather than genre:

- *W. R. J. Barron* (1987): 'what distinguishes romantic fiction across the ages is the characteristic mode in which it presents human experience. Critics increasingly prefer to define the medieval romance in terms of mode rather than genre.'[6]
- *Ad Putter and Jane Gilbert* (2000): 'romance is a 'family-resemblance' category: we should think of [the romances] as forming a complex network of relationship and similarities, not as a set that can be defined on the basis of specific properties common to each of its members.'[7]

GENRE STUDIES AND CHAUCER'S *TROILUS AND CRISEYDE* Outside of the romances, genre studies in Middle English have also contributed extensively to the critical reception of Chaucer's five-book poem *Troilus and Criseyde*. Embracing such diverse genres as chronicle, epic, romance and tragedy, the generic richness of Chaucer's Trojan poem has inspired a continuous seam of critical writing. Barry Windeatt's 1992 *Guide* to the poem describes the 'special inclusiveness of genres in *Troilus*', explaining that 'this gathering of genres in the poem – the absorption, combination, quotation, and transcendence of genres – is a distinctive part of the nature and meaning of *Troilus and Criseyde*.'[8] Despite this inclusiveness, at least one of the genres associated with the poem by earlier critics would now surprise us. Prompted in part by the rich and detailed characterization of Chaucer's protagonists, early critics of the poem were largely content to describe *Troilus* as a verse novel. 'A great psychological novel', exclaimed George Lyman Kittredge; 'Its spirit and temper are that of the modern novel', concurred Robert Kilburn Root.[9] Only later would scholars move to view the work in the light of the generic label Chaucer himself attached to the poem – tragedy.

> In the critical writing of the last few decades Chaucer's *Troilus and Criseyde* has been described prevailingly as a psychological novel. Our most influential interpreters, that is to say, draw our attention primarily to the subtle exhibition of psychology in the personages of the poem, and to the resemblance of the descriptive background to what we ordinarily call real life. By emphasizing these aspects of the *Troilus* they bring it into association with our modern novel.[10]

1938: Karl Young surveys the trend for 'novelistic' literary criticism of *Troilus*

'Go, litel myn tragedye'. Chaucer's description of *Troilus* as tragedy was taken in greatest earnest by allegorical critic D. W. Robertson, Jr. In his 'Chaucerian Tragedy' of 1952, Robertson argued that *Troilus* is intensely realized as tragedy when read not literally but allegorically. On an allegorical plane, Roberston argued, the poem relates the Christian soul's distraction from divine to earthly love. By submitting to desire for the transient, mutable pleasures of the world, Troilus straps himself to the wheel of Fortune where he follows an inevitable course of rise and fall:

TROILUS AS TRAGEDY

> Troilus subjects himself to Fortune in Book I, rises to the false heaven of Fortune's favor in Books II and III, and finally descends to a tropological Hell in Books IV and V . . . The three stages of tragic development – subjection to Fortune, enjoyment of Fortune's favor, and denial of providence – correspond to the three stages in the tropological fall of Adam: the temptation of the senses, the corruption of the lower reason in pleasurable thought, and the final corruption of the higher reason.[11]

This radical allegorical reading was widely contested (and on the opposition to Robertson's 'exegetical criticism' more generally, see chapter 5). But Robertson's labelling of *Troilus* as *tragedy* prompted other critics to take up the question of how Chaucer and his contemporaries might have conceptualized this genre. In 1960 Curry was confident: '*Troilus and Criseyde* is a tragedy, strongly deterministic in tone',[12] but in 1973 Ruggiers was more tentative, advancing 'Notes Towards a Theory of Tragedy in Chaucer'.[13] By 1978 McAlpine's book-length study on the genre of *Troilus* found a single generic label insufficient and the narrator's own labelling of *Troilus* as 'tragedye' questionable. The poem emphasizes love 'and love is not the usual subject of medieval tragedy',[14] observed McAlpine, a view supported by Clough's 1982 description of the poem as 'a hybrid form, which I label "romance tragedy"'.[15]

The effect of these critical moves in romance studies and Chaucer studies was to broaden critical awareness of the generic fluidity of medieval English texts. Old texts were looked at afresh in relation to genres and traditions with which they had not previously been linked. Only as a result of genre studies

of Chaucer could Matthews' 1960 study of the alliterative *Morte Arthure* call
for the poem to be 'set side by side with *Troilus and Criseyde* as a classic of the
medieval tragedy of fortune'.[16]

> Actually, it seems that Langland never could decide what form he was using,
> and from beginning to end, part of the difficulty of *Piers* to its readers is its
> confusion and even clash of genres.[17]
>
> Langland's shifting generic commitments form the real plot of the *Visio* and
> carry the burden of the initial search for Saint Truth. He moves through his
> genres to an explicit imitation of biblical narrative.[18]

1962, 1988: Morton W. Bloomfield and Stephen Justice explore the genre of
Piers Plowman

THE INFLUENCE OF HANS ROBERT JAUSS AND RECEPTION AESTHETICS

The most theorized critical work on genre in Middle English makes use of
the 'reception aesthetics' or 'reader-reception theory' first set out by Hans
Robert Jauss. Genre is vital to this theory of literary production and reception
since, in Jauss's view, it is only within a clearly circumscribed 'horizon of expectations' that the individual literary text can be comprehended and evaluated.
For Jauss, the triangulation of author, text and reader is a dynamic one in which
the reader plays a crucial role in the meaning process by bringing this horizon
of expectations to bear: 'In the triangle of author, work, and public the last is
no passive part, no chain of mere reactions, but rather itself an energy forma-
tive of history. The historical life of a literary work is unthinkable without the
active participation of its addressees.'[19]

From such a critical stance, genre is in no way a rigid concept applied
anachronistically to the literary work: it is germane to textuality at the very
moment of production and reception: 'A literary work, even when it appears
to be new, does not present itself as something absolutely new in an informa-
tional vacuum, but predisposes its audience to a very specific kind of reception
by announcements, overt and covert signals, familiar characteristics, or implicit
allusions.'[20] From this perspective, reading is viewed very much as an *act* or
event: by heeding those textual announcements, signals, characteristics and
allusions, the reader actively enables the text to *mean*. Because of the retrospective nature of this activity, genre criticism becomes in turn a kind of
historical criticism.

Jauss's ideas are applied and developed in our first extract on genre. In
'Middle English Narrative Genres', Paul Strohm sets out a taxonomy or
scheme of the major Middle English genres using the historically attested
generic labels of Middle English literary culture: *comedie, tragedie, cronicle,*

ensample and others. Complementing his other important work on genre (including contributions to genre studies of romance),[21] Strohm demonstrates how setting this taxonomy of genres in place allows the critic to measure the uniqueness of an individual work against the 'horizon of expectations' associated with its genre(s). For Strohm, as for Jauss, an important historical dimension inheres in genre criticism of this kind. Arguably, the modern reader who follows generic cues and who aligns generic expectations with those of medieval readers and audiences is a reader who can thereby 'draw closer to the experience of the work in its own historical time'.

Extract from Paul Strohm, 'Middle English Narrative Genres', *Genre* 13 (1980), 379–87.

1   *A Taxonomy of Middle English Narrative Terms*
This discussion might properly begin with a brief taxonomy of narrative terms, solidified when convenient by reference to standard Middle English glossaries:[1]

COMEDIE/TRAGEDIE (cf. Lat. *comoedia, tragoedia*). As we know from short Latin poems of the twelfth and thirteenth centuries and from Dante's *Commedia*, these terms were in no way restricted to theatrical performance. As Chaucer's Monk well reminds us, they could refer to any narrative with a pronounced rise or fall in the fortunes of its protagonist. Yet the theatrical sense could also be incorporated, as in the *Promp. Parv.*[a] definitions of *tragedia* ('Pley that begynnythe wythe myrthe, and endythe wythe sorowe') and *comedia* ('*Pley that begynnythe wythe mornynge and sorow, and endythe wythe myrthe*').

CRONICLE (cf. Lat. *cronica*, OF *cronique*). Implies some of the historicity of *storie* (see below), but in more particular reference to a bare, factual recital. *Promp. Parv.* translates ME *cronicle* as either *cronica* or *historia*.

ENSAMPLE (cf. Lat. *exemplum*, OF *ensample, essample*). While *ensample* often refers in a non-literary sense to any sort of illustrative 'instance', it may have generic force in reference to a particularly venerable, historical, or otherwise sanctioned incident, worthy of repetition for purposes of edification. [. . .] With its implication of brevity, it often refers to a narrative within a longer narrative or within a collection.

---

[a] *Promptorium Parvulorum*, an early medieval dictionary.

FABLE (cf. Lat. *fabula*, OF *fable*). Based ultimately on the Latin rhetorical term for a narrative with an invented plot, *fable* retained this sense throughout the period. (*Promp. Parv.*: fable or tale: *Fabula*.) Chaucer's Parson, for example, uses the word in this sense. OF *fablel* and *fabliau* did not enter Middle English, though these terms probably originated through the addition of the diminutive *el* to OF *fable* to create a sense of a relatively brief, informal narrative with an invented plot.

GESTE (cf. OF *geste*, ML *gesta*, pl.). The general sense of *gestes* as 'deeds' fostered the implication of *geste* as a narrative replete with vigorous deeds or actions, martial or otherwise. Yet a sense also lingered from memories or accounts of the presentation of *chansons de geste*, in which the *geste* was thought to have an element of vigorous representation, either in mime or song. In *Promp. Parv.*, *gestowre* is equated with *gesticulator*, and in *Cath. Ang.*,[a] *geste* is associated with such terms as *carmen* and *liricum*.

LEGENDE (cf. Lat. *legenda*, OF *legende*). Lat. *legenda* originated as a neutral plural marginal designation for those portions of the life and/or passion of a saint 'to be read' in the liturgy. As such readings were gathered into special lectionaries and other service books, *legenda* was transferred as a feminine singular form to the lectionary itself or to any of its components. With the wide fourteenth-century distribution of Jacobus's[b] more popularly oriented *Legenda*, ME *legende* came to refer to that work and occasionally to other popular hagiographical collections.

LYF (equivalent to Lat. *vita*). Latin *vita* originated to describe the life and miracles of a confessor (as opposed to *vita et passio* for a life ending in martyrdom or *passio* for the events connected with the trial, suffering, and death of a martyr). ME *lyf* is closely equivalent but more inclusive, virtually incorporating ME *passioun*. Variants include *liflade*, a compound of *lif* and OE *lad*/ME *lade*, meaning 'life-path' or 'course of life'.

MYRACLE (cf. Lat. *miraculum*, OF *miracle*). Normally (like its Latin original) used to refer to miraculous events themselves, *miracle* occasionally achieved independent generic force as a term for a narrative describing such an event. While these terms might occasionally designate a theatrical event, theatrical representation is more often conveyed through association with terms like *repraesentatio* or *pleyinge* (as in 'tretise on miracles pleyinge').

[a] *Catholicon Anglicum*, an English–Latin wordbook.
[b] Jacobus de Voragine's *Legenda Aurea* (*Golden Legends*), a famous medieval collection of saints' lives.

PASSIOUN (cf. Lat. *passio*, OF *passion*). See LYF, above.

PLEY (equivalent to Lat. *ludus*). Used from the fourteenth century onward to describe represented actions. (*Promp. Parv.* distinguishes between *pley* as a dramatic representation or *ludus/pley* as a game or spectacle.)

PROCES, PROCESSE (cf. Lat. *processus*, OF *proces*). Referring in many non-literary contexts to a sequence of actions or events, *proces* could refer by extension to a sequential narration. Often, a writer will refer to an unfolding narrative as 'this proces', and occasionally to the entire work in the same way. *Proces* probably retains more of the neutrality of the Lat. *narratio* than any other ME term, though it differs in its emphasis on step-by-step exposition.

ROMAUNCE (cf. OF *romans*). In its twelfth-century French and early fourteenth-century Middle English appearances, *romaunce* normally referred only to the language in which a work was written – in the vernacular and most often in French. In the later twelfth century in France and in the middle and later fourteenth century in England, it underwent an expansion of meaning to embrace those narratives to which it was often applied: accounts of the deeds of a single hero, with emphasis not only on martial but also on amatory and fanciful episodes. Yet another expansion of meaning was to embrace the form in which such narratives were couched; *Promp. Parv.* equates *romaunce* with *ryme* and *rithmichum*.

SPELLE (cf. OE *spel.*, MHG *spelle*; OE *spelian*, MHG *spellen*). Like ME *tale*, OF *conte*, and MHG *zal*, ME *spelle* retains a strong sense of verbal performance in the act of telling or narrating. Yet, while the meaning of *tale* expanded to include all sorts of narrative, the meaning of *spelle* contracted to confine itself to narratives of limited scope, immediate impact, and – by the later fourteenth century – popular or incidental appeal.

STORIE (cf. Lat. *historia*, OF *estoire*). In keeping with its etymology, ME *storie* refers principally to works which are either true or presumed to be true. (*Promp. Parv.*: story: *historia*.) *Storie* eventually embraced not only the factual tale (Lat. *historia*), but the invented tale with a plausible plot (Lat. *argumentum*), in the case of certain narratives of sufficient realism or venerability. (*Cath. Ang.*: story: *argumentum*, *historia* . . .) See above for CRONICLE, which also conveyed historicity but in reference to chronicle traditions rather than to literary narratives with strong plot lines.

TALE (cf. OE *talu*, MHG *zal*; OE *talian*, MHG *zalen*). Etymolgically, ME *tale* retains some of the sense of an oral or spoken narrative. (As an alternative to *tale*, *Promp. Parv.* offers 'mannys spekynge'.) In actual practice, since the great majority of narratives in the Middle English period were designed to be spoken aloud or read, *tale* has something of the inclusive sense of the Latin *narratio*, in referring impartially to all kinds of narrative, whether spoken or written, true or fictitious. (*Promp. Parv.* equates *tale* and *narracio*.) Late in the Middle English period, *tale* was occasionally equated with *fable*, to convey a sense of fictitiousness. (*Cath. Ang.* equates *tale* with *fabula* and *mitologia* as well as *narracio*.) See above for SPELLE, which has an analogous etymological history, but which mainly referred to narratives of limited scope and immediate impact.

TRETYS (cf. Lat. *tractatus*, OF *traitis*, *tretiz*). With its emphasis on the systematic or reasoned exposition of principles, *tretys* was often used to describe scientific, philosophical, or theological works. It often appears in connection with works which, unlike either *stories* or *fables*, eschew or come close to eschewing plot; Chaucer, for example, uses *tretys* to characterize only *Melibee*, the *Parson's Tale*, and *Treatise on the Astrolabe* among his complete narratives.

VISIOUN/AVISIOUN (cf. Lat. *visio*, OF *vision*). Middle English terms like *dreme*, *sweven*, and *visioun* more often refer in non-literary senses to the dreams or waking visions which are narratively described than to the narratives themselves. Nevertheless, *visio* had its own history as a marginal notation or chapter heading in Latin devotional narrative, and *visioun/avisioun* had at least a dimly generic sense in the *Pearl*-Poet's 'this veray[a] avysyoun' or Chaucer's 'Macrobeus, that writ the avisioun/ . . . of the worthy Cipioun'. 'Dream vision' is a modern coinage.

An interesting sidelight to this profusion of terms is that no one term embraced them all. Although *narratio* (with an inclusive sense similar to that of modern 'narrative') was available as a precedent throughout the Middle English period, 'narrative' did not actually enter the language in this sense until the sixteenth century. In the meantime, its place was taken by a variety of terms, each with its own particular shade of meaning: *spelle* and *tale* for oral narratives, *proces* for step-by-step narratives, *storie* for historical narratives and *fable* for invented narratives, *tretys* for systematic expositions which do not depend on plot, and so on. [. . .]

2   *Some Critical Applications*
In its historical lifetime, the debate over the status and utility of generic notions has veered between extremes. Classicizing critics have viewed genres as fixed

[a] genuine.

and immutable norms. Croceans,[a] new critics, and formalists have viewed genres as aesthetically meaningless categories which can only muddy the status of works which are ultimately singular and obedient only to their own rules. In recent decades, however, theorists of genre have developed a middle-ground position according to which genres are seen as 'provisional schemae' rather than immutable 'species concepts'.[2]

The persistence of such a compromise position on genre seems assured not only by its flexibility, but by its usefulness in the explanation of the complex and shifting relations between an audience and a literary work. Drawing analogies from the insights of linguistics into the ways we make sense of any utterance, contemporary theorists have cogently argued that provisional notions of genre are not only crucial to an audience's aesthetic experiences, but that they are necessary to render works *comprehensible*. E. D. Hirsch, for example, argues that 'an interpreter's preliminary generic conception of a text is constitutive of everything that he subsequently understands.'[3] H. R. Jauss argues in the same vein that 'every literary work belongs to a genre . . . which is to say an *ensemble* of pre-existing rules which orient the comprehension of a reader (or public) and permit his appreciative reception.'[4]

Once we have accepted the idea of genres as sets of intermediate rules or instructions which assist the reader in rightly interpreting a literary work, we have access to all sorts of new ways of understanding or using genre. One possibility is to devise our own generic schemae, founded on external form, function, form of discourse, or some other principle, and to use them heuristically as an aid to understanding similarities and differences in literary works. Yet the concept of genres as 'provisional schemae' which are neither timeless nor immutable has another possible implication as well. If we accept the idea that generic concepts live in time, that they have a diachronic as well as synchronic dimension, then we should not neglect their significations for particular audiences in particular places. If generic concepts do in fact come into use, sustain ceaseless modification and internal rearrangement, and finally pass into disuse, then we should not neglect the ways in which they live in history.

The attempt to understand a generic concept in reference to a particular audience, time, and place has special importance to those of us who believe that the most vital kind of literary history seeks to comprehend the reception of literary works by their contemporary audiences. This effort at comprehension, which Jauss has aptly charactered as reception-aesthetics, depends crucially on the reconstruction of the 'horizon' of literary expectations with which the contemporary audience approached a work (and on the kinds of 'horizon-change' which a work of art can require of its audience).[5]

---

[a] Followers of aesthetic theorist Benedetto Croce (1866–1952).

In seeking to reconstruct this horizon of expectations, the critic cannot afford to ignore the contribution of the audience's generic expectations. Every reader or hearer brings some generic expectations to a new work, as a result of his or her acquaintance with its tradition. And every literary work seeks from its opening lines to evoke, to substantiate, and [. . .] to modify these expectations.

This evocation of a horizon of generic expectations does not necessarily require the use of a generic term. We know from the beginning that *Pearl* is a vision, from such signals as its garden setting, from the information that the narrator's body lies 'in sweuen' while his spirit goes 'in auenture', and so on – little difference that we are told only in the closing lines that the poem is a *veray avysyoun*. Similarly, we know all along that *Gawain* is in a tradition of romance, because of its focus on the growth of the hero and its movement from martial to amatory testing to the 'other' spiritual world of the green chapel – and we are hardly surprised to learn at the end that the source of his adventures is 'the best boke of romaunce'.

At times, though, a work is so obliging as to come right out and label itself. When it does, we have an interpretative clue of special value. We have, as I have argued elsewhere, a sense of the 'silhouette' of the work; 'of where the narrative is likely to go, of what kinds of things are likely to happen – of the kind of expectations with which a contemporary reader might have approached the work'.[6]

Once the audience of the *Laud Troy Book* learned that the narrative is a *romaunce* rather than a *storie*, it knew that it could expect the increased importance of 'duke Ector of Troye' and the suppression of learned digression in favor of fast-paced narrative. Upon learning that *Kyng Alisaunder* is a noble *geste*, it would have expected a predominance of diverse actions over fantasy or amorous by-play. Upon learning that *Havelok* is a *spelle*, it would have expected a compact and immediate narrative. Once the audience of Chaucer's *Second Nun's Tale* learned that the tale is a *lif* and *passioun*, it knew where the tale was going and that it should not be amused by episodes like Cecilia's refusal of Valerian on their wedding night. Chaucer's clear advance designation of *Melibee* as a *tretys* would have prepared his audience for a tale which, however *murye*, would eliminate or restrict plot-elements in favor of the systematic development of an argument.

One could offer a lengthy catalogue of works which contain a fairly explicit generic designation, and which substantiate rather than challenge the expectations created by the designation. More interesting still are those works which [. . .] transcend particular generic categories, and which consequently contain a challenge to audience expectations. In fact, I am probably being too bland in using a word like 'interesting' to describe works which challenge their audience to revise its horizon of expectations, since the greatest medieval works invariably contain this element of challenge.

Piers Plowman, for example, starts out as a *visioun* or linked series of *visiouns*, but Morton Bloomfield has shown us how it goes on to embrace such additional genres as example, debate, complaint, sermon, and apocalypse.[7] The *Cursor Mundi*,[a] to choose a less familiar example, catches the attention of its audience with a catalogue of the matter of *geste* and *romaunce* and then shifts suddenly to sacred history illuminated by example, parable, sermon, and a variety of other forms. *Troilus* might be the best possible example of shifting generic expectations. It begins with a frank confession that it is a 'sorwful tale', but then moves so emphatically into the influence of Venus and devices of *romaunce* that the audience is jolted by the ultimate intervention of fortune and the reminder that it is in fact reading a *tragedye*. In each of these cases, the audience is forced constantly to revise its conception of the genre of the work as it unfolds.

Such instances of apparent generic instability in medieval works have raised methodological considerations for the presumptive genre critic. Because rhetorical techniques of amplification enabled medieval writers to achieve split-second generic redefinitions, rhetorically-oriented critics have questioned the utility of genre theory as a way of understanding the form of later medieval narrative.[8] Yet the fact that many medieval narratives violate and reconstruct generic expectations is hardly cause to abandon contemporary generic conceptions as a key to medieval literary form and experience. The possibility of internal shifts of generic conception has not only been fully entertained by twentieth-century theorists of genre, but is central to their work. As Tzvetan Todorov suggests in his essay on detective fiction, *every* major work 'transgresses the previously valid rules of [its] genre'.[9] Such licensed transgressions may, in fact, be seen as crucial to the entire literary enterprise. Through such transgressions, authors persistently modify received traditions in order that they may retain their challenge for new audiences in new social and historical situations. [. . .]

Notes

1 *Promptorium Parvulorum*, ed. A. Way, The Camden Society, vols 25, 54, and 89 (London, 1843, 1853, 1865); *Promptorium Parvulorum*, ed. A. L. Mayhew, EETS, OS, 102 (London: Kegan Paul, Trench, and Trübner, 1908); *Catholicon Anglicum*, ed. Sidney J. H. Herrtage, EETS, ES, 75 (London: N. Trübner, 1881).
2 E. D. Hirsch, Jr, *Validity in Interpretation* (New Haven, CT: Yale University Press, 1967), pp. 108–9.
3 Ibid., p. 74.
4 H. R. Jauss, 'Littérature médiévale et théorie des genres', *Poétique* 1 (1970), 82.

---

[a] *The Course/History of the World.*

5   H. R. Jauss, 'Literary History as a Challenge to Literary Theory', *New Directions in Literary History*, ed. Ralph Cohen (Baltimore, MD: Johns Hopkins University Press, 1974), pp. 11–27.

6   Paul Strohm, 'Passioun, Lyf, Miracle, Legende: Some Generic Terms in Middle English Hagiographical Narrative', Part 2, *Chaucer Review*, 10 (1975), 165.

7   Morton W. Bloomfield, *Piers Plowman as a Fourteenth-century Apocalypse* (New Brunswick, NJ: Rutgers University Press, 1961), pp. 3–43.

8   Such as Robert M. Jordan, 'Chaucerian Romance?', *Yale French Studies* 51 (1974), 223–34.

9   Tzvetan Todorov, 'The Typology of Detective Fiction', *The Poetics of Prose* (Ithaca, NY: Cornell University Press, 1977), p. 43.

TRANSFORM-
ATIONS OF
GENRE

Strohm's approach shares Jauss's aim to recover an historical understanding of Middle English genres. His suggestion that the boundaries of these genres are fluid is demonstrated in our second extract in which Piero Boitani examines the transformation of genre in the Middle English alliterative poem *Patience*. In its retelling of the Old Testament story of Jonah, the poem ostensibly falls into the literary genre of the *exemplum* – a short narrative used to make a moral point, widely used in preaching in the Middle Ages. Drawn from his 1982 study *English Medieval Narrative in the Thirteenth and Fourteenth Centuries*, Boitani's essay demonstrates how *Patience* breaks out of this exemplary genre in its transformation of the short scriptural story into a dramatic poem full of subtle detail and psychological observation. *Patience* cannot simply be classified alongside purely didactic Middle English writings. By following formalist and generic concerns in his approach, Boitani reveals the careful craftsmanship of the work ('a neat construction, as perfect as a Grecian urn') and the literary powers of the poet. His reading of *Patience* shows the transformations of genre achievable in Middle English writing, reminding us that any 'taxonomy of genres' must needs be fluid.

Extract from Piero Boitani, 'The Religious Tradition', in *English Medieval Narrative in the Thirteenth and Fourteenth Centuries*, trans. Joan Krakover Hall (Cambridge: Cambridge University Press, 1982), pp. 8–12.

[. . .] *Patience*,[1] which is only little over 500 lines long, is a neat construction, as perfect as a Grecian urn. Its theme is announced at once, and inserted into the context of the Beatitudes:

Pacience is a poynt, þaȝ hit displese ofte.
When heuy herttes ben hurt wyth heþyng oþer elles,   *scorn*
Suffraunce may aswagen hem and þe swelme leþe,   *lessen the bitterness*
For ho quelles vche a qued and quenches malyce.   *subdues every evil*

þay ar happen also þat con her hert stere,   *blessed; govern their hearts*
For hores is þe heuen-ryche, as I er sayde.

(1–4, 27–8)

At the end of the poem, the circle is closed: its 'point' has been proved:

For-þy when pouerte me enpreceȝ and payneȝ in-noȝe
Ful softly with suffraunce saȝttel me bihoueȝ;   *make peace*
For-þy penaunce and payne to-preue hit in syȝt
þat pacience is a nobel poynt, þaȝ hit displese ofte.

(528–31)

As in a sermon, the *exemplum* is recounted between the statement of the theme and the conclusion. The *exemplum* is constituted not by the proverbial story of Job but by the more indirectly related one of Jonah.[2] At first glance, the biblical text seems to deal with themes that are slightly different from that of patience: disobedience to the divine command; rejection of the heavy burden of prophecy; the omnipresence of God, who sees and hears everything, everywhere; divine mercy and human pettiness. Medieval allegorical interpretation saw in the three days and nights that Jonah spends in the whale's belly a prefiguration of the three days that passed between the Crucifixion and the Resurrection. A nineteenth-century interpretation within a novel, in the sermon preached by Father Mapple in *Moby Dick*, uses the story of Jonah to condemn sin, to demonstrate the omnipresence of God and to show the road to salvation through penance, thus indicating, in moral terms, the deeper meaning of the adventure that will take place in the book.[3] But the author of *Patience*, driven perhaps by personal circumstances,[4] is more subtle:

> The purpose of this poem is clear enough: to commend patience by an *exemplum* which first shows God's thwarting of impatience in a human being, and then expounds his own patience by contrast. The term 'patience', for which the poet's word is the same as ours, has a somewhat wider sense than it commonly possesses nowadays. It means both putting up with one's lot and being long-suffering towards folly and wickedness, rather than hasty to take vengeance on them. The first sense applies especially to man, the second especially to God.[5]

Patience moves from one meaning to the other: the first and longer part of the poem shows us God punishing Jonah's impatience; the second part, which is much briefer, shows us how God bears with the sins of Nineveh and how, as soon as its inhabitants repent, He spares the city. But the whole story can really be considered an ultimate test of divine patience. The Old Testament God, who normally punishes sinners pitilessly – who, as *Cleanness* will tell us, drowns the entire human race in the Flood and annihilates Sodom and Gomorrah – this God punishes Jonah, it is true, but He does so with great moderation. He saves him when the prophet invokes Him: He is a God who stops short of drastic action; He terrifies the sinner but, more than that, He humiliates him. He makes him pass three days and nights in the whale's stomach, dark, stifling, but, most of all, dirty and smelly. He ridicules him, teasing him almost, by making the shady bower for him and then destroying it – provoking Jonah's anger to then show up his pettiness, vanity and stupidity.

With regard to the biblical text, *Patience* is an *amplificatio*, following the rhetorical rules of the Middle Ages, but it is not merely a verbal *amplificatio*: it tends, like all homiletic literature,[6] towards a minute realism – that is, towards a description of details, of the objects that fill the story. But, more significantly, and beyond anything attempted in sermons, *Patience* shows a tendency towards a psychological characterisation of its protagonist. Whereas God remains the God of the Bible, the God who, according to Auerbach,[7] 'unexpected and mysterious, enters the scene from some unknown height or depth', Man takes his starting-point from moments of conflict and internal motivations, which Auerbach also finds in biblical characters but which are only hinted at in Scripture. And thus Man begins to become a character. To all this the author of *Patience* adds an extraordinary control of the technique he uses (that of alliteration) and of words.

Let me give a few examples of the processes I have just outlined. The first is of *amplificatio* pure and simple. The beginning of the *Prophetia Ionae* in the Vulgate is condensed and mysterious: 'Et factum est verbum Domini ad Ionam, filium Amathi, dicens: Surge, et vade in Niniven, civitatem grandem, et praedica in ea, quia ascendit malitia eius coram me' ('Now the word of the Lord came unto Jonah the son of Amittai, saying, Arise, go to Nineveh, that great city, and cry against it; for their wickedness is come up before me'). The author of *Patience* lengthens the text, he completes it rhetorically, with a clear homiletic and aesthetic intention:

Hit bi-tydde sum-tyme in þe termes of Jude,	
Jonas joyned watȝ þer-inne jentyle prophete;	*appointed; to the gentiles*
Goddes glam to hym glod þat hym vnglad made,	*speech; came*
With a roghlych rurd rowned in his ere:	
'Rys radly,' he says, 'and rayke forth euen;	
Nym þe way to Nynyue wyth-outen oþer speche,	
And in þat cete my saȝes soghe alle aboute,	*spread*
þat in þat place, at þe poynt, I put in þi hert.	

For iwysse hit arn so wykke þat in þat won dowelleӡ,   *town*
And her malys is so much, I may not abide,
Bot venge me on her vilanye and venym bilyue.
Now sweӡe me þider swyftly and say me þis arende.'   *message*

(61–72)

Here the voice of God has become 'a roghlych rurd', and His command – which in the Bible had been reduced to the bare minimum necessary for its function – has been divided into two stanzas; in the first it is articulated by the use of the relative clause, and in the second it is emphasised by repetition. The last verse of the second stanza then repeats the command given in the first one. This type of *amplificatio* is a mechanism that we find throughout the poem and in particular in the storm scene, on which the author naturally dwells: each of the salient points of the original narrative is expanded, in the ways I have pointed out. The storm's rising is followed, step by step, in a crescendo of descriptions, in which Turneresque brushstrokes are mingled with nautical language, agitated talk and invocations of every kind of god – an effect that Father Mapple and Herman Melville would no doubt have appreciated. Having thus prepared the scenic background (lines 129–80), the author concentrates his attention on Jonah, who, having taken shelter in his cabin, 'slypped vpon a sloumbe-selepe, and sloberande he routes'. At this point the action begins. Jonah is dragged by his hair onto the deck; the sailors question him anxiously and the prophet tells the truth. The sailors are terrified but make every effort to save the ship, themselves and their passenger. Finally, they beg God not to be angry with them for casting His prophet to the mercy of the waves and they throw Jonah overboard. The biblical narrative, which contains the bare skeleton of this episode, is exploited to the utmost, and its background, which has been merely sketched, is transformed into a literally and metaphorically dramatic scene (lines 180–244).

The scene that follows enlarges ten times over the biblical text, which merely states: 'Et praeparavit Dominus piscem grandem ut deglutiret Ionam; et erat Ionas in ventre piscis tribus diebus et tribus noctibus' ('Now the Lord had prepared a great fish to swallow up Jonah. And Jonah was in the belly of the fish three days and three nights'). The poet, instead, follows Jonah's steps through the whale's teeth, down its throat, beyond its gills and down to what seems to be the end of the road, to a cavern 'as brod as a halle':

And þer he festnes þe fete and fathmeӡ aboute,
And stod vp in his stomak þat stank as þe deuel;
þer in saym and in sorӡe þat sauoured as helle,
þer watӡ bylded his bour þat wyl no bale suffer.*

(273–6)

* *There was built the bower of the man who would suffer no hardship*

This is a stanza that shows the technique of the *Patience*-poet in miniature: the whale's stomach is rapidly sketched; it is made concrete mainly by its stench; its space is taken up by the figure of Jonah who has stumbled to his feet and is groping around. His situation is defined by a doublet that is enhanced if not created by alliteration – a touch of genius: 'in saym and in sorȝe' ('in the grease and filth') – but with the ambiguity that characterises 'sorȝe', the primary meaning of which is 'pain'. The two colloquial similes 'as þe deuel' and 'as helle' give the scene a touch of vulgarity, and at the same time provide a religious correlative to Jonah's condition: having rejected God and His message, he now finds himself in Hell. Finally, the author's ironic comment completes the picture by making Jonah ridiculous, when he had already been miniaturised, eight lines earlier, in the comparison with a 'mote in at a munster dor'. This technique, in short, can compress allusion, realism, ambiguity and irony, all invented out of whole cloth on the basis of biblical text, into a very small space.

Jonah has been treated from the first with the ironic detachment that belongs not only to the preacher or moralist but, most of all, to the novelist, and from the very beginning he is given a psychological depth [. . .] in this [. . .] he is a character typical of the *Gawain*-poet. When Jonah in the Bible disobeys God, the text does not waste words: 'Et surrexit Ionas, ut fugeret in Tharsis a facie Domini' ('But Jonah rose up to flee unto Tarshish from the presence of the Lord'). The *Patience*-poet, on the other hand, searches out Jonah's motives, which are, naturally enough, dictated mainly by fear, but, as he does so, he points out the man's rebellious spirit and his bad-tempered irony, which makes Jonah profoundly human. It is the first time in English literature that a man, a prophet of God, talks to himself about his God with such bitterness – in an interior monologue.

> When þat steuen watȝ stynt þat stowned his mynde,
> Al he wrathed in his wyt, and wyþerly he þoȝt:
> 'If I bowe to his bode and bryng hem þis tale,
> And I be nummen in Nuniue, my nyes begynes.   *troubles begin*
> He telles me þose traytoures arn typped schrewes;
> I com wyth þose tyþynges, þay ta me bylyue,
> Pyneȝ me in a prysoun, put me in stokkes,
> Wryþe me in a warlok, wrast out myn yȝen.   *foot-shackle*
> þis is a meruayl message a man for-to preche
> Amonge enmyes so mony and mansed fendes,   *accursed*
> Bot if my gaynlych God such gref to me wolde,   *gracious*
> For desert of sum sake, þat I slayn were.
> At alle peryles,' quoþ þe prophete, 'I aproche hit no nerre;
> I wyl me sum oþer waye þat he ne wayte after;
> I schal tee in-to Tarce and tary þere a whyle,

And ly3tly when I am lest he letes me alone.'
. . .

'Oure syre syttes,' he says, 'on sege so hy3e,
In his glowande glorye, and gloumbes ful lyttel   *worries*
þa3 I be nummen in Nunniue and naked dispoyled,
On rode rwly to-rent with rybaudes mony.'

(77–96)

This is a man who is so terrified that he even doubts God's word; a man who imagines the most frightful punishments, a man who reasons (though in a way that seems perverse in the context of the Bible) like a rational being. Jonah the man is not at all a prophet of God: he is not even a patient servant of God. This can be taken as a synthesis of both the moral message and the artistic achievement of *Patience*. [. . .]

Notes

1 I have used the text of *Patience* as edited by J. J. Anderson (Manchester, 1969).
2 In the Vulgate, four brief chapters are dedicated to it, which correspond to two pages of a modern edition.
3 H. Melville, *Moby Dick*, chapter 9, 'The Sermon'.
4 See lines 35–6 and 528–9.
5 A. C. Spearing, *The Gawain-Poet: A Critical Study* (Cambridge, 1970), pp. 77–8.
6 See G. R. Owst, *Literature and Pulpit in Medieval England*, 2nd rev. edn (Oxford, 1961), chs 1 and 4.
7 E. Auerbach, *Mimesis*, English trans. (Princeton, 1968; 1st edn, 1958), p. 8.

Further Reading

The 'Critical Idiom Monographs' provide a good starting-point for this topic: Heather Dubrow, *Genre* (London: Methuen, 1982). For a thorough treatment of the history and theories of genre, see Alastair Fowler, *Kinds of Literature: An Introduction to the Theory of Genres and Modes* (Oxford: Clarendon Press, 1982). Northrop Frye has influential things to say about romance as a mode in his *Anatomy of Criticism: Four Essays* (Princeton, NJ: Princeton University Press, 1957).
In addition to the essays of Dorothy Everett and John Finlayson, key documents in the debate on romance and genre include Kathryn Hume's two essays, 'The Formal Nature of Middle English Romance', *Philological Quarterly* 53 (1974), 158–80, and 'Romance: A Perdurable Pattern', *College English* 36 (1974), 129–46; Robert M. Jordan's 'Chaucerian Romance?', *Yale French Studies* 51 (1974), 223–34; and Derek Brewer's, 'The Nature of Romance', *Poetica* 9 (1978), 9–48. Some genre criticism on

romance takes the particular case study of *Sir Gawain and the Green Knight*, as in Sacvan Bercovitch's, 'Romance and Anti-romance in *Sir Gawain and the Green Knight*', *Philological Quarterly* 44 (1965), 30–7.

On genre in *Piers Plowman*, see the landmark study by Morton W. Bloomfield, *Piers Plowman as a Fourteenth-century Apocalypse* (New Brunswick: Rutgers University Press, 1962), and the influential essay by Steven Justice, 'The Genres of *Piers Plowman*', *Viator* 19 (1988), 291–306.

Paul Strohm's essay on Middle English genres appeared in a special issue of the journal *Genre* where it has a companion piece in Mark E. Amsler's 'Literary Theory and the Genres of Middle English Literature', *Genre* 13 (1980), 389–96. Among many other subtle suggestions, the notion that literary texts 'participate' in genres but never inhere within them is set out in Jacques Derrida's, 'The Law of Genre', in Derek Attridge (ed.), *Acts of Literature* (London: Routledge, 1992), pp. 221–52.

Chapter Notes

1   W. P. Ker, *Epic and Romance: Essays on Medieval Literature* (London: Macmillan, 1897); Nathaniel Griffin, 'The Definition of Romance', *PMLA* 38 (1923), 50–70 (50).

2   Dorothy Everett, 'A Characterization of the English Medieval Romances', in Patricia Kean (ed.), *Essays on Middle English Literature* (Oxford: Clarendon Press, 1955), pp. 1–22 (p. 3).

3   John Finlayson, 'Definitions of Middle English Romance', *Chaucer Review* 15 (1980–1), 44–62, 168–81 (45).

4   Ojars Kratins, 'The Middle English *Amis and Amiloun*: Chivalric Romance or Secular Hagiography?', *PMLA* 81 (1966), 347–54; Hanspeter Schelp, *Exemplarische Romanzen im Mittelenglischen* (Göttingen: Vandenhoeck and Ruprecht, 1967); Susan Crane, 'Guy of Warwick and the Question of Exemplary Romance', *Genre* 17 (1984), 351–71.

5   Susan Wittig, *Stylistic and Narrative Structures in the Middle English Verse Romances* (Austin, TX: University of Texas Press, 1978); Carol Fewster, *Traditionality and Genre in Middle English Romance* (Cambridge: D. S. Brewer, 1987); Robert Burlin, 'Middle English Romance: The Structure of Genre', *Chaucer Review* 30 (1995), 1–14.

6   W. R. J. Barron, *English Medieval Romance* (London: Longman, 1987), p. 2.

7   Ad Putter and Jane Gilbert (eds), *The Spirit of Medieval English Popular Romance* (London: Longman, 2000).

8   Barry Windeatt, *Troilus and Criseyde: Oxford Guides to Chaucer* (Oxford: Clarendon Press, 1992), p. 138.

9   A list of similar comments is given in Karl Young's essay, 'Chaucer's *Troilus and Criseyde* as Romance', *PMLA* 53 (1938), 38–63 (38).

10   Karl Young, 'Chaucer's *Troilus and Criseyde* as Romance', *PMLA* 53 (1938), 38–63, (38).

11   D.W. Robertson, Jr, 'Chaucerian Tragedy', *English Literary History* 19 (1952), 1–37.

12 Walter Clyde Curry, *Chaucer and the Medieval Sciences*, 2nd edn (New York: Barnes and Noble. 1960), p. 241.

13 Paul Ruggiers, 'Notes Towards a Theory of Tragedy in Chaucer', *Chaucer Review* 8 (1973), 89–99.

14 Monica McAlpine, *The Genre of Troilus and Criseyde* (Ithaca, NY: Cornell University Press, 1978), p. 16.

15 Andrea Clough, 'Medieval Tragedy and the Genre of *Troilus and Criseyde*', *Medievalia et Humanistica* n.s. 11 (1982), 211–27.

16 William Matthews, *The Tragedy of Arthur: A Study of the Alliterative 'Morte Arthure'* (Berkeley, CA: University of California Press, 1960), p. 178.

17 Morton W. Bloomfield, *Piers Plowman as a Fourteenth-century Apocalypse* (New Brunswick, NJ: Rutgers University Press, 1962), p. 8.

18 Stephen Justice, 'The Genres of *Piers Plowman*', *Viator* 19 (1988), 291–306.

19 Hans Robert Jauss, *Toward an Aesthetic of Reception*, trans. Timothy Bahti (Brighton: Harvester, 1982), p. 19.

20 Ibid., p. 23.

21 Important pieces are '*Storie, Spelle, Geste, Romaunce, Tragedie*: Generic Distinctions in the Middle English Troy Narrative', *Speculum* 44 (1971), 348–59, and 'The Origin and Meaning of Middle English *Romaunce*', *Genre* 10 (1977), 1–20.

4

Language, Style, Rhetoric

Linguistic studies of Middle English texts. Early philology. Dialectology. Stylistic and rhetorical readings of Middle English texts. A. C. Spearing on the early medieval narrative style of King Horn; *Diane Watt on the 'household rhetoric' of the Paston letters; Thorlac Turville-Petre on the Middle English lyric and the trilingualism of medieval England.*

Language studies are the keystone of Middle English criticism. Whether it be detailed analyses of an individual writer's style (P. J. C. Field or Mark Lambert on Malory; Geoffrey Shepherd on the *Ancrene Wisse*; David Burnley or Christopher Cannon on Chaucer) or broader surveys of Middle English dialects and discourses (the work of Angus McIntosh, Norman Blake, Rita Copeland), language studies form a bedrock of scholarship, roughly separable into three areas. The foundations were laid by the Victorian and Edwardian philologists with their grammars, primers and dictionaries. Dialectology and contextual studies followed, illuminating the relations between Middle English language and literature. Finally, a tradition of close textual studies has sprung up around central authors in the tradition – Chaucer, the *Gawain*-poet, Malory and others. This chapter reviews these three phases and introduces three critical extracts which engage Middle English language and style from divergent approaches.

THE
PHILOLOGICAL
BACKGROUND
Alongside history, philology (the systematic study of etymology, grammar and syntax) defined early Middle English studies. When the central figure in Victorian medievalism, Frederick J. Furnivall, launched his Early English Text Society (EETS) in 1864, philology was at the heart of his mission statement:

> It is not fitting that the ruling tongue of the world should longer allow its history to be unknown, by leaving the documents of that history unprinted; it is not right that men who bathe in the full stream of English Literature should rest

content with not exploring, and making plain to all, the sources of the great river they enjoy.[1]

The EETS rapidly superseded the publication activities of antiquarian clubs like the Roxburghe (founded in 1812), Bannatyne (founded in 1823) and the Maitland (founded in 1828). It brought Middle English texts to a wide audience, effectively assembling the printed corpus of Middle English literature we inherit today. A large team of editors worked under the direction of Furnivall whose philological interests were reflected by his close involvement with the London Philological Society (founded in 1842). In selecting which texts to print, emphasis went as much on linguistic interest as on literary merit. For, unlike medieval manuscripts, printed books could be cited for consultation by the general reader, their vocabulary could be indexed and fed into the dictionaries of Middle and Modern English then in preparation (the Philological Society's *Dictionary on Historical Principles* got under way in the late 1850s: it would eventually develop into the *Oxford English Dictionary*). For a subscriber to the EETS in the 1860s, then, the morning's post could bring some diverse reading matter indeed: the Society's output for 1864 ranged from Richard Morris's edition of *Sir Gawain and the Green Knight* to Hall's edition of *Ane conpendious and breue tractate concernyng ye Office and Dewtie of Kyngis*. The first work would quickly move to the centre of the Middle English canon, the second to its margins. But for the Society's philological aims in 1864, *both* texts were important.

This precedence of linguistic over literary concerns remained clear twenty-eight years on in the note which prefaced the EETS's 1892 issues:

> During the twenty-eight years of the Society's existence, it has produced, with whatever shortcomings, an amount of good solid work for which all students of our Language, and some of our Literature, must be grateful, and which has rendered possible the beginnings (at least) of proper Histories and Dictionaries of that Language and Literature, and illustrated the thoughts, the life, the manners and customs of our forefathers and foremothers.[2]

By this date 'students of the language' were also starting to benefit from the appearance of a number of primers, dictionaries and glossaries: Richard Morris's *Specimens of Early English* of 1867; the Middle English dictionaries of Mayhew and Skeat in 1888 and Bradley and Stratmann in 1891; Emerson's *A Middle English Reader* of 1905, Kaluza's *Historische Grammatik der Englischen Sprache* of 1906 (German scholars dominated the field of Middle English philology at this early date, sometimes to Furnivall's chagrin).[3] The typical critical apparatus to these volumes is linguistic in character – and so was the emphasis in university study. It was volumes such as these that made up the

Middle English portion of the undergraduate's bookshelf in the early decades of the century, on hand for students to research essays more concerned with Norse loan words than narrators.

But philology in its broader sense has always implied more literary concerns. Once the documentation of Middle English language was under way, these were gradually readmitted into critical practice. We can see things beginning to shift in Kenneth Sisam's 1921 preface to his *Fourteenth Century Verse and Prose*, an influential volume that brought together a range of sample extracts and one that would go through many editions in the course of the century. Sisam's preface suggests that a philology that excludes literary concerns debars the critical reader from a full understanding of Middle English literature: 'the student of literature (in the narrower, modern sense of the word) brings a new range of interests.'[4] As Sisam was no doubt conscious, it was in no small part the achievement of Furnivall, who had died eleven years previously, that the Middle English studies of this period were now well equipped to turn to this new range of interests.

> It cannot be too strongly urged that the purpose of a worker in Middle English should be nothing less than to read sensitively, with the fullest possible understanding. Of such a purpose many *curricula* give no hint . . . That much may be accomplished by specialists following a single line of approach has been demonstrated by the philologists, who have burrowed tirelessly to present new materials to a world which seldom rewards their happiest elucidations with so much as a 'Well said, old mole!'

1921: Kenneth Sisam's *Fourteenth Century Verse and Prose* moves beyond a solely philological agenda.

CONTEXTUAL LANGUAGE STUDIES

How do Middle English language and literature inter-relate? The state of a language at any given time holds implications for literary varieties of that language. In the case of Middle English, language studies have stressed the significance of two key factors in the linguistic background to the literature: the trilingual situation of medieval England, and the lack of a standard form of medieval English language. In 1939, R. M. Wilson's *Early Middle English Literature* pioneered appreciation of the literature of such early Middle English texts as *The Owl and the Nightingale*, Laȝamon's *Brut* and *Ancrene Wisse*. But advocate as he was for this literature, Wilson made clear that its literary potentialities were constricted by the linguistic situation of medieval England (where Latin and French were the prestige languages, English their poor relation): 'the development of Anglo-French, though it helped to retard the development of English, nevertheless made possible a more intimate fusion of the two literatures, and the *Owl and the Nightingale* shows the possibilities inherent in the mingling of the strains.'[5] Shortly afterwards, in 1945, H. J. Chaytor's foundational study of medieval manuscript culture, *From Script to Print*, was likewise emphatic about the pre-eminence of French over English during the early Middle English period: 'While the number of Normans who came and settled in England has been variously estimated and often exaggerated, there is no doubt that Norman French was the official language of the country for some two centuries'.[6]

Such work helped to establish the framework of understanding within which later critics would approach questions of language, style, translation and authorship in Middle English texts. Another key part of that framework was awareness of the absence of a standard English for medieval writers and readers. Print culture was established only towards the end of the medieval period: William Caxton's press was set up at Westminster in 1476. Although print was to revolutionize medieval textual culture and would hasten the eventual establishment of a standard literary English based upon the East Midland dialect, for the greater part of the Middle English period no single dialect enjoyed prominence over the others. Texts would be copied into different dialects by different scribes: many of the texts we inherit today represent a mingling of diverse dialectal forms. Dialectology is the branch of Middle English studies dedicated to untangling these different threads, enabling scholars to make more confident judgements as to date and provenance of medieval texts. Middle English dialectology got under way in 1952, when Angus McIntosh initiated a University of Edinburgh project to investigate and document the various dialects which make up 'Middle English'. The early phase of the project was marked by the delivery of an address to The Philological Society in 1956:

> If we consider English as it was spoken in England around 1400 we may regard all its numerous forms as falling under the general description 'Later Middle English'. This term is an abstraction embracing under one convenient heading a large number of interrelated sub-species or varieties of the spoken language, and no single variety is to be regarded as more strictly or fittingly described by the term than the other. All evidently bore very marked resemblances; though the student of dialects will tend to be more concerned with the differences between them than with their resemblances.[7]

Thirty years later, these differences and resemblances had been fruitfully explored: the aims of the project were realized with the publication in 1986 of *A Linguistic Atlas of Late Medieval English*. Linguistic data could now shed more light on the language-use of major and minor Middle English authors than ever before.

A whole range of linguistic tools . . . becomes available to the modern writer, which by the nature of his language could not be used by his medieval counterpart. As manuscripts were freely transcribed from one dialect to the next and as their language was modified or modernized accordingly, the nuances which might have been indicated by spelling were not possible. Indeed the absence of a standard probably meant that although potentially there were more markers of social and geographical origin available in the medieval period, such markers could not be used in written documents.[8]

1979: Norman Blake reflects on the implications for literary study of the absence of a standard literary English for medieval writers.

STYLISTIC
STUDIES,
RHETORICAL
STUDIES

In this context of increasing awareness of the interplay between language and literature, detailed studies of major authors' language use have appeared, their pace quickening from the late 1950s when the influence of theories of 'close reading' registered widely in the field. An early example was the pioneering work of Charles Muscatine. In his *Chaucer and the French Tradition* of 1957, Muscatine sought to evolve a schema that would comprehensively describe the stylistic modes employed in Chaucer's poetry: 'If conventional styles are developed to support specific areas of meaning, what are the conventional traits of style in Chaucer? . . . To what degree does Chaucer depend on the historically given formulation of style, on its traditional area of expressiveness? To what extent does he exploit the relationship between styles?'[9]

Reflective of the same trend is Denton Fox's short 1959 article on the 'aureate' (self-consciously Latinate) style in the poetry of Dunbar: 'It is obviously a very narrow and specialised style, for which it has been condemned, but the fact that its limitations are more than compensated for by corresponding advantages has not, I think, been sufficiently recognised.'[10] Considerations of style and language use are also foregrounded in John Speirs's *Medieval English Poetry* of 1957, in Marie Borroff's stylistic and metrical study of *Sir Gawain* in 1962, in A. C. Spearing's *Criticism and Medieval Poetry* of 1964 and in the large body of scholarship on alliterative style produced throughout the 1950s and 1960s.[11] The 1970s opened with a highly influential study of Thomas Malory's style: P. J. C. Field's *Romance and Chronicle* scrutinized the Arthurian's prose style as never before: 'The basis of all Malory's story-telling is the simple declarative sentence or collocation of co-ordinate main clauses, and the expression by this of a sequence of actions, perceptions, or facts . . . His is the chronicle style.'[12]

RHETORIC

Ever since J. M. Manly addressed the British Academy on the theme of 'Chaucer and the Rhetoricians' in 1926, linguistic Middle English studies have also tended to stress the *rhetorical* basis of some texts, especially poetry.[13] The medieval *trivium* (core syllabus in medieval grammar schools) taught grammar, rhetoric and logic as inter-related and overlapping disciplines: students would be tutored both to discern and to deploy rhetorical figures in reading and writing Latin. They would be introduced to the notion, derived from classical rhetoric, that literary composition may be disposed into three distinct levels of style: the high (*grandis*), middle (*mediocris*) and the low (*humilis*). And so it is that the purple passages of Chaucer, Gower, the *Gawain*-poet, the *Ancrene Wisse*-author can be expounded according to the rhetorical principles, tropes and topoi enshrined in the classic medieval rhetorical handbooks by Matthew of Vendome, Geoffrey of Vinsauf and others:

* *Derek Pearsall* (1955): 'On the whole, it seems evident that some sort of relationship exists between rhetorical precept and the stylistic practice of *Gawain* and other alliterative poems.'[14]
* *John Finlayson* (1963): 'The purpose of this article is to examine the most widely used feature of medieval rhetorical art, the *descriptio loci*, in . . . the fourteenth-century alliterative *Morte Arthure*.'[15]
* *Robert O. Payne* (1963): 'What I want to emphasize here is the way in which style, by a variety of schematic and figurative devices – *digressio, apostrophe, sententia*, etc. – amplifies various elements in the structure so as to thread through them a common insinuation, and one which will provide the moral and aesthetic resolution for the poem [*The Book of the Duchess*].'[16]
* *A. C. Spearing* (1964): 'Thus the whole of any poem might be an intricate web of rhetorical devices, in the sense that the whole of it would be capable of being described in the terms of the *ars poetica*.'[17]

A foundational text for each of these critics is Ernst Curtius's European-wide study of medieval literary culture, *European Literature and the Latin Middle Ages*, a hugely influential work which had placed strong emphasis on the rhetorical basis of medieval composition: 'Merely from the rhetorical character of medieval poetry, it follows that, in interpreting a poem, we must ask not on what "experience" it was based, but what theme the poet set himself to treat.'[18] But rhetorical studies in Middle English are not limited to poetry: Geoffrey Shepherd's introduction to parts six and seven of the prose work *Ancrene Wisse* is a classic example of this variety of criticism. Focusing upon the section of the text that describes Christ's wooing of the anchoress' soul in the guise of a lover-knight, Shepherd shows how such rhetorical figures as *anaphora* and *epanados* (two forms of mannered repetition) and *paregmenon* (repetition of a word-stem with variant endings) are in play:

> Throughout this passage the use of figured language should be remarked: the repetition and emphatic positioning of the word *scheld* in *anaphora* (22, 11, 14,

18, 20); with *epanados*, 23; with *paregmenon*, 20. Alliteration is added, apparently, to supply the desired emotional tone to some phrases: *leoue licome* (11); on *s* and *f* [. . .] *Paregmenon* appears elsewhere: *cruneð*, *icrunet* (21, 23), *wil*, *willes* (24), *bohte*, *buð*, *bohte* (30, 31).[19]

Rhetorical studies have also formed the dominant critical approach to medieval English letters, both fictional (the letters of Troilus and Criseyde) and factual (the Paston letters, the Stonor letters and others). The studies of Norman Davis, editor of the medieval English Paston Letters, first set out the rhetorical principles upon which medieval epistles were constructed. In a mode of criticism that again emphasizes technical and structural properties of language, Davis illustrates the formulaic character of the fifteenth-century English letter, showing how each may be divided into seven distinct parts:

> [1] a form of address most commonly beginning with the word 'Right' and an adjective of respect ('worshipful', 'worthy', 'well beloved', &c.) and the appropriate noun ('sir', 'husband', 'father', &c.); [2] a formula commending the writer to the recipient, often accompanied by [2a] an expression of humility and, if the letter is to a parent, [2b] a request for a blessing – this usually introduced by a present participle and strengthened by an adverb or a phrase; [3] an expression of desire to hear of the recipient's welfare – this again introduced by a participle; [4] a prayer, introduced by a relative, for the continuation and increase of this welfare 'to your heart's desire', or the like; [5] a conditional clause deferentially offering news of the writer's welfare; [6] a report of the writer's good health 'at the making of this letter'; [7] thanks to God for it.[20]

The critical work of Davis and others showed how far such principles were in play in literary as well as genuine historical letters. John McKinnell's rhetorical breakdown of Criseyde's final letter in *Troilus* is one example:

> The structure of her letter is correct – a combined *salutatio* [greeting] and *benevolentiae captatio* [appeal to goodwill] (v, 1590–6); a *narratio*, relating her attitudes (V, 1597–1620); a *peticio* [request], asking Troilus for friendship and not to be angered by her brevity . . . a second *benevolentiae captatio*, using *sententiae* (proverbs) – a method advocated by the anonymous Orleans *ars dictandi* (1627–30); and a simple *conclusio* (1631). The poise of her rhetoric is almost too perfect, and seems closer to the arts of poetry than to the more mundane skill of *dictamen* – she opens, for example, with a fine apostrophe to Troilus (V, 1590–1) of the kind which Geoffroi de Vinsauf calls *exclamatio*, used, as he recommends it, to express grief.[21]

More recent critical work has focused upon the interplay between rhetorical theory and translation theory in the Middle Ages. A landmark text in this area is Rita Copeland's 1991 study, *Rhetoric, Hermeneutics, and Translation in the Middle Ages*, a study which aims: 'to define the place of vernacular translation within the systems of rhetoric and hermeneutics in the Middle Ages . . . it seeks to show how translation is inscribed within a large disciplinary nexus, a historical intersection of hermeneutical practice and rhetorical theory.'[22]

How have critics approached texts whose style lies outside the rhetorical tradition? Lyrics, ballads, romances often hail from popular rather than literary traditions, showing oral-derived features, appealing more to the ear than the eye. To root out rhetorical figures and flourishes in works of this kind would be to misrepresent the material itself – other approaches must be explored. Our first extract in this chapter represents a critical exploration of this kind as A. C. Spearing engages the elliptical and minimalist style of the early Middle English romance *King Horn*. Spearing, whose critical work is productively fluid and adaptable in methodology, makes use of linguistic terminology introduced into critical discourse by the Russian Formalists. In particular, Roman Jakobson's distinction between the metaphoric and metonymic modes of literary expression is put to work in Spearing's analysis of the terse style of the thirteenth-century poem. But Spearing also finds that this style requires a further analytical model and so draws on the discourse of film studies to describe the 'cross-cuts' and 'invisible cutting' of the narrative style.

OTHER APPROACHES TO LITERARY STYLE

Extract from A. C. Spearing, 'Early Medieval Narrative Style', in *Readings in Medieval Poetry* (Cambridge: Cambridge University Press, 1987), pp. 28–36.

[. . .] *King Horn*, like most narratives of its period, whether in English or in French, is written in rhyming couplets, but in this case the lines are unusually short. They are not the normal octosyllabics of French romance or their accentual English equivalent, but lines of only two or three stresses; and this gives the narrative an oddly lyrical quality, which is heightened by its frequent repetitions of phrases and its ballad-like abruptness of movement. The story, in a much abbreviated outline, is as follows. Horn, the son of the king of Suddene, is driven into exile by Saracen pirates who kill his father. He crosses the sea to Westernesse with two friends – Athulf who is faithful, and Fikenhild who is false. There, though Horn is unknown, the king's daughter Rymenhild falls in love with him. He says he must prove himself before they can get married. He kills many Saracens, but soon the king, Aylmar, is persuaded by the malicious Fikenhild that Horn has seduced Rymenhild, and he banishes him. Horn crosses the sea again to Ireland, and there kills a Saracen giant who had earlier killed his father. The king of Ireland offers Horn his daughter in marriage, but Horn remains true to Rymenhild. He is summoned back to Westernesse, where Rymenhild is about to be married to someone else. He arrives disguised as a beggar, identifies himself by puns and other signs, kills the unwanted suitor, and is accepted by Aylmar. Now Horn returns to Suddene to attempt to win back his kingdom. While he is away, Fikenhild attempts to force Rymenhild to marry him; but Horn once more returns, disguised this time as a harper, kills Fikenhild, marries Rymenhild, and settles down as king of Suddene. In this story, as often in traditional narrative and in myth, the same motif is repeated several times in variant forms;[1] and here one consequence is that the different sections of the narrative are divided up by sea-voyages. (The usual background to knightly adventure in medieval romance is the forest; even more than this, the sea seems to symbolize the dangerous realm of chance, the source both of death and of new life, that lies outside the walls of civilization.)

Comment on *King Horn*'s style can appropriately begin with mention of two features that are not present in it and the absence of which contributes largely to its unnoticeability. The first [is] metaphor. So far as I have been able to observe, there are no metaphors in *King Horn* – or at least (an important reservation) there are none which exist simply on the level of verbal style. There *is* a metaphor, and a very important one, but it functions structurally, or on the level of action. Rymenhild has a dream in which she goes fishing. Her net is burst by a 'gret fiss',[2] and she interprets this as meaning that she will lose the fish that she would choose for herself. Horn identifies the fish that tore the net as someone who will cause them suffering, and this turns out to mean Aylmar, whose banishment of Horn causes their separation (lines 658–64). Later, when Horn visits Rymenhild in disguise, he identifies himself to her by means of an extended metaphor in which he says that he is a fisherman who has left his net by the seashore and has now returned to see whether there is a fish in it. The fact that this metaphor originates in the ambiguous symbolism of a dream indicates how special metaphor is for the poet: it is the product of a mind working in a quite unusual way, irrational and perhaps inspired. If a pun counts as a metaphor, then the poem also contains a second metaphor on the level of action, in the form of a pun on Horn's name. Aylmar puns on it when he fist learns what Horn is called:

> Horn, thu lude sune
> Bi dales and bi dune![a]
> (209–10)

---

[a] [Your name] shall sound loudly / Across dales and downs.

And the pun is repeated in the same scene in which the disguised Horn alludes to Rymenhild's dream of fishing. She bears a drinking-horn to pour drink for the guests at the feast that is supposed to celebrate her wedding to the king who wishes to marry her, and Horn urges her to 'Drink to Horn of horne' (1145): These are, I believe, the only two figures in the poem that belong to the general category of metaphor, that is, of identification based on resemblance. It is striking that the fishing-metaphor and the pun on Horn's name should be clustered together in the same scene of the poem, a scene of disclosure and recognition, in which what was hidden is revealed. The poem's language alone is not enough to support metaphor.

Even the easier figure of simile is extremely rare in *King Horn*, and most of the few instances are similarly clustered together. They occur at the very beginning of the poem, in the initial description of the hero in his childhood:

> He was bright so the glas;
> He was whit so the flur;
> Rose-red was his colur.
> (14–16)

These comparisons are of course entirely familiar. Though we might expect them to be applied to a heroine rather than to a hero even in his childhood, they require no effort of interpretation, and they scarcely affect the transparency of the poem's style.

The second absence that helps to make the style of *King Horn* escape our attention is that of the narrator. He appears in the opening lines of the poem, to establish a relation with his listeners and announce his intention:

> Alle beon he blithe
> That to my song lythe![a]
> A sang ihc schal you singe
> Of Murry the kinge.

And he ends the poem by announcing the completion of his intention and thus the dissolution of the relation with the listeners into a generalized piety encompassing 'us alle':

> Her endeth the tale of Horn,
> That fair was and noght unorn.[b]
> Make we us glade evre among,
> For thus him endeth Hornes song.

[a] May all be happy / Who listen to my song!
[b] ugly.

> Jesus, that is of hevene king,
> Yeve us alle His suete blessing!

Between the beginning and the end the narrator very occasionally mentions himself in lines such as 'Also ihc you telle may' (30), but the narratorial 'I' seems a mere grammatical convention: his role is positional rather than personal, and 'his omniscience is largely situational'.[3] The story appears to tell itself, and even the narratorial comments on it, intended to arouse specific responses in the audience – 'Al to fewe he hadde tho!'[a] (50) or 'Of wordes he was bald' (90) – seem to have no personality behind them. The poet prefers whenever possible to dramatize rather than narrate the events of the poem. Nearly half of *King Horn* – almost 700 lines[4] – consists of direct speech by the characters; and the poet sometimes converts narrative into direct speech by having one of the characters tell another about some of the poem's events. Again, there are none of those explicit narratorial transitions that are so common in Chaucer and in later medieval narrative generally, such as

> Now wol I stynte[b] of Palamon a lite,
> And lete hym in his prisoun stille dwelle,
> And of Arcita forth I wol yow telle.
> *(Knight's Tale*, 1, 1334–6)

There are no references to sources or even to 'olde stories' (859), no modesty *topoi* –

> Who koude ryme in Englyssh proprely
> His martirdom? for sothe it am nat I;
> Therfore I passe as lightly as I may
> (1459–61)

– and no examples of *occupatio* (the listing of what is not going to be recounted) –

> And certes, if it nere[c] to long to heere,
> I wolde have toold yow fully the manere
> How wonnen[d] was the regne of Femenye . . .
> (875–7)

[a] then.
[b] stop.
[c] were not.
[d] conquered.

In short, there are none of the devices by means of which later medieval poets, even without necessarily personalizing the narrator, make us aware of a narrator distinct from the material of the narrative, who is consciously aiming to present that material to us in one way rather than another.

In *King Horn*, then, there is nothing to suggest to us any distinction between the story itself and the way in which the story is told. This is despite the fact that, as my summary will have indicated, the narrative structure is very complicated, involving three main settings (Westernesse, Ireland, and Suddene), each of which is visited several times; eight sea-voyages; and several cross-cuts from Ireland and Suddene to Westernesse and back again. But the voyages transport us along with the characters, without the narrator's seeming to be involved; and the cross-cuts are conducted with the utmost naturalness, often being masked by an association of ideas. For example, the first cross-cut is introduced by our being told that Horn stayed in Ireland for seven years without returning to Rymenhild in Westernesse or communicating with her; and this is the cue for the narrative to turn (at line 923) to Rymenhild in Westernesse. The effect is of what in film is sometimes called 'invisible cutting'. The transitions are seamless (or rather, the seams are concealed); there appears to be simply a continuous flow generated from within the story itself, and we need to make a conscious effort to notice that a narratorial intervention has in fact occurred.

'Invisible cutting' was an ideal of the classic Hollywood film, though it was of course achieved by different means, not usually by such associations of ideas. Another respect in which the narrative technique of *King Horn* resembles that of film is in its general avoidance of summary – also a device which, by implying that someone is doing the summarizing, tends to remind us of the existence of a storyteller. It is difficult for film narrative to summarize, simply because a cinematographic representation of a certain sequence of action occupies just the same amount of time as the sequence itself. Abbreviation has to be effected by elliptical editing; and something analogous to that is preferred by the poet of *King Horn*. What he does is to divide his action up into very small units and cut rapidly from one to another, effacing himself in the process. This can properly be considered a kind of verbal equivalent to elliptical editing in the film, though it must be remembered that, whereas the film-maker at the editing stage is literally cutting up pieces of film that have already been shot, discarding the unwanted parts, and joining the remainder in a certain order, for the poet there is unlikely to be any sharp distinction between 'shooting' (i.e. imagining) and cutting. That is so, at least, unless we may think of the poet as 'cutting' the material provided by a source. There is an Anglo-Norman analogue to *King Horn* which is over 5000 lines long; the English version gets exactly the same story into only some 1500 lines, and very short lines too. *King Horn* is probably not translated directly from *Horn et Rimen-*

hild, but it is possible that the English poet was working from some such lengthier source and cutting it as he went along. However it came about, the narrative style of *King Horn* is very similar to that of film in its effect. Short pieces of event are joined together in series; and the joining in both cases is simply a matter of juxtaposition. Like the language of dream, the language of film is paratactic. It has no means of indicating explicitly and unambiguously the relation between one film-piece and the next or the meaning of that relation; it cannot even distinguish between *and* and *but*, still less has it any equivalent to the subordinate clause. So it is in general with *King Horn*: there is simply a sequence of briefly narrated pieces of action, with few, if any syntactical links among them, and the listeners are left to supply the connections for themselves from their understanding of the content. To take a single, striking example, Horn's first return to Westernesse to save Rymenhild from an unwanted marriage is narrated as follows:

The word of Rymenhild's wedding began to spread. Horn was in the water; he could not have come later [i.e. he came at the very last moment]. He left his ship at anchor and went to land.

> The word bigan to springe
> Of Rymenhilde weddinge.
> Horn was in the watere;
> Ne mighte he come no latere.
> He let his schup stonde,
> And yede to londe.
>   (1017–22)

As with the *Chanson de Roland*, in calling attention to these features of narrative style, I am undoubtedly doing something other than the poet would have expected or probably wished. If one reads the poem without making a conscious effort to be analytical, the method of storytelling becomes unnoticeable; the effect, as I have remarked, is simply of naturalness. It is worth emphasizing that 'naturalness' is not intended to imply 'realism'. The world represented in *King Horn* is highly stylized; it is a world of extremes with no middle ground between them –

> Athulf was the beste
> And Fikenylde the werste
>   (27–8)

– a world more like that of fairytale than like that of everyday life. (I set aside for the moment the complications introduced by the possibility that people in the early Middle Ages may have perceived their real world as being more like fairytale than we do ours.)⁵ The illusion created by *King Horn* is not that the events represented are those of real life, but that there is no mode of representation intervening between us and them; or [. . .] that the poem is merely a transparent window through which we regard the events that make up its content.

So far this consideration of the style of *King Horn* has largely been in terms of absence; and that is how it presents itself to us so long as we assume that poetic style is essentially a matter of metaphor, or of the whole family of figures based on the resemblance of one thing to another and the transfer of meaning over this bridge of resemblance. That conception of poetic style, however, is challenged by the distinction, originating with the Russian Formalists, expounded systematically by Roman Jakobson, and developed further in relation to English literature by more recent theorists such as David Lodge, between metaphor and metonymy.⁶ On this alternative view, metaphor and metonymy are generated by opposed principles or axes of language itself, metaphor being derived from similarity and metonymy from contiguity. Metonymy in this sense proves to be of greater use than metaphor in enabling us to detect the features that are present in the narrative style of *King Horn*, as opposed to those that are not. The poem's style does intervene between us and its content – how could it not? – but it does so not through figures that compare its literal content to other objects, or that substitute those objects for it, but through figures that direct us to imagine the content itself in one way rather than another. Our response is controlled by the verbal medium (its transparency is indeed an illusion), but it is controlled as our response to the events of a film is chiefly controlled, by the choice of shots and angles. It must be noted, however, that Jakobson's concept of metonymy, as the general name for the whole class of figures based on contiguity, is an enlargement of the traditional meaning of the term in rhetoric. The latter is given by the definition in the *Oxford English Dictionary:* 'A figure of speech which consists in substituting for the name of a thing the name of an attribute of it or of something closely related.' An example would be the use of the word *crown* to mean 'king' or 'kingship' or, in a monarchy, 'the state'. Metonymy in this restricted sense is not at all characteristic of the style of *King Horn*. But included within Jakobson's enlarged concept of metonymy are many other figures based on contiguity, among them that traditionally known as synecdoche. The definition of this in the *Oxford English Dictionary* is: 'A figure by which a more comprehensive term is used for a less comprehensive or *vice versa*; as whole for part or part for whole, genus for species or species for genus, etc.' And synecdoche, especially in the form in which the part is substituted for the whole, is a major feature of the style of *King Horn*.

The visual synecdoche in which the part stands for the whole is also an extremely common feature of the narrative style of film. A shot of two hands clasping or shaking each other may indicate that two men or two parties have reached agreement; a shot of marching feet may represent the movement of a whole army; a shot of the turning wheels and moving pistons of a locomotive may symbolize the journey of a train or of someone on board it (and this may be accompanied by what could be called the auditory synecdoche of a whistle or siren). Though visual synecdoche and the close-up shot are not the same thing, there is a strong tendency for them to be used in conjunction; if the part is to stand for the whole, then it will have to dominate our attention, and that can most easily be achieved if it occupies the whole of the screen. In considering the narrative style of *King Horn* I shall use *synecdoche* to mean the substitution of part for whole; and I find it very helpful in practice to imagine its synecdoches as close-ups in a hypothetical film. The analogy is undoubtedly less than perfect, but, precisely because we are not yet accustomed to analyse non-metaphorical narrative styles, such analogies can be useful initial aids.

I shall begin with some very simple examples. Early in *King Horn*, when the Saracens seize the boy Horn and his young companions and decide to set them adrift to drown, we are told:

> The children hi broghte to stronde[a]
> Wringinde here honde.[b]
>
> (111–12)

The second of these lines implies a close-up shot of hands being wrung, and this stands in place of a possible more comprehensive description of the boys' grief. Again, when Horn has grown up and is fighting the Saracens in Westernesse, we are told:

> Horn gan his swerd gripe,
> And on his arme wipe.
>
> (605–6)

That implies two close-up shots, showing first Horn's hand gripping the hilt of his sword, then the blade being wiped on his arm; and those two shots stand in place of a possible far lengthier account of his preparations for battle. They also of course imply grim determination and perhaps ruthlessness, states of mind which we infer (as in real life) from the fragments of bodily gesture. There are many cases where synecdoche is no more than a normal way of referring to a certain action. Thus, when Horn and the other boys arrive in Westernesse, the poet says,

---

[a] they . . . see shore.
[b] wringing their hands.

Of[a] schup hi gunne funde[b]
And setten fout to grunde.
(133–4)

To 'set foot to ground' is doubtless a perfectly ordinary, idiomatic way of referring to the action of alighting from a boat or a horse, but it is nevertheless a synecdoche, implying a shot not of the whole of the boys' bodies as they clamber ashore but of a single foot touching the ground. In yet other cases, it may be that a mode of expression which could be thought of as synecdochic is the *only* way of referring to an action. When Horn kneels to Rymenhild, the poet says that 'On knes he him sette' (383) – and how could the poet have told us that he knelt without focusing briefly on his knees?

There is clearly a danger of calling attention to what is merely commonplace, a feature of language rather than of style. It is well known that medieval literature in general tends to convey emotions through bodily gestures, to present the subjective in objective terms. (So indeed does film; given that its medium is predominantly visual, it has no choice.) On the other hand, I am convinced that we need to learn to respond more sensitively to a narrative style – a narrative imagination – which is fundamentally synecdochic, which again and again substitutes the part for the whole, and thereby gains concentration without losing rapidity and transparency. [. . .]

Notes

1   For comment, see, for example, Edmund Leach, *Genesis as Myth* (London, 1969), pp. 7–8, and *Lévi-Strauss* (London, 1970), pp. 59–60; Anne Wilson, *Traditional Romance and Tale* (Ipswich, 1976), pp. 59–62; Derek Brewer, *Symbolic Stories* (Cambridge, 1980), pp. 64–6.

2   *King Horn* is quoted here and subsequently from the Cambridge text as given by the edition of Joseph Hall (Oxford, 1901).

3   Mary Hynes-Berry, 'Cohesion in *King Horn* and *Sir Orfeo*', *Speculum* 50 (1975), 652–70; (654).

4   According to Hynes-Berry (ibid., p. 652), the exact figure is 692.

5   As suggested, to take a single example, by the parallels between Orfeo's return from the land of fairy and resumption of his kingdom and the 'return' of the pseudo-Baldwin from supposed death and his acceptance as Count of Flanders in 1224–5 (see chronicle accounts summarized by Norman Cohn, *The Pursuit of the Millennium* [London, 1957], pp. 77ff).

6   Roman Jakobson, 'Two Aspects of Language and Two Types of Aphasic Disturbances', in Roman Jakobson and Morris Halle (eds.), *Fundamentals of Language*

[a] From.
[b] hasten.

(The Hague, 1956), pp. 69–96, and 'Closing Statement: Linguistics and Poetics', in Thomas A. Sebeok (ed.), *Style in Language* (Cambridge, MA, 1960), pp. 350–77; David Lodge, *The Modes of Modern Writing* (London, 1977), pp. 73ff.

STYLISTICS OF MEDIEVAL LETTERS

Our second extract also takes up the challenge posed by a particular stylistic mode – that of medieval letter-writing. As we have seen, medieval letters were bound by rhetorical convention and can be shown to adhere closely to pre-scribed models. Can the modern reader find more in such letters than a string of rhetorical figures? Diane Watt's 1993 essay on the letters of the Paston women was concerned with just this question. Watt's starting-point is the famous dismissal of the letters by Virginia Woolf: 'in all this there is no writing for writing's sake; no use of the pen to convey pleasure or amusement or any of the million shades of endearment and intimacy which have filled so many English letters since.'[23] In the light of this response, Watt's essay takes a fresh look at the issue of language use and individual expression. In 'The Language of Service and Household Rhetoric in the Letters of the Paston Women' Watt largely sets aside the models of the *ars dictaminis*, attending instead to a more loosely defined 'household rhetoric' in which she perceives some more indi-viduated and distinctive touches in the language use of Margaret and Agnes Paston. Watt's approach draws on philological and rhetorical studies of English letters, on historical work on the medieval household, and on theory treating relations between oral and written discourses. With this more creative notion of rhetoric in place, Watt's essay draws out contexts of 'dramatic prose' and orality to yield a fresh perspective on the women's letters.

Extract from Diane Watt, '"No Writing for Writing's Sake": The Language of Service and Household Rhetoric in the Letters of the Paston Women', in Karen Cherewatuk and Ulrike Wiethaus (eds), *Dear Sister: Medieval Women and the Epistolary Genre* (Philadephia: University of Pennsylvania Press, 1993), pp. 127–33.

[. . .] The Royal Court and the great households of England had their own 'language' or vocabulary through which was expressed the social relationship of service, one of the most important forms of political and social allegiance in England. The hierarchical social structure is formalized in conventions of address. Written appeals for patronage and protection ('good lord/ladyship') are formal and deferential, reflecting both the obsequious language spoken at court and the influence of the *ars dictaminis*. Included in the documents written in the hand of John Paston III is a poem of complaint to an unidentified lord.[1] The opening lines take the form of a petition:

> My ryght good lord, most knyghtly gentyll knyght,
> On-to your grace in my most humbyll wyse
> I me comand, as it is dew and ryght,
> Besechyng yow at leyser to aduyse
> Vp-on thys byll, and perdon myn empryse[a]
> Growndyd on foly for lak of prouydence
> On-to your lordshep to wryght wyth-owght lycence.
>
> (no. 351)

No Middle-English letter-writing manuals survive, but Norman Davis has shown that official and private letters written in English in the later Middle Ages conformed to certain precepts. These conventions were regularized in France, where the *ars dictaminis* was applied to letters written in the vernacular. With only minor variations, certain words and phrases follow an established sequence: this verse epistle opens with the word 'right' which is only found in English letters, but the writer's commendation and declaration of humility closely correspond to the French formulae 'se recommande' and 'treshumblement'.[2]

The greater the social divide between writer and recipient, the more exaggerated the formality of the language and the more extreme the writer's appeal to the condescension of the recipient. Having apologized for the presumption of writing, the suitor in the verse epistle goes on to describe the anguish suffered in the absence of the lord and entreats for the opportunity to wait attendance upon him.[3] The rhetorical skill of John Paston III allows him to exploit the conventions of this language. He humorously petitions Lord Fitzwalter for a dozen rabbits, describing himself in exaggerated self-deprecation as 'your dayly seruaynt and beedman John Paston, more kayteff[b] than knyght' and claiming that his own property is inadequate for his needs, 'More lyeke a pynnefold then a parke' while theft is impossible from Fitzwalter's well-protected estates (no. 390).

Well-rehearsed in court circles was the ability to promote oneself while at the same time reinforcing the self-esteem of one's patrons. John III expresses deference and loyalty to a superior through lavish praise 'of þe most corteys, gentylest, wysest, kyndest, most compenabyll,[c] freest, largeest,[d] and most

[a] undertaking.
[b] wretch.
[c] friendly.
[d] most generous.

bowntefous knyght . . . he is on the lyghtest, delyuerst,[a] best spokyn, fayirest archer, deuowghtest, most perfyght and trewest to hys lady of all the knyghtys that euer I was aqweyntyd wyth' (no. 352).[4] Such rhetoric was often criticized by contemporaries as insincere; the poet Hoccleve condemns the flattery of courtiers: 'Many a seruant vnto his lord seith þat al the world spekith of him honour, / Whan contrarie of þat is soothe in feith.'[5] Margaret Paston advises her son to be wary of the deception of those whose support he solicited too extravagantly, 'for though ye haue nede thei wull not be right redy to help you of there owyn' (no. 210).

The Paston women were not unacquainted with court and political life. John III is certain that if his mother were to attend the Duchess of Norfolk during her confinement, Paston affairs will be furthered (no. 371). Several years later his wife Margery offers to speak to the Duchess on her husband's behalf, arguing that, 'on word of a woman shuld do more than the wordys of xx men' (no. 418). Margaret Paston was even present during a visit of the Queen to Norfolk, but the excitement with which she describes the event reveals that this was for her a rare glimpse of court life. Margaret's cousin actually spoke with the Queen, but Margaret complains that she herself did not even have a necklace fit to be worn 'among so many fresch jantylwomman as here were at þat tym' (no. 146). Under normal circumstances the Paston women, unlike more privileged members of their sex, did not have the opportunity to attend the Royal Court and had only limited access to its culture. Consequently, the sophistication of court rhetoric and the creative self-consciousness so typical of the letters of John Paston III occur rarely in the correspondence of the women.

However, the language of service did infuse the vocabulary and imagery of many other social relations including the discourse of love and the rhetoric of the household. John III asks his elder brother to recommend him to Sir John Parre 'wyth all my seruys, and tell hym by my trouthe I longyd neuer sorer to se my lady then I do to se hys mastershepe. And I prey God that he aryse neuer a mornyng fro my lady his wyff wyth-owght it be ageyn hyr wyll tyll syche tyme as he bryng hyr to Ouyr Lady of Walsyngham' (no. 352).[6] By means of romantic playfulness, John III is able to express his esteem for his lord's wife with the deference appropriate to a retainer. Such eloquence suggests that he may well have been experienced in the courtly pastime of lover's conversation, termed 'luf-talkyng' by the Gawain-poet.

The same relationship of service is invoked in his private love letters. John III humbly offers life-long obedience to a potential bride:

> Mastresse, thow so be that I, vanqweyntyd wyth yow as yet, tak vp-on me to be
> thus bold as to wryght on-to yow wyth-ought your knowlage and leue, yet, mas-

[a] most agile.

tress, for syche pore seruyse as I now in my mynd owe yow, purposyng, ye not dyspleasyd, duryng my lyff to contenu the same, I beseche yow to pardon my boldness and not to dysdeyn but to accepte thys sympyll bylle. (no. 373)

He is willing to withdraw his attentions if they become burdensome, 'for I wyll no ferther labore but to yow on-to the tyme ye geue me leue and tyll I be suer that ye shall take no dysplesure wyth my ferther labore.' Yet, despite his protestations of honor, his letters betray insincerity. He begs one 'Mastresse Annes' to 'let me not be forgotyn when ye rekyn[a] vp all your seruauntys, to be sett in the nombyr wyth other' (no. 362), but elsewhere describes her as 'þe thyng' (no. 363). On hearing of his sister's marriage he writes to his brother, 'I prey yow aspye some old thryffty draffwyff in London for me' (no. 369). These flippant remarks indicate that John III accepts the prevalent attitude of the time that marriages should be socially or economically advantageous – he includes a wealthy widow on his long list of possible brides. It is not surprising that John II cynically remarks to John III and a friend, 'Yit weere it pyte þat suche craffty wowerys[b] as ye be bothe scholde speede weell but iff ye love trewly' (no. 287).

When Margery, John III's future wife, found herself separated from her fiancé while the families negotiated the dowry, she was justifiably concerned about her father's financial reticence. She appealed to her lover as a petitioner ('bedewoman'), describing the pain which she suffered as a result of their separation, and humbly pleading with him to accept her:

yf þat ȝe[c] cowde be content wyth þat good and my por persone, I wold be þe meryest mayden on grounde. And yf ȝe thynke not ȝowr-selfe so satysfyed, or þat ȝe myght hafe mech more good, as I hafe vndyrstonde be ȝowe afor, good, trewe, and lovyng Volentyne, þat ȝe take no such labure vppon ȝowe as to com more for þat mater; but let it passe, and neuer more to be spokyn of. . . . (no. 416)

Like so much of John III's own writing, Margery's letter is consciously creative – part of the letter is written in rhyming prose.[7] As a betrothed woman rather than a lover's 'mistress', Margery happily accepts the sovereignty of her future husband, and instead of holding herself aloof, she promises that, despite any opposition from her friends, 'yf ȝe commande me to kepe me true whereeuer I go/Iwyse I will do all my myght ȝowe to love and neuer no mo' (no. 415). The social convention which made John III 'servant in love' combined with the law of church and state to make him 'lord in mariage.'[8] There is no suggestion in any of the surviving letters that in the years to come Margery

[a] count.
[b] wooers.
[c] you.

ever seriously challenged the authority of the man who remained her 'owyn swete hert' (no. 418).

Address was formalized both in the extended household and within the family unit.[9] The Paston women as well as the men were addressed with humility by their employees and dependants. While Richard Calle, the trusted and respected family bailiff, addressed both his master and mistress quite informally, one Piers, a servant who had been imprisoned for theft, had to plead for favours, placing himself entirely at Margaret Paston's mercy (nos. 714, 715, 169). John Paston I had certain expectations of his household: 'euery gentilman that hath discrecion waytith[a] that *his ken[b] and seruantis þat levith be hym* and at his coste shuld help hym forthward' (no. 73). The symbiotic relationship of patronage and service even infiltrated the heart of the household – the nuclear family. As patrons, householders would protect the interests not only of their retainers, domestic servants and tenants, but also of their children. John II had to strive to regain John I's 'good faderhood' after a period of friction (for example, no. 178). Margaret Paston describes her cousin's dilemma over his mother's proposed marriage; he has done all he can to dissuade her but runs the risk of losing 'hyr gode modyrchep' (no. 152). Such a loss would indeed be serious. Margaret's daughter forfeited the 'good ore helpe ore kownfort' of her family and friends by marrying Richard Calle against their wishes, and Margaret went so far as to ban her from the house (no. 203). Family patronage extended beyond the relationship of parent and child. The head of the household also had a certain amount of responsibility for her or his younger siblings: Margaret asks her husband to be a 'gode brothere' to his sister Elizabeth in furthering negotiations for her marriage (no. 145).

In return for parental patronage, children were expected to show obedience and honor. When John II seeks his father's forgiveness, he complains of 'the peyn and heuynesse þat it hathe ben to me syn yowre departyng owt of thys contre' and begs for grace:

> I beseche yow of yowre faderly pyte to tendre þe more thys symple wryghtyng, as I schal owt of dowght her-afftere doo þat schal please yow to þe vttermest of my powere and labore. And if there be any servyce þat I may do, if it please yow to comaund me or if I maye vnder-stonde it, I wyl be as glad to do it as any thyng erthely, if it were any thyng þat myght be to yowre pleasyng. (no. 234)

John III's younger brother Edmond apologizes to his mother for his neglect in similar terms: 'And it plese ȝow to be so good and kynde modyre[c] to forgeue me and also my wyffe of owur leude[a] offence þat we haue not don owur dute, whyche was to haue seyn and ave waytyd vp-on ȝow ore now' (no. 399).

[a] expects.
[b] kin.
[c] mother.

Edmond recognizes that he must attend his mother just as a courtier is obliged to attend the sovereign.

Household Rhetoric and Plain Style

> Speketh so pleyn at this tyme, we yow preye,
> That we may understonde what ye seye.
> *The Clerk's Prologue*

Despite the pervasiveness of at least some degree of formality in the Paston correspondence, the predominant style which characterizes the letters as a whole is a plain one. According to medieval *ars rhetorica*, style ought to reflect context; 'high' style characterized by formal language and complex grammar was appropriate, as the Host observed to the Clerk, 'whan that men to kynges write.' In contrast, a 'plain' style would be fitting for general household correspondence. The sixteenth-century letter-writing manual of William Fulwood advises against 'rare and diffused phrases', recommending rather 'the common and familiar speache' of the vernacular.[10] This style could be described as 'colloquial', bearing a striking resemblance to, and having its origins in the spoken idiom.[11]

The often dramatic prose of Margaret Paston has many features of oral narrative. In one of her most lively letters, she describes an attack on the family chaplain which occurred while he was walking home from the town. The attacker, John Wymondham, stood at his gate with some of his men, while another man stood on the road 'by þe canell side':

> And Jamys Gloys come with his hatte on his hede betwen bothe his men, as he was wont of custome to do. And whanne Gloys was a-yenst Wymondham he seid þus, 'Couere thy heed!' And Gloys seid ageyn, 'So I shall for the.' And whanne Gloys was forther passed by þe space of iii or iiij strede, Wymondham drew owt his dagger and seid, 'Shalt þow so, knave?' (no. 129)

Margaret's own intervention in the brawl is signaled by a shift away from dramatic direct speech into indirect discourse:

> And with þe noise of þis a-saut[b] and affray my modir[c] and I come owt of þe chirche from þe sakeryng,[d] and I bad Gloys go to my moderis place ageyn, and

---

[a] foolish.
[b] assault.
[c] mother.
[d] consecration of the host during Mass.

so he dede. And thanne Wymondham called my moder and me strong hores.[a]
. . . And he had meche large[b] langage, as ye shall knowe herafter by my mowthe.

Such a movement from third-person to first-person narrative is characteristic of informal speech. In her analysis of the passage, Janel Mueller notes that by means of this grammatical transition Margaret controls the narrative, just as she took charge when she came upon the fight.[12] Margaret may have felt that she was invulnerable to assault. She mentions in her letter that the attack took place while she was in the church, exactly at the moment of the elevation of the host. According to popular belief, seeing the elevated host could protect one from dying suddenly and unprepared.

The colloquialism found in the writing of Margaret Paston could be explained by the fact that she dictated her letters to a secretary, were it not for the appearance of a similar narrative style in the autograph correspondence of the other writers. John III, who is capable of writing an 18-line complex sentence in one short letter of petition (no. 359), slips into a much simpler style when writing of a family disagreement to his elder brother:

> Many qwarellys ar pyekyd to get my brodyr E. and me ought of hyr howse. We go not to be[d] vnchedyn lyghtly.[c] All þat we do is ille doon, and all that Syr Jamys and Pekok dothe is well deon. Syr Jamys and I be tweyn.[d] We fyll owght be-for my modyr wyth 'Thow prowd prest' and 'Thow prowd sqwyer', my modyr takyng hys part, so I haue almost beshet þe bote as for my modyrs house. (no. 353)

In this letter Margaret is portrayed as a matriarchal figure dominating the household. John III expresses in energetic prose his anger at the abuse which he is forced to endure and at his own sense of powerlessness. The spontaneity of the tense-switching is analogous to the grammatical fluidity of spoken narrative.[13] To the modern reader, such apparent inconsistency stands out in a written context as ungrammatical.

Apart from syntactic characteristics, certain features of vocabulary and phrasing within the letters, in particular proverbs, idioms and neologisms (such as 'beshit the boat', meaning 'to make oneself unwelcome')[14] are indicative of a colloquial style.[15] Such speech-like forms are not merely typical of the women's writing but are found throughout the collection. One of the most striking examples of a proverbial style is seen in a letter written by Agnes Paston to her eldest son, following a period of strained relations. Agnes begins in somber tones offering him her blessing: 'þat blyssyng þat I prayed ӡoure

---

[a] whores.
[b] offensive.
[c] we never make it to bed without a telling-off.
[d] separated.

fadir to gyffe ȝow þe laste day þat euer he spakke, and þe blyssyng of all seyntes vndir heven, and myn.' She goes on:

> ȝoure[a] fadyr sayde, 'In lityl bysynes lyeth myche reste.' Þis worlde is but a þorugh-
> fare[b] and ful of woo, and whan we departe þer-fro, riȝth nouȝght bere wyth vs
> but oure good dedys and ylle. And þer knoweth no man how soon God woll
> clepe[c] hym, and þer-for it is good for euery creature to be redy. Qhom[d] God
> vysyteth,[e] him he louyth. (no. 30)

The gnomic wisdom of Agnes's husband is confirmed by the authority of the New Testament reminders of the transitory nature of earthly things (1 Tim. 6: 7), the inevitability yet unpredictability of death (Matt. 24: 44), and the consolation of God's greater wisdom (Heb. 12: 6).[16] The passage has the measured control of a medieval sermon and belies any suggestion that Agnes Paston is uneducated. [. . .]

Notes

1 John Paston III did not sign this poem and it is not certain that it is his composition. However, he is known to have written verses in Latin addressed to the Duke of Norfolk (no. 393).

2 Norman Davis, 'The *Litera Troili* and English Letters', *Review of English Studies* n.s. 16 (1965), 238.

3 Compare Dunbar's complaint, 'Schir, ye have mony servitouris' which remonstrates James IV for his neglect and seeks his favour, and Hoccleve's plea for money from his patron in 'La Male Regle' (note 5).

4 Norman Davis notes a resemblance between John Paston III's praise of his patron and Ector's eulogy for Sir Launcelot at the end of Malory's *The Morte Arthur*. Davis comments, 'Malory finished his book in 1470, and Paston's letter is dated 2 June 1472. It seems not very likely that he could have based it directly on Malory. More probably there were other texts . . . which both he and Malory knew', 'Style and Stereotype in Early English Letters', *Leeds Studies in English* n.s. (1967), 15.

5 'La Male Regle de T. Hoccleue' (ll. 217–18) in M. C. Seymour, *Selections from Hoccleve* (Oxford: Oxford University Press, 1981).

6 The pilgrimage to the shrine at Walsingham in Norfolk was extremely popular in the century before the Reformation.

---

[a] your.
[b] thoroughfare.
[c] call.
[d] Whom.
[e] visits [affliction upon].

7   John I and his eldest son also included informal verses in their correspondence (nos. 77, 270).

8   *The Franklin's Tale*, l. 793. All citations of Chaucer are from Larry D. Benson (ed.), *The Riverside Chaucer*, 3rd edn (Oxford: Oxford University Press, 1988).

9   Norman Davis describes the conventional formulae of medieval household correspondence in 'The *Litera Troili* and English Letters' (note 2), 233–44 and in 'A Note on *Pearl*', *Review of English Studies* n.s. 17 (1966), 403–5.

10   William Fulwood, *The Enimie of Idlenesse: Teaching How to Indite, Epistles* (n.p.: 1568), f.6ᵛ.

11   For an analysis of the problems of discussing colloquialisms in Middle English see D. Rygiel, '*Ancrene Wisse* and Colloquial Style: A Caveat', *Neophilologus* 65 (1981), 137–43.

12   Janel Mueller, *The Native Tongue and the Word: Developments in English Prose Style 1380–1580* (Chicago: University of Chicago Press, 1985), pp. 90–1.

13   See Suzanne Fleischman, 'Philology, Linguistics, and the Discourse of the Medieval Text', *Speculum* 65, 1 (January 1990), 23.

14   B. J. Whiting (ed.), *Proverbs, Sentences, and Proverbial Phrases from English Writing Mainly Before 1500* (Cambridge, MA: Harvard University Press, 1968), B423.

15   On the oral basis of Middle English prose see Mueller, *The Native Tongue and the Word*, pp. 85–110; and Norman Davis, 'The Language of the Pastons', *Proceedings of the British Academy* 40 (1954), 119–39.

16   For a detailed discussion of biblical and proverbial allusions in this passage see Norman Davis, 'Style and Stereotype in Early English Letters', *Leeds Studies in English* n.s. (1967), 10–15.

ENGLISH LANGUAGE AND ENGLISH IDENTITY It remains to mention a more recent dimension of Middle English language studies. Critical approaches in the tradition of cultural studies have considered how far medieval English authors articulate a regional, even national consciousness in their work. Does the relation between English language and literature gradually evolve a distinctively *English* (as distinct from Anglo-Norman) literary culture in the centuries following the Conquest? Our final extract explores these questions, looking at the interplay between language and identity. In a criticism grounded in the trilingualism of medieval England, Thorlac Turville-Petre explores how 'early survivals of an English tradition' may be gleaned from the body of English lyric poetry collected in the Harleian and other manuscripts. Acknowledging the indebtedness of many of these lyrics to French motifs and conventions, Turville-Petre nevertheless finds examples that transcend slavish imitation and translation by rooting conventional sentiment in images that are 'precise, detailed, and local' and pointing at an apparently heightened correlation between English language and English identity.

Extract from Thorlac Turville-Petre, 'Three Languages', in *England the Nation: Language, Literature and National Identity, 1290–1340* (Oxford: Clarendon Press, 1996), pp. 204–8.

> Bytuene Mersh ant Aueril
> When spray biginneþ to springe,
> þe lutel foul haþ hire wyl
> On hyre lud to synge.
> Ich libbe in loue-longinge
> For semlokest of alle þynge,
> He may me blisse bringe;
> Icham in hire baundoun.*
>
> (29.1–8)[1]

With its bounce and zip, this is no second-hand version of a French lyric, and yet the influences are deep and obvious: the spring opening of the *reverdie*, the carol form, and most of all that final expression *baundoun*, capturing in a single French word the whole subject/mistress relationship of courtly-love. The verse is alive with supple movement; muted alliteration combines with jaunty rhythm to build up to the exuberant refrain:

> An hendy hap ichabbe yhent,
> Ichot from heuene it is me sent,
> From alle wymmen mi loue is lent
> Ant lyht on Alysoun.†
>
> (29.9–12)

The poets of the love-lyrics show how English verse can now respond to European lyric traditions and yet remain thoroughly English.[2] The generic structures are those used in French: the *chanson d'aventure* (of which the *pastourelle* is a popular type), where man meets woman and attempts to persuade her to love; the *reverdie* or renewal of spring, heralding the growth of love, indicated by opening lines such as 'In May hit murgeþ when hit dawes' (item

---

* Between March and April, / When the twig begins to bud, / The little bird delights / To sing in her language. / I live in love-longing / For the most lovely of all / She can bring me happiness; / I am in her power.

† I've had wonderful good fortune – / I know it is sent me from heaven / My love is withdrawn from all other women / And has come down on Alison.

44) or 'When þe nyhtegale singes' (item 65). The poets use a wide variety of lyric stanza-forms that show strong Anglo-Norman and Continental influence, such as the tripartite ten-line stanza on two rhymes of 'Wiþ longyng y am lad' (item 30), and variations on the tail-rhyme stanza [. . .] which are particularly characteristic of Anglo-Norman.[3]

The structures are French, but the verse itself is English. The source of the dullness of the lament for Edward I is its imitation of the French octosyllabics, by which 'De la mort un rei vaillaunt' (3) leads metrically to 'Of a knyht þat was so strong' (47.5). English metre is based on stress more than syllable count, and the stress pattern may be picked out by alliteration:

> Ichot a burde in bour ase beryl so bryht.
> > (28.1)
> Heo glystnede ase gold when hit glemede.
> > (35.3)

Or less insistently:

> On heu hire her is fayr ynoh,
> Hire browe broune, hire eȝe blake;
> Wiþ lossum chere he on me loh,
> Wiþ middel smal ant wel ymake.
> > (29.13–16)

The rhythmic structure of the line ranges widely from fairly regular iambs with unobtrusive alliteration to accentual alliterative lines of variable syllabic shape. In one ambitious poem, the lines alliterate in pairs within a demanding stanza, and the opening eight lines all end on the same consonant:

> Weping haueþ myn wonges wet
> For wikked werk ant wone of wyt;
> Vnbliþe y be til y ha bet
> Bruches broken, ase bok byt,
> Of leuedis loue þat y ha let
> þat lemeþ al wiþ luefly lyt.
> Ofte in song y haue hem set
> þat is vnsemly þer hit syt.*
> > (33.1–8)

---

* Weeping has wet my cheeks / For my wicked deeds and stupidity; / I'll be miserable until I've made amends / For sins I've committed, as the Book tells us to / Over ladies' love that I've forfeited / Ladies who all shine with lovely light. / Often I've put them in songs, / And that's unfitting there.

Experimental examples of similar patterns that combine a stanza form with alliteration and pararhyme or identical rhyme were recorded over half a century earlier by a Cistercian at Stanlow Abbey in Cheshire, such as the love poem that begins:[4]

> I haue to a semly that I bi sete
> Send mine sonde selliche sete,
> þat is brithure in bur þen basote ant bete;
> Yif that burde haues broken, best is to bete.*

By comparison with the Harley lyrics, these are contrived and lumpish, but they offer rare early survivals of an English tradition which the Harley poets have developed.

Of all kinds, the love-lyric is surely the least concerned with society and its structures? Love is universal and eternal; it knows neither national nor social barriers – or so the lover would make us believe. Love is its own world, as Donne's lover expresses it:

> She is all States, and all Princes, I,
> Nothing else is.

So, too, in the Harley lyrics:

> When heo is glad,
> Of al þis world namore y bad
> þen beo wiþ hire myn one bistad
> Wiþoute strif.[†]
>
> (36.7–10)

But the Harley lovers' attempts to escape to a state of transcendence are constantly thwarted. There is nothing timeless about this passion; it arrives punctually with the urge of spring, 'Bytuene Mersh ant Aueril', when the world wakes from the dead sleep of winter:

> Lenten[‡] ys come wiþ loue to toune,[§]
> Wiþ blosmen ant wiþ briddes roune,[¶]
> þat al þis blisse bryngeþ;

* To a lovely one that I sat next to / I have sent my gift splendidly adorned, / Brighter in bower than basalt [?] and better still; / If that lady has rejected it [?] it's best to put it right.
[†] When she's happy / I'd ask for nothing more of all the world / Than to be alone with her / At peace.
[‡] *Lenten*: Spring.
[§] *toune*: the world.
[¶] *roune*: song.

Dayeseȝes in þis dales,
Notes suete of nyhtegales,
        Vch foul song singeþ.
þe þrestelcoc* him þreteþ oo,[†]
Away is huere[‡] wynter wo
        When woderoue[§] springeþ.
                (43.1–9)

The natural scene is a helter-skelter of movement and noise; the leaves are budding, drakes courting, the birds singing so loudly 'þat al þe wode ryngeþ' (43.12). Excluded from this universal ecstasy, the rejected lover wishes to turn his back on the world:

ȝef me shal wonte wille of on
þis wunne weole y wole forgon
Ant wyht in wode be fleme.[¶]
                (43.34–6)

Yet the poem allows him no escape, for the wood as it has been described is a world of vigorous involvement and not a place of exile.

The images and the references in these love-lyrics are precise, detailed, and local. In the five successive stanzas of *Annot and John* the lady is likened to jewels, flowers, birds, spices, and heroes and heroines. Such traditional idealizations tend to be undiscriminating; this matchless jewel resembles all other matchless jewels. In this case, though, the string of specific comparisons draws the reader to one lady in particular, who is bright as a beryl, pretty as a sapphire in silver, glowing like a jasp, like a garnet, a ruby, an onyx, a diamond, coral, emerald, margarite, and carbuncle. Who can this be, this special lady? Her name is revealed in a teasing pun:

He is þrustle þryuen ant þro þat singeþ in sale,
þe wilde laueroc ant wolc ant þe wodewale;
He is faucoun in friht, dernest in dale,
Ant wiþ eueruch a gome gladest in gale;
From Weye he is wisist into Wyrhale.
Hire nome is in a note of þe nyhtegale;

---

* *þrestelcoc*: thrush.
[†] *þreteþ oo*: chides the whole time.
[‡] *huere*: their.
[§] *woderoue*: woodruff.
[¶] If I fail to have my way with a certain person, / I'll abandon this lovely joy / And immediately become a fugitive in the woods.

In Annote is hire nome; nempneþ hit non!
Whose ryht redeþ, roune to Johon.*

(28.23–30)

The use of the place-names in this passage is typical of the lyrics. She is the finest, not in the world but from the Wye to the Wirral, or in Ribblesdale, the fairest girl 'Bituene Lyncolne ant Lyndeseye, Norhamptoun ant Lounde' (65.17). So love is located, and because it is here, in Lincolnshire, it is made possible; the chances of a kind word from the loveliest in the East Midlands are worth pursuing. [. . .]

Notes

1   Quotations from the Harley lyrics are taken from *Facsimile of British Museum MS Harley 2253*, introd. N. R. Ker (EETS 255, 1965).
2   The debts of the love-lyrics to French and Latin traditions merit much more detailed study than they have received. A start was made by Theo Stemmler, *Die englischen Liebesgedichte des MS Harley* 2253 (Bonn, 1962), and there are some stimulating remarks in Peter Dronke, *Medieval Latin and the Rise of European Love-Lyric*, 2 vols (Oxford, 1965–6), pp. 112–25. For the traditions in French verse, see Pierre Bec, *La Lyrique française au moyen âge*, i. *Études* (Paris, 1977).
3   There is a brief account of Anglo-Norman versification in David L. Jeffrey and Brian J. Levy (eds), *The Anglo-Norman Lyric: An Anthology* (Toronto, 1990), pp. 17–27.
4   Printed and discussed by O. S. Pickering, 'Newly Discovered secular Lyrics from Later Thirteenth-century Cheshire', *Review of English Studies* n.s. 43 (1992), 157–80.

Further Reading

While we are better equipped with dictionaries than Furnivall's Victorian editing team, there is still as yet no exhaustive *Middle English Dictionary*. Under the editorship of Hans Kurath, a comprehensive dictionary was set in train in 1952: it has recently reached the letter T. In the broad critical literature on Middle English language it is also important to keep sight of key work on the *orality* of medieval culture. Walter Ong's general introduction *Orality and Literacy: The Technologizing of the Word* (New York: Methuen, 1982) has influenced the specifically medieval studies of M. T.

---

* She is an exquisite thrush singing in the hall, / The wild lark, hawk and woodpecker, / She is a falcon in the grove, hidden most deeply in the valley; / Most cheerful in conversation with every man. / She is the wisest from the Wye to the Wirral. / Her name is in *a note* of the nightingale – / In Annote is her name! Let nobody mention it – / Whoever gets it right, whisper it to John.

Clanchy, *From Memory to Written Record: England 1066–1307*, 2nd edn (Oxford: Blackwell, 1993), and Mark C. Amodio (ed.), *Oral Poetics in Middle English Poetry* (New York: Garland, 1994). Christopher Cannon's recent book on Chaucer's English has brought about a major reconsideration of the role Chaucer played in enriching and adapting the literary language (a role Cannon shows was overplayed): *The Making of Chaucer's English: A Study of Words* (Cambridge: Cambridge University Press, 1998).

Chapter Notes

1   As cited in William Matthews, *The Making of Middle English, 1765–1910* (Minneapolis, MN: University of Minnesota Press, 1999), p. 148.
2   As cited in Peter Faulkner, '"The Paths of Virtue and Early English": F. J. Furnivall and Victorian Medievalism', in John Simons (ed.), *From Medieval to Medievalism* (Basingstoke: Macmillan, 1992), p. 148.
3   Richard Morris (ed.), *Specimens of Early English* (Oxford: Clarendon Press, 1867); A. L. Mayhew and W. W. Skeat (eds), *A Concise Dictionary of Middle English* (Oxford: Clarendon Press, 1888); Francis Henry Stratmann (ed.), *A Middle English Dictionary*, rev. Henry Bradley (Oxford: Clarendon Press, 1891); O. F. Emerson (ed.), *A Middle English Reader* (London: Macmillan, 1905); Max Kaluza, *Historische Grammatik der Englischen Sprache* (Berlin: Felber, 1906).
4   Kenneth Sisam (ed.), *Fourteenth Century Verse and Prose* (Oxford: Clarendon Press, 1921), p. xlii.
5   R. M. Wilson, *Early Middle English Literature*, 3rd edn (London: Methuen, 1968), p. 298.
6   H. J. Chaytor, *From Script to Print: An Introduction to Medieval Vernacular Literature* (London: Sidgwick and Jackson, 1945), p. 30.
7   Angus McIntosh, 'The Analysis of Written Middle English', *Transactions of the Philological Society* (1956), 26–55 (26).
8   Norman Blake, *The English Language in Medieval Literature* (London: Methuen, 1979), p. 43.
9   Charles Muscatine, *Chaucer and the French Tradition: A Study in Style and Meaning* (Berkeley, CA: University of California Press, 1957), pp. 3–4.
10   Denton Fox, 'Dunbar's *The Golden Targe*', *English Literary History* 26 (1959), 311–34 (312).
11   John Speirs, *Medieval English Poetry: The Non-Chaucerian Tradition* (London: Faber, 1957); Marie Borroff, *Sir Gawain and the Green Knight: A Stylistic and Metrical Study*, Yale Studies in English (New Haven, CT: Yale University Press, 1962); A. C. Spearing, *Criticism and Medieval Poetry* (London: Edward Arnold, 1964). See also Ronald A. Waldron's 'Oral-formulaic Technique and Middle English Alliterative Poetry', *Speculum* 32 (1957), 791–804.
12   P. J. C. Field, *Romance and Chronicle: A Study of Malory's Prose Style* (London: Barrie and Jenkins, 1971), p. 38.

13 J. M. Manly, 'Chaucer and the Rhetoricians', *Proceedings of the British Academy* 12 (1926), 95–113.

14 Derek Pearsall, 'Rhetorical "Descriptio" in *Sir Gawain and the Green Knight*', *Modern Language Review* 50 (1955), 129–34.

15 John Finlayson, 'Rhetorical "Descriptio" of Place in the Alliterative *Morte Arthure*', *Modern Philology* 61 (1963), 1–11 (1).

16 Robert O. Payne, *The Key of Remembrance: A Study of Chaucer's Poetics* (Westport, CT: Greenwood Press, 1963), p. 124.

17 Spearing, *Criticism and Medieval Poetry*, p. 58.

18 E. R. Curtius, *European Literature and the Latin Middle Ages*, trans. W. R. Trask (London: Routledge and Kegan Paul, 1953), p. 158.

19 Geoffrey Shepherd (ed.), *Ancrene Wisse: Parts Six and Seven* (London: Thomas Nelson, 1959), pp. lxxi–lxxii.

20 Norman Davis, 'The *Litera Troili* and English Letters', *Review of English Studies* n.s. 16 (1965), 233–44 (236).

21 John McKinnell, 'Letters as a Type of the Formal Level in *Troilus and Criseyde*', in Mary Salu (ed.), *Essays on Troilus and Criseyde* (Cambridge: D. S. Brewer, 1980), pp. 73–89 (p. 87).

22 Rita Copeland, *Rhetoric, Hermeneutics, and Translation in the Middle Ages: Academic Traditions and Vernacular Texts* (Cambridge: Cambridge University Press, 1991), p. 1.

23 Virginia Woolf, *The Common Reader*, 1st series (London: Hogarth Press, 1925), p. 37.

5

Allegory

The fourfold scheme of biblical exegesis and its use in Middle English criticism. The 'historical criticism' of D. W. Robertson, Jr. The opposing propositions of New Criticism: E. Talbot Donaldson on 'Patristic Criticism'. Contextual uses of pastoral and didactic literature: Siegfried Wenzel on the study of the morality play Mankind. *The limits of allegorical criticism: Kathryn Hume on* The Owl and the Nightingale. *An adjusted balance between allegory and literal sense: Jill Mann on* Passus XVIII *of* Piers Plowman.

Allegory: the term is so closely associated with the literature of the Middle Ages it is small wonder that it looms large in the Middle English criticism of the past hundred years. From C. S. Lewis's hugely influential *Allegory of Love* (1936) onwards, studies of this distinctive medieval and Renaissance mode have been legion. The study of allegory (briefly, that narrative mode in which surface meaning is accompanied by a latent or hidden meaning) has also led to much critical variance in Middle English studies. Scholars have disputed widely over the *kinds of texts* that might reasonably be investigated for allegorical meanings. In the case of personification allegories such as, say, the moral plays of *Everyman* and *Mankind* the matter seems clear cut. Here, readers will naturally enough be drawn to address allegorical features, perhaps looking at interactions of allegorical entities and their individual development in each text. What is less clear is whether allegorical meanings can reasonably be claimed for other or even *all* medieval English texts. Might allegory lurk in even the most frivolous of Middle English love lyrics? In romances? In Chaucer's bawdy tales? Over the last half-century and more, these questions have been posed repeatedly – and have prompted some forcible responses.

The seeds for debate were sown in the early decades of the twentieth century. At this stage, increased critical interest was focused on a fourfold scheme of exegesis (i.e. interpretation) applied by biblical scholars to scripture in the early Middle Ages. For these scholars, scripture embodied not just a manifest, literal meaning but *three additional levels of meaning* that might be teased out by exegesis. These were: the typological or allegorical, the tropological or moral, and the anagogical or mystical (to keep life sufficiently complicated each level went by two names!). Caplan's influential 1929 article in *Speculum* took readers through these four levels, applying them to the example of Jerusalem: 'Literally, it is the city of that name; allegorically, it represents Holy Church; tropologically, it signifies the faithful soul of whosoever aspires to the vision of eternal peace; anagogically, it denotes the life of the dwellers in Heaven who see God revealed in Zion.'[1]

As familiarity with this fourfold scheme spread in literary studies, scholars began to explore how far it might be applied to medieval *secular* narrative. After all, manuscript materials were expensive, the labour of the scribe onerous: could it be that such cost and labour were expended on secular texts because they too embodied Christian truths? In 1950 D. W. Robertson, Jr suggested exactly that, setting out his method of 'Historical Criticism'. This approach involved the reading of medieval secular literature in the light of theological and patristic writings (the writings of the early Church fathers) and maintained that beneath the literal meanings of these secular texts there did indeed lie a hidden allegorical meaning. For Robertson, this meaning was invariably reducible to a key Christian principle: the doctrine of divine love or *caritas*: 'Medieval Christian poetry, and by Christian poetry I mean all serious poetry written by Christian authors, even that usually called "secular," is always allegorical when the message of charity or some corollary of it is not evident on the surface.'[2]

The claim was a sweeping one and, as we shall see, provoked much debate. But one attraction of 'historical criticism' was its apparent ability to confer artistic unity on otherwise loosely structured works: 'When the method is applied . . . literary works which have heretofore seemed incoherent or meaningless become consistent, meaningful and aesthetically attractive' (see chapter 2).[3] One text whose structure had baffled many was *Piers Plowman*, and it was to *Piers* that Robertson, in collaboration with Bernard Huppé, turned his attention in 1951. The scholars' *Piers Plowman and Scriptural Tradition* argued that Langland's work was amenable to sustained critical analysis applying the fourfold exegetical method: 'the basic structure of *Piers Plowman* rests on contrasts which . . . are largely dependent upon an understanding of the application of the traditional levels of meaning.'[4]

Our first extract reveals how, shortly afterwards, Robertson's 'historical criticism' and more traditional humanist approaches were to collide head on. In the distinctive voice of New Critic E. Talbot Donaldson, Robertson's approach is challenged, even lampooned, for its eschewing of the unique, the distinctive and the particular in literary texts. A fundamental difference between the two

'HISTORICAL CRITICISM' VERSUS HUMANIST CRITICISM

Figure 1   Title page of the personification allegory, *Everyman*. (Reproduced by kind permission of the British Library, Huth 32)

scholars' outlooks and approaches is revealed by the extract. Robertson's approach posits a *rupture* or disjunction in poetic tradition and reception: sealed off from the thought-world of the Middle Ages, modern criticism must engage in a retrospective enterprise to recover the hidden meanings and lost contexts of medieval texts. For Donaldson, aesthetic values are more continuous: his humanist criticism alludes to Wordsworth's *Lucy* poems and the Middle English 'Maiden in the Moor Lay' in the same breath, implying a continuity of aesthetic sensibility and a transhistorical integrity to the literary work. The modern reader remains connected to the medieval past: patristic writings provide a context for medieval literature but they do not provide its interpretative key: 'to give a reader a flat injunction to find one predetermined specific meaning in Middle English poetry is anything but the ideal way of preparing him to understand something old and difficult and complicated.' Appearing originally in a collaborative volume which brought 'historical criticism' and New Criticism face to face, the extract bears witness to the two major critical approaches dominating the field of Middle English studies in the 1950s and 1960s.

Extract from E. Talbot Donaldson, 'Patristic Exegesis in the Criticism of Medieval Literature: The Opposition', in Dorothy Betherum (ed.), *Critical Approaches to Medieval Literature* (New York: Columbia University Press, 1960), pp. 1–5 , 20–4.

I am not aware of any valid theoretical objection to the use of patristic exegesis in the criticism of medieval literature: if, as D. W. Robertson, Jr, says,[1] it is true that all serious poetry written by Christians during the Middle Ages promotes the doctrine of charity by using the same allegorical structure that the Fathers found in the Bible, then it follows that patristic exegesis alone will reveal the meaning of medieval poetry, and it would be sheer folly to disapprove of the fact. And even if one disbelieves, as I do, that the generality of good medieval poetry is such single-minded allegory, it would still be foolish to ignore the influence of the patristic tradition on medieval poetry, including that of the great poets Chaucer and Langland. But to admit such influence is not at all the same thing as admitting either that poetry which is nonallegorical in manner must be allegorical in meaning or that allegorical poetry which does not seem to be promoting charity must in fact be promoting it. There may be a handful of such poems, but I doubt that they are very good, or, if they are good, that they are good because they are cryptically allegorical or charity-promoting. In any case, I know of no such poems in Middle English, which is the only field in which I am competent. The patristic influence on Middle English poetry seems to me to consist in providing occasional symbols which by their rich tradition enhance the poetic contexts they appear in, but which are called into use naturally by those contexts and are given fresh meaning by them.

It is scarcely necessary to reassert the right of a poem to say what it means and mean what it says, and not what any one, before or after its composition, thinks it ought to say or mean. The existence of this right gives me, I hope, the right to test the validity of a kind of criticism which, it seems to me, imposes a categorical imperative upon the critic to operate in a certain way regardless of how the poem is telling him to operate. Since I lack a theoretical objection to patristic criticism as such, I can justify my opposition to it only by the invidious method of analyzing specific patristic critiques; but surely the burden of the proof is on the proponents of the critical method, who deny that I can understand what I read without possessing their special knowledge. To excuse my invidiousness I shall invoke a passage from the Scriptures: By their works ye shall know them. This I shall apply with twofold reference – though not, I trust, allegorically: that is, I shall apply it not only to those who try to prove the necessity for patristic exegesis, but also to the works in which this necessity is supposed to exist. I shall try to suggest that to give a reader a flat injunction to find one predetermined specific meaning in Middle English poetry is anything but the ideal way of preparing him to understand something old and difficult and complicated; for in his eagerness to find what must be there he will very likely miss what is there; and in so doing he may miss a meaning arising from the poem that is better than anything that exegesis is able to impose upon it. I hope I shall not offend any one if I suggest that while charity is the most important of doctrines it is not the only subject worth writing about, and that many poems may conduce to charity without mentioning it either specifically or allegorically. I may say rather ruefully that one of the natural disadvantages of the opponent of patristic criticism is that he is constantly being put in the position of seeming to deny that the Fall of Man has any dominant importance in the history of man's thought just because he denies that it has any relevance in a specific literary work. There are, indeed, moments when I could wish that scholars in Middle English literature would remind themselves that they are not angels but anglicists.

Having gone so far, I might go on to suggest that the Fathers of the Church were less expert at devising rules for poets than they were at devising rules for Christians. I am not, however, entirely persuaded that they did devise rules for poets. The case for the generalization that medieval poets were enjoined by patristic authority to write nothing but allegories supporting charity seems rather less than crystal-clear. It was natural that the fourfold method of scriptural interpretation should exert an influence on secular poets, especially in view of its occasional extension to the great pagan poets; and of course some medieval poets were, like Dante, deeply interested in exalting Christian doctrine through their poetry and consciously used allegory – even, perhaps, four-level allegory – to do so. But this does not mean that they all felt obliged to behave like Dante. I may quite well be wrong, but I cannot find that any of the patristic authorities ever clearly exhorted secular poets to write as the Bible had been written, even though the inference is pretty strong that some of them would have so exhorted if they had got round to it. But it seems to me that in order to find a definite injunction the modern critic has consciously to make a large inference.[2] Nor do I think that the case is much supported by the fact that in medieval schools reading was taught with attention to three matters, the *littera* or text, the *sensus* or narrative statement, and the *sententia* or theme, since the identification of *sententia* with an allegory promoting charity is itself no more than an inference.[3] After all, competent poetry has always contained something more than words making a statement, something that might well be called *sententia*, and I should imagine that Greeks, Romans, Arabs, Jews, and other non-Christians might inevitably teach poetry according to the same system: does the *Iliad* have no *sententia* because it is not Christian? Finally, there is at least one dissenting vote in the roll call of theologians presumably enjoining poets to write allegory after the example of Scripture. As W. K. Wimsatt pointed out in a paper on this topic several years ago,[4] Thomas Aquinas makes the unequivocal statement that 'in no intellectual activity of the human mind can there properly speaking be found anything but literal sense: only in Scripture, of which the Holy Ghost was the author, man the instrument, can there be found' the spiritual sense – that is, the four levels of allegory.[5] While I recognize that St Thomas is not a Father and that his statement may be idiosyncratic (as I believe some scholars regard it),[6] nevertheless I think he ought to be honestly reckoned with. To date I have seen no real discussion of his opinion by supporters of patristic exegesis. Nor will I accept as reputable the excuse that because he was a friar St Thomas would hardly reflect the point of view of such medieval poets as favored the monks.[7]

[. . .] I shall conclude with one final analysis of patristic exegesis, Robertson's interpretation of the little lyric 'Maiden in the Moor'.[8] In this poem we have the barest of literal statements and almost no *sensus* at all; one must proceed directly from the letter to the *sententia*. The poem is short; therefore I quote it entire:

> Maiden in the moor lay,
>   In the moor lay,
> Sevenight ful, sevenight ful;
> Maiden in the moor lay,
>   In the moor lay,
> Sevenightes ful and a day.
> Wel [i.e., good] was hir mete.[a]
>   What was hir mete?
> The primerole[b] and the –

[a] food.
[b] primrose.

The primerole and the –
Wel was hir mete.
What was hir mete?
The primerole and the violet.
Wel was hir dring.[a]
What was hir dring?
The chelde[b] water of the –
The chelde water of the –
Wel was hir dring.
What was hir dring?
The chelde water of the welle-spring.
Wel was hir bowr.
What was hir bowr?
The rede rose and the –
The rede rose and the –
Wel was hir bowr.
What was hir bowr?
The rede rose and the lilye flowr.[9]

Of this charming little piece Robertson writes:

> On the surface, although the poem is attractive, it cannot be said to make much
> sense. Why should a maiden lie on a moor for seven nights and a day? And if
> she did, why should she eat primroses and violets? Or again, how does it happen
> that she has a bower of lilies and roses on the moor? The poem makes perfectly
> good sense, however, if we take note of the figures and signs in it. The number
> seven indicates life on earth, but life in this instance went on at night, or before
> the Light of the World dawned. The day is this light, or Christ, who said, 'I am
> the day.' And it appears appropriately after seven nights, or, as it were, on the
> count of eight, for eight is also a figure of Christ. The moor is the wilderness of
> the world under the Old Law before Christ came. The primrose is not a Scrip-
> tural sign, but a figure of fleshly beauty. We are told three times that the prim-
> rose was the food of this maiden, and only after this suspense are we also told
> that she ate or embodied the violet, which is a Scriptural sign of humility. The
> maiden drank the cool water of God's grace, and her bower consisted of the roses
> of martyrdom or charity and the lilies of purity with which late medieval and
> early Renaissance artists sometimes adorned pictures of the Blessed Virgin Mary,
> and, indeed, she is the Maiden in the Moor . . .[10]

I cannot find that the poem, as a poem, makes any more 'sense' after exegesis than it did before, and I think it makes rather more sense as it stands
than the critic allows it. Maidens in poetry often receive curiously privileged

[a] drink.
[b] chilled.

treatment from nature, and readers seem to find the situation agreeable. From the frequency with which it has been reprinted it seems that the 'Maiden in the Moor' must have offered many readers a genuine poetic experience even though they were without benefit of the scriptural exegesis. I do not think that most of them would find it necessary to ask the questions of the poem that Robertson has asked; indeed, it seems no more legitimate to inquire what the maiden was doing in the moor than it would be to ask Wordsworth's Lucy why she did not remove to a more populous environment where she might experience a greater measure of praise and love. In each case the poetic *donnée* is the highly primitive one which exposes an innocent woman to the vast, potentially hostile, presumably impersonal forces of nature; and the Middle English lyric suggests the mystery by which these forces are, at times, transmuted into something more humane, even benevolent, by their guardianship of the innocent maiden. The poetic sense is not such as necessarily to preclude allegory, and I shouldn't be surprised if medieval readers often thought of the Virgin as they read the poem, not because they knew the symbols and signs, but because the Virgin is the paramount innocent maiden of the Christian tradition: such suggestivity is one of poetry's principal functions. Robertson's hard-and-fast, this-sense-or-no-sense allegory, however, seems to me so well-concealed and, when explicated, so unrevealing that it can be considered only disappointing if not entirely irrelevant. The function of allegory that is worth the literary critic's attention (as opposed to cryptography, which is not) cannot be to conceal, but is to reveal, and I simply do not believe that medieval poets veiled their poems in order to hide their pious message from heretics and unbelievers. In allegory the equation is not merely *a* equals *b*, the literal statement reanalyzed equals the suggested meaning, but is something more like *a* plus *b* equals *c*, the literal statement plus the meaning it suggests yield an ultimate meaning that is an inextricable union of both. Patristically the primrose may be a figure of fleshy beauty, but actually (and the actual is what poetry is made of) it is one of the commonest of the lovely flowers which nature in its benevolent aspect lavishes upon mankind and, in this case, all-benevolent lavishes upon the maiden of the moor. Robertson asks the question 'Why should she eat primroses?' I hope that if I answer 'Because she was hungry', it will not be said of me that a primrose by the river's brim a yellow primrose was to him, and it was nothing more.

Notes

1   D. W. Robertson, Jr, 'Historical Criticism', in A. S. Downer (ed.), *English Institute Essays, 1950* (New York: Columbia University Press, 1951), p. 14.

2   See the historical treatment of the matter by Robertson in the essay cited above and in 'Some Medieval Literary Terminology, with Special Reference to Chrétien de Troyes', *Studies in Philology* 48 (1951), 669–92; also that by Robertson and B. F. Hulppé in the first chapter of *Piers Plowman and Scriptural Tradition* (Princeton, NJ: Princeton University Press, 1951). The evidence for a genuine claim by Dante that he was using fourfold allegory in the *Divine Comedy* seems weakened by such recent studies as R. H. Green's 'Dante's "Allegory of Poets" and the Mediaeval Theory of Poetic Fiction', *Comparative Literature* 9 (1957), 118–28.

3   See Robertson, 'Historical Criticism', p. 13, and Robertson and Huppé, *Piers Plowman*, p. 1.

4   W. K. Wimsatt, 'Two Meanings of Symbolism: A Grammatical Exercise', *Catholic Renascence* 8 (1955), 19: I am indebted to Mr Wimsatt's excellent paper for this reference to St Thomas.

5   *Quaestiones Quodlibetales*, VII, quaestio VI, art. XVI: Unde in nulla scientia, humana industria inventa, proprie loquendo, potest inveniri nisi litteralis sensus; sed solum in ista Scriptura, cujus Spiritus sanctus est auctor, homo vero instrumentum.

6   Green ('Dante's "Allegory of Poets"', p. 121) speaks of St Thomas's *effort* 'to restrict the term *allegoria* to the mode of Sacred Scripture'.

7   Robertson and Huppé (*Piers Plowman*, p. 10) say that they in general exclude the commentaries of friars because the poet was anti-fraternal.

8   Robertson, 'Historical Criticism', pp. 26–7.

9   For the poem in its original form, see R. H. Robbins (ed.), *Secular Lyrics of the XIVth and XVth Centuries* (Oxford: Clarendon Press, 1947), pp. 12–13.

10   Robertson, 'Historical Criticism', p. 27.

MORE OBJECTIONS TO EXEGETICAL CRITICISM   Donaldson's objections were widely echoed. He had also been anticipated by Robert Frank who in 1953 had suggested that scholarly use of the fourfold exegetical scheme had actually *waned* in the later Middle Ages and so argued for greater scepticism in its use by modern critics:

> It is easy, however, to over-estimate the prevalence of the four-fold method in medieval exegetical work . . . Something more substantial than an off-hand allusion to the 'four-fold method in the medieval period' must be supplied before the reader should feel obliged to look for four levels of meaning in a medieval symbol-allegory.[5]

In 1958 Morton W. Bloomfield had also questioned the value of the scheme: 'It seems to me that this method, while not totally wrong, is essentially erroneous as a method of understanding most medieval literary works historically.'[6] Bloomfield aptly noted that to ask the modern reader to be always on the look-out for four levels of meaning is unrealistic: 'in effect, no one can consistently apply the fourfold criterion except to a few hackneyed terms like Jerusalem.'[7]

Just the same, further exegetical studies appeared throughout the 1960s. Robertson and Huppé would raise the profile of exegetical criticism still further with the former producing *A Preface to Chaucer* (1962) and both collaborating on *Fruyt and Chaf: Studies in Chaucer's Allegories* (1963). In the second book, sustained allegories were set out for the greater part of the Chaucer canon, from shorter poems to long, early works to late. Even a poem embodying the most transhistorical of subject matter turns out to encode specific doctrinal meaning for Robertson and Huppé. So in their reading of Chaucer's poignantly realized elegy *The Book of The Duchess*, the bitter grief of the Man in Black at the death of his beloved White is revealed as not a lover's grief at all. What readers had long taken as a moving evocation of the wasting, halting journey any bereaved lover must make from grief to resolution was now to be read as allegory, with human concerns firmly to the periphery:

> The true reason for his [the Man in Black's] sorrow is error; the speaker had been temporarily misled to believe that the loss of another human was the cause of his grief. In Christian fact there can be no sorrow except that arising in separation from God. A man's love has two sides, one false (cupidity), the other true (charity); his grief has two sides, one *tristitia*, false grief caused by the loss of an object of desire, the other a true grief caused by his enforced bodily separation from God. What the speaker had taken as grief was itself false worldly vanity.[8]

Humanist criticism this is not – and responses and rebuttals were again plentiful. Many reviewers and respondents were quick to acknowledge the rigour and scope of Robertson and Huppé's scholarship, but the consistent assertion of the non-literal level of meaning as pre-eminent brought repeated methodological objection, like this from Derek Brewer in 1965:

> The point is that such symbolization is not falsifiable, because of the authors' premiss that the poet does not say what he means . . . Statements that are not falsifiable may be quite meaningful: indeed such statements constitute literature itself: but they are not scientific, that is, they are neither criticism nor scholarship.[9]

Or this from Paul Beichner in 1967:

> I do not think that a search for a *sensus spiritualis* in secular literature similar to that sought by exegetes in the Bible can be more than a pious exercise of ingenuity. To interpret non-allegorical literature in these ways is like looking for faces or pictures in the clouds; anyone with a vigorous imagination can see what he wishes.[10]

Particular discomfort was felt with the interpretative free-for-all that could be prompted by allegorical criticism. As Bloomfield said, 'With sixteen mean-

ings for the peacock, who is to decide between them?' Or, as Beichner maintained, 'Not every lion encountered in a story represents either Christ, or
St Mark the Evangelist, or the devil, or a vice: some lions represent only
themselves.'[11]

> In the controversy so far, the most telling weakness of Professor Robertson's
> adherents has been a neglect of the precise and skeptical argument necessary to
> convince oneself as well as others; that of his opponents has been a lack of first-
> hand acquaintance with the Biblical commentaries and other exegetical texts
> whose relevance they are disputing. One hopes for an improvement of both in
> the debates that doubtless lie ahead.[12]

1963: R. E. Kaske takes stock of the debate over 'exegetical criticism'

CRITICISM
ON
PERSONIFICA-
TION
ALLEGORY

While debate raged as to the value of reading for fourfold allegory, a less con-
tentious issue was the place in Middle English studies of careful readings of
personification allegories. Many of these allegories showed close links with
Middle English sermons, pastoral literature and didactic literature: they invited
a kind of contextual criticism that crossed traditional literary boundaries. This
move produced such work as Siegfried Wenzel's *The Sin of Sloth: Acedia in
Medieval Thought and Literature*. Wenzel's 1967 study traced how representations of sloth, or *acedia*, moved from homiletic treatments in Middle English
devotional and pastoral writing to the vivid personification allegory of
medieval morality plays like *Mankind*. Wenzel's contextual criticism brings a
specific set of clerical intertexts to bear, arguing for the significance of Middle
English *didactic* writing ('catechetical literature', 'monastic literature', 'popular
instruction') as a context for reading *Mankind* and other moralities. His study
opened a route for later strands of Middle English criticism by demon-
strating the significance of clerical discourse and pastoral literature in the creation and reception of medieval English texts.

Extract from Siegfried Wenzel, 'The Poets', in
*The Sin of Sloth: Acedia in Medieval Thought and
Literature* (Chapel Hill, NC: University of
Carolina Press, 1967), pp. 147–54.

[. . .] In medieval morality plays the personification of the sins [. . .] is carried
one step further insofar as here the sins become true *dramatis personae* and

appear, speak, and act on stage. Unfortunately, of the earlier English moralities only one, *The Castle of Perseverance*, really presents the sins as actors; yet, although the evidence is so scanty, it neatly shows how the full dramatization of the vices grew out of didactic literature. A brief glance at *The Castle* is necessary in order to see how the later play *Mankind*, with which we shall be concerned, differs in technique from what historians of the English drama consider the pure type of medieval moralities, and how it uses the idea of spiritual sloth much more originally than the genuinely allegorical drama.

In *The Castle of Perseverance*, written in the first quarter of the fifteenth century, the seven deadly sins are distributed as helpers among the three enemies of man, the World, the Flesh, and the Devil, and in this conventional scheme 'Syr Slawth' belongs with Lechery and Gluttony to Flesh. In the beginning of the play, its hero, Mankind, chooses to follow the persuasions of his Bad Angel and enters the service of the World. He is enfeoffed to Avarice and the other deadly sins, who now appear for the first time and, in taking leave from their respective masters, reveal their characters by a set of appropriate speeches. Later, Mankind is converted and brought into the Castle of Perseverance. The seven virtues appear, and we learn that Sloth is opposed by Solicitudo or 'Besynesse' (ll. 1644–56). Eventually, all of man's enemies muster and besiege the castle. A verbal battle between vices and virtues for the possession of Mankind begins, surely accompanied by some appropriate stage action. Again, Sloth is pitted against Busyness. The vice carries a spade as his weapon:

> ACCIDIA: Ware,[a] war! I delue[b] with a spade;
> men calle me þe 'lord syr Slowe.'
> gostly[c] grace I spylle & schade;[d]
> fro þe watyr of grace, þe dyche I fowe. [clean]
> (ll. 2327–30)

This peculiar action of draining the ditch or moat of the water of grace occurred earlier in the allegorical battle of virtues and vices described in a fourteenth-century pastoral handbook, the second part of *Oculus sacerdotis*[e] (written before 1343) by William of Pagula. Here the vices engage in a series of consecutive military operations.

> In the army of the devil, pride carries the banner . . . Envy draws the arrows by backbiting other men. Wrath throws the stones, as it were, of cursing and scorn.

[a] Beware.
[b] dig.
[c] spiritual.
[d] pour off.
[e] *Eye of the Priest*, a fourteenth-century pastoral manual.

Then Accidia empties the ditches of the water of grace; for 'a sad mind dries up the bones' [Prov. 17: 22]. Avarice fills the empty ditches with the lust for earthly goods. Lechery lights a fire. Gluttony throws the fire and kindles it with the wood of food and drink.[1]

In *The Castle of Perseverance* all these actions except that of Avarice are used dramatically, though in different order.

The character of 'Syr Slawth' agrees closely with the popular image of the vice. Besides being a sin of the flesh, as in *Piers Plowman*, its main characteristic is to hinder man in God's service (ll. 990, 1238, 2344; cf. l. 69) by causing his bed, where he 'takes a sweat' (ll. 1218, 1227), or the ale-house (l. 2335) to be more attractive than the church. The other religious obligation in which faults of sloth are most common – receiving the sacrament of penance – is similarly stressed: Sloth causes delay of confession (ll. 2348–52; see also ll. 1349–57) and leaves the imposed penance undone (ll. 1222f). The sin rules men of religion as well as lords, ladies, and rogues (ll. 989–92).

In *The Castle* Man's antagonist is not so much the combined force of the seven deadly sins as it is World with his servant, Avarice.[2] As a matter of fact, the moral struggle of Mankind boils down to the choice between God and the World. For as soon as Mankind appears on the stage, poor and naked (ll. 285, 293), he is tempted by his Bad Angel to enter 'the world's service' (l. 342). In perplexity, but clearly understanding the alternatives of his choice, Mankind turns to the World with the argument that he is young and death is far away (ll. 424ff). It is only after this choice that the seven deadly sins approach the hero. Although they have been introduced to the audience before the true action begins (ll. 157–274), and although the sins together with the Three Enemies represent a formidable array of evil, the temptation proper of Mankind is realized in terms of avarice alone, that is, of undue desire for worldly goods, which are here materialized as rich clothes and money. In similar fashion, the great siege of the castle presents an impressive gathering of evil forces. But the vices fight only against personified virtues, whereas the true and decisive assault on Mankind himself is made by Avarice alone, who – unlike the vices that preceded him – refuses to debate with his opponent virtue and instead appeals to Mankind directly. I do not think it overly subtle to say that in the genuine moral action which the play dramatizes the seven deadly sins do not hold the center but act more as a filler or perhaps a means to create comic action.

In this play the psychological reality of man's fight against evil – his fall, conversion, and relapse – is thus dramatized by objectifying good and evil forces as personified abstractions who persuade, dispute, and occasionally engage in physical action. This technique of an allegorical battle for man's soul – customarily taken to be the essence of the English morality plays – is still

used to some extent in a later play, *Mankind* (*c.*1475). But here the temptation of man is handled with a significant difference. The 'hero' stands between
Mercy and Mischief, the latter accompanied by three good-for-nothings
(Newguise, Nowadays, and Nought) and aided by the devil Titivillus. After
receiving spiritual advice from Mercy, Mankind sets to work in the field, where
he is chaffed by the three scamps but remains firm in his proposal to work and
drives them off with some well-aimed blows of his spade. His enemies call
Titivillus to their aid, who eventually succeeds in inducing Mankind to give
up his work and join their evil fellowship. His final ruin is imminent, but in
the end Mankind is saved when Mercy appears with a scourge, drives off the
enemies, and by a reminder of God's mercy dissuades him from ending his life
in despair.

The temptation that leads to Mankind's eventual fall is of great interest to
our study because, although the word 'sloth' is not used in the play, the
temptation curiously follows the psychology of this vice as developed in
popular catechetical literature. Mankind appears as a peasant, carrying a spade
and engaged in digging up his field to sow grain. He looks like any other farm
laborer, until his reason for digging strikes a surprising note:

> Thys erth with my spade I xall assay to delffe;[a]
> To eschew ydullnes[b] I do yt myn own selffe.
>
> (ll. 321–2)

Manual labor in order to avoid idleness – precisely the spiritual, therapeutic
value given to work as one of the chief remedies against *acedia* in monastic literature and in popular instruction. Man must work in order to fulfill God's
injunction after the Fall; idleness not only opens the door to the Fiend but is
in itself a grave offense to man's Creator, as medieval preachers and confessors
never tired of emphasizing in their discussions of sloth. Realizing this,
Mankind can easily ward off the open attempts made by the three rogues to
draw him away from his work.

In contrast, the assault of the Devil is less easy to repel, and in fact Mankind
never suspects that it is the Fiend who now induces him to give up his service
of God. This gradual recession from God forms the psychologically most interesting section of the play. Titivillus buries a plank in the ground that Mankind
is digging up, with the purpose 'to yrke hym of hys labur' (l. 525); in other
words, the devil tempts Mankind to forsake 'hys goode purpose' (ll. 519, 573)
by making him feel the tedium and disgust of his work.

The temptation is a success. As soon as his spade strikes the
plank, Mankind exclaims: 'Thys londe ys so harde yt makyth wnlusty and

---

[a] shall attempt to dig.
[b] avoid idleness.

yrke'[a] (l. 538). Disgusted by a little hardship, Mankind decides to sow his grain
in winter 'and lett Gode werke' (l. 539). But the grain is gone – Titivillus has
meanwhile done away with it. In consequence, Mankind not only delays his
work but gives it up altogether, refusing to accept any hardship to his body.
Yet he still clings to God and, although he will not go to church,[3] kneels down
and recites the Pater Noster. But Titivillus is at hand again 'to make this fellow
yrke' (l. 549): He whispers in his ear that 'a short prayer pierces heaven', that
Mankind is already holier than the rest of his kin, and that in addition he must
follow an urge of his nature (ll. 551–3). And Mankind indeed abandons his
beads 'for drede of the colyke and eke of the ston' (l. 555), so that Titivillus
can rejoice at having diverted him from being 'besy in his prayers' and 'from
hys dyvyn seruyce' (ll. 558–9).

When Mankind returns, he has further advanced in *acedia*: Now evensong
seems much too long for him:

> I am yrke of yt: yt ys to longe be on myle.
> Do wey! I wyll no more so oft on the chyrche-style.[b]
>
> (ll. 575–6)

Thus he gives up, not only his work, but also his prayer with the remark, 'I
am nere yrke of both' (l. 578). The final step: He lies down to sleep, leaving
his mind open to evil instigations of the Devil. Of course, Titivillus is only too
ready with the Devil's first and last ruse: a handful of lies which he whispers
into Mankind's ear, denigrating the character of Mercy and leading Mankind
to believe that his spiritual father is dead. As a result, Mankind bids his former
master adieu and joins the company of the rogues.

The very plot of the temptation scene intimates that the author of the play
has used the vice of *acedia* as the hero's fault through which he is turned away
from good. Mankind falls through tedium in doing good work, which is caused
by the bodily hardship that accompanies good works, both physical and
spiritual. He gives in to sleep and thus becomes fully a prey to the Devil, who
then leads him to all sorts of sins and to Mischief.[4] Yet the suggestion that
Mankind's fall is motivated by *acedia* can be further substantiated by the terminology employed in this passage. Mankind's first reaction to physical hardship includes two very revealing key terms: 'Thys londe ys so harde yt makyth
wnlusty and *yrke*' (l. 538). The first, 'wnlusty', is an equivalent for 'slothful'. In
Ayenbite[c] the noun 'onlosthede', and in *Vices and Virtues* as well as the *Ormulum*[d] the noun 'vnlust' are used as synonyms of 'sloth', in addition to which

---

[a] [my work] dull and irksome.
[b] stile over the church wall.
[c] *Ayenbit of Inwit* ('The Biting Back of Conscience'), a fourteenth-century penitential manual.
[d] A collection of early thirteenth-century verse homilies.

Jacob's Well[a] defines: 'Slowthe is whan þou art vnlustig of þi-self to seruyn god or þe world'.[5] The second term, 'yrke', which occurs five times in the temptation scene of some eighty lines, is the Middle English equivalent for Latin *taedere* or *fastidire*, both verbs commonly used to characterize the nature of *acedia*. 'Yrken' and derivatives appear frequently in Middle English works in close connection with the sin of sloth. Thus, the prose *Mirror of St Edmund* in the Thornton manuscript (1430–1440), for example, says of sloth that it 'makes man's heart heavy and slow in good deeds, and causes man to irk in prayer or holiness, and puts man in the wickedness of wanhope, for it slackens the liking of ghostly love'.[6] Similarly, Rolle[b] admonishes the would-be lover of God 'not to be noyd with irksumness [*tedio*], nor with ydilness to be takyn . . . Cees not ȝit to rede or pray, or ellis some oder gude dede inward or outward do, þat not in-to idilnes or sleuyth [*ociositatem vel accidiam*] þou scryth [fall]. Many sothely irksomnes has drawen to idilnes, and ydilnes to necligens and wikkydnes.'[7] And in some versions of the *Speculum Christiani*[c] the verses on *Accidia* begin: 'I yrke full sore with goddes seruyce.'[8]

As in theological discussions of *acedia*, tedium in doing good leads Mankind to delay of confession and eventually to wanhope or despair. When Mercy tries to regain Mankind, his admonition is shrugged off, Mankind apparently being unaware of the warner's identity: 'I xall speke with thee a-nother tyme; to morn, or the next day' (l. 720). But when Mercy approaches a second time, now with a scourge, Mankind falls into despair (ll. 793ff) and is helped by his evil companions in his attempt to hang himself. He is saved, but remains in the state of not hoping for God's mercy for himself because he deems his sins greater than God's willingness to forgive, until Mercy finally succeeds in reviving his hope. It is noteworthy that in his lengthy speech Mercy attacks not only wanhope but also its opposite, overhope or vain trust (ll. 837–47), a combination occasionally also found in treatments of *acedia*.[9]

If the notion of *acedia* thus lies at the heart of Mankind's fall, it equally penetrates into other aspects of the play and gives them a peculiar slant. The first three tempters, for example, are shown to be allegorical figures by their names, Newguise, Nowadays, and Nought, but their precise meaning is uncertain and they cannot easily be fitted into standard medieval patterns of temptation and evil. Unfortunately, their introductory speeches have been lost. But near the end of the play, Mercy enlightens Mankind and us that in the familiar scheme of Flesh, World, and Devil as man's three enemies they represent the world (ll. 876ff). Yet their own activities in the play make it a little hard to be identified as such at first sight. They tempt Mankind by idle speeches

---

[a] A fifteenth-century doctrinal manual.
[b] Richard Rolle, fourteenth-century author of mystical and devotional writings.
[c] *The Mirror of the Christian.*

and songs to let go his work, and their further enterprises make them look very much like Langland's wastours, who were also closely related to sloth: they drink and steal, murder and fornicate. Could it be that in this play the conventional enemy World has been given predominantly those aspects that appeal to Man's penchant for idleness and sloth? In Lydgate's *Pilgrimage* Dame Ydelnesse reveals it as one of her functions to

> Studye ffor to ffynde off newe
> Devyses mad off many an hewe,
> ffolk to make hem fressh & gay,
> And hem dysguyse in ther array:
> Thys myn offys, yer by yere.
>   (ll. 11,667–71)

This would make at least Newguise a blood brother to Idleness.

If the temptation from the World is thus curiously slanted toward idleness and sloth, the same is also true of the Devil. I am now not thinking of his approaches to Man, already analyzed, but of his name. The choice of 'Titivillus'[10] for the subtle archenemy of Man in this play has puzzled critics, especially since a devil by the same name has, in the Last Judgment play of the Towneley cycle, only a very minor function. But the name fits the Devil's role in *Mankind* very well as soon as one sees here the temptation of *acedia*. It is well known that in medieval literature from the fourteenth century on the proper function of Titivillus was to watch out for idle talk in church and for the overskipping of syllables and words in the divine service. This is exactly the occupation by which he identifies himself in the Towneley cycle.[11] Also in the *exemplum* which narrates the vision of a fiend carrying a sack of overskipped syllables, the Devil is sometimes identified as Titivillus.[12] This *exemplum* was occasionally told as a warning against the sin of sloth.[13] Although I know of no text which mentions Titivillus himself in connection with *acedia*, the faults of jangling in church and of 'syncopating' were standard aspects of the sin.[14] If, therefore, the author of *Mankind* did use the concept of *acedia* to motivate Man's fall, what devil's name would have suggested itself more naturally than that of Titivillus, traditionally associated with faults of sloth?

The motivation of Man's fall by *acedia* also fits very well into the over-all meaning or moral of the play. Whether or not Sister M. P. Coogan's thesis is correct – that the play is a dramatized invitation to confession and penance performed during Shrovetide[15] – the fact remains that *Mankind* is concerned with the instability of man whose spiritual integrity is endangered by the conflict between body and soul, and who needs firm reliance upon God's mercy in order to be saved. The play shows Man's absolute need for Mercy to teach, to guide and, ultimately, to save him, since his own nature proves untrustworthy and 'unstabyl'.[16]

> Mankend ys wrechyd; he hath sufficyent prowe; [proof]
> There-fore God kept yow all *per suam misericordiam*.[a]
>
> (ll. 904–5)

Thus the declared moral of the play. But reliance upon God's mercy is frustrated by despair, and the sin which traditionally opens the way to despair is *acedia*, beginning with boredom in the fulfillment of one's duties and leading to negligence, abandonment of God's service, and the turn to sinful delights.

The remarkable fact about *Mankind*, therefore, is its utilization of the medieval concept of *acedia* for dramatic purposes in a way that is quite unprecedented. Here is not the allegorical figure of Sloth approaching Mankind from the outside, as it does in *The Castle of Perseverance*, but sloth forms Mankind's inner disposition to which the three scamps and Titivillus appeal and which only gradually, after the Devil employs various kinds of deceit (invisibility, the buried plank, theft, and lies), responds positively. Man's fall is then presented as a gradual descent from grace to sin, or from Mercy to Mischief, and the steps on this descent correspond to psychological stages on the downward path of *acedia*, with despair at the end.

Notes

1   William of Pagula, *Oculus sacerdotis*: 'Superbia in exercitu diaboli vexillum portat . . . Invidai sagittas trahit detrahendo aliis. Ira quasi petra iactat lapides blasphemie et improperii. Accidia fossa tum evacuat ab aquis gratie. "Spiritus enim tristis exsiccat ossa" [Prov. 17: 22]. Avaricia implet fossata per terrenorum cupiditatem. Luxuria ignem succendit. Gula hunc ignem incutit et accendit apponendo ligna cibariorum [sic] et potuum' (MS BM Royal 6.E.i, fol. 46r). In *The Castle*, the vices appear under the leadership of Devil, Flesh, and World in this order: Pride (ll. 2070–82), Wrath (ll. 2109–21), Envy (ll. 2148–60); Gluttony (ll. 2249–61), Lechery (ll. 2288–2300), Sloth (ll. 2327–39); Covetousness (ll. 2428–40). W. K. Smart noticed parallels between the siege of the vices in *The Castle* and those in the *Reply of Friar Daw Topias* and *Piers Plowman*, B.XX, but was unable to find a source; 'The *Castle of Perseverance*: Place, Date, and a Source', in *The Manly Anniversary Studies in Language and Literature* (Chicago, 1923), pp. 42–53.
2   Cf. J. W. McCutchan, 'Covetousness in *The Castle of Perseverance*', in *English Studies in Honor of James Southall Wilson* ('University of Virginia Studies', vol. IV [Charlottesville, 1951]), pp. 175–91.

[a] by his mercy.

3   Richard Fitzralph, Archbishop of Armagh, says in a sermon given on Ash
     Wednesday of 1346 that one must pray in church because there prayer is more
     laboriosa (and thus more pleasing to God), 'because it is more toilsome to go to
     church than to rest at home, and it is said to man, "In the sweat of thy face
     . . .", and, "Man is born to work . . ."' (MS BM Lansdowne 393, fol. 37r).

4   The name Mischief for the antagonist to Mercy has caused some perplexity. See
     the ingenious suggestion by Sister M. P. Coogan, *An Interpretation of the Moral
     Play, 'Mankind'* (Washington, 1947), pp. 59ff. But in the play this figure clearly
     represents something like wickedness or the state of sin and functions as the
     spiritual counterpoint to Mercy. The word bears this meaning of 'wickedness' in
     Malory ('By thy meschyef and thy vengeaunce thou hast destroyed the mooste
     noble knyght') and in Coverdale's translation of Gen. 6: 5 ('Ye earth was corrupte
     in ye sight of God and full of myschefe'; both quotations from *OED*); and
     in *Ludus Coventriae* the verb *myscheven* seems to denote 'to fall into sin' (e.g.,
     'on man þat is myschevyd haue compassyon', EETS, ES, 120, p. 100, l. 76;
     see also p. 127, l. 100). Sister Coogan also recognized this meaning (p. 59 and
     note).

5   *Ayenbite*: 'Onlosthede þet is sleuþe' (p. 31; cf. p. 163); *Vices and Virtues*, p. 3;
     Ormulum, ll. 2633, 4562, 4746; *Jacob's Well*, p. 103. In the poem 'Jesus appeals to
     Man by the Wounds', sloth is called *vnlust* (C. Brown, *Religious Lyrics of the
     Fourteenth Century* [2nd edn; Oxford, 1952], p. 227). *The Cloud of Unknowing*
     defines 'slewþ' as 'a weriness and an vnlistiness of any good occupacion' (EETS
     218, p. 37).

6   EETS 26, p. 25.

7   Rolle, *Incendium amoris*, in the translation of Richard Misyn (1435), Bk I, ch. xi
     (EETS 106, p. 23).

8   *Speculum Christiani*, EETS 182, p. 65. Cf. Mary's words, 'In Goddys servyse I xal
     nevyr irke!' in the Purification play of *Ludus Coventriae* (EETS, ES, 120) l. 194.
     The *Promptuarium parvulorum* gives 'Hirkyn: ffastidio . . . , accidior . . .' (EETS,
     ES, 102, col. 245).

9   For example: *Cursor mundi*, 27784ff and 27800ff; and esp. 28341–50 (wanhope)
     and 28351–9 ('presumpciun'); *Ménagier de Paris*, fifth and sixth branch of sloth
     (pp. 40ff); Brunetto Latini, *Il Tesoretto*, ll. 165–80.

10   The existing studies on Titivillus are not very clear on which *exempla* identify the
     fiend by name, nor even describe and classify relevant *exempla* very accurately.
     Good collections of relevant *exempla* are given by T. F. Crane, *The Exempla of
     Jacques de Vitry* (London, 1890), pp. 141 and 233; and J. Bolte, 'Der Teufel in der
     Kirche', *Zeitschrift für vergleichende Literaturgeschichte*, N.F., XI (1897), 249–66.
     For occurrences of 'Titivil' in English works, see *OED*, XI, 78. Some pictorial rep-
     resentations from medieval England are listed in M. D. Anderson, *Drama and
     Imagery in English Medieval Churches* (Cambridge, 1963), pp. 173–7. Sister Mary
     Emil Jennings in her MA thesis, 'A Study of the Literary Career of the Devil
     Tutivillus' (University of North Carolina, 1966), has collected a large number of
     passages from medieval and Renaissance sources which refer to Titivillus and the
     two *exempla*.

11 Play XXX, ll. 249–52 (EETS, ES, 71). But notice that already in the Towneley play Titivillus' role is expanded: He captures souls 'at the ale-house' and at plundering (l. 217), and others that are too much interested in new fashions (ll. 233ff). Originally, however, his province were people who talked in church and who syncopated their prayers. See the following example:

> Janglers cum Jappers, Nappers, Galpers, quoque Drawers,
> Momlers, Fforskippers, Overrenners, sic Overhippers,
> Ffragmina verborum Tutivillus colligit horum.

(MS BM Lansdowne 763, fol. 6or; printed in *A Catalogue of the Lansdowne Manuscripts in the British Museum* [London, 1819], p. 170). See also item 179 in Brown, *Religious Lyrics of the Fifteenth Century.*

12 MS BM Arundel 506, fol. 46v; Bromyard, *Summa praedicantium*, 'Ordo clericalis', II, xxvi; a somewhat different vision of the same devil, ibid., 'Ferie', VII, xxi; *The Mirror of Our Lady*, I, xx (EETS, ES, 19, p. 54); *Sermones quadragesimales Thesauri Novi*, sermo 13 (Augsburg, 1487) [. . .]

13 Thus in *Jacob's Well*, pp. 114–15.

14 One text for many: 'Accidia quidem est displicentia boni . . . Si est clericus, si negligens est in officio suo . . . Item, laicus si venit ad ecclesiam in festis et loquitur in eclesia cum alliis'. Raymundus of Pennaforte (?), *Summa de vitiis*, MS University of North Carolina 5 (written 1459), cap. xv.

15 Coogan, *An interpretation of 'Mankind'*, *passim*, following a suggestion made by W. K. Smart, 'Some Notes on *Mankind*', *Modern Philology* 14 (1916), 45ff.

16 The theme of instability is stated in ll. 207, 274ff, 739 (see Coogan, *An Interpretation of 'Mankind'*, p. 107), (902–3). Notice that in Play 24 of *Ludus Coventriae*, 'The Woman Taken in Adultery' – a play similarly concerned with Mercy – 'vnstable' is synonymous with 'sinful' (p. 208, l. 261; p. 201, l. 27).

THE LIMITS OF ALLEGORY: THE CASE OF *THE OWL AND THE NIGHTINGALE*

The story of allegory studies in Middle English must also take account of the great amount of ink spilled on the early Middle English debate poem, *The Owl and the Nightingale*. It is a text upon which many an allegorical reading has come to grief, ranging as it does so widely over such diverse subject matter. In the long critical history of the poem, allegorical readings of the two debating birds have tended to be convincing only for localized episodes, never for the work as a whole. The following extract from Kathryn Hume's 1975 book, *The Owl and the Nightingale: The Poem and its Critics* shows us just how many allegorical readings of the poem had been floated and foundered down to 1975. Hume's study, which itself goes on to offer an allegorical reading, highlights the limitations of allegorical approaches which make exclusive recourse to extrinsic contexts to interpret a work. In rehearsing so many competing readings of the poem, the extract tells us something about the *limits* of allegory.

Extract from Kathryn Hume, 'Intellectual and Religious Interpretations', in *The Owl and the Nightingale: The Poem and its Critics* (Toronto: University of Toronto Press, 1975), pp. 51–9.

What is *The Owl and the Nightingale* really about? In 1948 Albert C. Baugh denied that the poem was 'anything more than a lively altercation between two birds',[1] and almost every critic since has gone out of his way to protest this assessment. And it *is* difficult to believe that a poem of such length and quality should be merely a *jeu d'esprit*. Failure to see its meaning has driven critics to try explaining the poem by means of external contexts; in other words, to reading it allegorically. [. . .] The question is what kind of reading the poem demands. Must the audience extrapolate to allegorical referents to make sense of the work? Is the poem naturally suited to this approach? Can we hope the poem will yield to allegorical assault in the future if past attempts have failed?

The most common and least allegorical of the usual approaches is that which tries to explain the poem in terms of 'outlook on life'. The birds' outlooks have been classified as 'beauty, brilliancy, youth, cheerfulness' for the Nightingale, and 'serious, gloomy, sullen old age' for the Owl, or pleasure and asceticism (both descriptions are Ten Brink's); gaiety and gravity (Saintsbury); Art and Philosophy (W. P. Ker); joyous and solemn (Stanley); and aesthetic and serious (Wells).[2] Though these terms reflect differing emphases, the nature of the dichotomy discerned by these critics is clear: essentially it is a contrast between gloom and joy, modified by those human interests which the critic thinks to be involved allegorically; thus the Owl's gloom is not mere sourness, but is linked by several critics to religious asceticism.

[. . .] Clearly there is good cause to think of the Nightingale as interested in pleasure, gaiety, art, joy, aesthetics, sex, and perhaps in the sort of 'new' religion based on love and joy that was popularized by the Franciscans.

With this evidence before us, we can readily understand why so many critics have interpreted the poem as a conflict between some type of joy and gloom. This approach has the considerable virtue that it demands almost no extension beyond the text. We may extrapolate from such indirect statements as the Owl's periodic night songs to the canonical hours if we wish to add a religious touch, but that is hardly a great leap. The birds' comments on human concerns like adultery surely warrant our assuming there is some connection between them and man.

One substantial objection to general-outlook interpretations, however, is the peripheral placement of the evidence. Virtually all of it appears in the first half of the poem, much indeed before line 500. As the arguments unfold, it becomes clear that the controversy centres on service to mankind, and outlook proves of little relevance to the points scored or issues discussed. Indeed, the outlooks seem at odds with the birds' later pronouncements on astrology and fornication. Arrangement of the evidence in this fashion suggests that details about outlook, many of which are extensions of bird lore, were used to endow the birds with personality, not to define the meaning of the whole debate.

Another objection to interpreting the poem by outlook is our inability to equate the birds with consistent human philosophies. The Owl's characterization is straightforward: she represents all that is conservative, ascetic, and solemn, and may readily be labelled priest, philosopher, or monk.[3] Handling the Nightingale in the same fashion though, translating her traits and actions into human terms, results in a contradiction: half of her personality establishes her as secular opposition to the Owl; her strong connection with sexual love and her defence of maidens who slip make her seem a lay figure. But her claims to helping clergy of various descriptions (729–42) and her theological opinions on how to get to heaven designate her as a 'new' religious figure of the Franciscan or proto-Franciscan type. This duality greatly reduces our hope of identifying her with a consistent human stance, and with that any hope of interpreting the poem solely by means of outlook. One might also question whether female birds would have been chosen to represent serious religious philosophies.[4]

The contradictions inherent in the characterization of the Nightingale seem to me clearest evidence that this debate is not an exploration of two outlooks or philosophies of life. Such an approach leaves too much of the poem out of account; many an avian detail cannot be translated into human terms, and many subjects such as astrology and sexual lapses seem ill-suited to this interpretation of the birds. And since the work's focus shifts from personality to serving mankind, we cannot dismiss the poem as a simple confrontation for confrontation's sake like the quarrels between seasons. We can only conclude that outlooks are of secondary importance, not the key to the poem.

Since study of the birds' philosophies of life does not tell us what *The Owl and the Nightingale* is about, critics have attempted to find out by examining the issues debated. Some, attempting to avoid allegoresis as much as possible, have combed the text for commentary on any issue which might seem substantial enough to pass for the subject of the whole. Though the kaleidoscopic nature of the arguments discourages such approaches, two have been put forward: Bertram Colgrave proposes music as the theme, and A. C. Cawley astrology.[5]

Colgrave's argument can be broken into three contentions: (1) that the debate concerns musical practices; (2) that the Owl and the Nightingale represent respectively Gregorian chant and troubadour-influenced music; and (3) that the good man from Rome is John the Archchanter, who went to England about 680 to teach the barbarian Englishmen how to sing Gregorian music. The first is simply not adequate. It builds on a relatively small portion of the text, and ignores a great number of other issues. Gloom, joy, lechery, and romantic love all have some relevance to a discussion of music, but the birds' diets and nesting habits do not. Neither do the references to astrology or the Owl's crucifixion. Singing may be *an* issue, but it is not *the* issue. Colgrave's identification of the birds is equally questionable. He ignores the fact that the Owl helps men sing *conduts* at Christmas (481–4), yet the *condut* or *conductus* is a motet based, by definition, on a *non*-Gregorian melody. As for the man from Rome, Colgrave's identification contradicts his own contentions. The Nightingale says (1015–20) that this mysterious figure taught northerners good customs, which Colgrave interprets as 'good music', but the music John the Archchanter taught was Gregorian plainsong, the very type of music the Nightingale is supposedly trying to argue down in the figure of the Owl! All in all, this attempt to interpret the poem as a treatise on singing seems unconvincing.

A. C. Cawley, working outward from some intriguing observations on the specific meaning of the prophecy passage (1145–330), suggests that the poem is about astrology. The Nightingale has the 'traditionally hostile attitude of the Church towards astrology' while the Owl seems to be something like an 'apologist of a Christianized astrology'. Each of the disasters mentioned by the birds is indeed attributable to one of the malign planets, and Cawley's observations on this material are fascinating. It is unfortunate for his argument though that the Owl never cites the stars as her source of information; nor does the Nightingale seem to think astrology nonsense: 'Ich habbe iherd, & soþ hit is, / þe mon mot beo wel storrewis' (1317–18). She is merely denying that the Owl can read stars meaningfully, and accuses her of prophesying by means of witchcraft (1301).

Laying this objection aside for a minute, though, we can assess the interpretation's general utility. It explains the Owl quite as adequately as any other reading: her liking for darkness befits a star-gazer; her mournful 'wailawai' is appropriate for conveying warning of disasters. The Nightingale though resists identification as usual. Her cheer, the welcome flowers give her, her connection with sex, are all irrelevant to any stand on astrology she may care to take, and so are details of diet and nest sanitation. Though the Owl can be linked to astrology in general, and the Nightingale to Venus, there is nothing in the Nightingale's chief characteristics to motivate her hostility to astrology, and on these grounds I think Cawley's general reading breaks down.

Cawley and Colgrave confine their attentions to issues mentioned directly in the poem, and can be said to read allegorically only in so far as they translate the birds' comments on music and astrological prophecy into human terms. The other principal subject to be mentioned directly – the birds' rela-

tive usefulness to mankind – has rarely seemed important enough to constitute the *raison d'être* of so long a poem. It is no wonder therefore that a more
elaborately allegorical approach has attracted so many critics.

Atkins and Owst appear, at first glance, to have worked along lines similar to
Colgrave's, but they interpret the poem in terms of completely allegorical
referents, not issues mentioned in the text. They take a poem dealing with
birds' appearances, birdsong, bird diets, nest building, and birds' deaths (with
human adultery and astrology thrown in) and say, in effect, 'Aha! Obviously
this all has to do with old didactic and new courtly poetry writing' (Atkins)
or 'old thunderous and new joyous preaching' (Owst). These are rather long
leaps, though in fairness we must admit that they are not impossible.[6]

Atktins identifies the Owl as the gloomy defender of didactic poetry,
the Nightingale as the cheerful lay defender of the new courtly, secular poetry.
He depends for evidence on all the passages concerning singing, working on
the hypothesis that singing is to birds what poetry is to man. His approach
explains the Owl no better than do those of Colgrave and Owst: in all three
she emerges as the defender of the old and gloomy, be it music, preaching, or
poetry. But in its ability to handle the Nightingale, Atkins's view has much to
recommend it. Her habit of singing outside bowers where lords and ladies are
in bed can be explained as a reflection of courtly poetry's concern with the love
affairs of the highborn. So can her participation in the clash between the
jealous knight and his wife, a role played by a nightingale in one of Marie de
France's most courtly lais. Her unwillingness to sing in northern countries,
which is a natural fact but is treated as a matter of choice, can be explained as
her knowing that there was no courtly culture in the north and hence no place
for her.[7]

Furthermore Atkins's approach has one advantage which no other
can match: we can feel certain that the author of *The Owl and the Nightingale*
did have some interest in poetry writing. Whether he loved music or was
tone deaf, was stirred by one type of sermon or another, we can never know.
But he *must* have been interested in secular poetry or presumably he never
would have written such a long specimen. His, indeed, is one of the very few
poems not overtly didactic to have been preserved from the pre-Chaucerian
age.

But the disadvantage in this interpretation is that, like all the other single-
theme theories, it does not account satisfactorily for all the turns the birds'
arguments take. Astrology and prophecy lie outside such an explanation, as do
all passages related to the protagonists as birds. Nor is there any direct connection between the Owl's crucifixion and didactic poetry. Inevitably, with this
approach, we stumble over the irreducibly avian part of the poem which will
not adapt itself to intellectual issues.

Do we gain any more satisfying insights by trying to explain the debate in terms of preaching techniques? G. R. Owst has suggested the possibility, though he does not explore it in depth:

> Perhaps no modern commentator yet has hit upon the real significance of that remarkable Old-English poem known as *The Owl and the Nightingale*. Is it not, after all, intended to be an allegory of the age-long rivalry in the preaching of medieval Christendom between those who upheld the gentler themes of love and bliss and an ever-forgiving Redeemer, and those who preferred on the other hand to thunder of sin and Judgment and the Wrath to come? There is certainly evidence that this very problem was continually weighing upon the minds of contemporary churchmen. In the pulpits, at all events, the note of the Owl is heard most often.[8]

The lines which suggest this reading constitute a substantial part of the poem, but not all of it. Like other single-theme interpretations, this one has trouble encompassing all of the issues raised. Again, astrology and adultery do not fit, nor do such details of avian life as diet and nest-construction. It is to the credit of these critics that they do not desperately twist the poem to make it agree with their constructs, but this honesty only makes clearer the weaknesses of this type of approach. [. . .]

Notes

1   Albert C. Baugh, general editor and author of the Middle English portion, *A Literary History of England*, 2nd edn (New York: Appleton–Century–Crofts, 1967), p. 155.

2   Bernhard Ten Brink, *History of English Literature* (London: George Bell and Sons, 1904), p. 215; George Saintsbury, *A Short History of English Literature* (New York: Macmillan, 1898), p. 60; W. P. Ker, *Medieval English Literature* (1912; reprint, London: Oxford University Press, 1962), p. 135; E. G. Stanley (ed.), *The Owl and the Nightingale* (London: Nelson and Sons, 1960), p. 22; and J. E. Wells (ed.), *The Owl and the Nightingale* (Boston: D. C. Heath, 1907), p. xli.

3   The Owl's views on wives' adultery are not altogether in line with her austere characterization, although most readers welcome this lapse in logic for the humanity it signifies. If the Owl is meant to be a monk – and this is the most usual identification – we may be able to go further and call her a Cistercian. H. B. Hinckley (in *PMLA* 47 [1932], 304) points out that we may deduce the Owl to be white from her disparagement of the Nightingale for her dusky coloration (577 ff). But, of course, the birds accuse each other of faults they themselves share: the Nightingale, for example, loudly berates the Owl over her diet, only to be proven far from fastidious herself.

4   Their sex may reflect linguistic rather than physical gender, as seems to be the case with the falcon, so it is unsafe to base an interpretation on that characteristic.

5 Bertram Colgrave, '*The Owl and the Nightingale* and the "Good Man from Rome"', *English Language Notes* 4 (1966), 1–4; and A. C. Cawley, 'Astrology in "The Owl and the Nightingale"', *Modern Language Review* 46 (1951), 161–74. Richard E. Allen, in 'The Voices of *The Owl and the Nightingale*', *Studies in Medieval Cultures* 3 (1970), 52–8, supports Colgrave's musical interpretation throughout most of his argument, but suggests as a further possibility a connection to epic and romance.

6 J. W. H. Atkins (ed.), *The Owl and the Nightingale* (Cambridge: Cambridge University Press, 1922); G. R. Owst, *Literature and Pulpit in Medieval England*, 2nd edn (Oxford: Blackwell, 1961).

7 Norway, for instance, was eventually to embrace courtly works, but the stirrings of interest in that sort of literature in the north are not documented until 1226 when King Hakon ordered translated the Tristram story and then Marie's lais.

8 Owst, *Literature and Pulpit in Medieval England*, p. 22.

Hume's book shows how far, by 1975, Middle English allegory studies had been generally detached from the debate around 'exegetical criticism'. In the same year, David Aers was also seeking 'to resolve the long-standing debate about the relations between exegesis, homily and poetry', this time in the case of William Langland's elaborate allegory *Piers Plowman*.[13]

REBALANCING ALLEGORICAL AND LITERAL MEANINGS

Also focused upon *Piers*, our final extract reflects how recent studies of signs and symbols in Middle English literature have moved well beyond the dichotomies of the Robertson–Donaldson controversy. In 'Allegorical Buildings in Mediaeval Literature', Jill Mann highlights the range of allegorical meanings in play in Passus XVIII of Langland's poem, balancing these against textual detail and literal sense. A climactic sequence of the poem, Passus XVIII centres upon the parallel scenes of Christ's entry to Jerusalem on Palm Sunday and his triumphant liberation of the captive souls in hell ('the harrowing of hell'). By pointing to medieval pageantry as an important context for Langland's treatment of these scenes, the extract eloquently demonstrates that historical and literal facets need not be set aside in allegorical studies. The allegorical meanings of the *passus* are closely intertwined with the material or physical character of what is being described, imagery of enclosure, capture, light, breath, and release. Literal sense works in tandem with allegory, enhancing and enriching textual meaning.

Extract from Jill Mann, 'Allegorical Buildings in Mediaeval Literature', *Medium Ævum* 63 (1994), 204–6.

[. . .] Passus XVIII opens with a recapitulation of Christ's triumphal entry into Jerusalem on Palm Sunday: the dreamer sees in his vision a figure 'semblable to the Samaritan, and somdeel to Piers the Plowman' who rides 'Barefoot on an asse back' to 'juste[a] in Jerusalem' (10–14, 19). In the Gospel narratives, the entry into Jerusalem is a nodal point around which building-images cluster. Matthew (xxi.12–13) and Mark (xi.15–17) follow it with the account of Jesus casting the money-changers out of the temple, as does Luke, who adds between the two Christ's prophecy of the future destruction of the earthly Jerusalem (xix.41–4). The glory of the city and its total destruction are intimately entwined in this narrative sequence. John does not describe the Palm Sunday entry, but when he recounts the purging of the temple elsewhere, he follows it with Christ's claim to rebuild the temple, if it is destroyed, within three days, and interprets this as a reference to the temple of Christ's body (ii.19–21; cf. Matthew xxvi.61, xxvii.40; Mark xv.29). Langland gives prominent place to this claim in the trial scene which follows his account of the entry (41–5), and it is important to bear in mind this identification of temple and Christ's body, as well as the dual image of destruction and re-creation, in examining what happens to the building-image in the rest of Passus xviii.

As the passus proceeds, the temple gives place to a far grimmer building, the prison of hell. It is never described, but its menacing presence makes itself felt throughout the debate of the Four Daughters of God as to whether mankind can ever be released from its confines. And, as the passus progresses, there is an accumulating emphasis on the metaphors of locking and unlocking, opening and closing, which were associated with the building-image in Passus v. There is the 'unspering' of Longius' eyes (86), there is the eclipse that 'closeth' the sun (135), the sun 'locking' its light in itself as God dies (245), there is Book's prophecy that Jesus' resurrection will 'unjoynen and unlouken' the joy of the Jews (257). Again they work in both directions, the Crucifixion precipitating a double movement of present closure and promised unlocking. These metaphors converge on the central problem of the passus, which is forcibly expressed in Righteousness's words to Peace:

> Levestow[b] that yond light unlouke myghte helle
> And save mannes soule? Suster, wene[c] it nevere!
> (188–9)

With these words, the problem fleetingly glimpsed in Passus v is fully confronted: the problem not of keeping the Devil out of one's own stronghold, but of getting out of his.

The attack launched on the gates of hell by the light that is Christ takes the form of a verbal challenge:

[a] joust.
[b] Do you believe.
[c] believe.

'Suffre we!'[a] seide Treuthe, 'I here and see bothe
A spirit speketh to helle and bit[b] unspere the yates:
"Attolite portas."[c]
A vois loude in that light to Lucifer crieth,
"Prynces of this place, unpynneth[d] and unlouketh!
For here cometh with crowne that kyng is of glorie.'"

(xviii.260–4)

Here, good is no longer on the defensive, immobilized within the safety of the castle by the threats from outside. Here Christ is on the attack, and it is the devils, huddled together and hurriedly making whispered plans behind their gates, who are forced back into defence. And a new motif enters as well: Christ's words to Lucifer not only suggest an attack on a stronghold, they also imply the triumphal entry of a king into a place he claims as his own – 'here cometh with crowne that kyng is of glory'. The humble entry into Jerusalem on an ass's back prefigures the glorious entry of the King of Heaven into his own.

The moment when the gates of hell break open to admit the King of Heaven is the high point of Langland's poem. The problem posed by Right-eousness – can a light unlock hell? – is a problem of physics, and Langland does not leave the physical plane in finding an answer to it:

Eft[e] the light bad unlouke, and Lucifer answerde,
'*Quis est iste?*'[f]
What Lord artow?' quod Lucifer. The light soone seide,
'*Rex glorie*,[g]
The lord of myght and of mayn[h] and alle manere vertues –
Dominus virtutum.[i]
Dukes of this dymme place, anoon undo thise yates,
That Crist may come in, the Kynges sone of Hevene!'
    And with that breeth helle brak, with Belialles barres –
For any wye or warde,[j] wide open the yates.
    Patriarkes and prophetes, *populus in tenebris*,[k]

[a] Let us be quiet.
[b] bids.
[c] Lift up your gates!
[d] undo.
[e] Again.
[f] Who is this?
[g] King of Glory.
[h] power.
[i] Lord of Hosts.
[j] In spite of any man or guard.
[k] the people who walked in darkness.

> Songen Seint Johanes song, '*Ecce Agnus Dei!*'ᵃ
> Lucifer loke ne myghte, so light hym ablente.ᵇ
> And tho thatᶜ Oure Lord lovede, into his light he laughte.ᵈ
>
> (xviii.315–27)

Hell is broken open at Christ's word – but it is the word in its *physical* aspect, as 'breeth' or 'broken air', that accomplishes its destruction.[1] The insubstantial element of air, which seemed the most ethereal of the elements in Kind's castle, here swells to the force of a hurricane. Langland's reference to the great wind that 'puffed' pear-trees to the ground, at the opening of Passus v (14–20), foreshadows this startling escalation of power from a mere exhalation to a mighty whirlwind. The apparently immovable solidity of the building yields instantly and exhilaratingly to mere breath. And the light that seems merely a pale gleam in the darkness gathers force until it blinds Lucifer. The miracles of the physical world are for Langland as great as those of the spiritual.

In this dramatic moment, Langland allows us the excitement of breaking through the stasis represented by the building, the excitement of destruction (seen from the outside), the breaking-out from claustrophobia (seen from within). Yet the building-image is not destroyed along with hell. The breaking-open of hell's gates realizes not only the destruction of the old order but also the creation of the new. I suggested earlier that Christ's challenge to hell represented not only the knight's attack on a castle but also the king's triumphal entry into a city. That Langland had himself seen such entries is suggested by the scene in the Prologue where the angel speaks to the king, which recalls the scene at Richard II's coronation entry in 1377 when a mechanical angel bent from a stage castle to offer him a crown.[2] The comments of Ernst Kantorowicz on the structure of ideas lying behind the imagery traditional in early mediaeval versions of such civic entries can alert us to the full implications of the moment of the Harrowing in *Piers Plowman:*

> whenever a king arrived at the gates of a city, celestial Jerusalem seemed to descend from heaven to earth. It is as though, through the magic balm of the Anointed, both king and city are transformed as they approach one another; every terrestrial city becomes another Jerusalem at the Advent of the Anointed, and the ruler at his entry becomes more and more a likeness of Christ. In other words, the liturgical celebration of an *Adventus* reflects, or even stages, the Christian prototype of Messianic entries, that is, the Lord's triumphant Entry as king into Jerusalem on Palm Sunday.[3]

ᵃ Behold the Lamb of God!
ᵇ blinded.
ᶜ those who.
ᵈ caught up.

The re-enactment of the Palm Sunday entry in Christ's *adventus* at the gates of Hell I have already commented on. Kantorowicz's words suggest in addition that it is not only the earthly Jerusalem but also the heavenly that we ought to have in mind: 'whenever a king arrived at the gates of a city, celestial Jerusalem seemed to descend from heaven to earth.' According to Kantorowicz, the liturgical rituals which celebrated 'the living mystery of the descent to earth of the Celestial Jerusalem . . . began to wane in the Gothic and Renaissance ages',[4] but Gordon Kipling has recently shown that this strain of apocalyptic imagery persists in the civic pageantry of fourteenth-century London.[5] A chronicler describing the reception of Edward II and Queen Isabella in 1308 speaks of the city as 'ornamented with jewels like New Jerusalem'.[6] The castle from which the angel offered Richard II the crown in 1377 represented, according to Kipling, the heavenly city – as became even clearer when the pageantry was repeated for Richard's reconciliation with the city of London in 1392, and the castle was suspended by ropes in mid-air, mimicking the vision of Jerusalem descending out of heaven in Revelation.[7] That passus xviii of *Piers Plowman* has an apocalyptic dimension is readily evident; Christ's triumphal speech to Satan anticipates his Second and Final Coming:

> For I that am lord of lif, love is my drynke,
> And for that drynke today, I deide upon erthe,
> I faught so, me thursteth yet, for mannes soule sake;
> May no drynke me moiste, ne my thurst slake,
> Til the vendage[a] falle in the vale of Josaphat,
> That I drynke right ripe must, *resureccio mortuorum*.[b]
> And thanne shal I come as a kyng, crouned, with aungeles,
> And have out of helle alle mennes soules.
>
> (xviii. 366–73)

The final reaping of the grapes which are trodden in the winepress of the wrath of God recalls Revelation xiv; it is part of the final scenario that leads to the 'new heaven and new earth', and the vision of the heavenly Jerusalem. The Christ who challenges the gates of hell in the words of the Psalms, '*Attollite portas*' (Psalm xxiv.9), is also the God of Revelation (iii.20) who announces his coming with the words 'Behold I stand at the door, and knock.' And if we look more closely at the breaking-open of hell, we shall see that it is an apocalyptic moment, realizing an eternal present as a dimension of a historical event. As Prudentius'[c] temple realizes the heavenly Jerusalem as a living present in

---

[a] vintage.
[b] the resurrection of the dead.
[c] Fourth-century Latin author of the Christian allegory of *Psychomachia*.

the human soul, so Christ's entry into hell transforms it momentarily into the New Jerusalem. I quote again:

> And with that breeth helle brak, with Belialles barres –
> For any wye or warde, wide open the yates.
>   Patriarkes and prophetes, *populus in tenebris*,
> Songen Seint Johanes song, *'Ecce Agnus Dei!'*
> Lucifer loke ne myghte, so light hym ablente.
> And tho that Oure Lord lovede, into his light he laughte.
>
> (xviii.322–7)

Patriarchs and prophets sing *'Ecce Agnus Dei'*, as the four and twenty elders in John's vision sing the glory of the Lamb (v.9).[8] In the heavenly Jerusalem, there is no temple, for the temple is embodied in the Lamb. Neither is there any need 'of the sun, neither of the moon, to shine in it: for the glory of God did lighten it, and the Lamb is the light thereof . . . And the gates of it shall not be shut at all by day: for there shall be no night there.' So in this climactic moment of the Harrowing, hell is transformed into Jerusalem: its temple is Christ's resurrected body, its light is the light of the Lamb, and – most important of all – all its gates are open.

Notes

1   Donatus and Priscian define the basic unit of speech ('vox') as 'broken air' (aerictus'): see *Grammatici Latini*, ed. H. Keil, 7 vols (Leipzig, 1857–80) II, 5; IV, 367. The Eagle in Chaucer's *House of Fame* repeats this definition when he explains: 'Soun ys noght but eyr ybroken;/And every speche that ys spoken,/In his substaunce ys but air' (765–8).

2   See Glynne Wickham, *Early English Stages 1300 to 1660*, 4 vols (London and New York, 1959–81), I, 54–5; the entry is described in the *Historia Anglicana* of Thomas Walsingham, ed. Henry Thomas Riley, Rolls Series, 2 vols (London, 1863–4), I, 331–2. For the proposal that Langland had this occasion in mind, see E. T. Donaldson, *Piers Plowman: The C-Text and its Poet*, 2nd edn (London, 1966), p. 118. Langland may well have been influenced also by the staging of Christ's Entry into Jerusalem in the mystery plays; the surviving York and Chester cycles, although later in date than Langland, represent it as a civic entry by a great lord. Conversely, the naturalness of the religious imagery in a secular context is shown by Walsingham's account of Peter de la Mare's triumphant return to London after Richard on his accession had released him from prison: he was greeted by crowds of citizens crying 'Benedictus, qui venit in nomine Domini' (*Historia Anglicana*, ed. Riley, II, 384).

3   Ernst H. Kantorowicz, 'The "King's Advent" and the Enigmatic Panels in the Doors of Santa Sabina', *Art Bulletin* 26 (1944), 207–31 (210). See also his *Laudes*

Regiae: *A Study in Liturgical Acclamations and Medieval Ruler Worship* (Berkeley and Los Angeles, 1958), pp. 71–2, 145–6.

4 Kantorowicz, *Laudes Regiae*, p. 146.

5 Gordon Kipling, 'Richard II's "Sumptuous Pageants" and the Idea of Civic Triumph', in David M. Bergeron (ed.), *Pageantry in the Shakespearean Theater* (Athens, GA, 1985), pp. 83–103. I am grateful to Professor Kipling for reading this paper in typescript and sending me a copy of his article.

6 *Chronicles of Edward I and II*, ed. William Stubbs, Rolls Series (London, 1882), p. 152. Quoted in Kipling, 'Richard II's "Sumptuous Pageants"', p. 88.

7 This latter ceremony is too late to have influenced the B-text of *Piers Plowman*, but it helps to make clear some of the ideas implicit in the earlier civic entry. Richard Maidstone's verse description of this occasion (*De concordia inter Ric. II. et civitatem London.*) was edited by Thomas Wright for the Camden Society (London, 1838); extracts are printed in Edith Rickert, *Chaucer's World* (New York and London, 1948), pp. 35–9; and Wickham, *Early English Stages*, I, 67–70.

8 Kipling, 'Richard II's "Sumptuous Pageants"', p. 91, points out that the liturgy of Advent not only celebrates the first coming of Christ, heralded by John the Baptist, but also looks forward to his Second Coming. Thus in the 1392 ceremony Richard II was welcomed by a figure representing John the Baptist who bore the written legend '*agnus et ecce Dei*' (p. 86). Langland similarly uses the proclamation of Christ's First Coming in an apocalyptic context which suggests his Second.

Further Reading

A handy overview of literary allegory through the ages appears in the 'Methuen Critical Idiom' series: John MacQueen, *Allegory* (London: Methuen, 1970). Medieval–Renaissance continuities in allegorical narrative are traced by Rosamund Tuve, *Allegorical Imagery: Some Medieval Books and their Posterity* (Princeton, NJ: Princeton University Press, 1966) and there is a very useful chapter on medieval allegory in Pamela Gradon's *Form and Style in Early English Literature* (London: Methuen, 1971), pp. 32–92.

Critical treatments of Middle English allegories tend to draw upon two foundational studies that address allegory more broadly: Eric Auerbach, *Scenes from the Drama of European Literature*, trans. R. Manheim (New York: Meridian Books, 1959), and E. R. Curtius, *European Literature and the Latin Middle Ages*, trans. W. R. Trask (London: Routledge, 1953). A useful general collection of essays on the topic is edited by J. Stephen Russell: *Allegoresis: The Craft of Allegory in Medieval Literature* (New York: Garland Press, 1988), and a good Chaucer-specific volume is S. H. Rigby, *Chaucer in Context: Society, Allegory and Gender* (Manchester: Manchester University Press, 1996).

The ability of *The Owl and the Nightingale* to thwart a consistent hermeneutic formed the starting-point for a famous essay applying reader-reception theory to the text: R. Barton Palmer, 'The Narrator in *The Owl and the Nightingale*: A Reader in the Text', *Chaucer Review* 22 (1988), 305–21. A recent study of *Pearl* which, like Jill

Mann's reading of *Piers*, retains emphasis on the materiality of signs and symbols is Helen Barr's '*Pearl* – or The Jeweller's Tale?', *Medium Ævum* 69 (2000), 59–79, reprinted in *Socioliterary Practice in Late Medieval England* (Oxford: Oxford University Press, 2001).

Now held responsible for a fair few exaggerations and distortions, C. S. Lewis's *The Allegory of Love: A Study in Medieval Tradition* (Oxford: Oxford University Press, 1936) remains an important text – best read alongside more recent writing on the topic.

Chapter Notes

1 Harry Caplan, 'The Four Senses of Scriptural Interpretation and the Medieval Theory of Preaching', *Speculum* 4 (1929), 282–90.

2 D. W. Robertson, Jr, 'Historical Criticism', in A. S. Downer (ed.), *English Institute Essays, 1950* (New York: Columbia University Press, 1951), p. 14. Robertson also advanced his views in two articles the following year: 'Some Medieval Literary Terminology', *Studies in Philology* 48 (1951), 669–92, and 'The Doctrine of Charity in Medieval Literary Gardens', *Speculum* 26 (1951), 24–49.

3 Robertson, 'Historical Criticism', p. 19.

4 D. W. Robertson, Jr and Bernard Huppé, '*Piers Plowman' and Scriptural Tradition* (Princeton, NJ: Princeton University Press, 1951), p. 236.

5 R. W. Frank, 'The Art of Reading Medieval Personification Allegory', *English Literary History* 20 (1953), 237–50 (248).

6 Morton W. Bloomfield, 'Symbolism in Medieval Literature', *Modern Philology* 56 (1958), 73–81 (74).

7 Ibid., 76.

8 D. W. Robertson, Jr and Bernard Huppé, *Fruyt and Chaff: Studies in Chaucer's Allegories* (Princeton, NJ: Princeton University Press, 1963), p. 55.

9 D. S. Brewer, 'Review of Robertson and Huppé', *Review of English Studies* n.s. 16 (1965), 305.

10 Paul Beichner, 'The Allegorical Interpretation of Medieval Literature', *PMLA* 82 (1967), 33–8 (38).

11 Bloomfield, 'Symbolism', p. 8; Beichner, 'Allegorical Interpretation', p. 38.

12 R. E. Kaske, 'Chaucer and Medieval Allegory', *English Literary History* 30 (1963), 175–92.

13 David Aers, *Piers Plowman and Christian Allegory* (London: Edward Arnold, 1975), p. 1.

6

Literature and History

Antiquarianism and the traditional historicism of early Middle English scholars. Biographical criticism. History and mythology. The lull in historicist studies in the mid-twentieth century. Their resurgence in the 1970s and 1980s. The contemporary debate around 'critical historicism'. John M. Bowers (on Pearl*); Helen Barr (on* Hoccleve).

Do Middle English texts bear witness to an enduring *human condition* or to specific and ever-changing *historical conditions*? Around this question have formed some of the central critical traditions in the field. From early antiquarianism to the contemporary debate over 'critical historicism', scholars have continually returned to the question of how far Middle English literature can or should be related to the historical and social contexts within which it was produced and first received.

When the subject was in its infancy, an historical dimension was intrinsic to medieval English scholarship. For the antiquarians of the eighteenth century the value of medieval texts lay first and foremost in the window they gave onto medieval customs, manners, even costumes. It was this historicist spirit that moved Sir Thomas Percy to rescue the manuscript that now forms our most important source for medieval English ballad poetry from the flames of Sir Humphrey Pitt's hearth-fire: 'I saw it lying dirty on the floor under a Bureau in ye parlour: being used by the maids to light the fire.'[1] In 1765 Percy would publish the poems and ballads of this tattered manuscript as *relics* of ancient English poetry, prized less for literary merit than for the simple fact of their antiquity:

> In a polished age, like the present, I am sensible that many of these reliques of antiquity will require great allowances to be made for them. Yet have they, for the most part, a pleasing simplicity, and many artless graces, which in the opinion of no mean critics have been thought to compensate for the want of higher

beauties, and, if they do not dazzle the imagination, are frequently found to inter-est the heart.[2]

In getting medieval texts out of danger and into print, Percy and contem-poraries Thomas Warton (1728–90) and Joseph Ritson (1753–1803) laid an historicist foundation for later scholarship. Warton's *History of English Poetry* (1774–81) placed the same emphasis on manners and mores: 'the pictures of ancient manners presented by these early writers, strongly interest the imagination'.[3] And some of these 'ancient manners' provoked more than inter-est: a scandalized Warton protested at 'gross and open obscenities' in, of all things, the mystery plays: 'In a play of the Old and New Testament, Adam and Eve are both exhibited on the stage naked, and conversing about their nakedness.'[4]

Today, many medievalists look back on the labours of the antiquarians with mixed feelings. Indebted as we doubtless are to Percy, Warton and their con-temporaries for preserving so many texts, scholars are increasingly conscious of how these same antiquarians bequeathed to literary history a view of the Middle Ages as alien, remote, discontinuous with later epochs. As David Matthews points out, this emphasis on obsolete customs, curious habits and abstruse prac-tices painted the age as fundamentally 'other': 'The paradox of the study of medieval literature was that "ancient" texts were always hypostasized in a distant, irretrievably other, historical past, from which the editor and reader had to pluck the familiar, that which would speak to their own age.'[5] And here it seems the antiquarians simply sustained the bad press given to the period by the Renaissance humanists, who had cast the Middle Ages as a drab intermis-sion between the high-points of classical and Renaissance culture.

THE EARLY TWENTIETH CENTURY   Victorian and early twentieth-century medievalism generally took up the anti-quarians' view that medieval literature reflected medieval life. So in 1906, a literal-minded J. S. P. Tatlock was calculating 'how many days Chaucer con-ceived his Canterbury pilgrimage as occupying',[6] while the following year, J. W. H. Atkins looked to the verse romances for light on the medieval past: 'In certain respects [the] romances may be said to reflect the age in which they were written.'[7] Also representative are the comments on the romances by Ker and Eagleson, written twenty years apart:

- *W. P. Ker* (1912): 'The longer romances are really modern novels – studies of contemporary life, characters and emotions, mixed up with adventures more or less surprising.'[8]
- *Harvey Eagleson* (1932): 'In the matter of costume the writers of the metrical romances in England were realistic, changing the dress of their characters as that of their readers changed.'[9]

Equally characteristic is the 1933 opinion of Nellie Slayton Aurner that Sir Thomas Malory was as much historian as romancer: 'A faithful son of fifteenth-century England, he made his book the classic expression of his epoch.'[10]

As so often in Middle English studies, developments in Chaucer criticism of this date provide an index of the major currents that were overtaking the wider field. Kittredge and Manly, pre-eminent Chaucer critics of the early twentieth century, show a strong biographical and historicist emphasis in their reception of Chaucer's work. While recognizing the writer's indebtedness to literary convention, to sources and analogues, both scholars return again and again to the suggestion that written work reflects lived experience. Consider Kittredge's 1915 treatment of the Canterbury pilgrims:

> Chaucer had no need to borrow or invent: he needed only to observe . . . Pilgrims were as familiar sights to Chaucer as commercial travellers are to us. There is not one chance in a hundred that he had not gone on a Canterbury pilgrimage himself. And pilgrims did, for a fact, while away the time in story-telling. Newton did not learn that apples fall by reading treatises on pomology.[11]

In 1922 Manly would go even further. Not only, he observed, would our poet have had experience of real-life pilgrims, it was even possible to suggest positive historical identifications for various figures among the Canterbury cohort. Following others, Manly had turned up evidence that there really was a Harry Bailly, innkeeper of Southwark, at the end of the fourteenth century: 'We may therefore safely conclude that the host of the Tabard in Chaucer's day actually was named Harry Bailly and consequently that the Host of the *Canterbury Tales* was modeled upon him.'[12] From this historicist stance, art did indeed hold a mirror up to nature; literature and life were drawing very close indeed.

Only the more important documents have so far been published, except, perhaps, in the case of some recent issues of the Early English Text Society. We have long waited for a proper edition of the *Ludus Coventriae*, which has only just appeared. Professor Knott says that controversy over the authorship of *Piers Plowman* can reach no satisfactory conclusion until for that poem we have a completely representative and scholarly edition with which to work. Professor Emerson recently suggested that it was time for a new edition of the *Ormulum*; and one might add that publication with a convenient apparatus of introduction and notes is still to be desired for *Gawain and the Green Knight* and even Layamon's *Brut*. So much material on these poems has appeared in scattered notes that we need a compendium of the best of it. Still to be properly edited are such romances as the *Avowying of King Arthur*, the *Weddynge of Sir Gawen*, *Kyng Alisaunder*, *Sir Amadas*, *Sir Degare*, and *Roberd of Cisyle*.[13]

1924: Howard R. Patch surveys the state of the field

Running alongside the historicist work of this period was a current of scholarship concerned less with *history* than with mythology. Interest in mythic and folkloric origins for medieval texts focused in particular on Arthurian literature and, most of all, on *Sir Gawain and the Green Knight* whose many sources and analogues in French, Irish and English were brought to wide notice by G. L. Kittredge's landmark study of 1916.[14] The book encouraged a flurry of further studies, helped along by the definitive early edition of the poem by Tolkien and Gordon in 1925.[15] Kittredge's work had been influenced by Jessie L. Weston's monograph of 1897, *The Legend of Sir Gawain: Studies upon its Original Scope and Significance*.[16] This study of mythic elements of the legend had suggested divine origins for Gawain, outlining an original role for the figure as a sun god. Followers of Kittredge's school were also influenced by a second study by Weston, *From Ritual to Romance*.[17] Appearing in 1920, the book argued for mythic and folkloric origins for the Grail legend. And so *Gawain*-studies led the way in the early part of the century for those scholars who were concerned with source study and the tracing of story motifs in medieval literature. Thus in 1936 one critic from the Kittredge–Weston school maintained:

> such stories as Sir Gawain and the Green Knight cannot be understood unless we are willing to keep our minds open to the idea that, in addition to literary documents, popular ceremonies and rites may be of first-class importance in considering not only the derivation of a story but also the significance or 'myth' that originally produced it.[18]

A prolific critic working in this tradition was R. S. Loomis whose study on *Celtic Myth and Arthurian Romance* appeared in 1927,[19] and who produced related studies on Laȝamon's *Brut*[20] and the English Gawain poems throughout the 1930s and 1940s.[21]

The dominance of these concurrent approaches of historicism and literary anthropology was to exasperate some commentators. George Kane's 1951 study of *Middle English Literature* is prefaced with an appeal for a critical approach that considers the texts 'as something more than quarries for the production of historical topicalities, sources and analogues, foreign influences, ancient mythological figures in disguise, folk-lore motives, history of doctrine, social customs or phonological forms'.[22]

The stream of historicist Middle English studies lessens in the two decades from 1950: why is this? This was the period during which close textual studies of individual texts were in the ascendant. The influence of 'new' or 'practical criticism' registered strongly in the field at this time, resulting in some classic close textual studies: John Speirs's *Medieval English Poetry* of 1957; A. C.

Spearing's *Criticism and Medieval Poetry* of 1964; John Burrow's *A Reading of 'Sir Gawain and the Green Knight'* of 1965; Trevor Whittock's *A Reading of the Canterbury Tales* of 1968; the books of P. M. Kean (1967) and Ian Bishop (1968) on *Pearl*.[23] The slighter number of historicist readings from this period also reflects the shifts in critical landscape brought about by the arrival on the scene in 1951 of D. W. Robertson's 'Historical Criticism'.[24] Inclined to view all medieval literature as allegorical in mode and Christian in meaning, Robertson's brand of criticism directed readers to a very selective and specific set of historical contexts: the Bible and the writings of the Church Fathers, particularly Augustine. The debate that raged at this time between Robertson's 'Historical Criticism' and New Criticism (on which see chapter 5) played its own part in diverting critical currents from the historicism of the early decades of the century.

A twentieth-century reader cannot identify himself with a reader of the fourteenth or seventeenth century: his sense of the earlier context would always be abstract and acquired, not part of the air he breathes. Furthermore, and perhaps more important, he would have to renounce the poem's relevance to his own life and age, and forgo much that the poem could teach him about his own experience.[25]

1968: Trevor Whittock's close reading of the *Canterbury Tales* disavows a need for historicism

All the same, some critical minds were still at work on the question of how medieval literature and history inter-relate. Margaret Schlauch's 1956 survey of *English Medieval Literature and its Social Foundations* included observations that the romances were far from being the realistic reflections of medieval life the antiquarians had once taken them for: 'The Saracens as a whole are represented as primitive, ignorant, polytheistic, and often drunk, whereas they were in fact sober, abstemious, strictly monotheistic and very often more cultured than their opponents.'[26] And R. H. Robbins's 1959 preface to a collection of historical and political poems finds that the relation between literature and history is more nuanced than earlier commentators had sometimes assumed: 'the value of these poems is not just as the handmaiden of History. Admitting the importance of literature for historical research, one must place equal or greater reliance on documents – charters, parish records, wills, inventories, and so forth – and suggest that History illuminates Literature.'[27]

But for extensive literary–historical studies we must wait until the 1970s and the appearance in 1971 of V. J. Scattergood's *Politics and Poetry in the Fifteenth Century*. The work's first principles were markedly more cautious than those of the earlier generation of historicist commentators. Where once scholars had trusted fictional medieval texts to provide a window on the medieval world, Scattergood questioned the ability of even 'historical poems' to give anything but a partial view of that world:

> to look for accuracy of detail in these poems is almost certainly to look for some-thing with which the poet was not primarily concerned. Nor is a poet's analysis of contemporary events and society usually meant to be definitive. His response to a situation is usually immediate, primarily personal or sectional, and above all, to some degree biased.[28]

This is a notion sustained into the most recent 'critical historicism': Paul Strohm's 1992 study of fourteenth-century texts talks of the 'skepticism' as well as the 'respect' the historicist critic ideally brings to the medieval text, wary of that text's complicity in transmitting particular and partial historical perspectives:

> At the center of my inquiry is the text itself, with the cryptic and paradoxical information it both offers and withholds . . . This inquiry recognizes our reliance on the written record for what we can know of the past and seeks to approach texts with an appropriate mixture of skepticism and respect. It views texts not as finalized 'sources' but as argumentative and interpretative documents in their own right, as historical contestants and objects of contestation.[29]

Scattergood's literary–historical study thus reflected a growing critical recognition that the relation between medieval literature and medieval life was a more complex one than the early historicists had often assumed. Also appear-ing in 1971 was John Burrow's influential *Ricardian Poetry*, a work that had borrowed the historians' classification of a 'Ricardian' period (the reign of Richard II, 1377–99) and had applied this to the central English poets of the reign: Chaucer, Gower, Langland and the *Gawain*-poet.[30] Drawing on this work, in 1978 Anne Middleton examined the overlap between the social and literary values of the epoch in her influential article 'The Idea of Public Poetry in the Reign of Richard II'. Middleton suggested that, while specific histori-cal concerns were indeed countenanced in this literature, Ricardian poetry was more generally preoccupied with relating social and historical conditions to a universal framework:

> The public poetry of the Ricardian period is best understood not as poetry 'about' contemporary events and abuses, whether viewed concretely or at a distance, from the vantage point of a universal scheme of ideal order – it is rarely occa-sional or topical, and it is indifferent on the whole to comprehensive rational systems of thought or poetic structure. Rather it is poetry defined by a constant

relation of speaker to audience within an ideally conceived worldly community, a relation which has become the poetic subject.[31]

The 1980s saw further diversification of the scholarly view of literature and history. First, the cultural context in which the poems of the *Pearl* manuscript were composed was vividly brought to life by Michael J. Bennett's, *Community, Class and Careerism: Cheshire and Lancashire Society in the Age of 'Sir Gawain and the Green Knight'* of 1983, a study that would open up the contexts of the poem for a range of new critical readings.[32] The following year, Janet Coleman's entry in Raymond Williams's *English Literature in History* series focused upon the medieval readers and writers of 1350–1400. Coleman showed how much of the literature of this period was deeply implicated in framing historical perspectives for those same readers and writers:

[W]hat we can say about the factual history of the period after 1350 (which concerns the war with France, the financial problems resulting from this war and the ravage of the plague on the English landscape, the practices and ideals of Edward III's and Richard II's courts, the 'peasants' revolt' of 1381) arises again as subjects of the contemporary poetry. Not only may we examine the vernacular poetry as an art form of increasing brilliance, but we may also interpret much of its message as the poetic reformulation of contemporary social and religious concerns of authors and audience alike; for this was a period in which the perception of such 'realities' was determined less by men's memories than by the written word.[33]

As this more nuanced picture of the interplay between literature and history took hold, there registered in some critical quarters a sense of an obligation to historicize. Suspicion grew of critical approaches that celebrated 'timeless', transhistorical aspects of literary art: did not these approaches risk sanctioning ideologies that construct belief systems, social structures, gender roles as 'natural', 'enduring', 'timeless'? In the collaborative volume of 1986 edited by David Aers, *Medieval Literature: Criticism, Ideology and History*, Derek Pearsall explains how the enduring critical reception of Chaucer as 'for all time' served the interests of a particular class of readers:

It is an educated class, in which reading is instilled as an expected occupation, and with money enough to buy books; its view of society is a stable and 'natural' hierarchy of relationships; literature will be seen to endorse those socially cohesive categories and declare their permanence through its portrayal of 'general nature'; even those who do not share the benefits of the class will aspire to its views. The denial of history will be acclaimed: the poet transcends the 'merely historical' and communicates with all ages by connecting up to the current of the universal.[34]

In the same spirit and in the same year, Stephen Knight's Marxist-influenced re-reading of Chaucer showed the same sociohistorical emphasis: 'To re-read the Chaucerian texts in terms of their social and historical meaning is to be constantly aware of the political role of all culture in all periods.'[35]

> Although these poems cannot be understood without regard to their historical and literary context, an approach that skirts formal and poetic matters is equally inadequate. The four poems are neither tracts nor sermons; they are the work of a poet who organized his material carefully and who, for the most part, allowed his themes to remain unstated, implicit in his organization.[36]

1984: Lynn Staley Johnson's study of the *Gawain*-poet balances historicism and formalism.

A recurrent theme of 1990s' historicism was the notion that the modern scholar must remain aware of his or her own historical situation and of how this predisposes us to seek particular qualities in the texts of another age. The 'new' or 'critical' historicism of Lee Patterson and others stresses how the critic engages in an active dialogue with history: 'The goal of a self-assertive medievalism must be not the denial of the historicity of the past it seeks to recover but the affirmation of the historicity of the present in which it practices: the Middle Ages is indeed the realm of the historical, but so is every other period, including our own.'[37]

THE DEBATE OVER 'CRITICAL HISTORICISM'   Our two extracts represent recent historicist work, offering us an opportunity to consider some of the methodological issues raised by contemporary 'critical historicism'. The first extract centres upon the fourteenth-century poem *Pearl*. Until very recently, critical reception of this poem was dominated by ahistorical studies in the tradition of New Criticism. The poem's craftsmanship seemed to court these approaches: structure, symmetry and style in *Pearl* made the work fully congenial to critical approaches that would sever the link between text and context, literature and history. John Bowers's recent study changed direction. Bowers uncovers *The Politics of Pearl*, grounding the text within precise historical and cultural contexts (the many detailed footnotes to the extract demonstrate just how painstakingly this critical aim is pursued). The following extract looks at a central episode of the poem: the Pearl-Maiden's narration of the Parable of the Vineyard. Bowers's reading of this section aims to demonstrate that the parable functions not simply at an immediate thematic level as part of the Pearl-Maiden's theological instruction of the Dreamer, but at a more topical, inter-textual level as a textual intervention in an energized contemporary debate regarding labour, price and value. The inter-texts cited are various and range from the traditionally 'literary' to the 'non-

Figure 2 The capture of Richard II, prior to his deposition in 1399. No longer viewed as simply reflective of history, medieval texts are increasingly viewed as productive of historical understanding. (Reproduced by kind permission of the British Library, MS 1319. fol. 44)

literary' documentary sources of sermon, parliamentary petition and statute. This dissolution of traditional boundaries reflects the critical historicist notion that literary texts are inevitably rooted in the historical and cultural forces that produce them. Whether such an approach, for all its merits, can give sufficient acknowledgement to the literary and aesthetic qualities of the poem remains a pressing question.

Extract from John M. Bowers, 'Economics', in *The Politics of Pearl: Court Poetry in the Age of Richard II* (Cambridge: D. S. Brewer, 2001), pp. 41–8.

Pearl incorporates the Parable of the Vineyard from Matthew 20: 1–16 to make the point that the rewards of Heaven are equally divided despite the age of the individual.[1] This traditional interpretation can be traced back to St Augustine as part of his insistence upon God's prevenient grace in the work of salvation, and it was the subject of a homily by Gregory the Great [. . .] The Pearl Queen herself points to this liturgical context:

As Mathew mele3 in your messe	As the tale in the Gospel of Matthew goes
In sothfol gospel of God almy3t,	In the mass that blesses the bread and wine,
In sample he can ful graypely gesse,	In parable his words propose
And lykne3 hit to heuen ly3te.	A likeness to the realm divine.[2]

(lines 497–500)

Bolstered in the homiletic tradition by Pope Innocent III (*PL* 217: 351–2),[3] the parable was used by English churchmen such as Bishop Thomas Brinton in his sermon of 1376.[4] Preaching the English sermon *Redde Racionem Villicacionis Tue*[a] at St Paul's Cross in the tumultuous year 1388, Thomas Wimbledon proposed an all-encompassing morality that fused the spiritual and social: 'For ri3t as 3ee seeþ þat in tilienge of þe material vine þere beeþ diuerse laboreris . . . Ri3t so in þe chirche beeþ nedeful þes þre offices: presthod, kyn3thod, and laboreris.'[5] The Gospel of St Matthew offered no fewer than fifteen parables explaining the nature of Heaven, including the Parable of the Pearl of Great Price (Matt. 13: 45–6) more thematically suited to *Pearl* but granted far less space in the text (lines 730–2). It is therefore worth enquiring why the poet chose to grant such an extended treatment amounting to a tenth of the entire text (lines 497–612) to the parable in which Heaven is likened to a lord overseeing his harvest. Certainly not everyone in fourteenth-century England would have been so quick to compare Heaven to a country landlord.

It has become almost axiomatic that much of the social history of England in the second half of the fourteenth century is dominated by the Black Death and its economic consequences. With a drop in the rural work-force, peasants who had previously been bound by feudal indenture discovered that they had the power to bargain with their local lords. Others, lured by the prospect of cash payment, deserted the land and became migrant farm-workers offering their services to the highest bidders. The landed gentry struck back with the 1351 Statute of Labourers in an effort to enforce feudal contracts and to freeze wages at pre-plague levels. The great magnates as well as the lesser householders and religious landowners – particularly the old Benedictine monasteries, such as St Werburgh's Abbey in Chester – led a rear-guard action against these natural economic consequences, striving hard to keep dependents tied to the soil while asserting seignorial rights to the fullest. A great contest had begun.[6]

[. . .] The literal agricultural sense of the Parable of the Vineyard, which was carefully respected even by St Augustine in his homily on Matthew 20

[a] Pay your labourer's due sum.

(*PL* 38: 530–9), remains constant in the Dreamer's interpretative reactions and countermoves. Political considerations naturally followed a vernacular rendering that drew so vividly upon the immediate scene in ways typical of the period's more naturalistic representations. 'This direct approach evidenced also by the contemporaneous Bible translations', Walter Ullmann has remarked, 'powerfully stimulated the pictorial representation of gospel stories, with the result that they came to be set in natural surroundings which actually meant the environs with which the artist himself was familiar.'[7] At immediate issue here is the lord's absolute right to enforce labor contracts and to determine the wage-level for the laborers hired for the summer harvest. 'More, weþer louyly is me my gyfte / To do wyth myn quat-so me lykeȝ!'[a] (lines 565–6), the lord proclaims loftily to his hired hands. Bertha Putnam's foundational work on the enforcement of the Statutes of Labourers discovered that the cases brought before the justices of the peace concerned exactly these two provisions: contract agreements, and the workers' demands for wages other than those stipulated under law.[8] There were complaints in the late 1380s that farm laborers wanted two pence a day and a free dinner.

Naturally these workers had the best leverage for bargaining at harvest time, which is specified as the time-setting for *Pearl*: 'In Auguste in a hyȝ seysoun / Quen corne is coruen wyth crokeȝ kene'[b] (lines 39–40).[9] As early as Richard II's first Parliament, one of the most pressing complaints of the Commons against farm laborers concerned the severe losses caused by their failure to reap corn.[10] At harvest time, landowners were anxious that their crops might rot in the fields if not promptly gathered. Since they were sometimes forced to accept demands from day-laborers for as much as four pence a day,[11] it is no coincidence that *Pearl* translated the biblical *denarius* as 'a pené on a day' (line 510). This rate of a penny per day accorded with the statutory level of just wages – or 'resonabele hyre' (line 523) as the poet calls it – set by the Cambridge Parliament of 1388 and restated in commissions issued to the justices of the peace in 1390, even though it was an entirely unrealistic wage well below pre-plague levels of the 1340s.[12] Modern research has concluded that England enjoyed unusually abundant harvests during the years 1374–94, so that farm workers had good reason to expect to share in the bounty produced through their labors.[13] Beginning around 1395, however, agricultural production began a decline which acerbated the tensions between those who held the land and those who worked the land.

Pressures exerted by these social conflicts help to account for the length of *Pearl's* biblical paraphrase, which becomes a noticeable distention of text in a poem otherwise so scrupulously proportioned in respect to line-count and dis-

---

[a] Moreover, is not my gift-giving lawful to me, / To do with however I please?
[b] In August festival time / When corn is cut with sharp sickles.

position of stanzas.[14] The lord of the parable has no patience with shirkers in the marketplace – 'Why stande ȝe ydel?' (line 515) – but he is careful to observe the Statute of Labourers by hiring no men who had fled their feudal masters. He offers work only to those who give assurances 'her hyre watȝ nawhere boun'[a] (line 534). Most of all, he maintains his authority to enforce prior covenants by resisting the complaints of those workers who came early at the first hour. The significance of the poet's handling of contemporary details overall has been finely registered by Jim Rhodes: 'the *Pearl* Poet proves, through his artful appropriation of biblical parables, that he is engaged with the social and political issues that beset his church and society. Biblical hermeneutics is simply the way he chooses to inscribe crisis into his poetry.'[15]

This fantasy of feudal authority strenuously resisted the economic reality that labor had become a commodity whose monetary value was a function of supply and demand. This cherished fiction may have been sanctified by the Parable of the Vineyard and asserted legally, over and over again, by the parliamentary Statutes of Labourers, but it could only really exist in the cordoned-off space of an official literary discourse such as *Pearl*. In a poem that organizes, harmonizes, and neatens up everything, the relations between laborer and landlord have been rendered almost entirely unproblematic. Complaints from the field-workers are set aside. The standardized wage of a penny per day is rigorously enforced. And the landlord has the last word in commanding submission from his harvesters.

Notes

1 The centrality of the Vineyard Parable has been emphasized by Ian Bishop, '*Pearl* in its Setting (Oxford: Blackwell, 1968), pp. 122–5; Anne Douglas Wood, 'The *Pearl*-Dreamer and the *Hyne* in the Vineyard Parable', *Philological Quarterly* 52 (1973), 9–19; Kevin Marti, *Body, Heart, and Text in the 'Pearl'-Poet* (Lewiston NY: Edwin Mellen, 1991), pp. 83–99; and Ad Putter, *An Introduction to the Gawain-poet* (Harlow: Longman, 1996), pp. 168–77.

2 For longer passages from *Pearl*, I cite Marie Borroff's translation from *The Norton Anthology of English Literature* 7th edn, ed. M. H. Abrams (New York: Norton, 2000), pp. 299–328.

3 *Patrologia Latina*, ed. Jacques–Paul Migne (Paris: Migne, 1844–55), hereafter *PL* in text.

4 *The Sermons of Thomas Brinton, Bishop of Rochester (1373–1389)*, ed. Sr Mary Aquinas Devlin, 2 vols (London: Camden 3rd ser., no. 86, 1954), 2: 330–5.

5 See the edition by Nancy H. Owen, 'Thomas Wimbledon's Sermon: "Redde racionem villicacionis tue"', *Medieval Studies* 28 (1966), 176–97 (178). See

---

[a] Contracted to no [other] place.

Andrew W. Cole, 'Trifunctionality and the Tree of Charity: Literary and Social Practice in *Piers Plowman*', *English Literary History* 62 (1995), 1–27.

6 M. M. Postan, 'Medieval Agrarian Society in its Prime: England', in *The Cambridge Economic History of Europe*, vol. 1: *The Agrarian Life of the Middle Ages*, 2nd edn (Cambridge: Cambridge University Press, 1966), esp. 'Freedom and Servility', pp. 604–10; Rodney H. Hilton, *The Decline of Serfdom in Medieval England*, 2nd edn (London: Macmillan, 1983), pp. 23–47; 'Peasant Movements in England before 1381' (1974) rept. *Class, Conflict and the Crisis of Feudalism* (London: Hambledon, 1985), pp. 122–38, esp. 135–8; Barbara A. Hanawalt, 'Peasant Resistance', in F. X. Newman (ed.), *Social Unrest in the Late Middle Ages* (Binghamton, NY: Center for Medieval and Renaissance Texts and Studies, 1986), pp. 23–47; and Steven A. Epstein, *Wage Labor and Guilds in Medieval Europe* (Chapel Hill, NC: University of North Carolina Press, 1991), pp. 232–48. H. J. Hewitt, *Mediaeval Cheshire* (Manchester: Manchester University Press, 1929), pp. 148–50, deals with labor abuses at harvest time specifically in the hundred of Macclesfield.

7 See Walter Ullmann, *The Medieval Foundations of Renaissance Humanism* (Ithaca, NY: Cornell University Press, 1977), p. 84.

8 Bertha Haven Putnam, *The Enforcement of the Statutes of Labourers during the First Decade after the Black Death, 1349–1359* (New York: Columbia University Studies in History, Economics and Public Law, no. 32, 1908), pp. 153–218. See also May McKisack, *The Fourteenth Century* (Oxford: Clarendon Press, 1959), pp. 339–40.

9 On the symbolic significance of the August setting, see P. M. Kean, *The Pearl: An Interpretation* (New York: Barnes and Noble, 1967), pp. 48–52, and Lynn Staley Johnson, 'The *Pearl* Dreamer and the Eleventh Hour', in Robert J. Blanch, Miriam Youngerman Miller and Julian N. Wasserman (eds), *Text and Matter: New Critical Perspectives of the Pearl-poet* (Troy, NY: Whitston, 1991), pp. 3–15.

10 McKisack, *The Fourteenth Century*, p. 338.

11 Nora Kenyon, 'Labour Conditions in Essex in the Reign of Richard II', *Economic History Review* 4 (1934), 429–51 (438). Hewitt, *Mediaeval Cheshire*, p. 149, notes that offenders were usually described as harvesters who disappeared in autumn; the phrase that recurs in the rolls of indictments is 'exierunt a patria tempore autumpni'. Christopher Dyer, *Standards of Living in the Later Middle Ages: Social Change in England c. 1200–1520* (Cambridge: Cambridge University Press, 1989), pp. 158–9, makes the point that harvest workers deserved more because they worked harder within severe constraints of time, and needed more food to sustain these hard physical efforts.

12 Kenyon, 'Labour Conditions', 432–3. Her Appendix B-II 'Harvest Workers' makes it obvious that the wage-level of a penny per day would have been outrageously low even before the arrival of the Black Death.

13 Dyer, *Standards of Living*, pp. 261–5.

14 The poet's fastidious concern for proportion has been the focus of many studies: Coolidge Otis Chapman, 'Numerical Symbolism in Dante and the *Pearl*', *Modern Language Notes* 54 (1939), 256–9; Maren-Sofie Røstvig, 'Numerical Composition in *Pearl*: A Theory', *English Studies* 48 (1967), 326–32; and John V. Fleming, 'The Centuple Structure of the *Pearl*', in Bernard S. Levy and Paul E. Szarmach (eds), *The Alliterative Tradition in the Fourteenth Century* (Kent, OH: Kent State University Press, 1981), pp. 81–98.

15   Jim Rhodes, 'The Dreamer Redeemed: Exile and the Kingdom in the Middle English *Pearl*', *Studies in the Age of Chaucer* 16 (1994), 119–42.

BALANCING
TEXT AND
CONTEXT

Not all critics would follow Bowers in his treatment of literary and non-literary texts within the same frame of reference. The frequent objection levelled against 'critical historicism' or 'new historicism' is that such approaches, for all their helpful interrogation of the cultural and ideological forces underpinning texts, tell us little about the 'literariness' of literature. If New Criticism was too strident in severing text from context, does critical historicism risk losing sight of text in a welter of context, missing the wood for the trees?

In the light of this question, our second extract strikes a different balance, drawing on sociolinguistics and speech-act theory in order to place a greater focus on the question of literary practice. Helen Barr's 'Constructing Social Realities' reconceptualizes the literary language of medieval texts as a *social discourse*, replete with social resonance for contemporary audiences, and capable of being read back into the varieties of discourse – clerical, legal, civil – from which it is derived. The extract focuses upon a short poem which enjoys a precise and well-documented historical context. Thomas Hoccleve's *To Sir John Oldcastle* was written following the 1413 rebellion against the Lancastrian regime of Henry IV (who had himself come to power by deposing Richard II in 1399). Oldcastle, a sympathizer of Lollard religious views, appeared to be implicated in the rebellion; Hoccleve's poem calls for the knight to recant and reform.

Key to the extract is Barr's sense of poem as *practice*. In line with 'speech-act theory', the literary text is viewed as an intervention in a wider textual (and social) debate around dissidence, hierarchy and social order. The text is seen as proactive; it 'performs' discursive manoeuvres. Reconceived as a social discourse, literary language bears the marks of history at every turn, playing its own part in producing historical and cultural understanding. From such a critical stance, text and context, literature and history no longer represent binary opposites but, rather, two sides of the same coin.

Extract from Helen Barr, 'Constructing Social Realities', in *Socioliterary Practice in Late Medieval England* (Oxford: Oxford University Press, 2001), pp. 27–34.

[. . .] The poem was written after the rebellion in 1413 which the Lollard knight Oldcastle was reputed to have organized. Paul Strohm has recently argued that Oldcastle was framed by the Lancastrian regime as a threat to social order and that the revolt in 1413 was fathered upon him as part of an attempt to bolster Lancastrian rule. Dogged by the shadow of usurpation following the deposition of Richard II in 1399, Henry IV and his advisers needed to find ways to construct the new regime as one that was legitimate. By casting Lollards in general, and Oldcastle in particular, as a menace to the realm, the Lancastrian regime could deflect scrutiny about its own legitimacy by projecting questions of order, threat, and stability onto perceived heretics. Oldcastle was useful for the Lancastrians as a figure of insurgence. Through being seen as defenders of the security of the realm, and punishing anyone who threatened social stability, the Lancastrian regime authorized its right to rule.[1]

Hoccleve's poem is entirely complicit in this Lancastrian framing of Oldcastle. Ostensibly, the poem is an appeal to the knight to recant his heretical views. The terms in which it does so re-create the Lancastrian project to present Henry's rule as God-given and sanctioned, while Lollardy is seen as evil perfidy. The narrator calls on Oldcastle to quench his 'pryde' and 'presumpcioun', diction which frames Oldcastle as a Lucifer figure.[2] Mercy, however, is still available to the errant knight: 'it renneth al in brede' (70). A well of mercy is a figure familiar from religious lyrics[3] which Hoccleve here reregisters to present the Lancastrian regime as one that is ever merciful, willing to take even their Luciferian son back into their bosom.[4]

Hoccleve also mobilized the diction of Christian knighthood in order to effect an opposition between Oldcastle's disobedience and the God-sanctioned chivalry of the Lancastrian regime. The narrator calls on Oldcastle to be Christ's champion (69). This is a deeply resonant image. The poem was written as Henry V was embarking on a voyage to wage war against the French, and the conclusion of the poem implores Oldcastle to resume his knightly ways; to join the king in the war (509–12). Hoccleve legitimizes the military campaign against the French by framing Oldcastle, a figure who is cast as a threat to God-given social order, as one who ought to know his duty in joining the campaign, but who has preferred instead to abandon his rightful social duties. The narrator reminds Oldcastle that there was a time when if knighthood was being practised, then he would have been there (505–7). The lines explicitly yoke chivalry with 'manhode' (506), a quality which Oldcastle has abandoned because he has changed his 'gyse' (508) by aligning himself with the devil rather than the king. By deploying diction from a mixture of religious, chivalric, and gendered registers, the poem figures Oldcastle as unruly, feminine, and fiendish. All of this stands in stark contrast to the bold chivalry of the manly champion of Christ, Henry V, who is, as the poem states, 'our cristen Prince' (499). The first-person plural pronoun is important in constructing the writer and his audience as loyal to the king while Oldcastle stands outside this discourse of Christian allegiance.

The strategy of casting Oldcastle as an 'outsider', or as a threat to a benign and proper order is omnipresent. What is especially interesting about this poem is how these tropes of civil obedience are explicitly related to literary practice:

> Bewar Oldcastel & for Cristes sake
> Clymbe no more in holy writ so hie!
> Rede the storie of Lancelot de lake
> Or Vegece[a] of the aart of Chiualrie
> The seege of Troie, or Thebes thee applie
> To thyng þat may to thordre of knyght[b] longe![c]
> To thy correccioun now haaste and hie,
> For thow haast been out of ioynt al to longe.
>
> If thee list[d] thyng rede of auctoritee,
> To thise stories sit[e] it thee to goon:
> To Iudicum, Regum and Iosue,[f]
> To Iudith[g] & to Paralipomenon,[h]
> And Machabe & as siker as stoon,[i]
> If þat thee list in hem bayte thyn ye[j]
> More autentike thing shalt thow fynde noon,
> Ne more pertinent to Chiualrie.

(193–208)

Social rectitude is explicitly aligned with appropriate reading matter. As a knight, Oldcastle has transgressed by reading Holy Writ.[5] The use of diction such as 'clymbe so hie', and 'correccioun' figures Oldcastle's reading activity as presumptuous, anti-hierarchical, and disobedient. These lines offer up a model of policed reading: Oldcastle should read only those parts of the Bible which pertain to Christian knighthood. Such matter will, of course, implicitly provide Oldcastle with a mirror of his own liege lord, the Christian soldier knight, King Henry, after whom he should fashion his own behaviour. Throughout the poem, civil upset is figured as dissident reading. An earlier passage in the poem proleptically aligns Oldcastle's transgressive reading with the unruly female body:[6]

[a] Vegetius, Roman writer on military strategy.
[b] the order of knighthood.
[c] belong.
[d] desire.
[e] behoves.
[f] Judges, Kings and Joshua.
[g] (Apocryphal) Book of Judith.
[h] Chronicles.
[i] solid/trusty as stone.
[j] If you wish to feast your eye on them.

Some wommen eeke, thogh hir wit^a be thynne,
Wole argumentes make in holy writ!
Lewde calates!^b sittith doun and spynne,
And kakele of sumwhat elles, for your wit
Is al to feeble to despute of it!
To Clerkes grete apparteneth^c þat aart
The knowleche of þat, god hath for yow shit;^d
Stynte and leue of for right sclendre is your paart.
Oure fadres olde and modres lyued wel,
And taghte hir children as hemself taght were
Of holy chirche and axid nat a del^e
'Why stant this word heere?' And 'why this word there?'
'Why spake god thus and seith thus elles where?'
'Why dide he this wyse and might han do^f thus?'
Oure fadres medled no thing of swich gere:^g
þat oghte been a good mirror to vs.

(145–60)

The imperative and axiomatic tone of these stanzas is characteristic of the whole poem. There is little use of modality in the verbs used in this poem; and an absence of conditionality or possibility.[7] Hoccleve makes one propositional statement after another, which orders the conviction that society is set out unconditionally and immutably in a fixed pattern which it is dissident to alter. Subjects must unquestioningly obey according to social rank; they should not meddle.

In these stanzas, women are characteristically seen as lacking the intellect to argue points of Christian doctrine. It is noteworthy that Hoccleve attributes direct speech to them, emphasizing their orality rather than their literacy. And their orality is animalistic; like hens, they cackle. No reading matter is allocated to women, in contrast to the chivalric syllabus enjoined on Oldcastle. Rather, they must clothe the menfolk and the children. They must sit (a verb which emphasizes keeping very firmly in their place), and spin.[8] Reading and intellectual argument is not for them. For a woman to open a book is to contravene God's authority and to usurp the learned discourse of the clerics.

Lines 152–60 picture a social vignette of correct reading practice in which a stable society nourishes infantilized reading. Hoccleve mobilizes the

^a intelligence.
^b ignorant fools!
^c pertains.
^d shut off.
^e questioned not at all.
^f have done.
^g in such matters.

conventional trope of an idealized past as a foil against the corruptions of the present[9] to describe how good-living parents taught children as they themselves were taught. Socially correct reading is figured as an activity in which no questions are asked. There is no swerving from axiomatic truth and no interrogation of narrative order or interpretation. To query the arrangement of words or tensions of meaning between different passages is to unfix social and ecclesiastical order.

Rather, the meaning of a text is passed on in a kind of patrilinear succession. The family provides a stable frame to secure unmediated interpretation. While it is initially both fathers and mothers who teach their children, the ultimate exemplary figures are fathers: good mirrors to sons. Any construction of individuality or subjectivity is repressed. When a child looks into a mirror, what it sees is not its own reflection, but the authority of the father. In developing this model, texts are seen as property which is to be passed on to father and son:

> If land to thee be falle of heritage,
> Which þat thy fadir heelde in reste & pees,
> With title iust and treewe in al his age,
> And his father before him brygelees,[a]
> And his and his, & so foorth, doutelees,
> I am ful seur,[b] whoso wolde it reue,[c]
> Thow woldest thee deffende & putte in prees;[d]
> Thy right[e] thow woldest nat, thy thankes, leue.
>
> (161–8)

In these lines, Hoccleve selects diction from legal discourse: 'title . . . treewe'; 'his and his'; 'deffende'; 'right', and 'reue'[10] to argue that to disturb patrilinear succession is to break the law. To intervene in a patrilineal practice of interpretation is figured as a kind of 'breaking and entering'; an act of theft. A society which is a model of rectitude requires an unbroken succession of fathers all concerned to defend the sacred text of the Bible from violent appropriation by criminals. Hoccleve is on dangerous ground here. For, of course, the violation of patrilinear descent was exactly what the Lancastrians were anxious to deny they had committed in succeeding to the throne after Richard's deposition. By projecting such an act onto Oldcastle, Hoccleve exculpates the contemporary regime from such a charge and indicts a conveniently constructed menace with the crime instead.[11]

[a] undisputed.
[b] sure.
[c] remove.
[d] enter the fray.
[e] legal entitlement.

The correct use of literary texts envisaged in this poem is one that endorses normative social hierarchy. The third estate is excluded from access to authoritative texts; if a bailiff, a man of craft, or a reeve try to prove Christian faith by reason, they 'dote or raue' (144). To usurp social position in attempting to question what is beyond interrogation is seen to be an act of madness. Yet again, Hoccleve mobilizes an oppositional discourse; here, one which separates the mad from the sane, the unruly from the civilized.[12] There are no grey areas in this poem: dissident conduct is set at odds with an immutably proper civil order.

Throughout this poem Hoccleve images an unbendingly fixed picture of social relationships which are rooted in obedience to the Christian king and are organized around a rigid model of decorous reading practices. Several discourses are mobilized to endorse quietistic consumption of literary texts. In order to demonize (quite literally) unauthorized readings of the Bible, Hoccleve deploys figurative diction and analogies which yoke together discourses of patrilinear descent, transfer of property, legal ownership, land law, the normative model of the three estates, and conservative relations between men and women. These discourses of social rectitude are reinforced by a series of binary oppositions: Christ and Lucifer; past and present; reason and madness; high and low; movement and stillness; and obedience and disorder. The sheer number of normative discourses used, and their accretive interlayering, is a measure of the force of the threat that Hoccleve seeks to neutralize. This, together with the insistent use of propositional statements, and absence of modality, creates a style that is so over-determined and obstinate that the very strenuousness of the assertions bespeak a high level of anxiety. There is rather too much protestation which points, ironically enough, not to the naturalness of the model of civic order which Hoccleve presents, but to its constructedness. Hoccleve's over-assertion of his message, and the inflexibility of the reading he permits, expose how his normative language of social description is under pressure from contemporary processes and practices. The picture which he presents has a material reality, but it is forged from literary motifs whose dominance had already been effectively challenged by newly emergent civil and religious discourses. The sheer conservatism of Hoccleve's imagery and diction is an index of how besieged a position he adopts politically. For all the discursive manoeuvres to bridle unruliness which the poem performs, both the strident inflexibility of its literary materials and the evident anxiety about unpoliced reading, show that Hoccleve is closing the stable door after the horse has bolted.

When viewed alongside some of Hoccleve's other writings, the positionality of the stern moralizing in *Oldcastle* seems almost comic. From the *Oldcastle* poem, we are led to believe that the only socially obedient reading which Hoccleve sanctions is that which is undigested, unruminative, unexamined, and uninterpreted. But Hoccleve knew only too well, of course, that reading matter passed from fathers to sons was not ingested open-mouthed and swallowed wholesale. In *Regement of Princes* he creates for himself a literary persona which explicitly models himself as the son of Chaucer, and the ways that Hoccleve plays with the father–son poetic legacy[13] show only too clearly that the infantilized reading figured in *Oldcastle* is a piece of political opportunism:

> O maister deere, and fadir reuerent!
> Mi maister Chaucer, flour of eloquence,
> Mirour of fructuous entendement[a]
> O, vniversal fadir in science![b]
>
> (1961–4)

It is noteworthy that the image of the mirror which Hoccleve uses to suggest Oldcastle fashion himself after King Harry is here deployed to create a flattering image of Hoccleve's own poetic skills.[14] Hoccleve selects just those qualities about Chaucer's writing which can be seen to legitimize his own poetic project: learnedness, eloquence, knowledge. This is a highly selective and sanitized view. There is no mention of anything which might compromise the moral seriousness of this universal father. But Hoccleve was clearly aware of such elements in Chaucer's poetry. In lamenting Chaucer's death Hoccleve writes:

> Mi dere maistir – god his soule quyte![c]
> And fadir, Chaucer, fayn wolde han me taght;
> But I was dul and lernéd lite or naght.
>
> (2077–9)

The last line shows very clearly one thing that Hoccleve learnt from his illustrious father, the construction of a naive and ingenuous persona as narrator.[15] While the joke is ostensibly on Hoccleve himself, and his dull-wittedness, there are broader implications for reading the social poetics of Hoccleve's writing. Awareness of narrative positionality has potentially radical implications. To place an unreliable narrator at the heart of a work is to render its propositionality provisional and unstable. Such a narrative consciousness invites exactly the kind of readerly intervention in the text that Hoccleve is so anxious to deplore in *Oldcastle*. Far from the narrator telling the reader exactly what to think (even if ultimately, the constructedness of that position is self-evident), a self-effacing narratorial presence points, not to fixed statements, but to the arbitrariness of utterance. And once arbitrariness is placed at the

[a] fruitful instruction.
[b] knowledge.
[c] reward.

centre of textuality, then social relations and processes are placed in the melting pot. [. . .] [B]ecause language is itself a social process, to play with textuality is to play with social paradigms. [. . .]

Notes

1 Paul Strohm, *England's Empty Throne: Usurpation and the Language of Legitima-tion* (New Haven, CT, 1998), pp. 65–86.

2 *To Sir John Oldcastle*, in *Hoccleve's Works: The Minor Poems*, ed. F. J. Furnivall and I. Gollancz, rev. Jerome Mitchell and A. I. Doyle (EETS ES 67, 73 1970), l. 66. In the play of *Lucifer* in *The Chester Mystery Cycle*, ed. R. M. Lumiansky and David Mills (EETS SS 3 1974), Lucifer declares himself to be 'pearlesse and prince of pride' (184); 'pearlesse' figures his revolt socially as well as theologically.

3 For example, Douglas Gray (ed.), *A Selection of Religious Lyrics* (Oxford, 1975), nos. 35 and 42.

4 Cf. Hoccleve's *Regement of Princes*, ed. F. J. Furnivall (EETS ES 72 1987), where the beggar states that Henry, as prince of Wales, was present at John Badby's burning and begged him to recant his heretical views to avoid punishment, ll. 295–322.

5 Cf. *Against the Lollards* in *Historical Poems of the XIVth and XVth Centuries*, ed. R. H. Robbins (New York, 1959), pp. 152–7, where it is stated that it is 'unkyn-dely for a kniȝt / þat shuld a kynges castel kepe, / To babel þe bibel day & niȝt', 25–8.

6 Strohm (*England's Empty Throne*, pp. 184–5) notes how Hoccleve's accusation that Oldcastle lacks manhood is reflected in his reading practice.

7 Fowler analyses modality as an aspect of social discourse, in Roger Fowler, *Liter-ature as Social Discourse* (London: Routledge 1981), pp. 89–91.

8 Cf. *The Book of Margery Kempe*, ed. S. B. Meech and H. E. Allen (EETS OS 212 1940), p. 129/35–6, where the people of Beverly tell Kempe to go and 'spynne & card as oþer women don'.

9 Thomas J. Elliott discusses this conventional topos in 'Middle English Complaints Against the Times: To Contemn the World or to Reform It?', *Annuale Medievale* 14 (1973), 22–35 (23). Se also V. J. Scattergood, *Politics and Poetry in the Fifteenth Century* (London, 1971), pp. 309–10.

10 See *MED* 'treue-title' 13(e); 'his' pron (2); I(a); 'defenden' 5(b)' 'right'(n) 5(a); 'reven' I (a).

11 This is discussed by Strohm, *England's Empty Throne*, pp. 183–4.

12 Michel Foucault discusses how the division between reason and madness is one of the procedures for regulating discourse, in 'The Order of Discourse', In Robert Young (ed.), *Untying the Text* (London: Routledge and Kegan Paul, 1981), pp. 53–4, a subject he treats at length in *Madness and Reason: A History of Insanity in the Age of Reason*, trans. Richard Howard (New York, 1965).

13 Strohm discusses the Lancastrian implications of these lines in *England's Empty Throne*, pp. 147–8 and 182. See also Derek Pearsall, 'Hoccleve's *Regement of*

Princes: The Poetics of Royal Self-representation', *Speculum* 69 (1994), 386–410 (403–4).

14   Hoccleve uses the image of the mirror at several points in his poems; James Simpson analyses its use in the *Series* poems, 'Madness and Texts: Hoccleve's *Series*', in Julia Boffey and Janet Cowen (eds.), *Chaucer and Fifteenth Century Poetry* (London, 1991), pp. 15–26, as part of Hoccleve's exploration into ways of establishing himself as a figure of authority, pp. 24–5.

15   See T. W. Machan, 'Textual Authority and the Works of Hoccleve, Lydgate and Henryson', *Viator* 23 (1992), 281–99, repr. in Daniel Pinti (ed.), *Writing after Chaucer: Essential Readings in Chaucer and the Fifteenth Century* (New York and London, 1998), pp. 177–96 (178), where he observes that the numerous autobiographical passages show an awareness – perhaps learnt from Chaucer – of a narrator's rhetorical presence in his own narration. See also D. C. Greetham, 'Self-referential Artefacts: Hoccleve's Persona as a Literary Device', *Modern Philology* 86 (1989), 242–51.

LITERATURE AND HISTORY: AN ONGOING DEBATE   The debate over critical historicism is a defining feature of contemporary Middle English studies, returning readers to the basic question of how text and context inter-relate. For all their misconceptions regarding the Middle Ages, perhaps the early antiquarians were not so very wide of the mark in viewing the issue of literature and history as an especially pointed one for medieval texts. As David Wallace's comment at the close of the last millennium suggests, the historical context of medieval literature is in one sense inescapable: 'Medieval literature cannot be understood (does not survive) except as part of transmissive processes – moving through the hands of copyists, owners, readers and institutional authorities – that form part of other and greater histories (social, political, religious and economic)'.[38] As readers of medieval texts, the past is always with us.

Further Reading

David Matthews gives an informative and entertaining account of the 'invention' of Middle English by the antiquarians and the Victorian medievalists: *The Making of Middle English, 1765–1910* (Minneapolis, MN: University of Minnesota Press, 1999). Lee Patterson's *Negotiating the Past: The Historical Understanding of Medieval Literature* (Madison: University of Wisconsin Press, 1987) supplies both a detailed analytical history of medievalist historicism and an exemplary model of modern critical historicism. Patterson also edited a volume of collaborative essays employing critical historicist approaches: *Literary Practice and Social Change in Britain, 1380–1530* (Berkeley, CA: University of California Press, 1990). An extract from Patterson's *Chaucer and the Subject of History* (London: Routledge, 1991) appears in chapter 8.

In the 1970s the journal *New Literary History* published some important articles on the question of the 'alterity' of the Middle Ages, the most influential being Hans Robert Jauss's 'The Alterity and Modernity of Medieval Literature', *New Literary History* 10 (1978–9), 181–229. An important study of Middle English dissident writing in the period of the 'peasant's revolt' is Stephen Justice's *Writing and Rebellion: England in 1381* (Berkeley, CA: University of California Press, 1994), and for a wide-ranging collaborative volume on literature and history, see David Aers (ed.), *Medieval Literature and Historical Enquiry* (Cambridge: D. S. Brewer, 2000).

Chapter Notes

1 BL Add MS 27879, cited in David Matthews, *The Making of Middle English, 1765–1910* (Minneapolis, MN: University of Minnesota Press, 1999), p. 9.

2 Thomas Percy, *Reliques of Ancient English Poetry*, Vol. I (London: J. Dodsley, 1765), p. 8.

3 Thomas Warton, *The History of English Poetry* (London: Ward Lock and Co, 1870), p. 34.

4 Ibid, p. 162.

5 Matthews, *The Making of Middle English*, p. 15.

6 John S. P. Tatlock, 'The Duration of the Canterbury Pilgrimage', *PMLA* 21 (1906), 478–85 (478).

7 J. W. H. Atkins in A. W. Ward and A. R. Waller (eds), *The Cambridge History of English Literature*, Vol. I (Cambridge: Cambridge University Press, 1907), p. 317.

8 W. P. Ker, *English Literature: Medieval* (London: Williams and Norgate, 1912), p. 112.

9 Harvey Eagleson, 'Costume in the Middle English Metrical Romances', *PMLA* 47 (1932), 339–45.

10 Nellie Slayton Aurner, 'Sir Thomas Malory – Historian?', *PMLA* 48 (1933), 362–91 (391).

11 George Lyman Kittredge, *Chaucer and his Poetry* (Cambridge, MA: Harvard University Press, 1915), p. 149.

12 J. M. Manly, *Some New Light on Chaucer* (New York: Henry Holt and Co., 1926), p. 82.

13 Howard R. Patch, 'Desiderata in Middle English Research', *Modern Philology* 22 (1924), 27–34 (30–1).

14 George Lyman Kittredge, *A Study of Sir Gawain and the Green Knight* (Cambridge, MA: Harvard University Press, 1916).

15 J. R. R. Tolkien and E. V. Gordon (eds), *Sir Gawain and the Green Knight* (Oxford: Oxford University Press, 1925).

16 Jessie L. Weston, *The Legend of Sir Gawain: Studies upon its Original Scope and Significance* (London: David Nutt, 1897).

17   Jessie L. Weston, *From Ritual to Romance* (Cambridge: Cambridge University Press, 1920).

18   William A. Nitze, 'Is the Green Knight Story a Vegetation Myth?', *Modern Philology* 33 (1936), 351–66 (365).

19   R . S. Loomis, *Celtic Myth and Arthurian Romance* (New York: Columbia University Press, 1927).

20   R. S. Loomis, 'Notes on Laȝamon', *Review of English Studies* 10 (1934), 78–84.

21   R. S. Loomis, 'Gawain, Gwri, and Cuchulainn', *PMLA* 43 (1928), 384–96; 'The Visit to the Perilous Castle: A Study in the Arthurian Modifications of an Irish Theme', *PMLA* 48 (1933) 1000–35; 'More Celtic Elements in *Sir Gawain and the Green Knight*', *Journal of English and Germanic Philology* 42 (1943), 149–84.

22   George Kane, *Middle English Literature* (London: Methuen, 1951), p. vii.

23   John Speirs, *Medieval English Poetry: The Non-Chaucerian Tradition* (London: Faber, 1957); A. C. Spearing, *Criticism and Medieval Poetry* (London: Edward Arnold, 1964); John Burrow, *A Reading of 'Sir Gawain and the Green Knight'* (London: Routledge and Kegan Paul, 1965); Trevor Whittock, *A Reading of the Canterbury Tales* (Cambridge: Cambridge University Press, 1968); P. M. Kean, *The Pearl: An Interpretation* (New York: Barnes and Noble, 1967); Ian Bishop, *Pearl in its Setting* (Oxford: Blackwell, 1968).

24   D. W. Robertson, Jr, 'Historical Criticism', in A. S. Downer (ed.), *English Institute Essays, 1950* (New York: Columbia University Press, 1951).

25   Trevor Whittock, *A Reading of the Canterbury Tales* (Cambridge: Cambridge University Press, 1968), p. 14.

26   Margaret Schlauch, *English Medieval Literature and Its Social Foundations* (Oxford: Oxford University Press, 1956), p. 184.

27   R. H. Robbins (ed.), *Historical Poems of the XIVth and XVth Centuries* (New York: Columbia University Press, 1959), p. xxiii.

28   V. J. Scattergood, *Politics and Poetry in the Fifteenth Century* (London: Blandford Press, 1971), pp. 10–11.

29   Paul Strohm, *Hochon's Arrow: The Social Imagination of Fourteenth-century Texts* (Princeton, NJ: Princeton University Press, 1992), pp. 6–9.

30   John Burrow, *Ricardian Poetry: Chaucer, Gower, Langland and the 'Gawain'-poet* (Harmondsworth: Penguin, 1971).

31   Anne Middleton, 'The Idea of Public Poetry in the Reign of Richard II', *Speculum* 53 (1978), 94–114 (95).

32   Michael J. Bennett, *Community, Class and Careerism: Cheshire and Lancashire Society in the Age of 'Sir Gawain and the Green Knight'* (Cambridge: Cambridge University Press, 1983).

33   Janet Coleman, *Medieval Readers and Writers 1350–1400*. English Literature in History (London: Hutchinson, 1981), pp. 15–16.

34   Derek Pearsall, 'Chaucer's Poetry and its Modern Commentators: The Necessity of History', in David Aers (ed.), *Medieval Literature: Criticism, Ideology and History* (Brighton: Harvester, 1986), pp. 132–3.

35 Stephen Knight, *Geoffrey Chaucer* (Oxford: Blackwell, 1986), p. 6.
36 Lynn Staley Johnson, *The Voice of the Gawain-poet* (Madison: University of Wisconsin Press, 1984), p. xvi.
37 Lee Patterson (ed.), *Literary Practice and Social Change in Britain, 1380–1530* (Berkeley, CA: University of California Press, 1990), p. 5.
38 David Wallace 'General Preface', in David Wallace (ed.), *The Cambridge History of Medieval English Literature* (Cambridge: Cambridge University Press, 1999), p. xxi.

7

Gender

An introduction to the background and context of three Middle English gender studies: Sheila Delany's Marxist–feminist reading of The Wife of Bath *and* The Book of Margery Kempe; *Elizabeth Robertson's feminist approach to the body and identity in the* Ancrene Wisse *and Julian of Norwich's* Showings; *Laurie A. Finke and Martin B. Schichtman's gender study of masculinity and violence in Malory's* Morte Darthur.

When did Middle English gender studies first emerge? An answer will depend on our definition of key terms. For theoretically informed and politically aligned critical work on feminism, gender and sexual identity, we must wait until the boom period of the 1970s and 1980s. But if, for example, 'feminist study' is defined more loosely as any work committed to increasing knowledge of the place, status and condition of women in the Middle Ages we can point to examples of such scholarship from an encouragingly early date. Hope Emily Allen was writing on the origins and authorship of the *Ancrene Wisse* as early as 1918;[1] Eileen Power was researching medieval women's religious communities in 1922.[2] One writer on the development of feminism and medievalism suggests that we might even look back as far as 1893 for our starting-point, when Florence Buckstaff published an article on the legal rights of married women in medieval England.[3]

Though its origins may be difficult to pinpoint, today the presence of a flourishing gender studies is one of the most distinctive features on the map of Middle English studies. Perhaps more than any other critical school represented in this book, feminist and gender studies are one of the most dynamic and fast-growing areas of the field, pushing forth the boundaries of scholarship both in print and on the web (while you are reading this chapter, postings and updates on the many sites devoted to medieval gender are busy putting it out of date). Any brief review of so rich and diverse a field must be general. But the story of the development of gender studies can be told through the examples of the three extracts given in this chapter. The first, Sheila Delany's essay on Chaucer and Margery Kempe, dates from the early 1980s, and reflects the radical re-reading of central Middle English texts in the light of feminist theory. The second, Elizabeth Robertson's essay on *Ancrene Wisse* and Julian of Norwich's *Showings*, shows how the feminist criticism of the early 1990s made increasing use of theoretical work on gender, the body and individual identity. Drawn from the close of the 1990s, our final extract, Laurie A. Finke and Martin B. Schichtman's reading of Malory's *Morte Darthur*, shows the increasing diversification of gender studies that took place throughout the last decade of the twentieth century, including the rise of masculinity studies and queer theory.

The strange bedfellows of Chaucer and Margery Kempe have formed the most fruitful subjects for feminist and gender studies in Middle English. Chaucer's text speaks to us from the centre of a male-dominated literary canon, Margery's from its margins. The questions asked of Chaucer's works by gender studies are enduring ones: how far do these texts simply replicate the dominant gender ideology of the late fourteenth century, how far do they subvert it? Do Chaucer's women transcend the stereotyping of the medieval misogynist tradition? Was Chaucer, indeed, 'evir womanis frend' as sixteenth-century poet Gavin Douglas saw it? The questions asked of Margery's text are similar. Does Margery internalize the invidious gender ideology of her own age or does the fluid and visionary prose of her spiritual autobiography somehow subvert it? The critical debate concerning both authors' gender politics is a lively one.

By the time Sheila Delany came to link Margery Kempe with the Wife of Bath, rival camps had already formed in arguing for the pro- or anti-feminist Chaucer. In 1971, Daniel Murtaugh's essay on 'Women and Geoffrey Chaucer' considered that the poet 'may seem "ahead of his time" in his firm insistence that women are the moral equals of men'.[4] By contrast, Hope Phyllis Weissman was writing four years later of 'Antifeminism in Chaucer's Characterization of Women'.[5] Delany's essay nevertheless had a radical impact when it appeared in the *Minnesota Review* of 1975 and again, eight years later, in the book *Writing Woman*. Here, the frame of interpretation was explicitly Marxist–feminist: key references in this reading of Chaucer would not be to Kittredge and Manly but to Marx and Engels. The essay's socio-economic emphasis is germane to its feminism: it is as oppressed women within their specific economic class that the fictional wife and the historical Margery are considered. Literary and historical text are placed in dynamic relation to one another. In Delany's view, Margery's account of her experience can be used to uncover what is excluded, marginalized or simply not seen in Chaucer's text: 'the remarkable

Book of Margery Kempe gives us a social reality that Chaucer could neither observe firsthand nor sympathize with if he saw' (a suggestion which, contentiously for some, rests on a view of Chaucer as principally a court poet). The result is a landmark re-reading of Middle English texts in the light of their gender politics and their socio-economic contexts. Hindsight shows Delany's essay to be in the vanguard of the more radical, politically aligned currents of Middle English criticism that were to flourish in the 1980s and beyond.

Extract from Sheila Delany, 'Sexual Economics, Chaucer's Wife of Bath, and *The Book of Margery Kempe*', in *Writing Woman: Women Writers and Women in Literature: Medieval to Modern* (New York: Schocken, 1983), pp. 80–91.

[. . .] Let us begin with the specifics, by placing Margery Kempe in her social milieu. The exact dates of her birth and death are not known, but they can be safely estimated at about 1373 and 1438.[1] Her home was Lynn, Norfolk – Bishop's Lynn, as the city was called, after its ecclesiastical overlord, the Bishop of Norwich.[2] Because of its strategic location at the mouth of the Ouse River, and its function as the only port for the trade of seven shires (especially the Scandinavian trade), Lynn had by the thirteenth century established itself as one of the richest and most important commercial cities in England. It was also one of the staple towns for wool, that is, one of certain few designated towns where wool could be officially weighed, taxed, and shipped.

These two distinctive features, an ecclesiastical overlord and a thriving commercial base, meant that in Lynn, class struggle took on an even sharper and more protracted character than in most other English towns. For the effort of the upper bourgeoisie to gain political control of the city and establish its independence of the feudal aristocracy was met by more than the usual resistance. As A. S. Green points out:

> Prelates of the Church professed to rule with a double title, not only as feudal lords of the soil, but as guardians of the patrimony of St Peter, holding property in trust for a great spiritual corporation . . . Leaning on supernatural support for deliverance from all perils, it could the better refuse to discuss bargains suggested by mere political expediency.[3]

Such spiritually sanctioned intransigence led to many confrontations, both legal and physical. It is possible that as a child Margery witnessed the riotous expulsion of the bishop in 1377 by the armed populace of Lynn.[4]

It is important that we not misjudge Margery by viewing her through eighteenth-century spectacles. During the eighteenth century, such individualistic religious enthusiasm as Margery's was practiced largely by the lower-middle-class and proletarian members of dissenting sects. Though we may see Margery as a forerunner of later developments, she remained nonetheless an orthodox Catholic and member of the upper bourgeoisie of Lynn. Her father, John Brunham, was, she tells us, 'mayor five times of that worshipful borough, and alderman also many years'.[5] [. . .] Margery's husband also belonged to the upper ranks of the bourgeoisie who, by their wealth, qualified for the name of burgess (in contrast to the lower bourgeoisie and artisans who, as *inferiores*, were excluded from municipal government). Though John Kempe was not as consistently in the public eye as Brunham, he was also one of the first citizens of Lynn and was elected chamberlain in 1394.

In a passage that recalls the Wife of Bath's status-conscious love of finery (*General Prologue*, 448–52), Margery recounts 'her pride and pompous array' as a daughter of what Henri Pirenne has called 'the urban patriciate':

> for she wore gold pipes on her head, and her hoods, with the tippets, were slashed. Her cloaks also were slashed and laid with divers colors between the slashes, so that they should be the more staring to men's sight, and herself the more worshipped. (p. 12)

To become even richer – 'for pure covetousness and to maintain her pride', as the author puts it – Margery went into business for herself: first brewing, 'and was one of the greatest brewers in the town for three years or four, till she lost much money' (p. 13), then into grinding corn, with two horses and a hired employee, until that enterprise failed as well. Yet these ventures by no means impoverished Margery. She remained a rich woman despite her business losses, more solvent than her husband apparently, for when Margery asked her husband to remain chaste he countered by asking her to pay his debts (p. 31). Still later, the records of Lynn give notice of a Margeria Kempe being admitted to the Trinity Guild.

In brief, then, Margery Kempe was what the Wife of Bath would have liked to be: socially prominent and well-to-do, a member of one of the most prominent families in one of England's richest towns. It is with a grain of salt, then, that we must take R. W. Chambers' somewhat patronizing remarks about 'poor Margery',[6] even if we do not take 'poor' in its economic sense. Yet, of course, there is a kernel of truth in Chambers' epithet, inasmuch as what he was responding to – and what I suspect we respond to even more sympathetically – is the quality of personal agony in Margery's book. Margery's spiritual autobiography is, according to Chambers, disappointing and even 'from certain points of view, painful'. It is not a book of devotion; we are constantly aware of Margery in relation to her society; and it is the peculiar quality of her religious experience – unsatisfying for Chambers, fascinating for us – that it is so inadequate an instrument of transcendence.

We learn nothing of Margery's childhood – an omission to be regretted by psychoanalytic critics and social historians alike. The book opens with the fact of Margery's marriage at the age of twenty. Her first pregnancy occurred 'within a short time, as nature would'. Both pregnancy and labor were difficult, and during the pregnancy she was 'ever hindered by her enemy, the devil', so that she often did penance by fasting and prayer. After the birth of her child she 'went out of her mind', because of fear of damnation, for a period of eight months, during which time she suffered diabolical hallucinations. She was kept from suicide only by being bound night and day. Her remission came spontaneously with a vision of Jesus who, clad in a mantle of purple silk, sat by her bed and said, 'Daughter, why hast thou forsaken me and I forsook never thee?' (p. 11).

The next twenty-five years were an amalgam of worldly and religious experience; her business ventures, her prideful array, the temptation to adultery with a close friend who rejected her after he had made the initial advance, the bearing of fourteen children, and several serious illnesses including dysentery. Interspersed with these worldly concerns were visions of paradise; conversations with Mary and Jesus and SS Peter, Paul, and Catherine; auditory, olfactory, and other sensory hallucinations with religious import; diabolical fantasies of men (including priests) showing her their genitals; revulsion against 'fleshly communing' with her husband and repeated efforts to persuade him to abstain from sexual intercourse; travels to local and foreign shrines; and, in Jerusalem, the onset of what came to be her best-known trait, her 'crying', the uncontrollable sobbing and shouting that overcame her at moments of religious intensity, especially through pain and sorrow in contemplation of the Passion of Christ.

Eventually John Kempe was won over to the chaste life and took up separate residence in order to avoid gossip. In old age John fell downstairs in his own house, suffering a head injury that left him senile and incontinent. With characteristic split attention to physical detail and spiritual values, Margery describes their pathetic last years together:

> Then she took home her husband with her and kept him years after, as long as he lived, and had full much labour with him; for in his last days he turned childish again, and lacked reason, so that he could not do his own easement by going to a seat, or else he would not, but, as a child, voided his natural digestion in his linen clothes, where he sat by the fire or at the table, whichever it were; he would spare no place.
>
> And therefore was her labour much the more in washing and wringing, and her costage in firing; and it hindered her full much from contemplation, so that

many times she would have loathed her labour, save she bethought herself how she, in her young age, had full many delectable thoughts, fleshly lusts, and inordinate loves to his person.

It is easy enough to say, then, that the remarkable *Book of Margery Kempe* gives us a social reality that Chaucer could neither observe firsthand nor sympathize with if he saw. As a man, as a devout Catholic, as a highly placed civil servant and courtier, as a poet in the continental courtly tradition, he could scarcely be expected to see the bourgeois woman in other than the conventional doctrinal and literary terms. Chaucer shows us one version of the internalization of mercantile capitalism, the commodification of sexuality, but his neat schema is far too simple. The analogy between sexual and economic realms is engaging, in part because of its simplicity, and it helps Chaucer to expose what from the courtly point of view constitute the 'vices' of the bourgeoisie. Yet Margery's story shows that the bourgeois woman was far less likely to be a successful entrepreneur in her domestic life than she was to be an exploited worker; as Friedrich Engels remarked, 'Within the family the husband is the bourgeois and the wife represents the proletariat.'[7] Of course, Margery is far from being literally a proletarian, but the function of Engels' metaphor is to call attention to the special oppression of woman in class-structured society. It may be difficult to see Margery as an oppressed person when she is wealthy and seems to hold her own so well. Nonetheless I want to suggest that her book is precisely a document of the special oppression of women in early capitalist society. Despite her class position, and to some extent because of it, Margery is exposed to and has internalized the most damaging aspects of bourgeois society.

This is not to negate the significance or validity of other approaches to the book. Hope Emily Allen, first editor of the text, showed its indebtedness to the continental tradition of 'feminine mysticism', especially to the works of St Bridget of Sweden (who died in 1373 and was canonized in 1391, and whose chapel Margery visits in Rome), and Blessed Dorothea of Prussia.[8] Admittedly this tradition offered Margery a vocabulary and a form for the expression of her own experience, but it offers no understanding of the genesis of that experience. Nor is a psychoanalytic approach fully adequate to the task of explaining Margery and her book. Everyone agrees that she was 'neurotic'; Allen's diagnosis emphasizes hysteria, and to this we may add postpartum psychosis, wish-fulfillment, infantile regression, and reaction formation as obvious neurotic syndromes revealed in the book. Yet because psychoanalysis generally omits the social factor in the development of neurosis, suspending the individual in artificial isolation, it cannot provide a real understanding of neurosis, which is not, after all, an answer but the very thing to be explained. Both source study and psychoanalytic criticism must be supplemented with a methodology that places the individual in a social context and also provides as full as possible a definition of 'social context'. By placing Margery Kempe in time, place, and class, I have merely provided some of the data necessary to such an effort. I have not gone beyond the phenomena of history to the laws of history, nor have I dealt with the question of how Margery's internalization of the ethos of early capitalism is manifested in her book. I now want to focus on three aspects of the book that help us to address those problems. They are the author's constant awareness of money, her perception of herself as property, and the alienated quality of her relationships.

The transition from feudalism to capitalism during the later Middle Ages was the transition from an economy based on use value to one based on exchange value. The feudal manor produced goods (mainly agricultural) that were used or else exchanged for other goods. Feudal dues were generally paid in labor or in kind, and the manor's surplus was used by its producers or its owners. In such an economy money was not a prime necessity, and while it was never wholly absent in the earlier Middle Ages, it played a very limited role in the economy of Europe. The development of industry and of mercantile capitalism meant that goods were no longer being produced for immediate use, but rather for sale in domestic and foreign markets; they were to be exchanged not for other goods but for money. Money could be accumulated then reinvested for profit or lent at interest; large fortunes could be rapidly made; the big bourgeoisie could subsidize kings and impoverished aristocrats, buy titles and estates, and successfully compete with the feudal aristocracy for political power. Serfs and villeins left the manor to become free workers and artisans in the towns; those remaining began to demand the commutation of feudal dues and taxes and the establishment of money wages – in other words the abolition of feudalism, as in the English rebellion of 1381, the Bohemian Taborite rising of 1420, and the Peasant Wars in Germany during the first part of the sixteenth century. It was a lengthy process, which Marx and Engels characterize in their famous sentences from the *Communist Manifesto*:

> The bourgeoisie, wherever it has got the upper hand, has put an end to all feudal, patriarchal, idyllic relations. It has pitilessly torn asunder the motley feudal ties that bound man to his 'natural superiors', and has left remaining no other nexus between man and man than naked self-interest, than callous 'cash payment'.[9]

With Margery Kempe, one is kept constantly aware of the 'cash nexus'; it pervades her consciousness as it pervaded her world, part of every human endeavor and confrontation. No one is immune from money consciousness. From lowest to highest we see everyone pinching pennies, whether his own or someone else's: even the Archbishop of York squabbles over the fee to be paid Margery's escort (p. 167). Jesus denounces such concern for lucre (p. 209), but it is nonetheless the backdrop to Margery's religious devotion. The economics of pilgrimage is laid before us almost as prominently as its spiritual motivation. Thus we learn of the public financial settlement that Margery made before embarking for the Holy Land; of her expenditures for food, wine, bedding, lodging, and transportation; of the groat she paid a Saracen to bring her to the Mount where Jesus fasted forty days; of wage negotiations with the humpbacked Irishman who became Margery's servant. We hear continually of her fear of being robbed and her anxiety at being delayed in Rome because of insufficient funds, and are as relieved as she when gold finally arrives – proof that God is with her. With account-book scrupulosity Margery registers every gift, whether alms, cloth for a dress, or payment for her stories. Perhaps the most revealing single passage is the conversation in which Margery asks Jesus to be her executor:

> Lord, after thou hast forgiven me my sin, I make thee mine executor of all the good works that Thou workest in me. In praying, in thinking, in weeping, in going on pilgrimage, in fasting, or in speaking any good words, it is fully my will, that Thou give Master N. [Margery's confessor] half of it to the increase of his merit, as if he did them himself. And the other half, Lord, spread on Thy friends and Thine enemies, and on my friends and mine enemies, for I will have but Thyself for my share.
>
> Daughter, I shall be a true executor to thee and fulfill all thy will; and for the great charity that thou hast to comfort thy fellow thou shalt have double reward in heaven. (pp. 26–7)

It is a spiritual economics as schematic as anything produced by the Puritans: good deeds and prayer the commodity, transferable and administered by Jesus (with the legal/psychological pun on 'will'), invested in Master N. and other projects, and producing an enviable profit in heaven of 100 percent.

Yet despite this profound awareness of money, with Margery we are far from the aristocratic acceptance of wealth as a natural thing, or from the aristocratic virtue of largesse and the continual circulation of goods that is so prominent a feature of the courtly romance. On the contrary, the dominant tone of her concern is anxiety: the fear of loss of money or goods and the fear of being unable to provide for herself. This anxiety reflects not only Margery's personal experience of business failure but also that of her class, whose fortunes depended on speculation and investment and were therefore always subject to loss. This anxiety appears especially in her ambivalent attitude toward poverty. Margery views poverty as a spiritually glorifying condition, and she yearns in the Franciscan manner to imitate the poverty of Jesus. Yet once she is moneyless, moving among the common people of Rome without the security and social advantages conferred by wealth, she is deeply frightened.

And indeed this was the paradox of wealth for the medieval woman: that it created and destroyed at once. The creative power of money is that it compensates for the deficiencies of nature: The ugly person can buy a beautiful mate; the stupid person can buy intelligent employees; the bad person is honored for his or her social position.[10] Thus money creates socially, and Margery is created a valuable piece of property, a good match for the burgess John Kempe and with a social position entirely unrelated to her desires or talents. Yet it is precisely as a piece of valuable property that Margery is most profoundly destroyed, for she can never attain full humanity while she has no power to dispose of herself as she pleases. Like any medieval woman, Margery is born the property of her father; on her marriage this right is transferred to her husband. While she is owned by someone else, she remains alienated from herself – and I am using the verb *alienate* here in its original sense: to transfer the rights of ownership to another person.

Early in the book, Margery recounts an incident that poignantly reveals her understanding of this impotence. After her first vision of paradise, she urges her husband to continence. Yet having no right of property over her own body, Margery must endure legal rape when persuasion fails:

> She said to her husband, 'I may not deny you my body, but the love of my heart and my affections are withdrawn from all earthly creatures and set only in God.'
>
> He would have his will and she obeyed, with great weeping and sorrowing that she might not live chaste. . . . Her husband said it was good to do so, but he might not yet. He would when God willed. And so he used her as he had done before. He would not spare her. (p. 16)

Like the Wife of Bath, Margery is free to own property, run a business, and enter a guild, but she is not free to dispose of her person. Oppressed within her class, she participates in the economic advantages of the class but not in the full range of personal freedom extended to the bourgeois man. The incident recounted above reminds us that rape – *raptus* – sometimes means theft; here, the theft of one's person. It is not, of course, only Margery's husband who is guilty of this most fundamental form of theft, but the laws of religion and society that gave a husband authority over that piece of valuable property, his wife. And it is not only Margery who is victimized by these laws, but John as well, who is forced into the unpleasant choice of abusing his wife or abusing himself. For he cannot be divorced; neither can he find a normal sex life elsewhere. Luckily for Margery, though, her husband was the complete bourgeois:

more committed to his needs than to those of his wife, but even more committed to financial than to physical necessity. Thus, when Margery offers to pay his debts, John finally agrees to let her take the vow of chastity (p. 32). In this way Margery, like any serf, buys manumission from her lord: the human property whose service she removes has its price.

Margery is as alienated from spiritual selfhood as she is from physical, for without her husband's consent she cannot obey the urging of her soul to go on pilgrimage. Luckily John Kempe grants his wife permission to go. Her confessor, too, has the right to deny permission and is angry that she does not ask. Yet even in her travels, Margery has only jumped out of the frying pan into the fire, for she is as plagued with fear of rape throughout her journey as she is with fear of theft; indeed, on one occasion she is threatened with rape and only narrowly manages to dissuade her assaulter.

The alternatives were few in medieval society for the woman who resented the alienation of self. One was violence against the most immediate oppressor, the husband, and it has recently been suggested that the Wife of Bath availed herself of this alternative in disposing of her fourth husband.[11]

We may read a thinly veiled death-wish against her husband when Margery has a vision in which Christ promises to slay him.[12] But more often the internalization of oppression led to self-inflicted punishment, which, as mortification of the flesh, brought the social advantage of ecclesiastical approval. Thus, in the Middle English translation of the *Vita* of the French mystic Marie d'Oignies, we read, 'And for she [Marie] hadde not openly power of hir owne body, she bare prively under hir smok a fulle sharpe corde, with the whiche she was girded ful harde.'[13] Margery, too, internalizes the special oppression of women through self-inflicted punishment: not only is she continually obsessed with the desire to die, but she practices fasting, waking, and other forms of asceticism, and also wears a hair shirt under her clothes every day for several years.

With substantial limitation on her personal freedom, the medieval bourgeoise remained far more dependent than her husband on personal relationships for a sense of fulfillment. Yet even in this realm Margery seems to find little to sustain her. Her children are never mentioned as a source of stability, security, or comfort, with the exception of one son whom Margery converts from a profligate life. Likewise, there is no reference to Margery's relation with her parents. It is through her marriage that we get some sense of what 'normal' family relations were like. Though Margery wore a hair shirt for several years, her husband never knew about it, even though, as the author emphasizes, 'she lay by him every night in his bed and wore the haircloth every day, and bore children in the time' (p. 17). Plainly, the absence of intimacy and communication seems as awful to Margery as it does to us.

Now John Kempe was not a cruel or an evil man, nor does Margery accuse him of monstrosity: he neither beat her nor had her put away as insane nor denounced her publicly. He was distressed by his wife's eccentricity, though more, it seems, because it interfered with his sex life than for any other reason. Yet considering the measures at his disposal and the social standards of the time, John Kempe was a fairly reasonable man. He was, of course, a very busy man, extremely concerned with profit and loss, getting and spending, office and status; we have already seen that while he could not be persuaded to live chastely, he could be bribed to do so. A busy man, too, was Margery's father, five times mayor of Lynn, and doubtless no less money-minded than John Kempe. Even the clergy emerge from Margery's moral account-book as busy, ambitious, and often greedy. This, then, is the normal world in which Margery moves. Its normalcy is grotesque, not unlike our own, and its relationships are often deformed and dehumanized. In such a world, Jesus is the only male authority figure who is neither busy nor ambitious but always available and ready to love. Thus Jesus becomes ideal father, promising 'all manner of love that thou covetest', and ideal husband as well, united with Margery in mystical marriage (p. 112) and demanding only virtue.

Though Karl Marx knew nothing of Margery Kempe, his remarks on religion read as if tailor-made for her:

> Religious distress is at the same time the *expression* of real distress and the *protest* against real distress. Religion is the sigh of the oppressed creature, the heart of a heartless world, just as it is the spirit of a spiritless situation. It is the opium of the people.[14]

Religion is Margery's way of asserting her ownership of herself, of overcoming alienation while simultaneously providing the most poignant testimony to that alienation. It is also her way of projecting into mental reality the loving relationships so fervently desired and so glaringly absent from her domestic life. One could also say that Margery discovered a way to use the system against the system – a way to leave home, travel, establish a name for herself, and meanwhile remain both chaste and respectable. Religion became her way of combatting the special oppression of women, which she in no way understood as oppression, though she suffered and rebelled against its experiential weight. [. . .]

Notes

1   A chronology of Margery Kempe's life and times, together with the evidence for these dates, is provided in the edition by S. B. Meech and Hope E. Allen (London, 1940; EETS, OS 212, vol. 1).

2   Only with the Reformation was the city's name changed to King's Lynn. For much of the following information about Lynn, I am indebted to Alice S. Green, *Town Life in the Fifteenth Century* (Boston, 1894), 2 vols.

3   Ibid., vol. 1, pp. 277–8.

4   Nearly a century later, feelings still ran high. Richard Dowbigging's account of a confrontation between the bishop and the mayor of Lynn concludes: 'And so then the Bishop and his squires rebuked the mayor of Lynn, and said that he had shamed him and his town forever, with much other language, etc. . . . And so at the same gate we came in we went out, and no blood drawn, God be thanked.' Item 200 in *The Paston Letters*, ed. John Warrington (London, 1924; Everyman edn. no. 752), 2 vols.

5   For the convenience of readers not familiar with Middle English I have taken quotations from the modernized edition of W. Butler-Bowden (London: Jonathan Cape, 1954).

6   In the introduction to the Bowden edition, p. xx.

7   F. Engels, *The Origin of the Family, Private Property, and the State* (New York: International Publishers, 1942), pp. 65–6.

8   See H. E. Allen's 'Prefatory Note' and textual notes to the Meech–Allen edition.

9   Karl Marx and Friedrich Engels, *Manifesto of the Communist Party*, in *Collected Works* (London: Lawrence and Wishart, 1976), vol. 6, pp. 486–7.

10 On the creative power of money, see Karl Marx, 'The Power of Money in Bourgeois Society', in *Economic and Philosophic Manuscripts of 1844* (Moscow: Foreign Languages Publishing House, 1961), pp. 136–41.

11 Beryl Rowland, 'On the Timely Death of the Wife of Bath's Fourth Husband', *Archiv* 209 (1972).

12 'I shall suddenly slay thy husband' (p. 27). In the manuscript a marginal note inserts after 'slay' the phrase 'the fleshly lust in'. This scribal insertion seems gratuitous, and especially unjustified in view of the contents of the next chapter. There Margery's husband poses a conundrum: If he were forced under pain of death to 'commune naturally' with Margery, would she consent, or see him killed? Her answer: 'I would rather see you being slain, than that we should turn again to our uncleanness' (p. 30). A few lines further on, Margery says, 'I told you nearly three years ago that ye should be slain suddenly. . . .' Clearly, she is speaking of her husband's life, not his lust. Meech also believes that the emendation is 'quite wrong'.

13 Cited in the Meech–Allen edition, p. 261.

14 From the introduction to Marx's *Contribution to the Critique of Hegel's Philosophy of Right*, in *Marx and Engels on Religion* (New York: Schocken Books, 1964). Emphasis in original.

FEMINIST STUDIES OF CHAUCER

Feminist studies of Chaucer gathered pace in the years following Delany's essay. Though in 1990, Priscilla Martin would reflect in the preface to her *Chaucer's Women: Nuns, Wives, and Amazons*, 'As I write this Introduction there are no full-length studies available of the women in Chaucer's poetry',[6] a spate of such studies was shortly to appear. In 1991 came Jill Mann's study, balancing feminist concerns with a traditional humanist mode of criticism – 'I have tried to describe Chaucer's "feminism" in his own terms rather than ours'[7] – and in 1992 came Elaine Tuttle Hansen's, *Chaucer and the Fictions of Gender*, a study that was unpersuaded of the case for the protofeminist Chaucer: 'the attempt to recuperate a feminist Chaucer . . . based on the assumption that Chaucer is sympathetic to women's problems and that we hear in his poetry either a female voice or an *écriture féminine* (in the vernacular of the fourteenth-century East Midlands), is misguided.'[8]

> Feminist work in medieval studies is a thriving enterprise with a distinguished past and a promising future. Although the medieval-studies community is often indifferent and sometimes hostile to this feminist scholarship, the blending of medievalism and feminism works to the mutual benefit of feminist studies and medieval studies.[9]
>
> The broad contours of a dimly perceived landscape are, perhaps, beginning to emerge. Yet, as with any comparable project, the completion contains within itself the suggestion of a new beginning. It would, for example, be rewarding to compare texts from the same genre, but written by male authors and female authors, to see whether there is any discernible bias in the construction of female characters, or in themes treated; or to investigate 'particular moments and scenarios' in order to arrive at a fuller understanding of the complex of social, historical and literary influences at work.[10]

1993: Gender studies in the 1990s: in two separate surveys, Judith M. Bennett and Carol M. Meale review the state of the field.

FEMINIST READINGS OF LITERATURE BY AND FOR MEDIEVAL WOMEN

By the early 1990s the attention of increasing numbers of feminist scholars had also turned to non-Chaucerian texts. Study of the relatively few Middle English women writers was bolstered by the appearance of such anthologies as Alexandra Barratt's *Women's Writing in Middle English* and Alcuin Blamires' *Woman Defamed and Woman Defended* (both 1992).[11] In their 1994 collaborative volume, *The Wife of Bath and All her Sect: Feminist Readings in Middle English Literature*, editors Ruth Evans and Lesley Johnson noted the slow start to non-Chaucerian feminist studies: 'There has been a great deal of very sophisticated feminist work on Chaucer (Carolyn Dinshaw, Elaine Tuttle Hansen, Louise Fradenburg); much less, for various institutional reasons, on other areas such as the medieval drama.'[12] The mid-1990s also saw a burgeoning of interest in the corpus of Middle English devotional writings composed by and for medieval women (an interest reflected by our second extract).

Study of *The Book of Margery Kempe* continued in the volume of essays edited by Sandra J. McEntire in 1992 and in Lynn Staley's *Margery Kempe's Dissenting Fictions* of 1994.[13] This period also saw increased study of such works as the *Ancrene Wisse*, the 'Katherine Group' of Saints' Lives and devotional texts, the *Revelations* or *Showings* of Julian of Norwich. Many critical studies of these texts took up their preoccupation with the physical body: Julian and Margery describe bodily as well as spiritual experiences; concerned with the bodily virginity of his charges, the *Ancrene Wisse*-author writes at length about the disciplining and regulation of the body. Scholars made a fruitful connection between these texts and theoretical work concerned with the body. Karma Lochrie's 1991 study, *Margery Kempe and Translations of the Flesh* pioneers this approach:

> My point is that the body is not something we can take as a 'given', nor something which is the same for the Middle Ages as it is for us in the 1990s. The body, particularly the female body, is itself a construct of science, medicine, theology, literature, education, the clothing industry, advertising, and fitness centers. Except for the last two industries, the same is true for the Middle Ages. The female body, put simply, has a history, and that history is determined by social and religious values, institutions, and patriarchal power structures.[14]

By 1993, the date of Elizabeth Robertson's essay extracted below, theoretical work on the body was increasingly applied to medieval texts (the special gender-based issue of the journal *Speculum* produced that year included an essay on 'Genders, Bodies, Borders').[15] Robertson's essay on 'Medieval Medical Views of Women' applies the insights of this critical approach to the *Ancrene Wisse* and the *Showings* of Julian of Norwich. A starting-point for Robertson's essay is a conviction that the cultural meanings attached to the human body are not fixed and transhistorical but are contingent and culturally determined, shifting through time. The opening of the essay thus surveys the meanings attached to gendered bodies in medieval medical texts where, in a tradition deriving from the classical writer Galen, the bodies of men were associated with qualities of heat and dryness, those of women with qualities of coldness and moisture. Robertson views these essentialist views of femininity as informing both writing *for* medieval women (the *Ancrene Wisse*) and writing *by* medieval women (Julian's *Showings*).[16] Controversially for some readers, her argument proposed that an 'idiosyncratically female' dimension informs the spirituality of these two extraordinary medieval prose works.

Extract from Elizabeth Robertson, 'Medieval Medical Views of Women and Female Spirituality in the *Ancrene Wisse* and Julian of Norwich's *Showings*', in Linda Lomperis and Sarah Stanbury (eds), *Feminist Approaches to the Body in Medieval Literature* (Philadelphia: University of Pennsylvania Press, 1993), pp. 150–9.

[. . .] A religious guide written by a man for women, the *Ancrene Wisse*, is illustrative of the ways in which biological views of women shape the author's representation of female spirituality.[1] Indeed, the work as a whole reflects notions of the female body; as the work progresses, the author develops an idea of the anchorhold as a womb, a place that the anchoress must prepare for Christ's entry. Especially prominent in the last three chapters of the work, 'Confession', 'Penance', and 'Love', is an interwoven pattern of imagery that focuses on blood. In 'Confession', for example, the anchoress is told that 'We ahen him blod for blod. ant ure blod þah aȝein his bold þ he schedde for us. were ful unefne change . . . ant ure lauerd nimeð ed us ure teares aȝein his blod. ȝ is wilcweme.' ('We owe Him [Christ] blood for blood, and even so, our blood for His blood which He shed for us, would be a very unequal exchange . . . And our Lord accepts our tears from us in exchange for His blood, and is well pleased').[2] As in the medical texts, moistures, here blood and tears, are seen as interchangeable. It is, of course, a Christian commonplace to speak of Christ's blood as redemptive. The emphasis on the inferiority of the blood given in payment, however, is particularly apt for women whose excess blood was seen as especially impure. Furthermore, the *Wisse* author develops the image of blood graphically. The author tells the anchoress to contemplate the cross and see how 'swa swiðe fleaw þ ilke blodi swat. of his blisfule bodi. þ te streames urnen dun to þer eorðe . . . þus lo þe hale half ȝ te cwike dale droh þ uvele blod ut. frommard te unhale. ȝ healde swa þe seke' (60–1) ('the bloody sweat flowed so freely and in such quantity from His blessed body that it ran in streams to the ground . . . Thus the living, healthy part drew out the bad blood from that which was diseased and so healed that which was sick') (49–50). The association of women with excess moisture purged through menstruation makes these images, resonant though they are for both men and women, especially redemptive for women. Purgation, viewed in medical accounts as necessary for women's physical health, is here presented to female readers as necessary for spiritual health as well.

Redemption, in the *Ancrene Wisse*, is made possible not only through the purgation of excess feminine moisture, but also through heat, the heat brought about through sexual union with Christ. While heat, or the fire of love, the *incendium amoris*, is a motif that pervades twelfth-century affective works, the centrality of a sexual union with Christ in this particular work suggests the male author's concern to address the perceived needs of his female readers, including their biological need for heat met through union with the male. In the next chapter, 'Penance', the work paves the way for the anchoress's union with Christ by introducing an image of the fetid, wounded body to be redeemed by Christ. Such a focus is particularly apt for a female audience seen to be trapped in deficient bodies. The chapter then introduces the image of the fiery wheel and the flaming sword, establishing a sexualized and bodily framework for the anchoress's spiritual apotheosis. Elijah's wheel is red: 'Fur is hat ȝ read. I þe heate is understonden euch wa þ eileð flesch. Scheome bi þe reade' (181) ('Fire is hot and red. By the heat is signified every pain that afflicts the body. By the redness dishonour') (157). The wheel is transformed into a flaming sword, which stands for both the sun and the cross: 'Ne kimeð nan in to pareis. bute þurh þis leitinde sweord þe wes hat ȝ read' (181) ('No one enters paradise but by this flaming sword, which was hot and red') (157). God will thus win the anchoress with his implicitly erotic flaming sword.

Cleansed by penance, the anchoress is then ready for contemplation of her union with Christ, presented in this work as a literal marriage to a Christ Knight. Christ is particularly associated with fire, the fire of desire presented in medical texts as necessary for conception. What the anchoress conceives through union with Christ is her spiritual self. That the author intends the anchoress to equate union with Christ with sexual union with an earthly man is made explicit at the end of this section, where he introduces images of heat in the context of a discussion of the inadequacies of earthly sexual intercourse in comparison with union with Christ.

The work then culminates in an unusual catachretic image that has never been adequately accounted for, an image that compares God's love to Greek fire. Bringing together biological ideas of women's innate desire, need for heat, and excess moisture, this graphic, even incendiary image suggests that the anchoress may achieve spiritual fulfillment through the explosive transformations of Christ's blood. After discussing the need to kindle sticks to promote desire, the author directs the anchoress: 'Grickisch fur is imaket of reades monnes blod. ȝ þ ne mei na þing. bute Migge. ant Sond. ȝ eisil. as me seið acwenchen. þis grickisch fur is þe luve of iesu ure lauerd. ȝ ȝe hit schule makien of reade monnes blod. þ is iesu crist ireadet wið his ahne blod o þe deore rod' (205) ('Greek fire is made from the blood of a red man and cannot be quenched, it is said, except with urine, sand and vinegar. This "Greek fire" is the love of Jesus our Lord, and you shall make it from the blood of a red man, that is, Jesus Christ, reddened with His own blood on the precious cross') (178). The emphasis here on Christ's redness underscores his suitability as an object of female contemplation since, like women who are suffused with blood, Christ was believed to have a sanguine temperament.

In its emphasis on heat and moisture, this unusual image of Greek fire reflects biological views of women. The author as before relies on the medieval belief that bodily moistures are interchangeable: the bad blood of the earlier passage becomes the urine or vinegar that threatens the redemptive blood of Christ. Urine was the focus of diagnosis in medieval medicine; here the ill moisture of the body, urine, is transformed and redeemed by the moisture of Christ. Janet Grayson writes of this passage:

> The uncontrollable wildfire, the bloodied Christ . . . the specifics of urine and vinegar that threaten to smother the consuming Greek fire – all converge here into the emotional, highly concentrated repetitions and refinements of the power of sacrifice. And the pervasiveness of redness (initially the color of fire) provides a definite focus for the Passion, the *memoria Christi*, the affective influence of Christ crossed that kindles the *incendium amoris* between anchoress and Christ, between lady and Christ-knight.[3]

This image particularly intensifies the image of heat, that quality deemed most needed by women, for as Ian Bishop points out, comparing God's love to an incendiary device used in war would be like comparing God's love to napalm.[4] The explosiveness of the image might even suggest orgasm, which the medical texts considered necessary for women both to conceive and to help purge moisture.

The peculiar aptness of this image for women readers is further underscored by the author's departure from his sources, in which Greek fire is equated with lust; here it is equated with its opposite, Christ's love.[5] Perhaps this change can be attributed to the author's assumption that his female audience cannot escape its essentially lustful female nature. By equating Christ with a substance usually associated with lust, however, the author suggests to the readers that lust itself need not be transcended, rather, it must be properly directed. The female reader's innate lust is thus potentially redeemable not through its transcendence, but through its redirection to a suitable object, Christ. As the culminating image of the work, Greek fire crystallizes the overall theme: the anchoress's bodily realization of union with Christ.

What I believe is significant about this passage and different from medieval conceptions of male spirituality is that for women, union with Christ occurs not as an allegory of the ascent of the mind to God, but as concretized erotic experience, one that redeems her fleshliness and her excess moisture through orgasm. Erotic imagery does, of course, appear in male mystical works, but eroticism seems to be constructed differently for men and women. While some male writers may graphically describe their physical union with Christ (consider, for example, the Monk of Farne's description of plunging himself into Christ's wounds to achieve orgasm, or Rupert of Deutz's homoerotic description of passionately kissing Christ), such erotic imagery seems less driven by the physiological need for redemption of the flesh than do analogous meditations in female texts.[6] Often in male texts, eroticism is chiefly a tool to enhance the mind's contemplation of God, whereas in female mystical works, erotic union with Christ is itself often the end of the meditation.

Further work needs to be done on the similarities and differences between male and female spiritual desire in relationship to received views about male and female experiences of physical desire. The *incendium amoris* – the fire of love for God – is an erotic image equally available to male and female contemplatives in part because early biological views, as Laqueur has pointed out,[7] stress the importance of simultaneity of orgasm for men and women and the necessity of heat for conception. Nevertheless, women are by nature more conditioned by desire for the incarnate Christ both beccause their essential material nature denies them any other access to God and because their perceived biological natures place them in a condition of perpetual desire.[8]

In the work of Julian of Norwich there are distinctive features that I believe are influenced by her encounter with the standard medieval medical views outlined above. The sensual and physical permeate her work. In particular, running throughout the text is the idea that her body is redeemed through the body of Christ, who is figured in feminine terms. Like her, Christ, as God incarnate, is dominated by physicality. Indeed, Julian's meditations are prompted by notions of physicality. She says at the beginning of her work: 'I desyrede three graces be the gyfte of god. The fyrst was to have mynde of Cryste es passionn. The seconnde was bodelye sycknes, and the thryd was to have of goddys gyfte thre wonndys' ('I desired three graces by the gift of God. The first was to have recollection of Christ's Passion. The second was a bodily sickness, and the third was to have, of God's gift, three wounds') (125).[9] Julian's revelations thus spring from experiences of the body. She identifies with Christ as someone who, like herself, is wounded. While her stated desires are also common in works of male mystics, the fact that they are central in Julian's work not only reflects her sense of herself as rooted in the body but accentuates her work as distinctively feminine.

Furthermore her revelations are permeated with images of blood. She writes, 'with him I desyred to suffer, livyng in my deadly bodie, as god would give me grace . . . And in this sodenly I saw the reed bloud rynnyng downe from under the garlande, hote and freyshely, / plentuously and lively, right as it was in the tyme that the garland of thornes was pressed on his blessed head' (long text, ch. 3, 293, and ch. 4, 294) ('I desired to suffer with him, living in my mortal body, as God would give me grace . . . And at this, suddenly I saw the red blood running down from under the crown, hot and flowing freely and copiously, a living stream, just as it was at the time when the crown of thorns was pressed on his blessed head' [181]). Here Christ's blood, like menstrual blood, is purged, matching her own natural purgation of excess. Elsewhere Julian expands this image so that the blood is even more evocative of menstrual blood. Contemplating the crown of thorns, she says, 'And in the comyng ouȝte they were browne rede, for the blode was full thycke; and in the spredyng abrode they were bryght rede' (long text, ch. 7, 311) ('as they [the drops] issued they were a brownish red, for the blood was very thick, and as they spread they turned bright red' [187]). Like menstrual blood, 'The bledyng contynued' (long text, ch. 7, 311) ('the bleeding continued' [188]) and, as she explains of this vision in the short text, 'this ranne so plenteuouslye to my syght that me thought, ȝyf itt hadde bene so in kynde, for þat tyme itt schulde hafe made the bedde alle on blode and hafe passede onn abowte' (short text, ch. 8, 277) ('I saw this blood run so plentifully that it seemed to me that if it had in fact been happening there, the bed and everything all around it would have been soaked in blood' [137]).

Julian's image of blood, evocative of menstrual flow, also suggests blood lost in losing virginity; the blood of Christ is even explicity connected with her own bed. Furthermore, the fact that the age viewed menstrual blood and semen as homologous underscores the erotic implications of the image. Christ's blood is linked with all kinds of moisture, all redemptive of feminine excess: 'God had made waterse plentuouse in erthe to oure servyce and to owre bodylye ese, for tendyr love that he has to us. Botte ȝit lykes hym bettyr that we take fullye his blessede blode to wasche us with of synne; for thare ys no lykoure that es made that hym lykes so welle to gyffe us. For it is plenteuouse and of oure kynde" (short text, ch. 8, 227) ('God has created bountiful waters on the earth for our use and our bodily comfort, out of the tender love he has for us. But it is more pleasing to him that we accept freely his blessed blood to wash us of our sins, for there is no drink that is made which pleases him so well to give to us; for it is so plentiful, and it is of our own nature' [137]). Excess moisture is thus redemptive, and thereby so is femininity itself.

In order to highlight Julian's extraordinary and idiosyncratically female uses of blood imagery, let me digress for a moment to consider a contemplation of Christ's blood by her male contemporary, Richard Rolle. In comparing the two works, we should not overemphasize their differences since it is unclear for whom Rolle wrote his meditations. Indeed, Wolfgang Riehle speculates that many of the Middle English writings of the late medieval English mystics were intended for female readers. Furthermore, meditations on the passion are generically different from mystical revelations. Nonetheless, as we shall see, Rolle's meditation on blood differs quite markedly from that of a woman writer.

> A, Lord, þe pite þat I now se: þi woundys in þi streynynge reche so wyde, þi lymes and þi nayles are so tendre, þou lyst rowyd and reed streyned on þe cros, þe kene crowne on þin hed, þat sytteth þe so sore; þi face is so bolnyd, þat fyrst was so faire; þi synwes and þi bonys styrten owte starke, þat þi bonys may be nowmbryd; þe stremys of þi reede blood rennyn as þe flood; þi woundys are for-bled and grysly on to se; þe sorewe þat þi modur makyth encresuth þi woo.[10]

> (Ah, Lord, the pity that I see now: your wounds in your stretching-out stretch so wide, your limbs and the places where the nails pierced you are so tender, you lie, made raw and red, stretched on the cross, the sharp crown on your head sits on you so painfully, your face is so swollen, that once was so fair; your sinews and your bones stick out so starkly that your bones could be numbered; the streams of your red blood run as the flood; your wounds are covered with blood and are grisly to see. The sorrow your mother makes increases your woe.)

Whereas Julian's image of blood ultimately becomes confused with her own blood, here the picture of the suffering Christ evokes not so much identifica-tion as pity. If the viewer is to identify with anyone, it is with Mary, who is given much attention further on in the meditation. The blood produced by the crown of thorns is not mentioned, and the blood flowing from the wounds of the body is equally considered with the stretched limbs and swollen face, all of which evoke pity. The Rolle passage presents a systematic and inclusive analysis of Christ's suffering, one that details the shocking anatomy of the wounded body. Yet, despite the personal address to 'þou', and despite the affec-tive qualities shared by the Rolle and Julian passages, the Rolle passage lacks the immediacy and intimacy of Julian's description. The end of the passage shifts the focus away from the viewer to Mary. It is as if the male viewer cannot enter the body of the suffering Christ in the same way as can Julian, an impres-sion created in the Julian passage by the blurring of boundaries between Christ's blood and her own. Indeed, when male speakers describe entering the wounds of Christ, they recount a desire to possess Christ, whereas the female speakers tend to describe entering the wounds in order to merge with Christ. At the very least, we can say that excess moisture does not predominate in the Rolle passage as it does in that of Julian.

Another important aspect of Julian's work – that is, her emphasis on the sensuality of Christ – can be accounted for by considering it a reflection or even displacement onto Christ of medieval medical arguments about female sensuality. As Bynum points out in her discussion of the feminized Christ, Julian often figures Christ as a mother.[11] Julian further associates

Christ's feminized body, 'oure moder Cryst', with sensuality: 'he is oure moder of mercy in oure sensualyte takyng' (long text, ch. 58, 586) ('he is our Mother of mercy in taking our sensuality' [294]). And of Christ as the second part of the trinity she says 'The lower perty, whych is sensualyte, sufferyd for the salvacion of mankynd' (long text, ch. 55, 569) ('The lower part, which is sensuality, suffered for the salvation of mankind' [288]). The feminized body of Christ, rather than leading the contemplative to a transcendence of the sensual, redeems the sensual by uniting the contemplative's 'substance' with Christ's: 'for in oure moder Cryst we profyt and encrese, and in mercy he reformyth us and restoryth, and by the vertu of his passion, his deth and his uprysyng onyd us to oure substannce' (long text, ch. 58, 586) ('for in our Mother Christ we profit and increase, and in mercy he reforms and restores us, and by the power of his Passion, his death and his Resurrection, he unites us to our substance' [294]).

As far as I know, Julian's emphasis on the sensuality of Christ is distinctive. As Riehle writes,

> Julian's understanding of the image of God is that it embraces the whole man, including his bodiliness, a theory which has been put forward in traditional teaching, but not very frequently . . . It is thus possible to speak of God taking up his dwelling in man's *sensualite*. This is certainly Julian's most interesting contribution to the theme of the image of God.[12]

I suggest that Julian is speaking here not simply of a gender-neutral sensuality, but more specifically of woman's sensuality; moreover, the redemption she explores here, while a redemption of all mankind, is especially redemptive for women. Bynum has argued that the twelfth century's interest in the humanity of Christ, because of its celebration of the flesh, ultimately resulted in a reassessment of the value of femininity. In these passages on sensuality, Julian's emphasis is on Christ's redemption, not only of humanity, but also of that aspect of humanity which male writers repeatedly designate and condemn as particularly feminine, sensuality. While a woman author's association of Christ's redemption with her own feminine characteristics might well have resulted in a reassessment of femininity, it is important to recognize that Julian's approach carries with it at least her initial acceptance of the age's misogynistic views of the nature of her body. She celebrates the incarnated Christ because this is the only God that she can, according to the age's view of her limited nature, truly perceive.

The fact that Julian focuses in her writing so insistently on attributes of female physiology might make us wonder if other women mystical writers do the same. It would be useful to compare her writing to English and Continental female mystical writing. For the moment, let me consider briefly a near contemporary, Margery Kempe. Although I cannot here discuss Margery Kempe in detail, I would like simply to state the case that Margery's visions also are conditioned by her absorption of medieval views of the female body. In his analysis of Middle English mystics, Riehle is particularly troubled by Margery, whose habit of hyperbole he finds to be a sign of her 'pathologically neurotic traits': 'She is no longer capable of separating the sensual and spiritual and the former is indeed more important to her than the latter.'[13] For example, she literalizes her marriage to Christ: and writes that Christ says to her, 'þe mayst boldly, whan þu art in þi bed, take me to þe as for þi weddyd husband' ('you may boldly when you are in your bed take me to yourself as your wedded husband.')[14] She wants literally to hold and taste God. She is wounded with longing and, as one could not fail to notice in her account, cries to excess. Margery's behavior has led some critics to view her as exceptional, if not aberrant, in the history of female religious.[15] But far from being an exception to the female spiritual movement, she is rather at its center. For if we consider her writing in the context of the medieval assumptions about women we have been discussing here, we find that she has simply taken these assumptions, presented more covertly in other women's writing, to their logical extreme. Told by theory that she can only experience God through the body, Margery recounts extreme bodily experiences in her quest for union with God. Told that she has too much moisture, Margery cries excessively, which makes those around her, especially those in power who are challenging her authority, uncomfortable. The very excesses of her writing, her extremes of tears and sensual expressiveness, suggest a destabilization of those assumptions.

If we accept that gender is a sociocultural construct, then gendered subjectivity is an 'emergent property of a historicized experience'.[16] To understand medieval female subjectivity as it is constructed in texts written by and for women, I have argued here both that we must consider the discourses that shaped this subjectivity and that we should understand images of blood, tears, and other moisture – and indeed the general focus on the physical and sensual in female spiritual works – as internalizations of or reactions to prescriptive medical discourse about women's bodies. Furthermore, these medical views help shape the notion of writers that a woman's experience of union with Christ would be literal and concrete. There are many other examples of such literalization in spiritual writing by both men and women in England, and perhaps on the Continent as well; the erotic is stressed in the Monk of Farne's meditations, in Richard Rolle's writing, in Anselm's *Prayers and Meditations*, and in the work of Saint Bernard. A focus on the erotic is an important part of male spirituality. For female spirituality, it is central.[17]

The prevalence of images of blood, heat, and tears in works written for and by women suggests the writers' familiarity with medical ideology about women. We do not know whether or not these authors endorse this ideology, especially since we know very little about them other than what can be gleaned from the texts themselves.[18] What we do know does not provide us with enough information to determine precisely what the valence of certain signs in the text is. We might argue that Julian is an essentialist, that she has internalized misogynist medieval views about the nature of her body, and further, that through the contemplation of Christ's similarity to herself she redeems some attributes of the feminine. We do not know, however, how she responded to Aristotelian notions of femininity, since she does not tell us directly. (Indeed it is even difficult to determine how men reacted to these views. The thirteenth-century *Hali Meiðhad* tells us that some men viewed pregnancy and childbirth with disgust, but we have no analogous medieval text that describes a woman's view of such experiences.) We might go further and argue that Julian, rather than accepting male views of women, ultimately subverts them, and that rather than being an essentialist herself, she takes an 'essentialist' stance only as a strategy, in an Irigarayan sense: she mocks male views by mimicking and hyperbolizing them, and undoes them by overdoing them. [. . .]

Acknowledgements

In addition to the editors and readers, I would like to thank Gerda Norvig, Sarah Beckwith, and Jeffrey Robinson for their perspicacious editorial advice for the revision of this essay. I would also like to thank Karma Lochrie, whose astute reading of this essay at a late stage helped sharpen my thinking about the subject even though I was not able to respond fully to her comments.

Notes

1   For a full discussion of the ways in which the *Ancrene Wisse* represents a male construction of female spirituality, see chapter 4, 'The Rule of the Body: The Female Spirituality of the *Ancrene Wisse*', of my *Early English Devotional Prose and the Female Audience* (Knoxville: University of Tennessee Press, 1990), pp. 44–76.
2   J. R. R. Tolkien, *Ancrene Wisse: The English Text of the Ancrene Riwle* (Corpus Christi College Cambridge 402), EETS, OS 249 (London: Oxford University Press, 1962), p. 161. All further quotations are from this edition; page numbers are cited in parentheses in the body of my text. Following Tolkien, I have rendered the tironian ampersand as a 'z' with a hyphen through it. The translation is taken from the excellent work of M. D. Salu, *The Ancrene Riwle* (London, 1955; rpt, Notre Dame: University of Notre Dame Press, 1956), p. 139. All further translations will be taken from her work, and page numbers will be given in parentheses in my text.
3   Janet Grayson, *Structure and Imagery in the Ancrene Wisse* (Hanover, NH: University Press of New England, 1974), p. 205.

4   Ian Bishop, '"Greek Fire" in *Ancrene Wise* and Contemporary Texts', *Notes and Queries* 224 (1979), 170–99.

5   Bishop explains that the author, in his elaboration of the image of Greek fire, departs from his sources, which include the *Moralia super evangelia*, a work closely associated with the *Ancrene Wisse*.

6   According to Mary Wack, 'Rupert of Deutz (d. 1129) reports a dream in which he worshiped the Cross. The crucified Christ seemed to return his gaze and accept his salutation. Yet he wanted closer union with his Savior. Rushing to the altar, he embraced and kissed the image. "I held him, I embraced him, I kissed him for a long time. I sensed how seriously he accepted this gesture of love when, while kissing, he himself opened his mouth that I might kiss more deeply."' See Wack, *Lovesickness in the Middle Ages: The Viaticum and its Commentaries* (Philadelphia: University of Pennsylvania Press, 1990), p. 24. I am grateful to Karma Lochrie for drawing my attention to this passage. The Monk of Farne passage is described in Wolfgang Riehle, *The Middle English Mystics* (London: Routledge and Kegan Paul, 1981), pp. 46–7. Caroline Walker Bynum discusses some of the problems we face in interpreting male uses of imagery associated with the female in 'Women's Symbols' (in *Holy Feast and Holy Fast: The Religious Significance of Food to Medieval Women* [Berkeley, CA: University of California Press, 1987], ch. 10), and in *Jesus as Mother: Studies in the Spirituality of the High Middle Ages* (Berkeley, CA: University of California Press, 1982).

7   Thomas Laqueur, 'Orgasm, Generation and the Politics of Reproductive Biology', *Representations* 14 (Spring 1986), 1–41.

8   Given the fact that heat is more important physiologically to men than moisture, it is not surprising that the work of Richard Rolle's that is probably most clearly intended for male readers, the *Incendium amoris*, should focus primarily on the heat of desire rather than on moisture. There is barely a reference to moisture in the entire text. While women, too, might share in the praising of the acquisition of heat celebrated in the *Incendium*, the male mystic has an advantage over the female mystic in his quest for heat since he is by nature already in possession of it.

9   Julian of Norwich, *A Book of Showings to the Anchoress Julian of Norwich: Parts One and Two*, ed. with an introduction by Edmund Colledge and James Walsh (Toronto: Pontifical Institute of Medieval Studies, 1978), short text, ch. 1, p. 201. All further quotations will be taken from this edition; text, chapter, and page will be given in parentheses in the body of my text. Translations will follow those of Colledge and Walsh in their *Julian of Norwich: Showings* (NY: Paulist Press, 1978) and page numbers will be given in the body of the text.

10 Hope Emily Allen (ed.), *English Writings of Richard Rolle* (Oxford: Clarendon Press, 1931), p. 24. The translation is my own.

11 See Bynum, *Jesus as Mother*.

12 Riehle, *Middle English Mystics*, p. 148.

13 Ibid., p. 11.

14 *The Book of Margery Kempe*, ed. Sanford Meech and Hope Emily Allen, English Text Society, OS 212 (Oxford: Oxford University Press, 1990), p. 90. The

translation is taken from Barry Windeatt (ed. and trans.), *The Book of Margery Kempe* (Harmondsworth: Penguin, 1985), p. 126.

15   Although Margery is undergoing considerable critical reevaluation at the moment, few critics other than perhaps Karma Lochrie and Sarah Beckwith have argued that her behavior is a response to the ideologies of her age. See Lochrie's *Margery Kempe and the Translation of the Flesh* (Philadelphia: University of Pennsylvania Press, 1991), and Sarah Beckwith's *Christ's Body: Identity, Culture and Society in Late Medieval Writings* (London: Routledge, 1993). See also Sarah Beckwith, 'A Very Material Mysticism: The Medieval Mysticism of Margery Kempe', in David Aers (ed.), *Medieval Literature: Criticism, Ideology, and History* (Brighton: Harvester Press, 1986), pp. 34–57.

16   Linda Alcoff, quoted by Teresa de Lauretis in 'The Essence of the Triangle or, Taking the Risk of Essentialism Seriously: Feminist Theory in Italy, the US, and Britain', in Naomi Schor and Elizabelt Weed (eds), *The Essential Difference: Another Look at Essentialism, Differences* 1, no. 2 (Summer 1989), p. 12.

17   The fact that the Monk of Farne writes of plunging himself into the wounds of Christ to achieve orgasm suggests that Luce Irigaray's theory that the wounds of Christ are analogous to the female vulva is not simply a postmodern Freudian interpretation of Christ's wounds, but is also one that was prevalent in the Middle Ages. See Riehle, *Middle English Mystics*, pp. 46–7.

18   Colledge and Walsh summarize what we can guess about Julian's biography in their introduction to their edition of Julian. For a historical survey of the religious structure of Norwich in Julian's day, see Norman P. Tanner, *The Church in Late Medieval Norwich: 1370–1532* (Toronto: Pontifical Institute of Medieval Studies, 1984). An excellent essay that explores the subversive potential of a woman's use of physiological discourse much more thoroughly than mine is Karma Lochrie's 'The Language of Transgression: Body, Flesh, and Word in Mystical Discourse', in Allen J. Frantzen (ed.), *Speaking Two Languages: Traditional Disciplines and Contemporary Theory in Medieval Studies* (Binghamton: State University of New York Press, 1991), pp. 115–40. Without a fuller knowledge of Julian's relationship to the clergy I hesitate to call her use of such imagery subversive except insofar as the fact that her willingness to speak at all subverts medieval notions of the importance of female silence. The subversive potential of such imagery is certainly worthy of fuller consideration.

FURTHER STRANDS OF GENDER CRITICISM   By the date of our final extract, 1998, further diversification had taken place in the field of medieval gender studies. 'Feminist readings in Middle English' had never indicated a unitary school of approach: plurality and diversity of practice characterized the field. But, now, 'feminist study' in Middle English was increasingly shading into 'gender study', prompting enquiry into how far the gender ideologies inscribed in Middle English texts determine both feminine *and* masculine gender roles. This move had been anticipated at the end of the 1980s when, in her groundbreaking book on *Chaucer's Sexual Poetics*, Carolyn Dinshaw had noted in relation to the Pardoner that 'Chaucer suggests androcentrism takes its toll on men as well as on women, limits the idea of the "masculine" as well as the "feminine".'[17] In her introduction to the 1994 collaborative volume *Medieval Masculinities*, Clare Lees agreed: '[T]he important feminist contributions to medieval studies, which have necessarily concentrated on recovering and reconstructing women's history, now invite a complementary revision of what is often seen as the other side of this binary, asymmetric coin.'[18] The 1993 gender issue of *Speculum* stands as a landmark of this critical shift, bearing witness to the central place gender studies had assumed in Middle English criticism. As Allen Frantzen put it in his contribution to the *Speculum* volume, 'We cannot all be gender theorists, obviously, but everyone should examine gender critically – not only those who think about it all the time but also those who never seem to think about it at all.'[19]

Theoretical work on the body and identity continued to fuel gender study. Sarah Kay and Miri Rubin's collection *Framing Medieval Bodies* of 1994 reminded us:

> We are all born with bodies, but although they are thus native to us, and we innate to them, they are not thereby 'natural', distanced as they are from 'nature' by a multiplicity of psychic, sexual, social and political codes. This systematic coding of bodies means that they are as much the product, as the site, of experience.[20]

The theme of the sexual coding of bodies was to be pursued by increasing numbers of gender studies in the 1990s. As the editors of a 1997 volume on medieval sexuality put it, 'the study of medieval sexuality reminds us that sexuality is normative or queer only in relation to historically specific genders, bodies, and identities.'[21]

Around concerns of this kind has formed one of the most recent critical approaches to Middle English literature – queer theory. In the work of Carolyn Dinshaw, Glenn Burger, Steven Kruger and others, attempts are made to uncover the workings of gender ideology in medieval texts, at the same time hoping to reveal more about those of our own culture. Queer theory challenges many of the assumptions of the liberal humanist critical tradition. Its focus is not textual centres but margins. Those very things a text refuses to countenance, those things it relegates, suppresses or silences, form the starting-point for the queer reading. Dinshaw's reading of *Sir Gawain and the Green Knight* shows such a reading in action:

> [R]emember that if Gawain had succumbed fully to the lady's seduction *and* if he had honored the terms of his promise to the lord he would in fact have had to have sex with the lord – to yield his winnings, that is, his sexual conquest, in his own body, just as he has done with the kisses he received. Homosexual sex

is thus one hypothetical fulfilment – in fact we might say *the* logical end of the interlocking plots the lady and Bertilak play out – but it is a forbidden end. Or rather, not forbidden, but *unintelligible* within the heterosexual world of this poem. It is in this way fully *inside* the culture of the poem (it is produced by the game the three are playing) however apparently *outside* it (unreasonable, impossible: Gawain and Bertilak?).[22]

Queer theorists have offered radical re-readings of Chaucer, many of them taking their starting point from the ambivalent figure of the Pardoner in the *Canterbury Tales*. A continuous queer reception of Chaucer's Pardoner can be traced from Dinshaw's 'Eunuch Hermeneutics' in *Chaucer's Sexual Poetics* of 1989 to Glenn Burger's 'Kissing the Pardoner' of 1992 and Steven F. Kruger's 'Claiming the Pardoner: Toward a Gay Reading of Chaucer's Pardoner's Tale' of 1994.[23] (Each of these critics acknowledges a debt to the readings of the character given by Donald R. Howard in *The Idea of the Canterbury Tales* of 1976 and by Monica E. McAlpine's 1980 essay on 'The Pardoner's Homosexuality and How it Matters'.)[24] At the mid-point of the 1990s both Dinshaw and Burger published articles clarifying their approaches. In 'Chaucer's Queer Touches: A Queer Touches Chaucer', Dinshaw suggested that 'Queerness works by contiguity and displacement, knocking signifiers loose, ungrounding bodies, making them strange', while Burger's 'Gay Chaucer' argued that ' "queer" reading strategies . . . offer new possibilities for engagement with premodern subjects and the representation of medieval sexualities.'[25] Under the influence of these scholars, medieval queer studies would increasingly range beyond Chaucer at the close of the millennium. Allen Frantzen found an amenable subject in the *Gawain*-poet's *Cleanness*: 'it would be superfluous to try to queer *Cleanness* . . . the poet, one might say, has queered this poem himself',[26] and Dinshaw's wide-ranging *Getting Medieval: Sexualities and Communities, Pre- and Postmodern* provided queer medievalism with its first booklength study in 1999.[27]

Our final extract reflects these recent developments in gender studies. Drawn from a special gender issue of the journal *Arthuriana*, the extract performs a radical rereading of the matrix of violence, sexuality and gender identity at work in Sir Thomas Malory's *Morte Darthur*. Focusing on Malory's 'Tale of Sir Gareth', Laurie A. Finke and Martin B. Schichtman look closely at the relation between masculinity and violence in the treatment of Gareth's rise to knighthood and renown. Their reading is conducted in a rich theoretical framework (the social anthropologists Bourdieu and Goux are cited in addition to the gender theorists). The lens of masculinity studies reveals the subtle interplay of violence and identity; the lens of queer theory uncovers the homoerotic shades of Gareth's bedchamber battles with the unnamed knight. Crucially, the authors draw on the feminist theory of Judith Butler to describe

Figure 3   Medieval gender roles at large: Sir Gareth, the Red Knight, and Lynesse as depicted by Sir Arthur Rackham. (Mary Evans Picture Library)

gender as *performative*, residing not in an innate masculinity or femininity but in an individual's alignment of identity with socially constituted gender roles. Malory had been read in a variety of ways by the close of the twentieth century (historicism, formalism, genre studies and more). Finke and Schichtman's 1998 reading of the *Morte* suggests that some aspects of this familiar Arthurian work are only now coming to light.

Extract from Laurie A. Finke and Martin B. Schichtman, 'No Pain, No Gain: Violence as Symbolic Capital in Malory's *Morte Darthur*', *Arthuriana* 8 (1998), 118–25.

[. . .] What perhaps most sets Malory's *Morte d'Arthur* apart from other examples of Arthurian literature is its excessive violence. It is not quantitatively more
violent than other medieval versions of the legend, but it is often more gratuitously violent. As such, it makes a good test case for our claims about masculinity, and particularly about the relationship between masculinity and
violence in the medieval sexual economy. Our argument in this essay rests on
two seemingly contradictory claims. First, despite a tendency to link it with
random, impulsive, and unreflective behavior, violence often has a structure,
one that is oriented toward a purpose, in this case the construction of a hege-
monic masculinity based on martial prowess. We are particularly interested, in
this essay, in institutionalized forms of violence (state-sanctioned violence)
which, as Elaine Scarry has shown in *The Body in Pain*,[1] are structured through
a yoking of injury to some form of contest in the service of some officially
sanctioned goal. In the classical medieval romance, violence is carefully contained by well-established rules governing its application (the Beheading
Game in *Sir Gawain and the Green Knight* for instance). These rules – evident
in such medieval institutions as warfare, the hunt, the joust, single combat, and
juridical situations (trial by ordeal, trial by battle) – govern the times and places
at which violence can occur, the individuals who can participate, and the means
by which violence may be applied. *The Morte d'Arthur* does not deviate significantly from other romances in this regard. Violence provides the foundation for an elaborate structure of exchange which determines hierarchies
among men; it functions as a form of what anthropologist Pierre Bourdieu
refers to as symbolic capital, a system of social exchange in which such intan-
gibles as prestige, status, social control – and in this case violence – serve as
institutionalized (if unspoken) means of acquiring economic wealth.[2] In such
a system, violence serves to stabilize the social order represented by Arthur
and the Round Table, an idealized social order whose purpose is to represent
an emergent monarchical centralization. At the same time, however, (and this
is our second claim) violence in the *Morte* frequently escapes these authoritative discourses of containment and creates a perverse kind of carnival in which
the official goals of violence are subverted by many competing voices of
anarchy. Critics have argued that such a presentation of arbitrary violence in
the *Morte* reflects cultural and political upheavals in England during the War
of the Roses.[3] This reading has some merit, but it misses the extent to which

such social anarchy is not exceptional to the social order of chivalry, but endemic to it. The foundation of a social order on the exchange of violence creates the very chaos it is designed to hold at bay. Whatever its immediate cause, Malory's *Morte* represents violence not only as a centripetal force encouraging order, hierarchy, and centralization, but also as a centrifugal force that creates disorder, contention, and sometimes unbearable chaos. It recognizes both violence's potential for carnivalesque disruption as well as the possibility that this potential may be co-opted and used to foster social control.[4]

In *Symbolic Economies*, Goux suggests how the emergence of centralization out of 'earlier, more heterogeneous, and shifting social relations might depend on the stabilization of that heterogeneity around a "general symbolic equivalent," an idealized standard and measure of value that exists in an imaginary relationship of privilege and exclusion to all other elements which it governs and represents'.[5] In the political realm, the monarch functions as the general symbolic equivalent, the privileged representative and embodiment of the nation, just as in the realm of economics it is money, in the realm of signs it is language, and in the realm of sexuality it is the phallus. Malory's *Morte* describes a version of the process by which a multiplicity of patronage relationships among men is reduced to a single relationship, that between the monarch and his subjects, with the monarch – Arthur being Malory's most striking example – as the privileged and excluded bearer of all value.[6] By establishing patronal relations with his knights – by giving them 'ryches and londys'[7] – Arthur is able to impose a structure on the martial violence of his knights in the form of the 'oath' of the Round Table: he charges them 'never to do outerage nothir mourthir, and allwayes to fle treson, and to gyff mercy unto hym that askith mercy, uppon payne of forfiture [of their] worship and lordship of kynge Arthure for evirmore; and allwayes to do ladyes, damesels, and jantilwomen and wydowes [socour:] strengthe hem in hir ryghtes, and never to enforce them, uppon payne of dethe. Also, that no man take no batayles in a wrongefull quarell for no love ne for no worldis goodis'.[8] Note that this oath attempts to bring violence under the control of official institutions, not to eliminate it. This reformulation of the patron–client relationship around the general symbolic equivalent of the king, however, demands the exclusion of the monarch from participation in exchange – most notably the exchange of violence. While violence escalates with various knights competing with one another for recognition, Arthur retreats further and further from the action – at least until the end. As that which gives value to his subjects – the Knights of the Round Table – Arthur cannot himself be involved in the pursuit of value, but must be excluded. Ultimately, he becomes imaginary. Just as the image of gold, not gold itself, gives value to commodities in the economic sphere, so the image of the king, not necessarily the king himself, gives value to his subjects. Yet the maintenance of the imaginary symbolic equivalent requires the continued circulation of the very acts of violence that constitute it. Within the *Morte d'Arthur*, then, violence becomes a vicious circle, required to establish the rule of the monarch – even in his absence, and yet, in its carnivalesque excesses, destructive of centralized control of any kind.

Malory's 'The Tale of Sir Gareth of Orkney' romanticizes male initiation into the symbolic economy, and thereby contains the violence which determines the acquisition of capital in the Arthurian world. It does so through a dual structuration which requires violence directed at friends who, at least temporarily, become rivals and competitors as well as violence directed at enemies who, if the violence is successful, are brought into the circle of friends. Both forms of violence are designed to assign status (and wealth) to men in relation to other men. Gareth arrives at Arthur's court not as the fourth son of King Lot, Gawain's younger brother (and hence as one who has a place, however unexalted, at Arthur's court) but incognito as a mystery, an enigmatic sign to be read by the members of King Arthur's court. His status is very much in doubt. Some members of the court question whether Gareth is even eligible to participate at all in the violence sanctioned by the Round Table oath. When Arthur orders Kay to treat the mysterious stranger as if 'he were a lordys sonne,' Kay responds, 'That shall lytyll nede . . . to do suche coste upon hym, for I undirtake he is a vylayne borne, and never woll make man, for and he had be com of jantyllmen, he wolde have axed horse and armour, but as he is, so he asketh'.[9] Kay's statement that he 'never woll make man' suggests the extent to which the achievement of masculinity (becoming a man) is tied up with successfully negotiating the system of patronage that determined the homosocial relations between men (becoming Arthur's man by requesting horse and armour from him). A man is known by the gifts he seeks. The true knight, Kay argues, is known by his desire for 'worshyp,' while 'this desyryth ever mete and drynke and brothe'.[10] Disguising his identity in this way, however, frees Gareth from a system of genealogical relationships which favor the eldest son and produce rigid class differences between 'jantyllman' and 'vylayne'. It frees him to participate in a parallel system of patronage relations which open up spaces through which those disinherited and disadvantaged by birth – younger sons – might advance through the judicious application of violence.

When the time comes for Gareth's initiation and the quest that will establish his reputation, the court discovers that Gareth already has all the external trappings of knighthood – the armour – that he needs. He lacks only a shield and a spear (the phallus, for Goux the goal of the hero's initiation). These he acquires by defeating Sir Kay in the untried knight's first application of violence: 'with a foyne threste hym thorow the syde, that sir Kay felle downe as he had bene dede. Than Beawmaynes alyght downe and toke Sir Kayes shylde and his speare and sterte upon his owne horse and rode his way'.[11] This episode allows Gareth revenge for Kay's insults but constrains it within the scheme of capital accumulation that structures the romance.

The violence by which Gareth accumulates the external trappings of knighthood, however, is not enacted only on those members of Arthur's court who had insulted him. He also must fight his chief supporter and ally, Lancelot. The ritual structuration of aristocratic masculinity – at least in the romance – requires that combat with friends be as deadly serious as combat with enemies:

> ayther made hem redy and com togydir so fersly that eyther bare other downe to the erthe and sore were they brused . . . So they russhed togydyrs lyke two borys, trasyng[a] and traversyng[b] and foynyng[c] the mountenaunce[d] of an houre. And sir Launcelot felte hym so bygge that he mervayled of his strengthe, for so he fought more lyker a gyaunte than a kynght, and his fyghtyng was so passyng durable and passyng perelous. For sir Launcelot had so much ado with hym that he dred hymself to be shamed.[12]

There is nothing in the language to set this battle apart from the countless other single combats that litter the *Morte*, nothing to suggest it is any less deadly than a battle with the most villainous and treacherous opponent. Indeed, the language of violence both in this tale and throughout the *Morte* is monotonously repetitive, even ritualistic, drawing on a limited vocabulary and a small stock of rhetorical devices (the most obvious being animal imagery). Though the combat ends in a draw, with Lancelot declaring that 'your quarell and myne is nat grete but we may sone leve of',[13] what Gareth receives from Lancelot is nothing less than his knighthood, his acceptance into the order of chivalry. After this somewhat truncated initiation, Gareth is ready to set off on his quest.

During the quest, the increasingly violent encounters between this untried knight and his deadly opponents and friendly rivals constitute a series of exchanges through which Gareth accumulates the symbolic, material, and human capital that will earn him first a place at the Round Table and then a kingdom of his own through his marriage with Lyoness (the exchange of women). The message of this tale is encapsulated in a plea made by a number of earls, barons, and noble knights that Gareth spare the life of the Red Knight of the Red Lands. Perhaps the most dastardly of the villains Gareth confronts, the Red Knight attempts to demonstrate his value – ostensibly to Dame Lyoness – through an act of outrageous conspicuous consumption: he hangs

[a] treading.
[b] dodging.
[c] thrusting.
[d] space of time.

the fully armed bodies of forty knights he has killed on a tree beneath her window, displaying the products of his accumulated violence. After a particularly difficult battle, described using the same ritualistic language used to describe his battle with Lancelot – 'they yode[a] to batayle agayne, trasyng, traversynge, foynynge, and rasyng[b] as two borys'[14] – Gareth defeats the Red Knight and prepares to kill him – also ostensibly to demonstrate his worth to dame Lyoness – when he is persuaded otherwise: 'hit were fayrer of hym to take omage and feauté and lat hym holde his londes of you than for to sle hym, for by his deth ye shall have none avauntage, and his myssededys that be done may not be undone. And therefore make ye amendys for all partyes, and we all woll becom youre men and do you omage and feauté'.[15] The Red Knight is worth more to Gareth alive than dead. Not only does he pledge his own homage and fealty to Gareth, he offers him 'all tho erlys and barouns with hym'. As Gareth crosses the Arthurian countryside, he controls his capacity for violence – which, as he proves throughout the tale, is formidable – applying it judiciously to accumulate capital. As Gawayne notes, 'ye have sente mo worshypfull knyghtes this twelve-monthe than fyve the beste of the Rounde Table hath done excepte sir Launcelot'.[16] Indeed, Gareth's tale speaks to how the fourth son of a vanquished king – a very likely victim of the system of primogeniture – can amass wealth through the martial skill of his 'fair hands'. The only knights killed by Gareth apparently have nothing of value to offer him. Those to whom he grants mercy provide him with a powerful standing army and the material wealth necessary to become a powerful lord and patron.

Few episodes in any romance expose so blatantly the interconnectedness among exchanges of violence, women, and wealth as Gareth's courtship of Dame Lyoness. As part of his initiation into the role of general symbolic equivalent, Gareth must learn to channel his tendencies toward sexual aggression within the norms of monogamous heteronormativity. He tolerates Lynet's mocking his inadequacies easily enough, although other knights suggest that they would be far less patient with her. Refraining from sexual intercourse with Dame Lyoness, with whom he falls in love at a glance, however, proves more difficult for the young knight. The two lovers 'brente bothe in hoote love that they were acorded[c] to abate their lustys secretly'.[17] The excessive violence that marks their two love scenes threatens to escape the constraints of military structuration that dominate the romance. In the first scene, Lynet introduces an unnamed knight to deflect Gareth's 'hoote lustis', to work off his sexual energies by engaging him in violent bedside combat, thus preserving Lyoness'

[a] went.
[b] slashing.
[c] agreed.

chastity. The bedroom, however, is most definitely not a site marked out for institutional violence of the kind that enables Gareth simultaneously to prove his worth and amass wealth. Because it lays outside of the romance's structuration of violence, the two knights' engagement in this scene seems gratuitously violent, out of control:

> And whan the knyght sawe sir Gareth com so fersly uppon hym he smote hym with a foyne[a] thorow the thycke of the thygh, that the wounde was a shafftemonde[b] brode and had cutte a-too many vaynes and synewys. And therewithall sir Gareth smote hym uppon the helme such a buffette that he felle grovelyng, and than he lepe over hym and unlaced his helme and smote off his hede fro the body.[18]

The bedroom setting and Malory's overheated language suggest that this combat is tinged with more than a little homoeroticism, and along with it an attendant anxiety about the relationship between the male on male violence of the hero's initiation and same sex attraction.[19] The unnamed knight thrusts his 'long gyserne' into Gareth's thigh, dealing him a sexual wound that implies both sexual passivity and castration. Gareth responds by symbolically castrating his opponent, smiting off his head [. . .] Homosexual desire is produced by the metonymic linking of bedroom and battle, but it is also, at the same time, rendered unintelligible through Lynet's machinations to preserve heteronormativity intact. Only an externally imposed force – Lynet's magic – can reintroduce order to this violent scene that threatens all sorts of disruptions – political, sexual, military, economic – and that order is decidedly heterosexual. Her 'oyntemente' restores the decapitated knight's head (and later cures Gareth's sexual wound), bringing the violence under her control when Gareth proves too immature. Her restorative magic renders the exchange no more violent or destructive than the loss of a maidenhead, and indeed seems almost a parodic displacement of the intended deflowering.

The second love scene, ten nights later, substantially repeats the events of the first. This time, however, Gareth, to prevent Lynet from restoring the attacking knight a second time, 'hew the hede uppon an hondred pecis . . . and toke up all tho pecis and threw them oute at a wyndow into the dychis of the castell'.[20] Lynet collects the 'gobbettis of the hede' and glues them back together again. Lyoness' virginity – the basis of the heteronormative exchange of marriage and property – it seems, can be preserved intact for the wedding night only through the dismemberment of the nameless knight. The episode's comic ending in which Lynet painstakingly puts the dismembered knight back together again forestalls the threat of all those sexual desires that might undermine the economy of heterosexual exchange based on marriage, at the same

[a] thrust.
[b] handbreadth.

time it restores heterosexual masculinity – makes it whole – so it can continue to serve as 'an invisible cultural structure of normativity'.[21] All violations of bodily integrity – both dismemberment and deflowering – are rendered invisible by the magic 'oyntemente'.

Lynet's comic magic, then, insures that Gareth and Lyoness wait until their wedding to consummate their love. The wait is important. It legitimizes the marriage of Gareth and Lyoness and simultaneously legitimizes Gareth's claim to Lyoness' kingdom. Their 'overhasty' desire would compromise the political contract that is the real climax of this tale. When at the conclusion of the tale Arthur offers Lyoness to Gareth 'whether he wolde have this lady as peramour, other ellys to have hir to his wyff',[22] the choice is between the violent world of the knight and official world of king. Arthur, in effect, devalues Lyoness by offering her as a paramour; he makes the land she holds of no value to the knight requiring only a lover. In choosing Lyoness as a wife, Gareth revalues her, and takes on value himself as lord of her property. At the conclusion of his tale, Gareth becomes much like King Arthur, a powerful patron who is set apart from the violence engaged in by lesser men – usually bachelor knights seeking patronage – married, a powerful lord who can set the conditions that govern the violent acts of others. He can withdraw from his own wedding tournament to become the spectator whose presence gives value to the violence enacted for his pleasure; the knights he has defeated – Persaunte of Inde, the deuke de la Rouse, and the Rede Knyght of the Rede Laundis – become members of his household, his 'sewear cheyff,' his cup bearer, and his carver. Our students are often troubled by the virtual disappearance of Gareth from the *Morte d'Arthur* following his tale, disturbed that such a compelling figure who has elevated himself to fourth best among Arthur's knights should exclude himself from the action. In this respect, his military career takes a different trajectory from that of, say, Lancelot, who remains perpetually a bachelor knight in love with his patron's wife. 'Gareth', we would argue, enacts a different romance genre entirely, one in which the goal of the quest is the transformation of the knight-errant into the general symbolic equivalent whose power is both determined and marked by exclusion from the exchange of violence. [. . .]

Notes

1 Elaine Scarry, *The Body in Pain: The Making and Unmaking of the World* (Oxford: Oxford University Press, 1985).

2 Bourdieu's notion of symbolic capital is crucial to understanding the medieval political economy; see Pierre Bourdieu, *Outline of a Theory of Practice*, trans. Richard Nice (Cambridge: Cambridge University Press, 1977). Symbolic capital

in the form of honor, prestige, reputation, and status were as important as material wealth in medieval politics and business. The centrality of symbolic capital to success explains why a family of Norfolk lawyers and landowners like the fifteenth-century Pastons would invest so significantly to send one of their younger sons to court, literally to curry favor with more important men in hopes of furthering their business interests. And why, lacking any real symbolic capital to leverage, John Paston II could fail so miserably at court, 'for he is not bold enough to put himself forth' as his uncle Clement writes; see H. S. Bennett, *The Pastons and their England: Studies in an Age of Transition* (Cambridge: Cambridge University Press, 1932), pp. 83–4. The romance only mystifies what the Paston letters discuss so openly, the struggle to accumulate symbolic capital and to convert it to financial capital.

3 Felicity Riddy, for example, writes that 'early readers of both manuscript and print must . . . have had a very specific understanding of the instability and division on which the *Morte Darthur* rests.' She writes of Malory himself as 'an unstable and divided figure': Felicity Riddy, *Sir Thomas Malory* (Leiden: E. J. Brill, 1987), p. 2.

4 On the relationship between centripetal and centrifugal forces in social formations see M. M. Bakhtin, *The Dialogic Imagination*, trans. Michael Holquist and Caryl Emerson (Austin, TX: University of Texas Press, 1981), pp. 270–5. On carnival see M. M. Bakhtin, *Rabelais and his World*, trans. Hélène Iswolsky (Bloomington, IN: Indiana University Press, 1984); and Peter Stallybrass and Allon White, *The Politics and Poetics of Transgression* (Ithaca, NY: Cornell University Press, 1986), esp. ch. 1.

5 Jean-Joseph Goux, *Symbolic Economies after Marx and Freud*, trans. Jennifer Gage (Ithaca, NY: Cornell University Press, 1993).

6 See Christopher Baswell, 'Men in the *Roman d'Eneas*: The Construction of Empire', in Clare A. Lees (ed.), *Medieval Masculiuities: Regarding Men in the Middle Ages* (Minneapolis, MN: University of Minnesota Press, 1994), pp. 149–50.

7 Thomas Malory, *Works* (Oxford: Oxford University Press, 1971), p. 75.

8 Ibid.

9 Ibid., p. 178.

10 Ibid.

11 Ibid., pp. 180–1.

12 Ibid., p. 181.

13 Ibid.

14 Ibid., p. 198.

15 Ibid., p. 200.

16 Ibid., p. 222.

17 Ibid., p. 205.

18 Ibid., p. 206.

19 In our discussion of same sex erotic relationships among bachelor knights we are following Leonard Barkan's characterization of homosexuality as 'erotic relations of any kind between those of the same gender, whatever mentality concerning psyche, society, or identity may accompany them': Leonard Barkan, *Transuming*

Passion: Ganymede and the Erotics of Humanism (Stanford: Stanford University Press, 1991), p. 22. This position avoids the extreme positions of Boswell (see John Boswell, *Christianity, Social Tolerance, and Homosexuality: Gay People in Western Europe from the Beginning of the Christian Era to the Fourteenth Century* [Chicago: Chicago University Press, 1980]), who argues for the possibility not only of homosexuality during the Middle Ages, but of a gay identity more or less continuous with modern gay identity, and Halperin, (see David M. Halperin, *One Hundred Years of Homosexuality and Other Essays on Greek Love* [New York: Routledge, 1990]), who argues that since sexuality itself was an invention of the nineteenth century, even if there were those who sought out sexual contact with others of the same sex, seeking homosexuality in history is anachronistic. See also Dinshaw (Carolyn Dinshaw, 'A Kiss is Just a Kiss: Heterosexuality and its Consolations in *Sir Gawain and the Green Knight*', *Diacritics* 24 [1994], 207), who argues that we can and should speak of sexuality in the Middle Ages as long as we historicize it with regard to 'psyche, society, and identity', and David L. Boyd, 'Sodomy, Misogyny, and Displacement: Occluding Queer Desire in *Sir Gawain and the Green Knight*', *Arthuriana* 8 (1998), 77–113.

20   Malory, *Works*, p. 207.
21   Dinshaw, 'A Kiss is Just a Kiss', p. 208.
22   Malory, *Works*, p. 223.

Further Reading

Further reading for this topic might best start online. Of the many medieval websites on gender two of the best are: *Feminae: Medieval Women and Gender Index* (http://www.haverford.edu) and *Medieval Feminist Forum: Sources for Medieval Feminist Scholarship* (http://www.smfs.uoregon.edu). Links from these sites also give access to issues of the *Medieval Feminist Newsletter* (inaugurated in 1984 by E. Jane Burns, Roberta Krueger and Elizabeth Robertson).
In hard copy, the special issue of *Speculum* on gender studies and medievalism forms an excellent starting-point to the topic, as do the various feminist anthologies; for example, Ruth Evans and Lesley Johnson (eds), *The Wife of Bath and All her Sect: Feminist Readings in Middle English Literature* (London: Routledge, 1994). Hot off the press is the collaborative volume edited by Carolyn Dinshaw and David Wallace, *The Cambridge Companion to Medieval Women's Writing* (Cambridge: Cambridge University Press, 2003). In 1998 *The Yearbook of Langland Studies* included a special section on gender and *Piers Plowman*: *The Yearbook of Langland Studies* 12, ed. Andrew Galloway and John A. Alford (Asheville: Pegasus Press, 1998).
Jeffrey Jerome Cohen has written about monstrous medieval bodies. His *Of Giants: Sex, Monsters and the Middle Ages* (Minneapolis, MN: University of Minnesota Press, 1999) looks at a variety of Middle English texts, viewing the figure of the giant as 'a violently gendered body'. In the genre of Arthurian literature, there is a cluster of intriguing feminist re-readings of *Sir Gawain and the Green Knight*, including Geraldine Heng's, 'Feminine Knots and the Other *Sir Gawain and the Green Knight*',

PMLA 106 (1991), 500–14; and Sheila Fisher, 'Leaving Morgan Aside: Women, History and Revisionism in *Sir Gawain and the Green Knight*', in Christopher Baswell and William Sharpe (eds), *The Passing of Arthur: New Essays in Arthurian Tradition* (New York: Garland Press, 1988), pp. 129–51. Two foundational texts on theories of the body and gender identity are Elaine Scarry's book, *The Body in Pain: The Making and Unmaking of the World* (Oxford: Oxford University Press, 1985) and the radical gender study by Judith Butler, *Bodies that Matter: On the Discursive Limits of 'Sex'* (New York: Routledge, 1993). A foundational text for queer theorists is Eve Kosofsky Sedgwick's *Between Men: English Literature and Male Homosocial Desire* (New York: Columbia University Press, 1985).

Chapter Notes

1 Allen's contribution to medieval scholarship is evaluated by John C. Hirsch in *Hope Emily Allen: Medieval Scholarship and Feminism* (Norman, OK: Pilgrim Books, 1988).

2 Eileen Power, *Medieval English Nunneries* (Cambridge: Cambridge University Press, 1922).

3 Judith M. Bennett, 'Medievalism and Feminism', *Speculum* 68 (1993), 309–31 (314).

4 Daniel M. Murtaugh, 'Women and Geoffrey Chaucer', *English Literary History* 38 (1971), 473–92 (492).

5 Hope Phyllis Weissman, 'Antifeminism in Chaucer's Characterization of Women', in George D. Economou (ed.), *Geoffrey Chaucer* (New York: McGraw-Hill, 1975), pp. 93–110.

6 Priscilla Martin, *Chaucer's Women: Nuns, Wives and Amazons* (London: Macmillan, 1990), p. xii.

7 Jill Mann, *Geoffrey Chaucer* (London: Harvester Wheatsheaf, 1991), p. xii.

8 Elaine Tuttle Hansen, *Chaucer and the Fictions of Gender* (Berkeley, CA: University of California Press, 1992), p. 12.

9 Judith M. Bennett, 'Medievalism and Feminism', *Speculum* 68 (1993), 309–31 (310–11).

10 Carol M. Meale (ed.), *Women and Literature in Britain, 1150–1500* (Cambridge: Cambridge University Press, 1993), p. 4.

11 Alexandra Barratt (ed.), *Women's Writing in Middle English* (London: Longman, 1992); Alcuin Blamires (ed.), *Woman Defamed and Woman Defended: An Anthology of Medieval Texts* (Oxford: Clarendon Press, 1992).

12 Ruth Evans and Lesley Johnson (eds), *The Wife of Bath and All her Sect: Feminist Readings in Middle English Literature* (London: Routledge, 1994), p. 6.

13 Sandra J. McEntire (ed.), *Margery Kempe: A Book of Essays* (New York: Garland Press, 1992); Lynn Staley, *Margery Kempe's Dissenting Fictions* (University Park: Pennsylvania State University Press, 1994).

14 Karma Lochrie, *Margery Kempe and Translations of the Flesh* (Philadelphia: University of Pennsylvania Press, 1991), p. 3.

15   Kathleen Biddick, 'Genders, Bodies, Borders: Technologies of the Visible', *Speculum* 68 (1993), 389–418.

16   An important earlier study in this vein was Vern L. Bullough's, 'Medieval Medical and Scientific Views of Women', *Viator* 4 (1973), 485–501.

17   Carolyn Dinshaw, *Chaucer's Sexual Poetics* (Madison: University of Wisconsin Press, 1989), p. 182.

18   Clare A. Lees (ed.), *Medieval Masculinities: Regarding Men in the Middle Ages* (Minneapolis, MN: University of Minnesota Press, 1994), pp. xv–xvi.

19   Allen J. Frantzen, 'When Women Aren't Enough,' *Speculum* 68 (1993), 445–471 (471).

20   Sarah Kay and Miri Rubin (eds), *Framing Medieval Bodies* (Manchester: Manchester University Press, 1994), p. 1.

21   Karma Lochrie, Peggy McCracken and James A. Schultz (eds), *Constructing Medieval Sexuality* (Minneapolis, MN: University of Minnesota Press, 1997), p. xvii.

22   Carolyn Dinshaw, 'A Kiss is Just a Kiss: Heterosexuality and its Consolations in *Sir Gawain and the Green Knight*', *Diacritics* 24 (1994), 204–26 (206).

23   Dinshaw, *Chaucer's Sexual Poetics*, pp. 156–84; Glenn Burger, 'Kissing the Pardoner', *PMLA* 107 (1992), 1143–54; Steven F. Kruger, 'Claiming the Pardoner: Toward a Gay Reading of Chaucer's Pardoner's Tale', *Exemplaria* 6.1 (1994), 115–39.

24   Donald R. Howard, *The Idea of the Canterbury Tales* (Berkeley, CA: University of California Press, 1976); Monica E. McAlpine, 'The Pardoner's Homosexuality and How it Matters', *PMLA* 95 (1980), 8–22.

25   Carolyn Dinshaw, 'Chaucer's Queer Touches: A Queer Touches Chaucer', *Exemplaria* 7.1 (1995), 75–92 (76); Glenn Burger, 'Gay Chaucer', *English Studies in Canada* 20 (1994), 153–69.

26   Allen J. Frantzen, 'The Disclosure of Sodomy in *Cleanness*', *PMLA* 111 (1996), 451–64 (452).

27   Carolyn Dinshaw, *Getting Medieval: Sexualities and Communities, Pre- and Postmodern* (Durham, NC: Duke University Press, 1999).

8

Identity

Divergent critical approaches to the question of individual identity in medieval English texts. Literary and theatrical approaches to dramaturgy and characterization in David Mills's critical prologue to mystery-play characters; Marxist-influenced studies of identity in the work of David Aers on Sir Gawain *and the* Green Knight; *historicism and psychoanalysis in Lee Patterson's study of subjectivity in* Troilus *and* Criseyde.

A final theme much revisited by Middle English criticism is that of character, identity, subjectivity or selfhood in medieval English literature. The literature of the period introduces us to some vivid, intensely realized characters: Langland's Will, Chaucer's Troilus, Malory's Lancelot. And it brings us into the putative presence of genuine historical subjectivities too: Margery Kempe, Julian of Norwich, Richard Rolle, Walter Hilton, the Paston family. Together, these texts have prompted some influential and enduring character studies, and have raised lively and enduring critical questions on the subject of identity. Are the subjectivities represented in Middle English texts continuous with those of later literature or are medieval identities somehow distinct from modern identities? Is Chaucer's Criseyde as amenable to sustained character study as Shakespeare's Cressida? Should a character study historicize, drawing on medieval humoural theory to explain the melancholy of Troilus or the Pearl-dreamer, or are modern psychoanalytic approaches to the constitution of subjectivity in fact better placed to reveal what is present (and tellingly absent) in medieval characterization?

> Next to Shakspere, Chaucer is the greatest delineator of character in our literature.
> Medieval characterization was almost purely typical. Chaucer vitalized the types. This great feat he accomplished, first by his humorous and pathetic realism, and, secondly, by his dramatic power, – by which I mean, of course, his ability to put himself into the place of various men and women, and then to express their nature in speech and action.[1]

1915: Early character-based criticism in the work of George Lyman Kittredge

Perhaps the best place to open the discussion is upon the medieval stage. Naturally enough, discussions of character, subjectivity and identity in English literature have repeatedly gravitated towards the great characters of drama. Renaissance drama, in particular, with its celebrated studies of character and its many soliloquies has attracted a long tradition of character-based criticism. But what were the dominant conceptions of dramatic character for medieval players where drama, on the basis of what has come down to us, was overwhelmingly religious in nature, where 'the stage' took the form of a pageant-wagon in the street – if not the street itself – where 'acting' often involved the impersonation, perhaps wearing a mask, of a biblical character, even a divine figure or, in the Morality plays, some abstract quality such as Mercy, Good Deeds, Everyman?

Our first extract by David Mills engages this question, offering a 'critical prologue' to the questions of character, identity and selfhood in the mystery cycles. Both literary and theatrical aspects of the question are considered. The extract moves from a survey of critical responses to medieval character to a performance-oriented consideration of whether Stanislavskian or Brechtian dramatic theory make best sense of the plays for a modern-day actor. (The journal from which the essay is drawn is slanted towards critical interpretation and performance: it informs modern productions of medieval drama such as the biennial staging of the mystery plays at York or the production of Tony Harrison's adaptation *The Mysteries*, last staged at the National Theatre in 2000.) As the extract concludes, Mills's literary-theatrical approach yields a key interpretative point for responding to character in medieval plays: both critic and actor alike must recognize that the basis for individual action in the plays is less human motivation than divine will: 'Actions originate in the will of God, not in the characters of men.'

Extract from David Mills, 'Characterisation in the English Mystery Cycles: A Critical Prologue', in *Medieval English Theatre* 5 (1983), 5–10.

As a critical term, *characterisation* is not much over a century old – OED records the definition 'creation of fictitious characters' only in 1866, although this meaning is an obvious development of the 1814 sense: 'description of characteristic or essential features, portrayed in words'. Thus 20th-century critics have the familiar problem of using a term with 19th-century overtones to analyse the drama of the Middle Ages.

A more serious problem, however, is that characterisation is not an exclusively 'theatrical' term. Its meaning is still bound up with character in the sense first exemplified by OED from 1749: 'A personality invested with distinctive attributes and qualities by a novelist or dramatist; also, the personality or "part" assumed by an actor on the stage' (OED, *character*, 17). This combination of literary and theatrical aspects points to the fact that dramatic characterisation is part of the fluid interrelationship of author, text, and actor which is present in all theatrical realisation. But it is sadly true that such interrelationships for the drama of the Middle Ages must today be a matter only for inference and speculation. And our awareness of subsequent theories of criticism and acting makes such speculation even more difficult.

But perhaps the major problem in using characterisation as a critical term can be found within OED's definition 11 of *character*, first exemplified from 1647: 'The sum of the moral and mental qualities which distinguish an individual or a race, viewed as a homogeneous whole; the individuality impressed by nature and habit on man or nation; moral constitution'. A concern for the hidden, elusive uniqueness which distinguishes each individual, which gives coherence and meaning to his/her every action, which may even make his/her reactions to some degree predictable, can lead us directly to the concerns, the techniques, and the language of the modern psychologist. The idea that the task of the actor is somehow to discover the inner uniqueness of the character he/she is playing has for long been seen as a goal of theatrical characterisation, as the anonymous treatise *The Actor* of 1750 suggests:

> The actor who is to express to us a peculiar passion and its effects, if he wou'd play his character with *truth*, is not only to assume the emotions which that passion wou'd produce in the generality of mankind; but he is to give it that peculiar form under which it wou'd appear, when exerting itself in the breast of such a person as he is giving us the portrait of.[1]

But our awareness of an unseen individuality must arise from its external expression, from the *characteristics* of the person in the sense of the distinctive marks, traits, or features; the distinguishing or essential peculiarities or qualities (OED 1664) by which the person is identified. On stage, the actor employs a collection of signals – a kind of rhetoric of bearing, gesture, movement, dress, etc. – which his audience can understand and interpret. An awareness of such signals may well underlie some prescriptions of dress or gesture in medieval stage directions; the preamble to the Anglo-Norman *Adam* is a suggestive example: 'Let all persons be coached thus, so that they may speak in an orderly manner and make gestures appropriate to the things of which they speak.'[2] Perhaps one source for the repertoire of such gestures may be found in rhetoricians' concerns for the delivery of set speeches. Geoffrey of Vinsauf, for example, offers the following advice:

A bellowing voice goes forth, the countenance is inflamed, and the demeanour disturbed: the external behaviour follows the internal, and the inner and outer man are identically moved. If you represent the person of this angry man, what, as a speaker, will you do? Imitate true rages. Yet be not yourself enraged: behave partially like the character, but not inwardly. Let your behaviour be the same in every detail but not to such an extent; and suggest wrath becomingly. You can also present the gestures of a rustic character and be humorous. Your voice may suggest the character's voice, your face his face, and your gestures his gestures – through little clues.[3]

This dualism between internalised individuality and external characteristics has become a focus for many modern critical discussions of medieval literature, particularly of Chaucer. In 1898 Saintsbury claimed:

[Chaucer's] characters are rather astonishingly brilliant types, individualised by the freshness and sharpness of the impression, rather than absolutely individual persons. It was indeed almost impossible, till the clutch of allegory had been finally shaken off, that the complete tyranny of the type should be shaken off likewise.[4]

But in 1915 Kittredge demanded that Chaucer's pilgrims be regarded not as types but as unique individuals:

[Chaucer] had the genius to create the Pilgrims, endowing each of them with an individuality that goes much beyond the typical . . . The Pilgrims do not exist for the sake of the stories, but vice versa. Structurally regarded, the stories are merely long speeches expressing, directly or indirectly, the characters of the several persons.[5]

The 'character *versus* type' debate thus becomes one of literary primacy, motivation, and thematic centre, and has continued in those terms to the present day. Thus J. B. Trapp seems to incline towards Kittredge:

[The pilgrims] are types, without doubt . . . Yet the characters are so individual that they seem to ride out of the pages. Are we to conclude that they are portraits drawn from life? . . . [Chaucer] may have taken hints from contemporary men and women who were known to him personally or by repute to diversify the types he was drawing.[6]

But D. W. Robertson, continuing Saintsbury's concern with type and allegory, argues:

Medieval men were likely to think of their problems as community problems and of their own behavior in moral rather than psychological terms. It is a mistake therefore to seek psychological profundity in medieval art or to expect characters to display personality in the modern sense of the word.[7]

But it is not only the awareness of an allegorical mode which leads some critics to deny a medieval concern with the individual. Some critics have also emphasised that the prescriptions for composing rhetorical portraits encouraged the perception of literary character in terms of rhetorical tricks employed in the service of persuasion. Pamela Gradon, discussing Matthew of Vendome's advice on the creation of such portraits, typifies this view:

> The author then has to assign a topic, or subject, to a matter, or person, by means of his attributes; that is to say, he must consider what kind of impression he wishes the character to convey, whether he wishes to praise or blame, and choose the details in accordance with this theme.[8]

Such a view of rhetorically appropriate details would obviously complement a thesis of rhetorically appropriate gesture.

These and other theories[9] are important for any attempt to define the dramatist's contribution to characterisation in the play-text, for he is the heir of that literary tradition and his writing is conditioned by the varying claims of naturalism, allegory, and rhetoric. But plays are performed by individual people. What is to become of their own individualities as they enter the plays?

Of the various answers possible to this question, two must be foremost in the mind of the modern actor. On the one hand, his task may be to occupy his part completely; as Stanislavsky puts it:

> [An actor] must fit his own human qualities to the life of this other person, and pour into it all of his own soul. The fundamental aim of our art is the creation of this inner life of a human spirit, and its expression in an artistic form.[10]

On the other hand, his task may be to make the audience aware of a disjunction, a *partial* fit, between his real self and the 'self' of the character he is playing: as Brecht puts it:

> The actor does not let himself be transformed into the man he presents so that nothing of himself is left. He is not Lear, Harpagon, or the good soldier Schweik – he is 'showing' them to an audience . . . Giving up the idea of complete transformation, the actor brings forward his text, not as an improvisation but as a *quotation*.[11]

Both approaches, of course, envisage actors who have been rigorously trained in ways that – we assume – medieval guildsmen were not. One medieval actor at least certainly used his role for self-display, to make the audience conscious of actor rather than role – Chaucer's Absalon:

Somtyme to shewe his lightnesse and maistrye, He pleyeth Herodes upon a scaf-
fold hye.[12]

I suspect that it is the unpredictable nature of a performance in the hands of
the actors which really underlies the objection to an analogy of religious drama
and religious painting expressed in *A Tretise of Miraclis Pleyinge*:

> But so ben nat miraclis pleyinge that ben made more to deliten men bodliy than
> to ben bokis to lewid men. And therfore yif they ben quike bookis, they ben
> quike bookis to shrewidnesse more than to godeness.[13]

I would certainly make the minimal assumption that the nature of the text and
the acting style should be compatible, and that a disconcerting tension might
result from applying Stanislavskian method to typological or allegorical drama.

[. . .] With the mystery cycles we enter a universe of moral order whose drama-
tised foundation is God. God ultimately can compel all morally meaningful
action. Hence characterisation is divorced from causation. Actions originate
in the will of God, not in the characters of men; and they are manifestations
of divine will, not of human individuality. Causation is thereby freed from the
necessity of plausibility, since an omniscient God is unknowable and unac-
countable, but axiomatically right. 'It is my will it shoulde be soe'[14] is reason
enough. A principle of moral disorder is admitted on licence into the morally
ordered universe by 'free will' and is initially located in Lucifer; mimesis
becomes the means by which he seeks to acquire the attributes of God, to
occupy the divine role completely instead of merely quoting it in selected
attributes.[15] Hence there exists, outside the historical action, as moving agents
in the moral universe, a set of strangely garbed, masked, supernatural beings
whose costumes conceal their human form and signal their detachment from
the norms of naturalistic – and hence predictable – conduct. [. . .]

Acknowledgement

This 'prologue' is a slightly revised version of a paper given at the Medieval English
Theatre Conference on the theme of 'Characterization in Medieval Drama' which was
held at the University of Salford, England, on 26 March 1983.

Notes

1   Quoted in Richard Boleslavsky, *Acting: The First Six Lessons* (London, 1949;
reprinted, 1966), p. 76.

2 'The Service for Representing Adam', in David Bevington (ed.), *Medieval Drama* (Boston, 1975), p. 81 (my italics).

3 'The New Poetics', in James J. Murphy (ed.), *Three Medieval Rhetorical Arts* (Berkeley, 1971), p. 108.

4 G. Saintsbury, *A Short History of English Literature* (1898; London, 1944), p. 128.

5 G. L. Kittredge, *Chaucer and his Poetry* (Cambridge, MA, 1915; 55th anniversary edition, 1970), pp. 154–5.

6 In Frank Kermode and John Hollander (eds), *The Oxford Anthology of English Literature*, vol. 1 (Oxford, 1973), p. 130.

7 D. W. Robertson, Jr (ed.), *The Literature of Medieval England* (New York, 1970), p. 239.

8 Pamela Gradon, *Form and Style in Early English Literature* (London, 1971), p. 239.

9 Among such theories one may note particularly the influence of humoural and affective physiognomy. See W. C. Curry, *Chaucer and the Medieval Sciences* (rev. edn, London, 1968), and John Block Friedman, 'Another Look at Chaucer and the Physiognomists', *Studies in Philology* 78, 138–52.

10 Constantin Stanislavski, *An Actor Prepares*, trans. Elizabeth Reynolds Hapgood (London, 1937; repr. 1967), p. 14.

11 Quoted in Toby Cole and Helen Crich Chinoy (eds), *Actors on Acting* (New York, 1949; repr. 1965), pp. 282–3.

12 'The Canterbury Tales', I 3383–4 in F. N. Robinson (ed.) *The Works of Geoffrey Chaucer*, 2nd edn (London, 1957).

13 Clifford Davidson (ed.), *A Middle English Treatise on the Playing of Miracles* (Washington, 1981), p. 45, lines 446–50.

14 R. M. Lumiansky and David Mills (eds), *The Chester Mystery Cycle* (EETS, SS, 3; London, 1974), vol. 1, p. 3.

15 See further R. W. Hanning, '"You Have Begun a Parlous Pleye": The Nature and Limits of Dramatic Mimesis as a Theme in Four Middle English "Fall of Lucifer" Cycle Plays', reprinted in Clifford Davidson et al. (eds), *The Drama of the Middle Ages: Comparative and Critical Essays* (New York, 1982), pp. 140–68.

Mills emphasizes the pre-eminence of God's will in shaping human action. Is it this that defines a more general difference between medieval and modern conceptions of character? Stephen Medcalf raised this question in the 1981 collaborative volume, *The Later Middle Ages*: APPROACHES TO CHARACTER

What is it to be a person? Is a person valuable or interesting in virtue of the essential singularity of his being? Or in virtue of what is universalizable in him, of his relation to a general type or to the categories of a code of ethics? Or in virtue of his relation to other people, to one other person, or to God? As with the idea of an artist, so with that of a person, one hypothesis would define the medieval view as the exact opposite of the romantic view. Kierkegaard in the nineteenth century maintained that a man's essential singularity and his relation to God are the same, essentially private thing: the hypothesis I refer to would say that the medievals identified the point of a person's being with his place in a public ethical scheme or social hierarchy.[2]

Some critical approaches to Middle English literature share this hypothesis, maintaining that so different was the thought-world of medieval writers and audiences that we are unjustified in seeking reflections of modern subjectivity in medieval works. Other critics strongly contest the notion that subjectivity was somehow chanced upon only with the dawning of the Renaissance or the Enlightenment. If this were so, they argue, why should the great characters of medieval literature speak to us so forcibly? Troilus, Crisyede, Gawain have repeatedly prompted the kind of close character-based criticism and psychological commentary usually exclusive to criticism of the novel. For answer, some scholars have suggested that it is actually *during* the medieval period itself that notions of selfhood undergo development and change. The conflicted, contradictory character traits of a Gawain or Troilus reveal the shifts in understanding taking place. For some commentators, this process amounts to nothing less than 'the discovery of the individual'. The process is described in a work on church and intellectual history of 1972:

> The discovery of the individual was one of the most important cultural developments in the years between 1050 and 1200. It was not confined to any one group of thinkers. Its central features may be found in many different circles: a concern with self-discovery; an interest in the relations between people, and in the role of the individual within society; an assessment of people by their inner intentions rather than by their external acts. These concerns were, moreover, conscious and deliberate. 'Know yourself' was one of the most frequently quoted injunctions.[3]

Attempts to locate the origin of this discovery in place and time have been various. Linda Georgianna's important study of the thirteenth-century *Ancrene Wisse* looked in detail at this question. Written as a spiritual guide for a group of female religious recluses, *Ancrene Wisse*'s emphasis upon the inner life makes it a rich subject for the search for the individual:

> The subtlety and specificity with which the *Wisse* author examines the inner life is ample evidence of his central interest in promoting individuality in the solitary life rather than the more traditional otherworldly goals usually set for solitaries. In this interest the author reflects the complex world of late twelfth-century and early thirteenth-century thought, a world in which various systems of thought first collided, then fused to produce a rather new set of values centering upon the individual rather than the community. In particular, the author writes at a time when the traditional distinction between an elite theology for monks and a theology for laymen collapses, resulting in a new moral theology,

equally applicable to all Christians because its field of study is the variety and individuality of human conduct. Once the world is viewed as inescapable, because it signifies not simply an outer reality, but a psychological reality that we all carry within us, then the whole notion of monasticism as withdrawal from the world is open to question, and the new religious ideal is dominated by the notion of conscience, the moral reflection of the outer world that exists in men at all times. The movement is away from a cloistered, static view of the world, away from any view that considers the world as separable from the self.[4]

If Georgianna is correct, 'the discovery of the individual' in Middle English writings takes place early. It might even coincide closely with the Fourth Lateran Council of 1215 – a council that is seen as significant by social historians given that its insistence upon annual lay confession created a whole tradition of confessional literature focused upon self-knowledge and self-understanding. By contrast, John Burrow's *Medieval Writers and their Work* of 1982 places 'the discovery of the individual' much later in the history of Middle English writings:

> The real discovery of the individual comes in English literature much later – with the great writers of the Ricardian period and their successors in the fifteenth century. The Gawain-poet preserves his anonymity; but his contemporaries, Chaucer, Langland, and Gower, are poets with names and identities who speak in distinctive voices. The same can be said of the next generation: Lydgate and Hoccleve, for instance. In this later medieval period, in fact, anonymity increasingly becomes characteristic of certain *types* of writing – ballad, for instance – while other types reveal more and more about their authors.[5]

Focused upon one of these fourteenth-century writers, our second extract takes up the question of individual discovery, arguing how self-knowledge is achieved at a considerable price in *Sir Gawain and the Green Knight*. David Aers's sociohistorical approach in *Community, Gender and Individual Identity: English Writing 1360–1430* looks at the social conflicts and ideological tensions inscribed in late Middle English texts. He views these as reflective of the break-up of traditional patterns of feudal social organization and their replacement by forms of social interaction and administration based around the emergence of the cash nexus of early capitalism (the approach followed is thus similar to that taken in Sheila Delany's essay in chapter 7).

In Aers's reading of *Sir Gawain and the Green Knight* the effect of these contesting social forces registers in the tension the hero encounters between collective and individual spheres of experience and modes of consciousness. Sent out on a quest as chief representative of Arthurian chivalry, Sir Gawain initially represents the values of the aristocratic collective, he is 'the honourman' in Aers's term, drawing on the work of social historian Mervyn James.

Put to the test at Hautdesert, Gawain's experience of sexual and moral temptation leads to a split in his consciousness: he uncovers aspects of his identity not expressed nor even countenanced in his public role at Camelot. As these areas of his experience and self-understanding become hived off from the collective, Gawain, according to Aers, experiences a 'privatization or interiorization of consciousness'. His self-knowledge is achieved at the price of his estrangement from the chivalric masculine identity he had previously epitomized. And when it is recalled that Gawain represents not just himself but the interests of the entire chivalric elite, the split he experiences starts to look portentous for late medieval feudalism.

The Marxist-influenced historicism of the extract is explicitly oppositional to an earlier school of Anglo-American *Gawain* criticism. From the 1960s onwards, several critical treatments of the poem emphasized what was seen as 'Gawain's fault' – his concealment of the green girdle from Bertilak and his presumed failure to make confession for the deed to his priest. Viewing this debate as extrinsic to the action and import of the poem, Aers joins with Stephen Knight in deploring the influence of 'a priestly caste of scholars' for (in their view) magnifying this moral dimension out of all proportion. A critical emphasis on 'Gawain's fault' makes the poem one of individual trial, suffering and redemption. Aers's reading employs a broader frame of reference: the individual is defined against the collective, public and private interrelate, the solitary hero acts within 'the ethos of his community'.

Extract from David Aers, '"In Arthurus Day": Community, Virtue and Individual Identity in *Sir Gawain and the Green Knight*', in *Community, Gender and Individual Identity: English Writing, 1360–1430* (London: Routledge, 1988), pp. 162–9.

[. . .] Within the network of the massive continuities between Gawain's home community and the Hautdesert which receives him as an ideal model stepping out of a courtesy book, certain discontinuities emerge. On these I now wish to focus. They are not in themselves presented as matter for lamentation, for celebration, or for moralistic censoriousness. But they do provide crucial elements of the plot and their significance is resonant as their consequences pervade the poem's ending. What their cultural and historical significance may be, we shall also consider. The discontinuities I have in mind can be characterized as the privatization or domestication of space, together with what that enables, and the privatization or interiorization of consciousness. Both of these are realized by some shift in poetic mode.

The privatization of space is one aspect of a complex social history.[1] At Hautdesert solitude is not just the effect of heroic mission in wild country but as much a potential of life within the castle as it was for Troilus in his community and palace. We are now shown Gawain alone, lying contentedly in bed, 'Vnder couertour ful clere, cortyned about' while daylight shines on the walls (1,178–81; see also 1,469–71, 1,731–2).[2] In the public world and its heroic word a domestic sphere has suddenly been opened out or, depending on one's perspectives, closed in. The poet did not make space or time at Camelot in which the knight could be described like this, or in which he could be found getting dressed alone or seeking a place to hide a gift (1,871–5). Given his grasp of the consequences such private spaces contained, the need to moralize about them would have been understandable – one may recall Langland's anger at the privatization of upper-class eating habits (*Piers Plowman*, X 97–103). But he never does. While this accords with the poem's avoidance of the prophetic and judgemental registers of *Piers Plowman* or *Cleanness*, perhaps the poet's immanence to court culture meant that even when looking back to Arthur's day he saw no point in already belated attempts simply to close the stable door with moralization, attempts such as Langland's. He did, however, dramatize the way such spaces could encourage interactions which would affect honourmen even in their public relations and roles.

One especially impressive example of this process will suffice here. It comes after Gawain has safely negotiated the difficulties presented to him by the lady's second visit to his bedroom. He is enjoying a typical courtly evening of 'al þe manerly merþe þat mon may of telle' (1,648–57), a characteristic celebration of the collective, the means and ends of heroic virtue. Customary decorum is maintained and the most honoured guest, 'oure luflych knyʒt' sits beside the lady (1,657). Suddenly the poet shifts the narrative's mode and focus (1,658–63):

> Such semblaunt[a] to þat segge[b] semly ho[c] made,
> Wyth stille stollen countenaunce, þat stalworth to plese,[d]
> þat al forwondered[e] watz þe wyʒe[f] and wroþ[g] with hymseluen,

[a] expression.
[b] man.
[c] she.
[d] secretive, surreptitious looks to please that bold [knight].
[e] bewildered.
[f] man.
[g] angry.

Bot he nolde not for his nurture nurne hir aȝaynez[a]
Bot dalt with hir al in daynté, how-se-euer þe dede turned
Towrast.[b]

On this passage A. C. Spearing comments that 'we are not left merely as observers of the behaviour of the Lady and Gawain, but are taken into Gawain's consciousness and given a most detailed and subtle account of the eddying conflict in his feelings'.[3] Privatization of space and interiorization of consciousness has disturbing implications. As with Troilus, Gawain's gender and class identity is bound up with a 'nurture' which includes 'daynté' and 'luf-talkyng' (927). What happens now is that the public identification-marks of an honourman become sources of serious difficulty, forcing the knight to direct his baffled anger against himself rather than the woman with whose 'stille stollen countenaunce' he colludes, and must collude. Gawain's public 'nurture' and the identity it guarantees has exposed him to forces in the private, domestic spaces which in turn bring distressing pressures to bear on him in the public domain itself. A troublesome private space is opened up within the collective and within the knight. The coherent, integrated heroic figure is thrown into unfamiliar self-division. The poet highlights the subtle and painful dialectic involved here by having Gawain's disturbance take place in the most public and symbolically central area of collective life, the great hall. It is here, before the leader's inner group withdraws to the 'chambre', that Gawain determines to pursue the contradictions now opening out in his 'nurture' and the identity it gives him, 'how-se-euer þe dede turned / Towrast'. In this desperate resolution we should not underestimate the man's baffled rage at finding how mastery of courtly discourses, a mastery that represents control of his world, including relations with females, now appears as a form which simultaneously enslaves him, 'how-se-euer þe dede turned / Towrast'.[4] In these new interactions between private and public, mastery becomes bondage and collective solidarities come under confusing pressures they themselves seem to sponsor. The knight's sense of contradiction, of self-division, potentially poses grave problems to the culture whose idealized self-image he represents.

This brilliant and resonant passage must stand here for the poem's increasing concern with Gawain's consciousness. The concern, by no means consistently sustained, is to evoke an identity in a mode which includes introspective activity and the possibility of sharp self-division. Other episodes, like the third temptation, display the features we have been analysing.[5] But rather than reiterate and reapply the kind of argument developed above, it will suffice to note that the pressures brought to bear on the heroic virtues lead to slippages in

---

[a] spurn her openly.
[b] But behaved courteously with her regardless of how this might be understood.

their language. In the private sphere Gawain ruminates how if the woman's girdle were to save his life 'þe sleȝt were noble' (1,855–9). In the public domain of the community to which Gawain belongs it would be impossible to categorize an action or a 'sleȝt' as 'noble' simply because it might enable an individual to live longer. The knight's terms represent an increasingly troublesome split between private and public, inner and outer. They probably account for a puzzling aspect of the third temptation: namely, why Gawain never mentions his public agreement with the woman's lord, his host, and why the poet never hints that 'hit come to his hert' (1,855). His motives for ignoring it when he hears the girdle might save his life are hardly obscure, but the case is different earlier in the scene. There he *is* attempting to extricate himself from the woman's 'luf' without showing any marks of being a 'craþayn' (a villein, a churl) lacking 'cortaysye' (1,772–3); there he *is* attempting to reject the ring (both literal and sexually symbolic). Why should he ignore an agreement which would allow him to disentangle himself from the woman's web, retain 'cortaysye' with mastery over discourse and woman, and simultaneously affirm the masculine bond between honourmen as well as his public identity? It seems that the splits between the private and the public have become such that the public game (whatever its legal terminology it remains a holiday game) seems so infinitely remote from the intimacy of the private sphere that it simply does not 'come to his hert' in any form, neither when it could help his purposes nor when it would impede them as a guilty thought. The split in domains and spaces has generated a split in forms of consciousness, a split in 'obligations', and, as we have outlined, divisions in the knight's identity.[6]

It is a consequence of just such splits that the hero can be represented as making what he assumes to be his final confession and returning to fulfil his social role with heroic gaiety, apparently now free from any introspective agonizings. One can see why scholars of the 'priestly caste' should turn to clerical texts on confession, trying to sort out whether Gawain's confession was 'consciously or unconsciously incomplete' and assessing his theological guilt. Perhaps the privatizations of space and consciousness at Hautdesert might seem to justify such a familiarly prying, inquisitorial anatomization, inviting readers to become confessor to this straying sheep, this 'learner' penitent.[7] But only 'might seem' to do so. For the poet makes the contrasts between different forms of representation quite sharp enough for us to respect them, and here one must respect the absence of introspective tremors such as those shown by Gawain as he sat next to the lady at dinner. When a community complete with court clerics, Bishop, and daily ecclesiastical service produces a pious knight who represents its idealized self-image, and when this paragon fails to classify an act as 'sin', fails apparently even to wonder whether it might be so classifiable, then it is quite irrelevant to categorize that failure as 'sin', whatever scholastic *Summae* or counter-reformation Catholic dogmatics might maintain. If the poet ever considered making such a judgement, something we cannot know, he certainly decided not to do so. Instead he keeps his imaginative attention on how habitual dispositions shaped by a network of cultural practices, including knightly Christianity, respond as they come under unfamiliar pressures in changed circumstances – new spaces, new splittings. It seems to me that here the poem figures forth aspects of a long historical change within the class which produced honourmen, a change which would, according to Mervyn James's study *English Politics and the Concept of Honour*, not be completed until the resilient and adaptable honour culture was superseded in the seventeenth century with the emergence of a ruling class whose composition, contexts, and dominant ideology was significantly different from its predecessors'.[8] Part of this history was the lay appropriation and cultivation of forms of privacy and inwardness stimulated for their own reasons by the scholastic élite (based especially in the universities).[9] It would, however, be a mistake to think that it is appropriate to fill in silences or seeming inconsistencies in a poem produced for a distinctly ruling class community living within and *making* this very historical process.

The poem's final section opens with a description of a wild winter dawn listened to by a sleepless Gawain (1,998–2,002). With the exception of one assistant he arms himself alone.[10] He then goes to take leave of his host community, reaffirming the virtues and vocabulary of Christian honourmen (2,052–68). He does so again on the way to the Green Chapel when the servant seeks to open up another private sphere within the public world of 'menske', promising Gawain a path to survival. Gawain confirms his heroic identity, the collectively endowed role which constituted him in the poem's first part. Becoming 'a knyʒt kowarde', seeking to avoid 'chaunce' and fate ('þe Wyrde') in flight would be worse than death (2,089–155). The context and the very mode of Gawain's assertion here blocks out the possibility of private spaces and self-divisions opened up at Hautdesert. When the servant seeks to conjure up ambiguity around 'lelly'[a] (echoing the lady) Gawain is totally unimpressed (2,124, 1,863). Speculations about his 'private' state in opposition to his 'exterior' or 'public manner' in this encounter are thus unwarranted, for in the mode and the heroic virtue it represents there is no such split.[11] When Gawain reaches the Green Chapel the poet certainly does evoke Gawain's perspectives in this desolate place (2,178–211). But if, as Spearing writes, 'we enter into Gawain's very mind', it is a mind directed outwards, one seeking to grasp the feel of the place and its significance.[12] There is no sign of a mind turned 'inwards', reflecting on its own movements, seeking to anatomize its religious state or experiencing any kind of split between inward and outward performance.

Under the axe itself the heroic virtues are displayed, Gawain's identity as their bearer tested in the most fearful way and confirmed. The poet mentions

[a] loyally.

the bare white flesh of the knight's neck to evoke the human vulnerability with which heroic traditions contend. In this test Gawain is not only being required to face death, but to turn himself voluntarily into a passive object, as one inanimate, already dead. That he only shrank a little with his shoulders, and only once, is a sign of the monumental self-discipline he has achieved within the ethos of his community (2,251–67). Still, it is enough for the Green Knight to taunt him (as the lady had done) with the most exacting demands of his social identity (2,270–3):

> 'Þou art not Gawayn,' quoth þe gome,[a] þat is so goud halden,[b]
> Þat neuer arȝed[c] for no here[d] by hylle ne be vale,
> And now þou fles for ferde er þou fele harmez![e]
> Such cowardise of þat knyȝt cowþe[f] I neuer here.'

This vocabulary neither seeks nor allows splits between public and private, inner and outer in its version of virtue, and the challenger goes on to claim that he has won the competition for honour which defines such communities as Gawain represents (2,274–7).[13] The knight fully accepts the challenger's terms, only pointing out that they compete under rather different conditions (2,280–3). As he stands absolutely still, rock-like, under the second stroke he shows total mastery over the fear of death, won in and through his total identification with the heroic ethos (2,291–3). The same identification is plain both in his challenge to the Green Knight after the latter has withheld his hand and in his reaction on surviving the third stroke (2,299–301, 2,314–30). It is just this that the Green Knight so appreciates as he admires Gawain's physical vitality and courage (2,331–5),[14] challenger and challenged bound together in a common culture the poet shares. What remains is for the Green Knight to unpack aspects of Gawain's trials that are still hidden from him, and for Gawain to return to his own community.

This unpacking proves extremely complex because it reactivates the split we have considered in discussing Gawain's time at Hautdesert, splits that the final journey to the Chapel and the encounter with the Green Knight had seemed to transcend so decisively. This is certainly not the Green Knight's purpose. His praise of Gawain is unambiguous and immense, finding him, 'On þe fautlest freke þat euer on fote ȝede', a pearl among 'oþer gay knyȝtez' (2,362–5). The lord of Hautdesert, Sir Bertilak, is as immanent to the ethos of the heroic virtues and the honour community as Arthur or Gawain. For

[a] man.
[b] held to be so good.
[c] took fright.
[d] warrior-band.
[e] you flee on account of fear before you're felt any injuries!
[f] knew.

him it is Gawain's commitment to *this* ethos that has been tested (2,345–68), one in which his retention of the girdle was only 'a lyttel' failing, based in an understandable love of life for which, 'þe lasse I yow blame' (2,368). This seems the authentic voice of that social élite with whom the poem is identified, the dominant groups in Michael Bennett's study of the poet's homeland or in Mervyn James's study of those bearing the concept of honour in English political practices.[15]

For 'a gret whyle' Gawain stands silent as he takes in the stunning information that what were private transactions in a private space are now brought into the public domain. The Green Knight's assurance that the failure was only 'a lyttel' matters less to him than its categorization as a failure in 'lewté'[a] (2,366) and its exhibition in a domain that to Gawain seems public, at least in contrast with the apparently private encounters with his host's wife. His anguish is painful (2,370–2):

> So agreued for greme he gryed withinne;[b]
> Alle þe blode of his brest blende in his face,
> Þat al he schrank for schome[c] þat þe schalk[d] talked.

Gawain responds as a chivalric hero for whom virtue is very much a matter of 'reputation' and the avoidance of any 'public sense of shame': 'it is not until Gawain realizes that he has been found out that he starts to feel guilty.'[16] Spearing's observations are correct and could apply with equal precision to the English men of honour described by Mervyn James, a fact which emphasizes Gawain's representative and normative status even here.[17] When his 'schome' allows him to speak it is to curse cowardice and covetousness, aligning 'vice' with 'vylany', a moral term which encapsulates the class perspective of his community's ethos and a specific social history (2,374–5). Once he has unfastened the girdle and fiercely ('broþely') flung it to Sir Bertilak (2,376–7), he turns against himself:

> For care[e] of þy knokke,[f] cowardyse me taȝt
> To acorde me with couetyse, my kynde[g] to forsake:
> Þat is larges[h] and lewté, þat longez to knyȝtez.

---

[a] loyalty.
[b] So inflamed with anger he shuddered inwardly.
[c] shame.
[d] man.
[e] fear.
[f] blow.
[g] nature.
[h] liberality.

In these words Gawain affirms the heroic virtues, the knightly honourman's code. His 'kynde' *is* his social identity, private and public seem so fused that the very distinction becomes irrelevant. Confronted with his transgression being classified as a lack of 'lewté', albeit a 'lyttel' lack, the knight feels his identity dissolving, his being disintegrating. [. . .]

Notes

1 The role of class (access to economic resources) is crucial here, but see Don E. Wayne, *Pensheerst* (London: Methuen, 1984), ch. 1; F. R. H. du Boulay, *An Age of Ambition* (Walton on Thames: Nelson, 1970), ch. 6; L. Stone, *The Family, Sex and Marriage in England* (London: Weidenfeld and Nicolson, 1977), ch. 4 and pp. 253–7; Stephen Knight, *Geoffrey Chaucer* (Oxford: Blackwell, 1986), ch. 2.

2 All quotations of *Sir Gawain and the Green Knight* are from Malcolm Andrew and Ronald Waldron (eds), *The Poems of the Pearl Manuscript* (London: Arnold, 1978).

3 A. C. Spearing, *The Gawain-poet: A Critical Study* (Cambridge: Cambridge University Press, 1970), p. 174, see also p. 202.

4 On this dialectic, see Toril Moi, chapter 1 in David Aers (ed.) *Medieval Literature and Historical Inquiry* (Cambridge: D. S. Brewer, 2000); Spearing, *Gawain-poet*, pp. 201–6.

5 See lines 1,750–871: Gawain's consciousness also evoked at lines 842–9, 943–6, 1,195–203, 1,651–2, 1,760–76, 1,855–9, 2,006–8, 2,163, 2,179–96, 2,205–11, 2,233, 2,257. On this topic, see Spearing, *Gawain-poet*, pp. 173–4, 191–219.

6 On the split in 'obligations', see John Burrow, *A Reading of Sir Gawain and the Green Knight* (London: Routledge and Kegan Paul, 1965), p. 104.

7 Ibid., p. 123 and Mary F. Braswell, *The Medieval Sinner* (New York: Associated University Presses, 1983), p. 96.

8 Mervyn James, *English Politics and the Concept of Honour, 1485–1642* (Past and Present Society, 1978).

9 For these aspects, see T. N. Tentler, *Sin and Confession on the Eve of the Reformation* (Princeton, NJ: Princeton University Press, 1977).

10 Lines 2,002–42. Much is made in the scholarly literature of Gawain's apparent forgetfulness of the pentangle, yet Gawain himself had never been shown as especially attentive to the pentangle. It was the poet who affirmed its special relation to Gawain (623–4) and interpreted its symbolism: why not foreground lines 611–12 as much as the religious symbolism?

11 For an example of this approach, see W. R. Barron, *Trawthe and Treason: The Sin of Gawain Reconsidered* (Manchester: Manchester University Press, 1980), p. 116.

12 Spearing *Gawain-poet*, p. 187.

13 On this competition, see James, *English Politics*.

14 Spearing, *Gawain-poet*, pp. 189–90.

15 Michael Bennett, *Community, Class and Careerism: Cheshire and Lancashire Society in the Age of Sir Gawain and the Green Knight* (Cambridge: Cambridge University Press, 1983); James, *English Politics*.

16 Spearing, *Gawain-poet*, pp. 226–7. See also the timely revisions to his influential
    book in chapter 7 of J. Burrow, *Essays on Medieval Literature* (Oxford: Oxford
    University Press, 1984), p. 118, n. 5 and p. 126.
17 James, *English Politics*, pp. 28–31.

PSYCHO-   Aers's concern with individual consciousness chimes with the psychoanalytic
ANALYTIC   criticism that has entered medieval English studies in the past two decades.
CRITICISM Exemplified in the work of such critics as Louise Fradenburg and H.
Marshall Leicester, psychoanalytic approaches draw upon the work of Jacques
Lacan in addressing the constitution of subjectivity in Middle English texts.
It is a critical approach inevitably on collision course with some of the *grands
récits* of intellectual history discussed above. As Louise Fradenburg has recently
pointed out, psychoanalysis must repeatedly challenge an older view of the
Middle Ages as an epoch of group rather than individual subjectivity:

> Group subjectivity was . . . zealously assigned to the Middle Ages by Enlight-
> enment thinkers, partly because it was the business of Enlightenment thinkers
> to critique group thought as unreasoning, slavish and superstitious. The idea that
> an age of faith in supernatural agency was to give way to an age of reason . . .
> assigned all uncanny zombies, resistance to change, and irrational beliefs, to the
> past and/or Catholicism. The Middle Ages becomes a time when beings of
> uncertain sentience . . . walked the earth in the shape of rational human beings.[6]

Fradenburg's own work on Chaucer, the Scottish Chaucerians and others, has
done much to challenge this notion, as has Leicester's 1991 study of subjectivity in the *Canterbury Tales*, a reading which argues that 'the poem is a set
of texts that are about the subjectivity of their speakers . . . Chaucer's subject
is the subject.'[7]

Identity can mean individuality or personality. In this sense, identity is that
which makes me particularly, distinctively, even uniquely me. But identity is also
used in current debates to mean something almost the opposite; it can mean
identity position. In this sense, my identity is that which signals group affilia-
tion – often race or biological sex but sometimes also statuses generally understood as socially shaped, such as class, language group, or religion. Finally,
identity can mean spatiotemporal continuity. In this sense, identity refers to the
fact that I am the same person I was a moment ago. This third understanding
of identity carries the connotation of oneness or integrity.[8]

2001: Caroline Walker Bynum on contemporary debates on identity.

Psychoanalytic theory also informs the final extract of this *Guide* in which Lee
Patterson revisits the subjectivity of one of the most compelling character portraits in medieval literature – Crisyede. Perhaps more character-based criti-

cism has been written on this figure than on any other Middle English character. Constructed by her own narrator as unknowable, maligned in literary tradition for the desertion of her beloved Troilus, the character has attracted more than her share of detailed studies of her 'entente', prompting a long debate over how far the character is to be blamed or excused. But as Patterson's essay demonstrates, the critical debate around Criseyde reflects a wider debate around the question of *agency*. How are the actions of historically and culturally situated individuals to be viewed: invariably as expressions of individual will, or as reflections in part of determining extrinsic forces? Humanist criticism emphasizes individual agency, the power of the individual to make coherent and logical choices and to pursue intrinsic motivations. Other approaches, particularly psychoanalytic and critical historicist approaches, emphasize the historical, discursive and cultural determination of the individual subject. Only certain permutations of selfhood are made available to the subject bound by historical time and place. Cultural imperatives and prescriptions impinge upon subjectivity.

Informed by both new historicist and psychoanalytic thought, Patterson's *'Troilus and Criseyde* and Subjectivity' recasts the complex characters of Chaucer's poem as a 'site' where 'many selves are in a ceaseless process of constitution'. Drawing on the propositions of Lacan, he views the characters' subjectivity as driven by a desire 'that at once includes sexuality and aspires to a satisfaction that sexual possession can never provide'. Patterson's reading of Criseyde thus departs sharply from traditional humanist approaches which emphasize her 'fault' or 'flaw', or from exegetical approaches that view her as symbolic of false felicity, the worldly snare of cupidinous desire. Instead, Patterson's Criseyde, as an historically, culturally, textually confined character, enjoys minimal individual agency. As the subject of (or in) history, Criseyde reveals the constancy of selfhood to be an illusion.

Extract from Lee Patterson, *'Troilus and Criseyde and the Subject of History'*, in *Chaucer and the Subject of History* (London: Routledge, 1991), pp. 142–50.

[. . .] To reduce the subjectivity of the *Troilus* to intentionality is to assume that human beings exist as singular, self-identical, and self-present individuals, an assumption that the poem throughout calls into question. Instead, we would do better to think of the subjectivity of the *Troilus* as a site where not one but many intentions – in effect, many selves – are in a ceaseless process of constitution. In one sense, the character who most ostentatiously displays the multiplicity of selves that typifies this subjectivity is the Janus-faced Pandarus. Mercurial in mood as in function, he alternates easily between modes of behavior that we usually think of as distinct: as he shuttles visitors in and out of Troilus's sickroom at Deiphoebus's house, for instance, he adopts and divests himself of a wide variety of roles, and in his manipulation of the consummation scene he is equally adept at assuming – and perhaps even experiencing – radically disparate forms of behavior. He is, moreover, equally at home at Troilus's 'beddes syde' (3, 236, 1589; 5, 294) or at Criseyde's (3, 682, 1555–82), and he displays throughout the narrative a sexual interest that is at once genderless and double-gendered, without specific affect and therefore capable of multiple cathexes. It is true that the very facility that makes it possible for Pandarus to transfigure himself as he manipulates others might render his subjectivity less rather than more problematic: in defining him as less than fully invested in any of his roles, the poem invites us to understand him as an instance of a simple, in the sense of deliberate and therefore wholly controlled, hypocrisy. But even this kind of simplicity is delusive. The turmoil of selves that he displays comes finally to surround a strange emptiness at the center – we never finally do understand his own motivation, and neither, so far as we know, does he.

Just as Pandarus is more of a mystery than he may at first appear, so too are the lovers; and while we (and they) are tempted to stress their difference from him, the narrative insists that they are to an important degree equivalent. That Criseyde is changeable is the central fact about her: linked imagistically to the moon, to 'slydynge fortune', and to the unstable world itself, she is an object of exchange whose subjectivity alters with her circumstances.[1] With Troilus she is a courtly lady anxiously aware that all worldly happiness is 'fals felicitee' (3, 814), aggrieved and saddened by her lover's jealousy, and yet finally prepared to yield herself wholly to him: 'And at o word, withouten repentaunce, / Welcome, my knyght, my pees, my suffisaunce!' (3, 1308–9). Yet immediately after this wholehearted yielding she engages in a notoriously ambiguous flirtation with Pandarus that causes even the narrator to turn away in embarrassment – 'I passe al that which chargeth nought to seye' (3, 1576) – and she finally becomes the woman whose self-interest allows her to accept the matching selfishness of Diomede's brutal protection. It is all too easy to decide that the last of these Criseydes is the real one, but to do so requires us to impeach all the rest by assuming a self-consistency – a constancy of selfhood – that the poem itself shows to be an illusion.

For not even Troilus, endowed (as Criseyde herself recognizes) with 'moral vertu, grounded upon trouthe' (4, 1672), is exempt from variableness. Two examples of his complexity – a complexity that he himself seeks to efface and that criticism has been equally reluctant to acknowledge – will suffice. After each of the dramatized meetings with his lady, Troilus engages in a conversation with Pandarus that reveals a sharply different self than had previously been in evidence. In the bedroom at Deiphoebus's house Troilus is a tongue-tied lover, unable to manage the elaborate game of role playing that Pandarus has fabricated: when Criseyde declines to be the courtly beloved but insists instead on acting the threatened victim pleading for protection, Troilus collapses into blushing silence (3, 78–84). Similarly, and even more drastically, at Pandarus's house the fiction of Horaste – and Criseyde's apparent belief in it – renders him not just silent but unconscious: unable to extricate himself from Pandarus's web, he faints.

But after each of these scenes he is a wholly different, and far less appealing, person. When Pandarus worries that he might be thought a bawd, Troilus provides not just the expected disclaimers but also an offer to be himself a bawd in return. Not only does this offer reinstate the sleaziness that he and Pandarus have been trying to deny, but it is delivered in a language far more blunt that any that Pandarus would use:

> I have my faire suster Polixene,
> Cassandre, Eleyne, or any of the frape[a] –
> Be she nevere so fair or wel yshape,
> Tel me which thow wilt of everychone,
> To han[b] for thyn, and lat me thanne allone. (3, 409–13)

Similarly, when after the lovers' night together Pandarus again comes to Troilus, not only does Troilus 'telle hym of his glade nyght' (3, 1646) but he is 'nevere ful to speke of this matere' (1661). 'This tale ay was span-newe[c] to bygynne, / Til that the night departed hem atwynne' (1665–66): for an entire day Troilus rehearses with his friend the night they have *together* (we unhappily remember) spent with Criseyde – men discoursing together about a woman they have, in some indefinable but nonetheless real way, already shared. Here it is Criseyde who is the mediating third term: at once present in memory and absent in fact, she is the means by which two men spend a day together – and a day apparently spent, moreover, in bed.[2]

We can, if we wish, draw a moral distinction between Criseyde's abandonment of Troilus and Troilus's talking about Criseyde with Pandarus, but we should not allow it to obscure the similarity between the two lovers. In fact, Chaucer continually insists that not one but both the lovers are simultaneously knowing and unknowing, at once conscious of the nature of their desire and the means of its fulfillment and yet profoundly, and necessarily, unaware. Criseyde must know, for example, that the meeting at Deiphoebus's house is not required by Poliphete's threat – which she herself has dismissed (2,

[a] company.
[b] have.
[c] brand new.

1477–8) – and both the secret pleasure she takes at the discussion of Troilus's illness and virtues ('For which with sobre cheere[a] hire herte lough' [2, 1592]) and her lack of surprise at the absence of Helen and Deiphoebus in his bedroom certainly suggest that she knows the true purpose of the meeting. But does this mean that her continued playing of the role of threatened victim is simply hypocrisy, an empty gesture toward conventions of seemliness? Or does it not rather express hesitations and anxieties that are deeply a part of her character? Similarly, the night at Pandarus's house where the lovers will, as the narrator delicately says, 'leiser have hire speches to fulfelle' (3, 510) is prepared for by innuendo and even outright suggestion (see, e.g., 3, 566–7); indeed, the very pretext that keeps Criseyde from going home – that it is raining – is itself empty, since it was raining not only before she came but when the invitation was first accepted (see 3, 562). Yet does that mean that Criseyde's shock on being awakened by Pandarus, and her protestations about receiving Troilus, are meaningless? If they are, why does Pandarus confect the story about Horaste in the first place? The fact is that this semi-awareness is a necessary condition for the love affair. No doubt Criseyde is in Pandarus's house because she wants to make love with Troilus: as she finally says to him, 'Ne hadde I er now, my swete herte deere, / Ben yolde,[b] ywis, I were now nought here!' (3, 1210–11). But because her world proscribes the explicit representation of female sexual desire, she cannot admit this want either to others or to herself. Indeed, the obsessive secrecy that surrounds and perhaps even dooms the affair is best understood as a metaphoric displacement of this need for *self-concealment*: it is less 'every pie[c] and every lette-game'[d] (3, 527) who threaten the affair than the guilt and shame with which sexuality, and specifically female sexuality, is invested.

When Chaucer describes how Criseyde falls in love, he shows not only that desire is experienced by her as an external force that comes upon her, but that even when it has become a part of her – when it has become *her* desire – she is unable to represent it to herself as her own. Aroused first by Pandarus's words, her feelings are intensified by the sight of Troilus returning from battle to the point where she can understand them only as a form of almost chemical change: 'Who yaf[e] me drynke?'[3] Retreating into her closet, she then retreats yet further into her own mind: by debating the question of love she hopes to gain a conscious purchase upon it. This process is not resolved but merely sealed by a series of symbolic events (all of them Chaucer's invention)

[a] expression.
[b] been given.
[c] magpie.
[d] spoilsport.
[e] gave.

that serve to present love, and specifically passion, as an entity at once a part of and apart from the female subject who experiences it. First there is the over-hearing of the *Canticus Antigoni* (as several manuscripts call it). A song of love as mutuality, it alienates Criseyde's desire from itself by its double vicarious-ness: it is not even Antigone's own song much less Criseyde's (and hence its difference from the *Canticus Troili* of the previous book) but the song of the unnamed 'goodlieste mayde / Of gret estat in al the town of Troye' (880–1). Then there is the 'lay / Of love' (921–2) sung by the nightingale in the cedar tree, a wordless song that by its oblique allusion to Philomela images passion as a function only of the rapacious male and so simultaneously invokes and mutes the female fear of desire. And finally there is the dream of the bone-white eagle with his 'longe clawes' (927), who in rending from her her heart and replacing it with his own fulfills the promise of mutuality offered in Antigone's song and so redeems the violence of the means: 'she nought agroos,[a] ne nothyng smerte'[b] (930). Criseyde remains the passive recipient of actions performed not only upon her body but with her will – and yet at no point does either body or will find representation. By this point, Criseyde has, as she will later, passively say, 'ben yold' (3, 1210), but her accession to that yielding – much less her desire for it – remains unspoken and unacknowledged. She knows and doesn't know that she desires: she has heard it and dreamed it, and the knowledge is at once part of and apart from her.

The unreflective, subterranean way in which love comes upon Criseyde is a function not of moral failure but of cultural necessity: all we need do to demonstrate this to ourselves is to try to imagine in what terms she might acknowledge her own sexuality. For then she immediately turns into a char-acter like the Miller's Alison, or Alison of Bath – and she perforce exits from the world of this poem. The precondition of Criseyde's existence as Criseyde, in other words, is that she *not* know the burden of that name.

Troilus's Oedipean blindness is also prescribed by cultural imperatives. After his sight of Criseyde in the temple he composes the *Canticus Troili*, asserting his utter passivity before the transcendent force that has possessed him. So too does Chaucer assert his passivity in receiving the translation of this song from 'myn auctour called Lollius' (1, 394). But just as the 'tonges dif-ference' (1, 395) that is the condition of all writing subverts the disingenuous claim of the poet, so do the circumstances of the lover's song call into ques-tion the singleness of his *entente*: it is one of the means by which Troilus will '*arten* hire to love' (1, 388), and its strategic value stands in awkward opposi-tion to its transcendent claims.[4] Neither poet nor lover is in touch with an origin (Love, Lollius) that legitimizes their analogous projects. Indeed, as soon

[a] was frightened.
[b] felt pain.

as the metaphor of Cupid shooting lovers with his arrows is invoked in the temple scene in Book 1 (206–10) it is immediately undone by the heavily sexualized eye play in which Troilus and Criseyde then engage. Troilus's 'eye percede, and so depe it wente, / Til on Criseyde it smot, and ther it stente'[a] (1, 272–3); but when she responds with her 'somdele deignous' glance, 'He was tho glad his hornes in to shrinke'[a] (300). Rather than proceeding from a transcendent source, desire is a function of human sexuality, and the metaphor of Cupid's arrows is revealed as a mystification of its physical source.

But if sexuality is the ground of Troilus's desire, it is in no sense its whole content. Indeed, if it were, the loss of Criseyde would be easily consoled. To 'arten' Criseyde solely for the purposes of sexual gratification would be as much a betrayal of Troilus's *gentilesse* as it would be to 'ravisshe' her out of Troy. Hence the necessity of Pandarus, whose function for Troilus is to enact those aspects of his *entente* to love that he cannot acknowledge. It is because Pandarus is available not only to handle the embarrassing details of the consummation but actually to undress Troilus and install him in Criseyde's bed that Troilus can afford to faint. The point is not, as D. W. Robertson has memorably said, that Troilus loves Criseyde for nothing more 'than her pleasing "figure" and surpassing competence in bed', but that his desire is initiated by and necessarily includes a sexuality that he wishes both to enact and, for reasons we are surely meant to admire, to disavow.[5]

Willful ignorance is thus the condition of the lovers' very existence. Endowed with a subjectivity that is irreducibly complex, and driven by a desire that at once includes sexuality and aspires to a satisfaction that sexual possession can never provide, their unification can only be accomplished by means of a go-between whose very presence necessarily betrays, and betrays it to, its own multiplicity. To acknowledge that Pandarus represents the mediated and therefore unsatisfactory gratification at which all desire arrives is not, however, to establish him as the cause of the failure. On the contrary, the tragedy of desire is that its efforts to recover that which has been lost serve to confirm how truly lost it is: the condition of desire is always to rebegin. This rebeginning is enacted by the lovers in Book 4, which repeats [. . .] the structure of the action of Books 1–3. An effort at closure, Book 4 not only, and necessarily, fails of its desire but then opens onto the saddest act of repetition of all, the parodic reenactments of the past that occupy Book 5. With Diomede Criseyde not only engages in a foreshortened and debased reenactment of her courtship with Troilus, but as the poem leaves her she recognizes that her fate is to be 'rolled . . . on many a tonge' (5, 1061) by historians who are the literary equivalent of Diomede with his 'tonge large' (5, 804). This is both a Dantesque vision of the endless historiographical recording in which she is

[a] stopped.

condemned to reenact her original crime and, with Chaucer's invocation of the 'tonge' with which both Diomede and historians like himself manipulate her, a disturbingly vivid reminder of the sexual abuse implicit in misogynist writing.

In describing Criseyde's betrayal, as with the other decisive moments of his poem, the narrator insists that the process by which actions unfold is so imperceptibly gradual and so compounded of motives and circumstances that the search for a single or simple explanation – 'the cause whi' – is inevitably thwarted. At the conclusion of Diomede's interview with Criseyde in her tent, 'he roos and tok his leve.'

> The brighte Venus folwede and ay taughte
> The wey ther brode Phebus down alighte;
> And Cynthea hire char-hors[a] overraughte[b]
> To whirle out of the Leoun,[c] if she myghte;
> And Signifer[d] his candels sheweth bright
> Whan that Criseyde unto hire bedde wente
> Inwith hire faders faire brighte tente,
>
> Retornyng in hire soule ay up and down
> The wordes of this sodeyn[e] Diomede,
> His grete estat, and perel of the town,
> And that she was allone and hadde nede
> Of frendes help; and thus bygan to brede
> The cause whi, the sothe for to telle,
> That she took fully purpos for to dwelle.
>
> (5, 1016–29)

The astronomical machinery represents not only the relentless passage of time – Criseyde had promised Troilus she would return 'Er Phebus suster, Lucina the sheene, / The Leoun passe out of this Ariete' (4, 1591–2) – but also the workings of forces that operate in ways that are necessarily not fully available to self-reflection. Now as the moon leaves Leo so does Criseyde leave the lover who has just been described as 'Yong, fressh, strong, and hardy as lyoun' (5, 830).[6] Venus is somehow in Diomede's train here, and she in turn dominates Phoebus Apollo: to say that love overcomes wisdom is a not inaccurate translation of the astronomical symbolism, but neither is it fully adequate as an account of Criseyde's decision. The Zodiac bears signs, but their meaning is not available to Criseyde, an ignorance that is both the condition of her very

[a] chariot horses.
[b] reached over.
[c] the constellation of Leo.
[d] the Zodiac.
[e] impetuous.

existence and a key constitutive of her decision – if 'decision' is the right word. Lying in bed, Criseyde 'returns' Diomede's words as the heavens turn, a scene that itself returns to the night some three years before when 'lay she stille and thoughte' (2, 915) of Troilus's words, of Pandarus's, and of Antigone's. Then she had heard the 'lay / Of love' sung by the nightingale, had dreamed the dream of the eagle, and had awakened (we were prepared to believe) in love.[7]

In deciding to stay with Diomede and abandon Troilus, Criseyde not only continues her earlier behavior but reveals her life to be a continuous process that cannot be endowed with a precisely demarcated beginning and ending, in the sense of either a single motive or an intended goal. If it were true, as Pandarus had said, that 'th'ende is every tales strengthe' (2, 260), now that we reach that conclusion we should be able retrospectively to evaluate the meaning of the events that have occurred: 'But natheles men seyen that at the laste, / For any thyng, men shal the soothe se' (5, 1639–40). Criseyde's liaison with Diomede ought then to tell us what her liaison with Troilus meant: at the end of her career in the poem her actions will have made clear what she meant at the beginning, just as when Troilus and Criseyde ended up in bed we knew (apparently) that this had always been 'the fyn of hir entente'. But in fact, far from clarifying the enigma of her character and motivation, much less of human actions in general, Criseyde's behavior in Book 5 serves to compound the difficulty: her end does not gloss but replicates her beginning.[8]

It seems that the narrator himself finds this narrative inconclusion painful. So, at least, we might judge from his last-minute attempt to suppress it. In the midst of Diomede's second and successful assault on Criseyde, he suddenly introduces into the poem portraits of the three protagonists. Technically, the presence of these portraits is sanctioned by the historiographical tradition: Dares, Benoît, and Joseph of Exeter all include similar passages in their histories, and Chaucer's version may owe some details specifically to Joseph.[9] But the point about their late appearance in *this* version of the story is that they evade the very problem of interpretation on which Chaucer has hitherto insisted. By substituting for the detailed representation of subjectivity woodenly externalized *effictiones* ornamented with brief judgements – Diomede has the reputation of being 'of tonge large' (804), Criseyde is, notoriously, 'slydynge of corage'[a] (825), Troilus is 'trewe as stiel in ech condicioun' (831) – the narrator suddenly implies that the relation of character to action has become self-evident. But the very narrative that these portraits mean to gloss belies such interpretive confidence. [. . .]

---

[a] changeable of spirit.

Notes

1 For these comparisons, see Donald W. Rowe, *O Love, O Charite! Contraries Harmonized in Chancer's Troilus* (Carbondale, IL: Southern Illinois State University Press, 1976), pp. 57–91.

2 When Pandarus first arrives he sits on the 'beddes syde' (1589) to talk with Troilus, but Troilus leaps up and gets on his knees in thanksgiving. Then, however, 'down in his bed he lay' (1615), and we never hear of him getting up again: just as the first conversation takes place with Pandarus on the 'beddes syde' (3, 236) and Troilus lying down, so too does this one.

3 That Criseyde has been prepared by Pandarus's words is suggested by the description of 'al hir meyne' rushing to welcome him with a cry of remarkably sexual suggestiveness: 'cast up the yates wyde! / For thorwgh this strete he moot to paleys ride' (615–16).

4 The verb *arten* is derived, according to the *MED*, from *arctare* and means to compel, force, or induce; but it also absorbs ominous connotations from its homonym, *art*.

5 D. W. Robertson, Jr, *A Preface to Chaucer*, (Princeton, NJ: Princeton University Press, 1962), p. 496.

6 And see also 1, 1074, where we are told that 'in the feld [Troilus] pleyde tho leoun'. The symmetry between Troilus the lion and his rival Diomede the boar perhaps derives from the *Thebaid*, where Adrastus is given a prophecy that his two daughters will be married to a lion (Polynices) and a boar (Tydeus); see Statius, *Silvae, Thebard, Achilleid*, trans. J. H. Mozley, 2 vols (London: Heinemann, 1928), vol. 1, pp. 395–400.

7 For an account of the symmetry between Criseyde falling in and out of love with Troilus, see Donald R. Howard, 'Experience, Language, and Consciousness: *Troilus and Criseyde*, II, 596–931', in Jerome Mandel and Bruce A. Rosenberg (eds), *Medieval Literature and Folklore Studies: Essays in Honor of Francis Lee Utley* (New Brunswick: Rutgers University Press, 1970), pp. 173–92.

8 As we would expect of a Troy poem, *Troilus and Criseyde* is saturated with the language of beginnings and endings: see, for example, 1, 377–78; 1, 973; 2, 671–72; 2, 790–91; 2, 1234–35; 2, 1565–66; 2, 1595–96; 3, 462; 4, 1282–84; 5, 764–65; 5, 1003–4; and 5, 1828–33.

9 Ever since R. K. Root's essay on 'Chaucer's Dare', *Modern Philology* 15 (1917–18), 1–22, it has been assumed that Chaucer knew Joseph of Exeter's *Ilias Daretis Phrygii* and used it in these portraits. But the evidence is very slight. There is also no firm evidence that Chaucer knew either Dares or Dictys directly, but given their assimilation into Benoît and Guido it is unlikely that we would be able to recognize their direct presence in Chaucer's poem in any case. It is possible, however, that his reference to Geoffrey of Monmouth as a Trojan historian in the *House of Fame* (1470) shows that Chaucer was misled by one of the several manuscripts of Geoffrey's *Historia* that was prefaced with Dares' *Historia* into thinking that Geoffrey was the author of the entire Trojan–British compilation. He may have read Dares' *Historia*, in other words, thinking it was by Geoffrey, and assumed that Dares' work was something else again. *Pace* Root, it seems unlikely that he would have

thought that Joseph of Exeter's tortuously stylized poem, with its several references to twelfth-century events, was Dares' eyewitness history. For a fourteenth-century version of this technique, see George B. Stow (ed.), *Historia vitae et regni Ricardi Secundi* (Philadelphia: University of Pennsylvania Press, 1977), in which the author includes a portrait of Richard II just after his death but prior to the end of the book (p. 161).

Further Reading

Where early studies asked 'What is it to be a medieval person?', more recent studies have explored what it means to be a particular *kind* of medieval person. Robert Bartlett has looked at 'Medieval and Modern Concepts of Race and Ethnicity' in *Journal of Medieval and Early Modern Studies* 31 (2001), 39–56, and Miri Rubin has looked at medieval conceptions of Jewish identity in *Gentile Tales: The Narrative Assault on Late Medieval Jews* (New Haven, CT: Yale University Press, 1999). On the question of collective identities you might consult Simon Forde, Lesley Johnson and Alan V. Murray's volume on *Concepts of National Identity in the Middle Ages* (Leeds: Leeds Studies in English, 1995).

An accompanying piece to David Mills's essay in *Medieval English Theatre* looks at the question of character in the Moralities, defining a 'demonstrative mode' of action for the characters: Sarah Carpenter, 'Morality Play Characters', *Medieval English Theatre* 5 (1983), 18–28. The villains of medieval drama have also attracted character studies: Arnold Williams, *The Characterization of Pilate in the Towneley Plays* (East Lansing: Michigan State College Press, 1950); Robert Brawer, 'The Characterization of Pilate in the York Cycle Play', *Studies in Philology* 69 (1972), 289–303; David Staines, 'To Out-Herod Herod: The Development of a Dramatic Character', *Comparative Drama* 10 (1976), 29–53; 13, 207–31; Lawrence M. Clopper, 'Tyrants and Villains: Characterization in the Passion Sequence of the English Cycle Plays', *Modern Language Quarterly* 41 (1980), 3–20.

David Aers and Lee Patterson have championed the case for locating the discovery of the individual in pre-Renaissance writing. Particularly persuasive is Aers's 1992 'A Whisper in the Ear of Early Modernists; or Reflections on Literary Critics Writing the "History of the Subject" ', in David Aers (ed.), *Culture and History, 1350–1600: Essays on English Communities, Identities and Writing* (London: Harvester Wheatsheaf, 1992), pp. 177–202. On the growing presence of psychoanalytic studies in the field, see Louise O. Fradenburg, ' "Be Not Far From Me": Psychoanalysis, Medieval Studies and the Subject of Religion', *Exemplaria* 7 (1995), 41–54.

Chapter Notes

1   George Lyman Kittredge, *Chaucer and his Poetry* (Cambridge, MA: Harvard University Press, 1915), p. 29.

2   Stephen Medcalf, 'On Reading Books from a Half-alien Culture', in Stephen Medcalf (ed.), *The Later Middle Ages* (London: Methuen, 1981), pp. 25–6.
3   Colin Morris, *The Discovery of the Individual 1050–1200*, Church History Outlines 5 (London: SPCK for the Church History Society, 1972), p. 158.
4   Linda Georgianna, *The Solitary Self: Individuality in the 'Ancrene Wisse'* (Cambridge, MA: Harvard University Press, 1981), p. 141.
5   John Burrow, *Medieval Writers and their Work: Middle English Literature and its Background 1100–1500* (Oxford: Oxford university Press, 1982), p. 40.
6   Louise O. Aranye Fradenburg, 'Amorous Scholasticism', in Robert F. Yeager and Charlotte C. Morse (eds), *Speaking Images: Essays in Honor of V. A. Kolve* (Asheville: Pegasus Press, 2000), pp. 27–53 (p. 28).
7   H. Marshall Leicester, Jr, *The Disenchanted Self: Representing the Subject in the Canterbury Tales* (Berkeley, CA: University of California Press, 1990), p. 15.
8   Caroline Walker Bynum, *Metamorphosis and Identity* (New York: Zone Books, 2001), p. 163, as cited in Phillipa Hardman (ed.), *The Matter of Identity in Medieval Romance* (Cambridge: D. S. Brewer, 2002), p. 1.

Afterword

'For a mixture of the modern and the mediaeval, of the practical and of the wildly fanciful, I think this is surely the limit,' said he. 'What do you make of it, Watson?'

The Adventure of the Sussex Vampire

It is possible to sketch the history of Middle English criticism as essentially adversarial, rooted in disagreements and sometimes heated differences of critical opinion: source study versus close reading, exegetics versus New Criticism, queer theory versus liberal humanism. Much of the editorial commentary in this book is likewise designed to emphasize *difference*, stressing disparity between approaches, taking issue with the assumptions and propositions they convey.

At the same time, it is as fair to view the relation between distinct approaches as one of *conversation* rather than entrenched opposition. As the chapters of this *Guide* have aimed to show, shared interpretative concerns are revisited again and again by starkly contrasting schools. Around such critical concerns as authorship, literature and history, gender, and identity, divergent critical traditions have formed, between them advancing our understanding and deepening our appreciation of the English literature of 1100–1500 (and beyond). The English literature of the Middle Ages continues to challenge all of its readers to read, write and debate in new and resourceful ways.

At the start of the twenty-first century, this critical conversation is rapidly breaking new ground. It is a conversation that increasingly questions period boundaries ('medieval' and 'Renaissance', 'pre-modern' and 'modern'), one that challenges received notions of the literary canon and literary history (what does it really *mean* to call Chaucer 'the father of English poetry'? Is the literature of the fifteenth century *really* marked by decline and decay?). It is a conversation which now ranges beyond the pages of printed journals and monographs into the electronic discussion forums and message-boards of the web. Middle English criticism is a continuing and rewarding conversation – one which, it is hoped, this *Guide* may encourage all critical readers to join.

Bibliography

The following book lists are not exhaustive: there is an inevitable element of overlap in the lists for each chapter. Abbreviations are avoided with the exception of *PMLA* (Publications of the Modern Language Association of America).

Foundational Middle English studies to 1960

Auerbach, Eric, *Mimesis: The Representation of Reality in Western Literature*, trans. W. R. Trask. Princeton, NJ: Princeton University Press, 1953.

Chaytor, H. J., *From Script to Print: An Introduction to Medieval Vernacular Literature*. Cambridge: Cambridge University Press, 1945.

Curtius, E. R., *European Literature and the Latin Middle Ages*, trans. W. R. Trask. London: Routledge, 1953.

Ker, W. P., *Epic and Romance: Essays on Medieval Literature*. London: Macmillan, 1897.

——, *Medieval English Literature*. Oxford: Oxford University Press, 1912.

Lewis, C. S., *The Allegory of Love*. Oxford: Oxford University Press, 1936.

Selected key studies post 1960

Allen, Judson Boyce, *The Ethical Poetic of the Later Middle Ages*. Toronto: University of Toronto Press, 1982.

Carruthers, Mary, *The Book of Memory: A Study of Memory in Medieval Culture*. Cambridge: Cambridge University Press, 1990.

Gellrich, Jesse, *The Idea of the Book in the Middle Ages: Language Theory, Mythology, and Fiction*. Ithaca, NY: Cornell University Press, 1985.

Green, Richard Firth, *Poets and Princepleasers: Literature and the English Court in the Late Middle Ages*. Toronto: University of Toronto Press, 1980.

Lewis, C. S., *The Discarded Image: An Introduction to Medieval and Renaissance Literature*. Cambridge: Cambridge University Press, 1964.

Medcalf, Stephen (ed.), *The Later Middle Ages*. London: Methuen, 1981.

Olson, Glending, *Literature as Recreation in the Middle Ages*. Ithaca, NY: Cornell University Press, 1982.

Pearsall, Derek, *Old and Middle English Poetry*. London: Routledge and Kegan Paul, 1977.

Spearing, A. C., *Criticism and Medieval Poetry*. London: Edward Arnold, 1964.

Zumthor, Paul, *Towards a Medieval Poetics*, trans. Philip Bennett. Minneapolis, MN: University of Minnesota Press, 1992.

'State of the field' essays and surveys

Baugh, A. C., 'Fifty Years of Chaucer Scholarship', *Speculum* 26 (1951), 659–72.

Bloch, R. Howard and Nichols, Stephen G. (eds), *Medievalism and the Modernist Temper*. Baltimore, MD: The Johns Hopkins University Press, 1996.

Bloomfield, Morton W., 'Continuities and Discontinuities', *New Literary History* 10 (1979), 409–16.

——, 'Present State of *Piers Plowman* Studies', *Speculum* 14 (1939), 215–32.

——, '*Sir Gawain and the Green Knight*: An Appraisal', *PMLA* 76 (1961), 7–19.

Brownlee, Marina S., Brownlee, Kevin and Nichols, Stephen G. (eds), *The New Medievalism*. Baltimore, MD: The Johns Hopkins University Press, 1991.

Burrow, John, 'The Alterity of Medieval Literature', *New Literary History* 10 (1979), 385–90.

Donaldson, E. Talbot, 'Designing a Camel: or, Generalizing the Middle Ages', *Tennessee Studies in English Literature* 22 (1977), 1–16.

Jauss, Hans Robert, 'The Alterity and Modernity of Medieval Literature', *New Literary History* 10 (1979), 181–228.

Patch, Howard R., 'Desiderata in Middle English Research', *Modern Philology* 22 (1924), 27–34.

Patterson, Lee, *Negotiating the Past: The Historical Understanding of Medieval Literature*. Madison: University of Wisconsin Press, 1989.

——, 'On the Margin: Postmodernism, Ironic History, and Medieval Studies', *Speculum* 65 (1990), 87–108.

Robinson, F. N., 'Anniversary Reflections', *Speculum* 25 (1950), 491–501.

Collections of critical approaches

Machan, Tim William (ed.), *Medieval Literature: Texts and Interpretation*. Binghamton, NY: Center for Medieval and Early Renaissance Studies, 1991.

Simons, John (ed.), *From Medieval to Medievalism*. London: Macmillan, 1992.

Trigg, Stephanie (ed.), *Medieval English Poetry*. London: Longman, 1993.

Chapter bibliographies

Authorship

Barthes, Roland, 'The Death of the Author', in *Image–Music–Text*, trans. Stephen Heath, pp. 142–8. New York: Hill and Wang, 1977.

Baugh, A. C., 'Documenting Sir Thomas Malory', *Speculum* 8 (1933), 1–29.

Bennett, H. S., 'The Author and his Public in the Fourteenth and Fifteenth Centuries', *Essays and Studies* 23 (1937), 7–24.

Benson, Larry D., *Malory's Morte Darthur*. Cambridge, MA: Harvard University Press, 1976.

Brewer, Derek (ed.), *Chaucer and Chaucerians: Critical Studies in Middle English Literature*. London: Thomas Nelson and Sons, 1966.

Burrow, J. A., 'Autobiographical Poetry in the Middle Ages: The Case of Thomas Hoccleve', *Proceedings of the British Academy* 68 (1982), 389–412.

——, *Medieval Writers and their Work*. Oxford: Oxford University Press, 1982.

——, *Ricardian Poetry*. London: Routledge and Kegan Paul, 1971.

——, *Thomas Hoccleve, Authors of the Middle Ages 4*. Aldershot: Variorum, 1994.

Cargill, O. and Schlauch, M., '*The Pearl* and its Jeweller', *PMLA* 43 (1928), 105–23.

Chambers, E. K., *Sir Thomas Malory*. Oxford: Oxford University Press, 1922.

Chapman, Coolidge Otis, 'The Authorship of *The Pearl*', *PMLA* 47 (1932), 346–53.

Coleman, Janet, *Medieval Readers and Writers, 1350–1400*. London: Hutchinson, 1981.

Copeland, Rita, 'Medieval Theory and Criticism', in Michael Groden and Martin Kreiswirth (eds), *The Johns Hopkins Guide to Literary Theory and Criticism*, pp. 500–8. Baltimore, MD: The Johns Hopkins University Press, 1994.

Davenport, W. A., *The Art of the Gawain-poet*. London: Athlone Press, 1978.

Donaldson, E. Talbot, 'Chaucer the Pilgrim', *PMLA* 69 (1954), 928–36.

Ferrante, Joan, 'Was Vernacular Poetic Practice a Response to Latin Language Theory?', *Romance Philology* 35 (1982), 586–600.

Field, P. J. C., *The Life and Times of Sir Thomas Malory*. Cambridge: D. S. Brewer, 1993.

Foucault, Michel, 'What is an Author?', in David Lodge (ed.), *Modern Criticism and Theory: A Reader*, pp. 196–210. London: Longman, 1988.

Gray, Douglas, *Robert Henryson*. Leiden: E. J. Brill, 1979.

Green, Richard Firth, *Poets and Princepleasers: Literature and the English Court in the Late Middle Ages*. Toronto: University of Toronto Press, 1980.

Hanna III, Ralph, *Pursuing History: Middle English Manuscripts and their Texts*. Stanford: Stanford University Press, 1996.

Hicks, Edward, *Sir Thomas Malory, his Turbulent Career*. Cambridge, MA: Harvard University Press, 1928.

Johnson, Ian, 'Vernacular Valorizing: Functions and Fashionings of Literary Theory in Middle English Translation of Authority', in Jeanette Beer (ed.), *Translation Theory and Practice in the Middle Ages*. Studies in Medieval Culture 38. Kalamazoo: Medieval Institute, 1997.

Johnson, Lynn Staley, 'The Trope of the Scribe and the Question of Literary Authority in the Works of Julian of Norwich and Margery Kempe', *Speculum* 66 (1991), 820–38.

Justice, Steven and Kerby-Fulton, Katherine (eds), *Written Work: Langland, Labor, and Authorship*. Philadelphia: University of Pennsylvania Press, 1997.

Kittredge, George Lyman, 'Who was Sir Thomas Malory?', *Harvard Studies and Notes in Philology and Literature* 5 (1896–7), 85–106.

Lehrer, Seth, *Chaucer and his Readers: Imagining the Author in Late Medieval England.* Princeton, NJ: Princeton University Press, 1993.

Lewis, C. S., *The Discarded Image: An Introduction to Medieval and Renaissance Literature.* Cambridge: Cambridge University Press, 1964.

Lumiansky, R. M., 'Sir Thomas Malory's *Le Morte Darthur*, 1947–1987: Author, Title, Text', *Speculum* 62 (1987), 878–97.

Machan, Tim William, *Textual Criticism and Middle English Texts.* Charlottesville: University of Virginia Press, 1994.

Martin, Alfred T., 'The Identity of the Author of *Le Morte Darthur*', *Archaeologica* 56 (1898) 165–77.

——, 'Sir Thomas Malory', *Athenaeum* 30 (1897), 353–4.

Matthews, William, *The Ill-framed Knight: A Skeptical Inquiry into the Identity of Sir Thomas Malory.* Berkeley, CA: University of California Press, 1966.

Middleton, Anne, 'The Idea of Public Poetry in the Reign of Richard II', *Speculum* 53 (1978), 94–114.

——, 'William Langland's "Kynde Name": Authorial Signature and Social Identity in Late Fourteenth-century England', in Lee Patterson (ed.), *Literary Practice and Social Change in Britain, 1380–1530*, pp. 15–81. Berkeley, CA: University of California Press, 1990.

Millet, Bella, 'Chaucer, Lollius, and the Medieval Theory of Authorship', *Studies in the Age of Chaucer* 1 (1984), 93–103.

Minnis, Alastair, 'The Influence of the Academic Prologue on the Prologues and Literary Attitudes of Late-medieval English Writers', *Medieval Studies* 43 (1981), 342–83.

——, *Medieval Theory of Authorship: Scholastic Literary Attitudes in the Later Middle Ages.* London: Scolar Press, 1984.

——, and Brewer, Charlotte (eds), *Crux and Controversy in Middle English Textual Criticism.* Cambridge: D. S. Brewer, 1992.

Moorman, Charles, 'The Role of the Narrator in *Pearl*', *Modern Philology* 80 (1955), 73–81.

Pearsall, Derek, *John Lydgate.* London: Routledge and Kegan Paul, 1970.

——, *Old and Middle English Poetry.* London: Routledge and Kegan Paul, 1977.

Perkins, Nicholas. *Hoccleve's Regiment of Princes: Counsel and Constraint.* Cambridge: D. S. Brewer, 2001.

Vinaver, Eugene, *Malory.* Oxford: Oxford University Press, 1929.

Watson, Nicholas, *Richard Rolle and the Invention of Authority.* Cambridge: Cambridge University Press, 1991.

Wimsatt, W. K., *The Verbal Icon: Studies in the Meaning of Poetry.* Lexington, KY: University of Kentucky Press, 1954.

Wogan-Browne, Jocelyn, Watson, Nicholas, Taylor, Andrew and Evans, Ruth (eds), *The Idea of the Vernacular: An Anthology of Middle English Literary Theory, 1280–1520.* Exeter: University of Exeter Press, 1999.

Woolf, Rosemary, *The English Religious Lyric in the Middle Ages*. Oxford: Clarendon Press, 1968.

Textual Form

Alford, John (ed.), *A Companion to Piers Plowman*. Berkeley, CA: University of California Press, 1988.

Baldwin, Ralph, *The Unity of the Canterbury Tales*. Copenhagen: Rosenkilde and Bagger, 1955.

Brewer, D. S., 'Form in the *Morte Darthur*', *Medium Ævum* 21 (1952), 14–24.

——, 'The hoole book', in J. A. W. Bennett (ed.), *Essays on Malory*, pp. 41–63. Oxford: Clarendon Press, 1963.

Bronson, B. H., '*The Parlement of Foules* Revisited', *English Literary History* 15 (1948), 252–60.

Brooks, Cleanth, *The Well Wrought Urn: Studies in the Structure of Poetry*, rev. 2nd edn, London: Dennis Dobson, 1968.

Cooper, Helen, *The Structure of The Canterbury Tales*. London: Duckworth, 1983.

Donner, Morton, 'The Unity of Chaucer's Manciple Fragment', *Modern Language Notes* 70 (1955), 245–9.

Dunning, T. P., 'The Structure of the B-text of *Piers Plowman*', *Review of English Studies* n.s. 7 (1956), 225–37.

Edwards, A. S. G., 'The Unity and Authenticity of *Anelida and Arcite*: The Evidence of the Manuscripts', *Studies in Bibliography* 41 (1988), 177–88.

Frank, Jr, Robert Worth, 'Structure and Meaning in The Parlement of Foules', *PMLA* 71 (1956), 530–9.

Frankl, Paul, *Gothic Architecture*, trans. Dieter Pevsner. Harmondsworth: Penguin, 1962.

Furnivall, Frederick J., *A Temporary Preface to the Six-text Edition of Chaucer's Canterbury's Tales*. Chaucer Society. London: Trubner, 1868.

Gerould, Gordon Hall, 'The Structural Integrity of the B-text of *Piers Plowman*', *Studies in Philology* 45 (1945), 60–75.

Howard, Donald R., *The Idea of the Canterbury Tales*. Berkeley, CA: University of California Press, 1976.

Jordan, Robert M., *Chaucer and the Shape of Creation: The Aesthetic Possibilities of Inorganic Structure*. Cambridge MA: Harvard University Press, 1967.

——, 'The Non-dramatic Disunity of *The Merchant's Tale*', *PMLA* 78 (1963), 293–9.

Kittredge, George Lyman, *Chaucer and his Poetry*. Harvard, MA: Harvard University Press, 1915.

Knight, Stephen, *The Structure of Sir Thomas Malory's Arthuriad*. Sydney: Sydney University Press, 1969.

Lacy, Norris J., 'Spatial Form in Medieval Romance', *Yale French Studies* 51: Approaches to Medieval Romance (1974), 160–9.

Lawlor, John, 'The Imaginative Unity of *Piers Plowman*', *Review of English Studies* n.s. 8 (1957), 113–26.

Lewis, C. S., *The Discarded Image: An Introduction to Medieval and Renaissance Literature*. Cambridge: Cambridge University Press, 1964.

Leyerle, John, 'Thematic Interlace in the *Canterbury Tales*', *Essays and Studies* 26 (1979), 107–21.

Lindahl, Carl, 'The Festive Form of the *Canterbury Tales*', *English Literary History* 52 (1985), 531–74.

Lumiansky, R. M., 'Chaucer's *Parlement of Foules*: A Philosophical Interpretation', *Review of English Studies* 24 (1948), 81–9.

—— (ed.), *Malory's Originality: A Critical Study of Le Morte Darthur*. Baltimore, MD: The Johns Hopkins University Press, 1964.

——, *Of Sondry Folk: The Dramatic Principle in The Canterbury Tales*. Austin, TX: University of Texas Press, 1955.

——, 'The Question of Unity in Malory's *Morte Darthur*', *Tulane Studies in English* 5 (1955), 29–39.

Mâle, Emile, *The Gothic Image: Religious Art in France of the Thirteenth Century*. New York: Harper, 1958.

Manly, John Matthews, *Some New Light on Chaucer*. London: G. Bell, 1926.

Moore, Arthur K., 'Medieval English Literature and the Question of Unity', *Modern Philology* 65 (1968), 285–300.

Moorman, Charles, *The Book of King Arthur: The Unity of Malory's Morte Darthur*. Lexington, KY: University of Kentucky Press, 1965.

Muscatine, Charles, *Chaucer and the French Tradition: A Study in Style and Meaning*. Berkeley, CA: University of California Press, 1957.

——, 'Form, Texture and Meaning in Chaucer's *Knight's Tale*', *PMLA* 65 (1950), 911–29.

——, *Poetry and Crisis in the Age of Chaucer*. Notre Dame, IN: University of Notre Dame Press, 1972.

Nolan, Barbara, *The Gothic Visionary Perspective*. Princeton, NJ: Princeton University Press, 1977.

Panofsky, Erwin, *Gothic Architecture and Scholasticism*. New York: Meridian Books, 1957.

Pearsall, Derek, *The Canterbury Tales*. London: Routledge, 1985.

Price, Thomas R., '*Troilus and Criseyde*: A Study in Chaucer's Method of Narrative Construction', *PMLA* 11 (1896), 307–22.

Reidy, John, 'Chaucer's Canon and the Unity of the *Canon's Yeoman's Tale*', *PMLA* 80 (1966), 31–7.

Robertson, Jr, D. W. and Huppé, Bernard F., *Piers Plowman and Scriptural Tradition*. Princeton, NJ: Princeton University Press, 1951.

Ruggiers, P. G., 'The Unity of Chaucer's *House of Fame*', *Studies in Philology* 50 (1953), 16–29.

Rumble, Thomas, 'Malory's *Balin* and the Question of Unity in the *Morte Darthur*', *Speculum* 41 (1966), 68–85.

Scala, Elizabeth, *Absent Narratives, Manuscript Textuality, and Literary Structure in Late Medieval England*. New York: Palgrave, 2002.

Simpson, James, *Sciences and the Self in Medieval Poetry: Alan of Lille's Anticlaudianus and John Gower's Confessio Amantis*. Cambridge: Cambridge University Press, 1995.

Spearing, A. C., *Criticism and Medieval Poetry*. London: Edward Arnold, 1964.

Stillwell, Gardiner, 'Unity and Comedy in Chaucer's *Parlement of Foules*', *Journal of English and Germanic Philology* 49 (1950), 470–95.

Strohm, Paul, 'Form and Social Statement in *Confessio Amantis* and *The Canterbury Tales*', *Studies in the Age of Chaucer* 1 (1979), 17–40.

Thompson, Francis J., 'Unity in *The Second Shepherd's Tale*', *Modern Language Notes* 64 (1949), 302–6.

Tupper, Frederick, 'Chaucer and the Seven Deadly Sins', *PMLA* 29 (1914), 237–371.

Wells, Henry W., 'The Construction of *Piers Plowman*', *PMLA* 44 (1929), 123–40.

White, Hugh, 'Divison and Failure in Gower's *Confessio Amantis*', *Neophilologus* 72 (1988), 600–16.

Wilson, R. H., 'How Many Books Did Malory Write?', *University of Texas Studies in English* 30 (1951), 1–23.

Wittig, Susan, *Stylistic and Narrative Structure in the Middle English Romances*. Austin, TX: University of Texas Press, 1978.

Genre

Amsler, Mark E., 'Literary Theory and the Genres of Middle English Literature', *Genre* 13 (1980), 389–96.

Barron, W. R. J., *English Medieval Romance*. London: Longman, 1987.

Bercovitch, Sacvan, 'Romance and Anti-romance in *Sir Gawain and the Green Knight*', *Philological Quarterly* 44 (1965), 30–7.

Bloomfield, Morton W., 'Episodic Motivation and Marvels in Epic and Romance', in *Essays and Explorations*, pp. 97–128. Cambridge, MA: Harvard University Press, 1970.

——, *Piers Plowman as a Fourteenth-century Apocalypse*. New Brunswick, NJ: Rutgers University Press, 1962.

Boitani, Piero, *English Medieval Narrative in the Thirteenth and Fourteenth Centuries*, trans. Joan Krakover Hall. Cambridge: Cambridge University Press, 1982.

Braswell, Laurel, '*Sir Isumbras* and the Legend of Saint Eustace', *Medieval Studies* 27 (1965), 128–51.

Brewer, Derek, 'The Nature of Romance', *Poetica* 9 (1978), 9–48.

Burlin, Robert, 'Middle English Romance: The Structure of Genre', *Chaucer Review* 30 (1995), 1–14.

Childress, Diana T., 'Between Romance and Legend: "Secular Hagiography" in Middle English Literature', *Philological Quarterly* 57 (1978), 311–22.

Clough, Andrea, 'Medieval Tragedy and the Genre of *Troilus and Criseyde*', *Medievalia et Humanistica* n. s. 11 (1982), 211–27.

Crane, Susan, 'Guy of Warwick and the Question of Exemplary Romance', *Genre* 17 (1984), 351–71.

Curry, Walter Clyde, *Chaucer and the Medieval Sciences*, 2nd edn. New York: Barnes and Noble, 1960.

Derrida, Jacques, 'The Law of Genre', in Derek Attridge (ed.), *Acts of Literature*, pp. 221–52. London: Routledge, 1992.

Dubrow, Heather, *Genre*. Critical Idiom Monographs. London: Methuen, 1982.

Everett, Dorothy, 'A Characterization of the English Medieval Romances', in Patricia Kean (ed.), *Essay on Middle English Literature*, pp. 1–22. Oxford: Clarendon Press, 1955.

Farnham, Willard, *The Medieval Heritage of Elizabethan Tragedy*. Berkeley, CA: University of California Press, 1936.

Fewster, Carol, *Traditionality and Genre in Middle English Romance*. Cambridge: D. S. Brewer, 1987.

Finlayson, John, 'Definitions of Middle English Romance', *Chaucer Review* 15 (1980–1), 44–62, 168–81.

Fowler, Alastair, *Kinds of Literature: An Introduction to the Theory of Genres and Modes*. Oxford: Clarendon Press, 1982.

Frye, Northrop, *Anatomy of Criticism: Four Essays*. Princeton, NJ: Princeton University Press, 1957.

——, *The Secular Scripture: A Study of the Structure of Romance*. Cambridge, MA: Harvard University Press, 1976.

Grady, Frank, 'The Lancastrian Gower and the Limits of Exemplarity', *Speculum* 70 (1995), 552–75.

Griffin, Nathaniel, 'The Definition of Romance', *PMLA* 38 (1923), 50–70.

Hume, Kathryn, 'The Formal Nature of Middle English Romance', *Philological Quarterly* 53 (1974), 158–80.

——, 'Romance: A Perdurable Pattern', *College English* 36 (1974), 129–46.

Jauss, Hans Robert, *Toward an Aesthetic of Reception*, trans. Timothy Bahti. Brighton: Harvester, 1982.

Jordan, Robert M., 'Chaucerian Romance?', *Yale French Studies* 51: Approaches to Medieval Romance (1974), 223–74.

Justice, Steven, 'The Genres of *Piers Plowman*', *Viator* 19 (1988), 291–306.

Kane, George, 'The Middle English Metrical Romances', in *Middle English Literature*. London: Methuen, 1951.

Ker, W. P., *Epic and Romance: Essays on Medieval Literature*. London: Macmillan, 1897.

Kratins, Ojars, 'The Middle English *Amis and Amiloun*: Chivalric Romance or Secular Hagiography?', *PMLA* 81 (1966), 347–54.

McAlpine, Monica, *The Genre of Troilus and Criseyde*. Ithaca, NY: Cornell University Press, 1978.

McCarthy, Terence, '*Le Morte Darthur* and Romance', in D. Brewer (ed.), *Studies in Medieval English Romances*, pp. 148–75. Cambridge: D. S. Brewer, 1988.

Matthews, William, *The Tragedy of Arthur: A Study of the Alliterative 'Morte Arthure'*. Berkeley, CA: University of California Press, 1960.

Mehl, Dieter, *The Middle English Romances of the Thirteenth and Fourteenth Centuries*. London: Routledge and Kegan Paul, 1968.

Pearsall, Derek, 'The Development of Middle English Romance', *Medieval Studies* 27 (1963), 91–116.

——, 'The English Romance in the Fifteenth Century', *Essays and Studies* n.s. 29 (1976), 56–83.

Putter, Ad and Gilbert, Jane (eds), *The Spirit of Medieval English Popular Romance*. London: Longman, 2000.

Reiss, Edmund, 'Romance', in Thomas Heffernan (ed.), *The Popular Literature of Medieval England*, pp. 108–30. Knoxville: University of Tennessee Press, 1985.

Robertson, Jr, D. W., 'Chaucerian Tragedy', *English Literary History* 19 (1952), 1–37.

Ruggiers, Paul, 'Notes Towards a Theory of Tragedy in Chaucer', *Chaucer Review* 8 (1973), 89–99.

Schelp, Hanspeter, *Exemplarische Romanzen im Mittelenglischen*. Göttingen: Vandenhoeck and Ruprecht, 1967.

Strohm, Paul, 'Middle English Narrative Genres', *Genre* 13 (1980), 379–88.

——, 'The Origin and Meaning of Middle English *Romaunce*', *Genre* 10 (1977), 1–20.

——, '*Storie, Spelle, Geste, Romaunce, Tragedie*: Generic Distinctions in the Middle English Troy Narrative', *Speculum* 44 (1971), 348–59.

Vinaver, Eugène, *The Rise of Romance*. Oxford: Oxford University Press, 1971.

Windeatt, Barry, *Troilus and Criseyde: Oxford Guides to Chaucer*. Oxford: Clarendon Press, 1992.

Wittig, Susan, *Stylistic and Narrative Structures in the Middle English Verse Romances*. Austin, TX: University of Texas Press, 1978.

Young, Karl, 'Chaucer's *Troilus and Criseyde* as Romance', *PMLA* 53 (1938), 38–63.

Language, Style, Rhetoric

Amodio, Mark C. (ed.), *Oral Poetics in Middle English Poetry*. New York: Garland Press, 1994.

Benson, C. David, *Chaucer's Drama of Style: Poetic Variety and Contrast in The Canterbury Tales*. Chapel Hill, NC: University of North Carolina Press, 1980.

Blake, Norman, *The English Language in Medieval Literature*. London: Methuen, 1979.

Borroff, Marie, *Sir Gawain and the Green Knight: A Stylistic and Metrical Study*. Yale Studies in English. New Haven, CT: Yale University Press, 1962.

Burnley, David, *The Language of Chaucer*. Basingstoke: Macmillan, 1983.

Cable, Thomas, *The English Alliterative Tradition*. Philadelphia: University of Pennsylvania Press, 1991.

Cannon, Christopher, *The Making of Chaucer's English: A Study of Words*. Cambridge: Cambridge University Press, 1998.

Chaytor, H. J., *From Script to Print: An Introduction to Medieval Vernacular Literature*. London: Sidgwick and Jackson, 1945.

Clanchy, M. T., *From Memory to Written Record: England 1066–1307*, 2nd edn. Oxford: Blackwell, 1993.

Copeland, Rita, *Rhetoric, Hermeneutics, and Translation in the Middle Ages: Academic Traditions and Vernacular Texts*. Cambridge: Cambridge University Press, 1991.

Crosby, Ruth, 'Chaucer and the Custom of Oral Delivery', *Speculum* 13 (1938), 413–32.

——, 'Oral Delivery in the Middle Ages', *Speculum* 11 (1936), 88–110.

Curtius, E. R., *European Literature and the Latin Middle Ages*, trans. W. R. Trask. London: Routledge and Kegan Paul, 1953.

Dalrymple, Roger, 'Reaction, Consolation and Redress in the Letters of the Paston Women', in James Daybell (ed.), *Early Modern Women's Letter-writing in England 1400–1700*, pp. 16–28. London: Palgrave, 2001.

Davis, Norman, 'Style and Stereotype in Early English Letters', *Leeds Studies in English* n.s. 1 (1967), 7–15.

Ellis, Roger (ed.), *The Medieval Translator: The Theory and Practice of Translation in the Middle Ages.* Cambridge: D. S. Brewer, 1989.

Enders, Jody, *Rhetoric and the Origins of Medieval Drama.* Ithaca, NY: Cornell University Press, 1992.

Faulkner, Peter, '"The Paths of Virtue and Early English": F. J. Furnivall and Victorian Medievalism', in John Simons (ed.), *From Medieval to Medievalism.* Basingstoke: Macmillan, 1992.

Field, P. J. C., *Romance and Chronicle: A Study of Malory's Prose Style.* London: Barrie and Jenkins, 1971.

Finlayson, John, 'Rhetorical "Descriptio" of Place in the Alliterative *Morte Arthure*', *Modern Philology* 61 (1963), 1–11.

Fisher, John H., 'Chancery and the Emergence of Standard Written English in the Fifteenth Century', *Speculum* 52 (1977), 870–99.

——, 'A Language Policy for Lancastrian England', *PMLA* 107 (1992), 168–80.

Fleischmann, Suzanne, 'Philology, Linguistics, and the Discourse of the Medieval Text', *Speculum* 65 (1990), 19–37.

Fox, Denton, 'Dunbar's *The Golden Targe*', *English Literary History* 26 (1959), 311–34.

Ganim, John, *Style and Consciousness in Middle English Narrative.* Princeton, NJ: Princeton University Press, 1983.

Gradon, Pamela, *Form and Style in Early English Literature.* London: Methuen, 1971.

Hanna, III, Ralph, 'Defining Middle English Alliterative Poetry', in M. T. Tavormina and Yeager, R. F. (eds), *The Endless Knot*, pp. 43–64. Cambridge: D. S. Brewer, 1995.

Lambert, Mark, *Style and Vision in Le Morte Darthur.* New Haven, CT: Yale University Press, 1975.

Lawrence, R. F., 'The Formulaic Theory and its Application to English Alliterative Poetry', in Roger Fowler (ed.), *Essays on Style and Language*, pp. 166–83. London: Routledge, 1966.

Lawton, David, 'The Diversity of Middle English Alliterative Poetry', *Leeds Studies in English* 20 (1989), 143–72.

—— (ed.), *Middle English Alliterative Poetry and its Literary Background.* Cambridge: D. S. Brewer, 1982.

McIntosh, Angus, 'The Analysis of Written Middle English', *Transactions of the Philological Society* (1956), 26–55.

McKinnell, John, 'Letters as a Type of the Formal Level in *Troilus and Criseyde*', in Mary Salu (ed.), *Essays on Troilus and Criseyde*, pp. 73–89. Cambridge: D. S. Brewer, 1980.

Manly, J. M. 'Chaucer and the Rhetoricians', *Proceedings of the British Academy* 12 (1926), 95–113.

Matthews, William, *The Making of Middle English, 1765–1910.* Minneapolis, MN: University of Minnesota Press, 1999.

Mueller, Janel, *The Native Tongue and the Word: Developments in English Prose Style 1380–1580.* Chicago: University of Chicago Press, 1985.

Murphy, James J., *Rhetoric in the Middle Ages: A History of Rhetorical Theory from St Augustine to the Renaissance*. Berkeley, CA: University of California Press, 1974.

Muscatine, Charles, *Chaucer and the French Tradition: A Study in Style and Meaning*. Berkeley, CA: University of California Press, 1957.

Oakden, J. P., *Alliterative Poetry in Middle English: A Survey of the Traditions*, 2 vols. Manchester: Manchester University Press, 1930, 1935.

Ong, Walter, *Orality and Literacy: The Technologizing of the Word*. New York: Methuen, 1982.

Payne, Robert O., *The Key of Remembrance: A Study of Chaucer's Poetics*. Westport, CT: Greenwood Press, 1963.

Pearsall, Derek, 'Rhetorical "Descriptio" in *Sir Gawain and the Green Knight*', *Modern Language Review* 50 (1955), 129–34.

Rothewell, William, 'The Trilingual England of Geoffrey Chaucer', *Studies in the Age of Chaucer* 16 (1994), 45–67.

Rygiel, Dennis, '*Ancrene Wisse* and Colloquial Style: A Caveat', *Neophilologus* 65 (1981), 137–43.

Shain, C. E., 'Pulpit Rhetoric in Three *Canterbury Tales*', *Modern Language Notes* 70 (1955), 235–45.

Shepherd, Geoffrey (ed.), *Ancrene Wisse: Parts Six and Seven*. London: Thomas Nelson, 1959.

——, 'The Nature of Alliterative Poetry in Late Medieval England', *Proceedings of the British Academy* 56 (1970), 57–76.

Sisam, Kenneth (ed.), *Fourteenth Century Verse and Prose*. Oxford: Clarendon Press, 1921.

Smith, J. J. (ed.), *The English of Chaucer and his Contemporaries: Essays by M. L. Samuels and J. J. Smith*. Aberdeen: The University Press, 1988.

Spearing, A. C., *Criticism and Medieval Poetry*. London: Edward Arnold, 1964.

——, *Readings in Medieval Poetry*. Cambridge: Cambridge University Press, 1987.

Speirs, John, *Medieval English Poetry: The Non-Chaucerian Tradition*. London: Faber, 1957.

Turville-Petre, Thorlac, *The Alliterative Revival*. Cambridge: Cambridge University Press, 1977.

——, *England the Nation: Language, Literature and National Identity, 1290–1340*. Oxford: Clarendon Press, 1996.

Waldron, Ronald, 'Oral-formulaic Technique and Middle English Alliterative Poetry', *Speculum* 32 (1957), 792–804.

Watt, Diane, '"No Writing for Writing's Sake": The Language of Service and Household Rhetoric in the Letters of the Paston Women', in Karen Cherewatuk and Ulrike Wiethaus (eds), *Dear Sister: Medieval Women and the Epistolary Genre*, pp. 122–38. Philadelphia: University of Pennsylvania Press, 1993.

Wilson, R. M., *Early Middle English Literature*, 3rd edn. London: Methuen, 1968.

Wogan-Browne, Jocelyn, Watson, Nicholas, Taylor, Andrew and Evans, Ruth (eds), *The Idea of the Vernacular: An Anthology of Middle English Literary Theory, 1280–1520*. Exeter: University of Exeter Press, 1999.

Allegory

Aers, David, *Piers Plowman and Christian Allegory*. London: Edward Arnold, 1975.

Astell, Ann W., *Political Allegory in Late Medieval England*. Ithaca, NY: Cornell University Press, 1999.

Auerbach, Eric, *Scenes from the Drama of European Literature*, trans. Richard Manheim. New York: Meridian Books, 1959.

Barr, Helen, '*Pearl* – or The Jeweller's Tale?', *Medium Ævum* 69 (2000), 59–79.

Beichner, Paul, 'The Allegorical Interpretation of Mediaeval Literature', *PMLA* 82 (1967), 33–8.

Bloomfield, Morton W., 'Symbolism in Medieval Literature', *Modern Philology* 56 (1958), 73–81.

Caplan, Harry, 'The Four Senses of Scriptural Interpretation and the Medieval Theory of Preaching', *Speculum* 4 (1929), 282–90.

Curtius, E. R., *European Literature and the Latin Middle Ages*, trans. W. R. Trask. London: Routledge, 1953.

Donaldson, E. Talbot, 'Patristic Exegesis in the Criticism of Medieval Literature: The Opposition', in Dorothy Betherum (ed.), *Critical Approaches to Medieval Literature*, pp. 1–26. New York: Columbia University Press, 1960.

Fowler, David C., *The Bible in Middle English Literature*. Seattle: University of Washington Press, 1984.

Frank, R. W., 'The Art of Reading Medieval Personification Allegory', *English Literary History* 20 (1953), 237–50.

Gillespie, Vincent, '*Doctrina et Predicatio*: The Design and Function of Some Pastoral Manuals', *Leeds Studies in English* n.s. 11 (1980), 36–50.

Gradon, Pamela, *Form and Style in Early English Literature*. London: Methuen, 1971.

Hume, Kathryn, *The Owl and the Nightingale: The Poem and its Critics*. Toronto: University of Toronto Press, 1975.

Huppé, Bernard F., *A Reading of The Canterbury Tales*, rev. edn. Albany, NY: State University of New York Press, 1967.

Justman, Stewart, 'Literal and Symbolic in *The Canterbury Tales*', *Chaucer Review* 14 (1979–80), 199–214.

Kaske, R. E., 'Chaucer and Medieval Allegory', *English Literary History* 30 (1963), 175–92.

Kellog, A. L., 'An Augustinian Interpretation of Chaucer's Pardoner', *Speculum* 26 (1951), 465–81.

Lewis, C. S., *The Allegory of Love: A Study of Medieval Tradition*. Oxford: Oxford University Press, 1936.

MacQueen, John, *Allegory*. Critical Idiom Series. London: Methuen, 1970.

Mann, Jill, 'Allegorical Buildings in Mediaeval Literature', *Medium Ævum* 63 (1994), 191–210.

Neuse, Richard, *Chaucer's Dante: Allegory and Epic Theater in The Canterbury Tales*. Berkeley, CA: University of California Press, 1991.

Owst, G. R., *Literature and Pulpit in Medieval England*, 2nd edn. Oxford: Blackwell, 1961.

Palmer, R. Barton, 'The Narrator in *The Owl and the Nightingale:* A Reader in the Text', *Chaucer Review* 22 (1988), 305–21.

Rigby, S. H., *Chaucer in Context: Society, Allegory and Gender*. Manchester: Manchester University Press, 1996.

Robertson, Jr, D. W., 'The Doctrine of Charity in Medieval Literary Gardens', *Speculum* 26 (1951), 24–49.

——, 'Historical Criticism', in A. S. Downer (ed.), *English Institute Essays, 1950*. New York: Columbia University Press, 1951.

——, *A Preface to Chaucer*. Princeton, NJ: Princeton University Press, 1962.

——, 'Some Medieval Literary Terminology', *Studies in Philology* 48 (1951), 669–92.

—— and Huppé, Bernard, *Fruyt and Chaff: Studies in Chaucer's Allegories*. Princeton, NJ: Princeton University Press, 1963.

—— and——, *Piers Plowman and Scriptural Tradition*. Princeton, NJ: Princeton University Press, 1951.

Russell, J. Stephen, *Allegoresis: The Craft of Allegory in Medieval Literature*. New York: Garland Press, 1988.

Tuve, Rosamund, *Allegorical Imagery: Some Medieval Books and their Posterity*. Princeton, NJ: Princeton University Press, 1966.

Wenzel, Siegfried, *The Sin of Sloth: Acedia in Medieval Thought and Literature*. Chapel Hill, NC: University of Carolina Press, 1967.

Literature and History

Aers, David, *Chaucer, Langland and the Creative Imagination*. London: Routledge and Kegan Paul, 1980.

——(ed.), *Medieval Literature and Historical Inquiry*. Cambridge: D. S. Brewer, 2000.

Aurner, Nellie Slayton, 'Sir Thomas Malory – Historian?', *PMLA* 48 (1933), 362–91.

Barr, Helen, *Socioliterary Practice in Late Medieval England*. Oxford: Oxford University Press, 2001.

Bennett, Michael J., *Community, Class and Careerism: Cheshire and Lancashire Society in the Age of 'Sir Gawain and The Green Knight'*. Cambridge: Cambridge University Press, 1983.

Benson, Larry D., *Malory's Morte Darthur*. Cambridge, MA: Harvard University Press, 1976.

Bishop, Ian, *Pearl in its Setting*. Oxford: Blackwell, 1968.

Bowers, John, *The Politics of Pearl: Court Poetry in the Age of Richard II*. Cambridge: D. S. Brewer, 2001.

Brown, Carleton, 'Another Contemporary Allusion in Chaucer's *Troilus*', *Modern Language Notes* 26 (1911), 208–11.

Burrow, John, *A Reading of 'Sir Gawain and the Green Knight'*. London: Routledge and Kegan Paul, 1965.

——, *Ricardian Poetry: Chaucer, Gower, Langland and the Gawain-poet*. Harmondsworth: Penguin, 1971.

Cantor, Norman, *Inventing the Middle Ages: The Lives, Works and Ideas of the Great Medievalists of the Twentieth Century*. New York: William Morrow, 1991.

Coleman, Janet, *Medieval Readers and Writers 1350–1400*. English Literature in History. London: Hutchinson, 1981.

Dobson, R. B. (ed.), *The Peasants' Revolt of 1381*. London: Macmillan, 1970.

Dyer, Christopher, *Standards of Living in the Later Middle Ages*. Cambridge: Cambridge University Press, 1989.

Eagleson, Harvey, 'Costume in the Middle English Metrical Romances', *PMLA* 47 (1932), 339–45.

Galloway, Andrew, 'Gower in his Most Learned Role and the Peasants Revolt of 1381', *Medievalia* 16 (1993), 329–47.

Hanawalt, Barbara A. (ed.), *Chaucer's England: Literature in Historical Context*. Minneapolis, MN: University of Minnesota Press, 1992.

—— and Wallace, David (eds), *Bodies and Disciplines: Intersections of Literature and History in Fifteenth-century England*. Minneapolis, MN: University of Minnesota Press, 1996.

Hanna, III, Ralph, *Pursuing History: Medieval Manuscripts and their Texts*. Stanford: Stanford University Press, 1996.

Howard, Donald R., 'Medieval Poems and Medieval Society', *Medievalia et Humanistica* n.s. 3 (1972), 99–115.

Jauss, Hans Robert, 'The Alterity and Modernity of Medieval Literature', *New Literary History* 10 (1978–9), 181–229.

Johnson, Lynn Staley, *The Voice of the Gawain-poet*. Madison: University of Wisconsin Press, 1984.

Justice, Steven, *Writing and Rebellion: England in 1381*. Berkeley, CA: University of California Press, 1994.

Kane, George, *Middle English Literature*. London: Methuen, 1951.

Kean, P. M., *The Pearl: An Interpretation*. New York: Barnes and Noble, 1967.

Ker, W. P., *English Literature: Medieval*. London: Williams and Norgate, 1912.

Kittredge, George Lyman, *Chaucer and his Poetry*. Cambridge, MA: Harvard University Press, 1915.

——, *A Study of Sir Gawain and the Green Knight*. Cambridge, MA: Harvard University Press, 1916.

Knight, Stephen, *Arthurian Literature and Society*. New York: St Martin's Press, 1983.

——, 'Chaucer and the Sociology of Literature', *Studies in the Age of Chaucer* 2 (1980), 15–51.

——, *Geoffrey Chaucer*. Oxford: Blackwell, 1986.

——, 'The Social Function of the Middle English Romances', in David Aers (ed.), *Medieval Literature: Criticism, Ideology and History*, pp. 99–122. Brighton: Harvester, 1986.

Loomis, R. S., *Celtic Myth and Arthurian Romance*. New York: Columbia University Press, 1927.

——, 'Gawain, Gwri, and Cuchulainn', *PMLA* 43 (1928), 384–96.

——, 'More Celtic Elements in *Sir Gawain and the Green Knight*', *Journal of English and Germanic Philology* 42 (1943), 149–84.

——, 'Notes on Layamon', *Review of English Studies* 10 (1934), 78–84.

——, 'The Visit to the Perilous Castle: A Study in the Arthurian Modifications of an Irish Theme', *PMLA* 48 (1933), 1000–35.

Manly, J. M., *Some New Light on Chaucer*. New York: Henry Holt and Co., 1926.

Matthews, David, *The Making of Middle English, 1765–1910*. Minneapolis, MN: University of Minnesota Press, 1999.

Medcalf, Stephen (ed.), *The Later Middle Ages*. London: Methuen, 1981.

Middleton, Anne, 'The Idea of Public Poetry in the Reign of Richard II', *Speculum* 53 (1978), 94–114.

Muscatine, Charles, *Poetry and Crisis in the Age of Chaucer*. Notre Dame, IN: University of Notre Dame Press, 1972.

Nitze, William A., 'Is the Green Knight Story a Vegetation Myth?', *Modern Philology* 33 (1936), 351–66.

Patch, Howard R., 'Desiderata in Middle English Research', *Modern Philology* 22 (1924), 27–34.

Patterson, Lee (ed.), *Literary Practice and Social Change in Britain, 1380–1530*. Berkeley, CA: University of California Press, 1990.

——, *Negotiating the Past: The Historical Understanding of Medieval Literature*. Madison: University of Wisconsin Press, 1987.

Pearsall, Derek, 'Chaucer's Poetry and its Modern Commentators: The Necessity of History', in David Aers (ed.), *Medieval Literature: Criticism, Ideology and History*. Brighton: Harvester, 1986.

Robbins, R. H. (ed.), *Historical Poems of the XIVth and XVth Centuries*. New York: Columbia University Press, 1959.

Scattergood, V. J., *Politics and Poetry in the Fifteenth Century*. London: Blandford Press, 1971.

Schlauch, Margaret, *English Medieval Literature and its Social Foundations*. Oxford: Oxford University Press, 1956.

Spearing, A. C., *Criticism and Medieval Poetry*. London: Edward Arnold, 1964.

Speirs, John, *Medieval English Poetry: The Non-Chaucerian Tradition*. London: Faber, 1957.

Strohm, Paul, *England's Empty Throne: Usurpation and the Language of Legitimation*. New Haven, CT: Yale University Press, 1998.

——, *Hochon's Arrow: The Social Imagination of Fourteenth-century Texts*. Princeton, NJ: Princeton University Press, 1992.

——, *Social Chaucer*. Cambridge, MA: Harvard University Press, 1989.

Tatlock, John S. P., 'The Duration of the Canterbury Pilgrimage', *PMLA* 21 (1906), 478–85.

Veeser, H. Aram (ed.), *The New Historicism*. New York: Routledge, 1989.

Wallace, David (ed.), *The Cambridge History of Medieval English Literature*. Cambridge: Cambridge University Press, 1999.

Ward, A. W. and Waller, A. R. (eds), *The Cambridge History of English Literature*. Cambridge: Cambridge University Press, 1907.

Watson, Nicholas, 'Censorship and Cultural Change in Late-medieval England: Vernacular Theology, the Oxford Translation Debate, and Arundel's Constitutions of 1409', *Speculum* 70 (1995), 822–64.

Weston, Jessie L., *From Ritual to Romance*. Cambridge: Cambridge University Press 1920.

——, *The Legend of Sir Gawain: Studies upon its Original Scope and Significance*. London, 1897.

Whittock, Trevor, *A Reading of the Canterbury Tales*. Cambridge: Cambridge University Press, 1968.

Gender

Aers, David, 'Criseyde: Woman in Medieval Society', *Chaucer Review* 13 (1979), 177–200.

Allen, Hope Emily, 'The Origin of the *Ancrene Riwle*', *PMLA* 33 (1918), 448–92.

Baker, Derek (ed.), *Medieval Women: Essays Dedicated and Presented to Rosalind M. T. Hill*. Studies in Church History. Oxford: Blackwell, 1978.

Barratt, Alexandra (ed.), *Women's Writing in Middle English*. London: Longman, 1992.

Bartlett, Anne Clark, *Male Authors, Female Readers: Representation and Subjectivity in Middle English Devotional Literature*. Ithaca, NY: Cornell University Press, 1995.

Baswell, Christopher and Sharpe, William (eds), *The Passing of Arthur: New Essays in Arthurian Tradition*. New York: Garland Press, 1988.

Beckwith, Sarah, 'A Very Material Mysticism: The Medieval Mysticism of Margery Kempe', in David Aers (ed.), *Medieval Literature: Criticism, Ideology and History*, pp. 34–57. Brighton: Harvester, 1986.

Beer, Frances, *Women and Mystical Experience in the Middle Ages*. Boydell: Woodbridge, 1992.

Bennett, Judith M., 'Medieval Women, Modern Women: Across the Great Divide', in David Aers (ed.), *Culture and History 1350–1600: Essays on English Communities, Identities and Writing*. New York: Harvester Wheatsheaf, 1992.

——, 'Medievalism and Feminism', *Speculum* 68 (1993), 309–31.

Biddick, Kathleen, 'Genders, Bodies, Borders: Technologies of the Visible', *Speculum* 68 (1993), 389–418.

Biller, Peter and Minnis, A. J., *Medieval Theology and the Natural Body*. Woodbridge: York Medieval Press, 1997.

Blamires, Alcuin, *The Case for Women in Medieval Culture*. Oxford: Clarendon Press, 1997.

——, with Pratt, Karen and Marx, C. W. (eds), *Woman Defamed and Woman Defended: An Anthology of Medieval Texts*. Oxford: Clarendon Press, 1992.

Boone, Joseph and Cadden, Michael (eds), *Engendering Men: The Question of Male Feminist Criticism*. London: Routledge, 1990.

Boswell, John, *Christianity, Social Tolerance, and Homosexuality: Gay People in Western Europe from the Beginning of the Christian Era to the Fourteenth Century*. Chicago: University of Chicago Press, 1980.

Boyd, David Lorenzo, 'On Lesbian and Gay/Queer Medieval Studies', *Medieval Feminist Newsletter* 15 (1993), 12–15.

——, 'Sodomy, Misogyny, and Displacement: Occluding Queer Desire in *Sir Gawain and the Green Knight*', *Arthuriana* 8 (1998), 77–114.

Bullough, Vern L., 'Medieval Medical and Scientific Views of Women', *Viator* 4 (1973), 485–501.

Burger, Glenn, 'Erotic Discipline . . . Or "Tee Hee, I Like my Boys to be Girls": Inventing with the Body in Chaucer's Miller's Tale', in Jeffrey Jerome Cohen and Bonnie Wheeler (eds), *Becoming Male in the Middle Ages*, pp. 245–60. New York: Garland Press, 1997.

——, 'Gay Chaucer', *English Studies in Canada* 20 (1994), 153–69.

——, 'Kissing the Pardoner', *PMLA* 107 (1992), 1143–56.

Butler, Judith, *Bodies that Matter: On the Discursive Limits of 'Sex'*. New York: Routledge, 1993.

——, *Gender Trouble: Feminism and the Subversion of Identity*. New York: Routledge, 1990.

Bynum, Caroline Walker, *Fragmentation and Redemption: Essays on Gender and the Human Body in Medieval Religion*. New York: Zone Books, 1991.

Cadden, Joan, *The Meanings of Sex Difference in the Middle Ages: Medicine, Natural Philosophy, and Culture*. Cambridge: Cambridge University Press, 1993.

Carruthers, Mary, 'The Wife of Bath and the Painting of Lions', *PMLA* 94 (1979), 209–22.

Chance, Jane, *The Mythographic Chaucer: The Fabulation of Sexual Politics*. Minneapolis, MN: University of Minnesota Press, 1995.

Clover, Carol, 'Regardless of Sex: Men, Women, and Power in Early Northern Europe', *Speculum* 68 (1993), 363–87.

Cohen, Jeffrey Jerome. *Of Giants: Sex, Monsters and the Middle Ages*. Minneapolis, MN: University of Minnesota Press, 1999.

Crane, Susan, *Gender and Romance in Chaucer's Canterbury Tales*. Princeton, NJ: Princeton University Press, 1994.

Delany, Sheila, 'Sexual Economics, Chaucer's Wife of Bath and *The Book of Margery Kempe*', in *Writing Woman: Women Writers and Women in Literature: Medieval to Modern*, pp. 76–91. New York: Schocken Books, 1983.

——, 'Womanliness in the Man of Law's Tale', *Chaucer Review* 9 (1974), 63–72.

Diamond, Arlyn and Edwards, Lee R. (eds), *The Authority of Experience: Essays in Feminist Criticism*. Amherst: University of Massachusetts Press, 1977.

Dinshaw, Carolyn, 'Chaucer's Queer Touches: A Queer Touches Chaucer', *Exemplaria* 7.1 (1995), 75–92.

——, *Chaucer's Sexual Poetics*. Madison: University of Wisconsin Press, 1989.

——, *Getting Medieval: Sexualities and Communities, Pre- and Post-modern*. Durham, NC: Duke University Press, 1999.

——, 'A Kiss is just a Kiss: Heterosexuality and its Consolations in *Sir Gawain and the Green Knight*', *Diacritics* 24 (1994), 204–26.

—— and Wallace, David (eds), *The Cambridge Companion to Medieval Women's Writing*. Cambridge: Cambridge University Press, 2003.

Dollimore, Jonathan, *Sexual Dissidence: Augustine to Wilde, Freud to Foucault*. Oxford: Oxford University Press, 1991.

Evans, Ruth and Johnson, Lesley (eds), *The Wife of Bath and All her Sect: Feminist Readings in Middle English Literature*. London: Routledge, 1994.

Finke, Laurie A. and Schichtman, Martin B., 'No Pain, No Gain: Violence as Symbolic Capital in Malory's *Morte Darthur*', *Arthuriana* 8 (1998), 115–33.

Fisher, Sheila and Halley, Janet E. (eds) *Seeking the Woman in Late Medieval and Early Renaissance Writings: Essays in Feminist Contextual Criticism*. Knoxville: University of Tennessee Press, 1989.

Foucault, Michel, *The History of Sexuality I: An Introduction*, trans. Robert Hurley. New York: Vintage, 1980.

Fradenburg, Louise O., 'The Wife of Bath's Passing Fancy', *Studies in the Age of Chaucer* 8 (1986), 31–58.

—— and Freccero, Carla (eds), *Premodern Sexualities*. New York: Routledge, 1996.

Frantzen, Allen J., 'The Disclosure of Sodomy in *Cleanness*', *PMLA* 111 (1996), 451–64 (452).

——, 'When Women Aren't Enough,' *Speculum* 68 (1993), 445–471 (471).

—— and Robertson, David A. (eds), *The Body in Medieval Art, History, and Literature*. Essays in Medieval Studies 11. Chicago: Illinois Medieval Association, 1995.

Galloway, Andrew and Alford, John A. (eds), *The Yearbook of Langland Studies* 12. Asheville: Pegasus Press, 1998.

Georgianna, Linda, *The Solitary Self: Individuality in the Ancrene Wisse*. Cambridge, MA: Harvard University Press, 1981.

Hansen, Elaine Tuttle, *Chaucer and the Fictions of Gender*. Berkeley, CA: University of California Press, 1992.

Heng, Geraldine, 'Feminine Knots and the Other *Sir Gawain and the Green Knight*', *PMLA* 106 (1991), 500–14.

Howard, Donald R., *The Idea of the Canterbury Tales*. Berkeley, CA: University of California Press, 1976.

Jacobus, Mary, *Reading Women: Essays in Feminist Criticism*. London: Methuen, 1986.

Kay, Sarah and Rubin, Miri (eds), *Framing Medieval Bodies*. Manchester: Manchester University Press, 1994.

Kinney, Clare R., 'The (Dis)Embodied Hero and the Signs of Manhood in *Sir Gawain and the Green Knight*', in *Medieval Masculinities: Regarding Men in the Middle Ages*, pp. 47–60. Minneapolis, MN: University of Minnesota Press, 1994.

Kruger, Steven F., 'Claiming the Pardoner: Toward a Gay Reading of Chaucer's Pardoner's Tale,' *Exemplaria* 6.1 (1994), 115–39.

Laskaya, Anna, *Chaucer's Approach to Gender in The Canterbury Tales*. Chaucer Studies 23. Cambridge: D. S. Brewer, 1995.

Lees, Clare A. (ed.), *Medieval Masculinities: Regarding Men in the Middle Ages*. Minneapolis, MN: University of Minnesota Press, 1994.

Lochrie, Karma, *Margery Kempe and Translations of the Flesh*. Philadelphia: University of Pennsylvania Press, 1991.

——, McCracken, Peggy and. Schultz, James A (eds), *Constructing Medieval Sexuality*. Minneapolis, MN: University of Minnesota Press, 1997.

McAlpine, Monica E., 'The Pardoner's Homosexuality and How it Matters', *PMLA* 95 (1980), 8–22.

McEntire, Sandra J., *Julian of Norwich: A Book of Essays*. New York: Garland Press, 1998.

——, *Margery Kempe: A Book of Essays*. New York: Garland Press, 1992.

McSheffrey, Shannon, *Gender and Heresy: Women and Men in Lollard Communities 1420–1530*. Philadelphia: University of Pennsylvania Press, 1995.

Mann, Jill, *Geoffrey Chaucer*. London: Harvester Wheatsheaf, 1991.

Margherita, Gayle, *The Romance of Origins: Language and Sexual Difference in Middle English Literature*. Philadelphia: University of Pennsylvania Press, 1994.

Martin, Priscilla, *Chaucer's Women: Nuns, Wives, and Amazons*. London: Macmillan, 1990.

Meale, Carol M. (ed.), *Women and Literature in Britain c.1150–1500*. Cambridge: Cambridge University Press, 1993.

Millet, Bella, 'The Audience of the Saints Lives of the Katherine Group', *Reading Medieval Studies* 16 (1990), 127–55.

—— and Wogan-Browne, Jocelyn (eds), *Medieval English Prose for Women: Selections from the Katherine Group and Ancrene Wisse*. Oxford: Clarendon Press, 1990.

Moi, Toril, *Sexual/Textual Politics: Feminist Literary Theory*. London: Methuen, 1985.

Murtaugh, Daniel M., 'Women and Geoffrey Chaucer', *English Literary History* 38 (1971), 473–92 (492).

Partner, Nancy F., 'No Sex, No Gender', *Speculum* 68 (1993), 117–42.

Power, Eileen, *Medieval English Nunneries*. Cambridge: Cambridge University Press, 1922.

Rigby, S. H., *Chaucer in Context: Society, Allegory and Gender*. Manchester: Manchester University Press, 1996.

Robertson, Elizabeth, 'Medieval Medical Views of Women and Female Spirituality in the *Ancrene Wisse* and Julian of Norwich's *Showings*', in Linda Lomperis and Sarah Stanbury (eds), *Feminist Approaches to the Body in Medieval Literature*, pp. 142–67. Philadelphia: University of Pennsylvania Press, 1993.

Rubin, Gayle, 'The Traffic in Women: Notes on the "Political Economy" of Sex', in R. R. Reiter (ed.), *Toward an Anthropology of Women*, pp. 157–210. New York: Monthly Review Press.

Savage, Anne, 'The Translation of the Feminine: Untranslatable Dimensions of the Anchoritic Works', in Roger Ellis and Ruth Evans (eds), *The Medieval Translator 4*, pp. 181–99. Exeter: Exeter University Press, 1994.

Scarry, Elaine, *The Body in Pain: The Making and Unmaking of the World*. Oxford: Oxford University Press, 1985.

Schibanoff, Susan, 'Taking the Gold out of Egypt: The Art of Reading as a Woman', in Elizabeth A. Flynn and Patrocinio P. Schweickart (eds), *Gender and Reading: Essays on Readers, Texts, and Contexts*, pp. 83–106. Baltimore, MD: The Johns Hopkins University Press, 1986.

Sedgwick, Eve Kosofsky, *Between Men: English Literature and Male Homosocial Desire*. New York: Columbia University Press, 1985.

——, *Epistemology of the Closet*. Berkeley, CA: University of California Press, 1990.

Smith, Lesley and Taylor, Jane H. M. (eds), *Women, the Book and the Godly: Selected Proceedings of the St Hilda's Conference, 1993*. Woodbridge: D. S. Brewer, 1995.

Staley, Lynn, *Margery Kempe's Dissenting Fictions*. University Park, PA: Pennsylvania State University Press, 1994.

Strauss, Barrie Ruth, 'The Subversive Discourse of the Wife of Bath: Phallocentric Discourse and the Imprisonment of Criticism', *English Literary History* 55 (1988), 527–54.

Voaden, Rosalynn, *God's Words, Women's Voices: The Discernment of Spirits in the Writing of Late-medieval Women Visionaries*. Woodbridge: York Medieval Press, 1999.

Watt, Diane, *Secretaries of God: Women Prophets in Late Medieval and Early Modern England*. Cambridge: D. S. Brewer, 1997.

Weisl, Angela Jane, *Conquering the Reign of Femeny: Gender and Genre in Chaucer's Romance*. Cambridge: D. S. Brewer, 1995.

Weissman, Hope Phyllis, 'Antifeminism in Chaucer's Characterization of Women', in George D. Economou (ed.), *Geoffrey Chaucer*, pp. 93–110. New York: McGraw-Hill, 1975.

Wilson, K. M. and Makowski, E. M. (eds), *Wykkyd Wyves and The Woes of Marriage: Misogamous Literature from Juvenal to Chaucer*. Albany, NY: State University of New York Press, 1990.

Identity

Aers, David (ed.), *Culture and History 1350–1600: Essays on English Communities, Identities and Writing*. London: Harvester Wheatsheaf, 1992.

——, *Community, Gender, and Individual Identity: English Writing 1360–1430*. London: Routledge, 1988.

Bartlett, Robert, 'Medieval and Modern Concepts of Race and Ethnicity', *Journal of Medieval and Early Modern Studies* 31 (2001), 39–56.

Beadle, Richard (ed.), *The Cambridge Companion to Medieval English Theatre*. Cambridge: Cambridge University Press, 1994.

Beckwith, Sarah, *Christ's Body: Identity, Culture and Society in Late Medieval Writing*. London: Routledge, 1993.

Benson, Robert L. and Constable, Giles, with Lanham, Carol (eds), *Renaissance and Renewal in the Twelfth Century*. Cambridge, MA: Harvard University Press, 1982.

Benton, John F., 'Consciousness of Self and Perceptions of Individuality', in Robert L. Benson and Giles Constable, with Carol Lanham (eds), *Renaissance and Renewal in the Twelfth Century*, pp. 263–95. Cambridge, MA: Harvard University Press, 1982.

Bhaba, H. K., 'Postcolonial Criticism', in Stephen Greenblatt and G. Gunn (eds), *Redrawing the Boundaries: The Transformation of English and American Literary Studies*, pp. 437–65. New York: Modern Language Association, 1992.

Bigson, Gail, *The Theatre of Devotion: East Anglian Drama and Society in the Late Middle Ages*. Chicago: University of Chicago Press, 1989.

Brawer, Robert, 'The Characterization of Pilate in the York Cycle Play', *Studies in Philology* 69 (1972), 289–303.

Burrow, John, *Medieval Writers and their Work: Middle English Literature and its Background 1100–1500*. Oxford: Oxford University Press, 1982.

Bynum, Caroline Walker, *Metamorphosis and Identity*. New York: Zone Books, 2001.

Carpenter, Sarah, 'Morality Play Characters', *Medieval English Theatre* 5 (1983), 18–28.

Clopper, Lawrence M., 'Tyrants and Villains: Characterization in the Passion Sequence of the English Cycle Plays', *Modern Language Quarterly* 41 (1980), 3–20.

Cohen, Jeffrey Jerome, *Medieval Identity Machines*. Minneapolis, MN: University of Minnesota Press, 2003.

——(ed.), *The Postcolonial Middle Ages*. New York: St Martin's Press, 2000.

Delany, Sheila, *Medieval Literary Politics: Shapes of Ideology*. Manchester: Manchester University Press, 1990.

Forde, Simon, Johnson, Lesley and Murray, Alan V. (eds), *Concepts of National Identity in the Middle Ages*. Leeds: Leeds Studies in English, 1995.

Fradenburg, Louise O. Aranye, 'Amorous Scholasticism', in Robert F. Yeager and Charlotte C. Morse (eds), *Speaking Images: Essays in Honor of V. A. Kolve*, pp. 27–53. Asheville: Pegasus Press, 2000.

——, '"Be Not Far from Me": Psychoanalysis, Medieval Studies and the Subject of Religion', *Exemplaria* 7 (1995), 41–54.

Georgianna, Linda, *The Solitary Self: Individuality in the Ancrene Wisse*. Cambridge, MA: Harvard University Press, 1981.

Hanning, R. W., *The Individual in Twelfth-century Romance*. New Haven, CT: Yale University Press, 1977.

Hardman, Phillipa (ed.), *The Matter of Identity in Medieval Romance*. Cambridge: D. S. Brewer, 2002.

Leicester, Jr, H. Marshall, *The Disenchanted Self: Representing the Subject in The Canterbury Tales*. Berkeley, CA: University of California Press, 1990.

Medcalf, Stephen (ed.), *The Later Middle Ages*. London: Methuen, 1981.

Mills, David, 'Characterisation in the English Mystery Plays: A Critical Prologue', *Medieval English Theatre* 5 (1983), 5–17.

Morris, Colin, *The Discovery of the Individual 1050–1200*. London: SPCK, 1972.

Patterson, Lee, *Chaucer and the Subject of History* London: Routledge, 1991.

Riddy, Felicity (ed.), *Regionalism in Late Medieval Manuscripts and Texts: Essays Celebrating the Publication of 'A Linguistic Atlas of Late Medieval England'*. Cambridge: D. S. Brewer, 1991.

Rubin, Miri, *Gentile Tales: The Narrative Assault on Late Medieval Jews*. New Haven, CT: Yale University Press, 1999.

Schmitt, Natalie Crohn, 'The Idea of a Person in Medieval Morality Plays'in Clifford Davidson and John H. Stroupe (eds), *Drama in the Middle Ages: Comparative and Critical Essays*, pp. 304–15. New York: AMS Press, 1982.

Simpson, James, *Sciences and the Self in Medieval Poetry: Alain of Lille's Anticlaudianus and John Gower's Confessio Amantis*. Cambridge: Cambridge University Press, 1995.

Smith, Paul, *Discerning the Subject*. Minneapolis, MN: University of Minnesota Press.

Staines, David, 'To Out-Herod Herod: The Development of a Dramatic Character', *Comparative Drama* 10 (1976), 29–53; 13, 207–31.

Turville-Petre, Thorlac, *England the Nation: Language, Literature and National Identity, 1290–1340*. Oxford: Clarendon Press, 1996.

Williams, Arnold, *The Characterization of Pilate in the Towneley Plays*. East Lansing: Michigan State College Press, 1950.

Index